THE HÉBERTISTES
TO THE GUILLOTINE

THE HÉBERTISTES
TO THE GUILLOTINE

ANATOMY OF A "CONSPIRACY" IN

REVOLUTIONARY

FRANCE

MORRIS SLAVIN

LOUISIANA STATE UNIVERSITY PRESS
Baton Rouge and London

Copyright © 1994 by Louisiana State University Press
All rights reserved
Manufactured in the United States of America
First printing
03 02 01 00 99 98 97 96 95 94   5 4 3 2 1

Designer: Amanda McDonald Key
Typeface: Palatino
Typesetter: G&S Typesetters, Inc.
Printer and binder: Thomson–Shore, Inc.

Library of Congress Cataloging-in-Publication Data

Slavin, Morris, 1913–
    The Hébertistes to the guillotine : anatomy of a "conspiracy" in
revolutionary France / Morris Slavin.
        p.   cm.
    Includes bibliographical references and index.
    ISBN 0-8071-1838-9
    1. France—Politics and government—1789–1799. 2. France—
History—Revolution, 1789–1799—Societies, etc.   3. Club des
Cordeliers—History. 4. Hébert, Jacques-René, 1757–1794—Death and
burial. 5. Revolutionaries—France—Death. 6. Guillotine.
I. Title.
DC183.5.S58   1994
944.04—dc20   93-45300
                                                              CIP

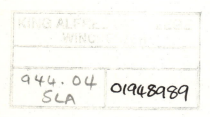

For Leon, Bess, Bernie, Steve, and Jeanne—and for Leslie and Michael

The advent of the Hébertistes was the advent of science and reason in its strongest and most popular form, but also in the shape that alone could assure its definitive triumph. The science that the Girondins . . . wanted to cloister in a literary oligarchy, was pulled out of the boudoir and cast into the public square.
> —G. Tridon, member of the Paris Commune of 1871,
> **Les Hébertistes**

Republicans, what has become of your oaths? . . . You have sworn a hundred times to die, well die then, for you no longer have any liberty.
> *—Letter of Robert, a member, to the Cordeliers,*
> *1 Germinal II (March 21, 1794)*

CONTENTS

ILLUSTRATIONS

PREFACE

Current events in Central and Eastern Europe remind us, yet again, that revolutions are made from below. Just as in 1789 it was the sans-culottes, the peasants, and the bourgeoisie—in short, the people—who launched the great *journées* that ended the Old Regime, so in 1989 it was the workers, students, and farmers who overthrew the *nomenklatura* that had ruled over them since the end of World War II. Observers and analysts of these current revolutions speak of "movements from below" or "revolutions from below" to explain the sudden destruction of entrenched regimes. Thus, politics in the grand sense has returned to history, and in doing so has demonstrated once again the validity of Aristotle's definition of man as a political animal.

This reemphasis on politics does not diminish the important studies of the French Revolution that have appeared in the last two decades. Investigations grounded in social history, in the evolution of philosophical concepts, in the role of ideology and ideas, and in that whole complex we call culture—from public festivals to popular folkways—all have enriched our understanding of the Revolution. Nevertheless, the study I present here reflects my own interests, which focus on the *political* struggles of 1793 and 1794.

Like other revolutions, the French contains its paradoxes. This study seeks to demonstrate that the struggle to the death between the Hébertistes and the Dantonistes ("radicals" versus "moderates") inevitably led to the demise of both. Neither understood that each could not exist without the other—if each was to frustrate the "single will" that Robespierre preached. If there was to be a balance in the body politic of revolutionary France, both factions had to exist. Once the Committee of Public Safety destroyed the Hébertistes it was forced to suppress the Dantonistes as well.

The second paradox is rooted in the first. The Convention and its two Great Committees felt they had to suppress the factional disputes that were undermining the unity of the Republic, for only unity, they believed, could lead to victory over the enemies of France. But in destroying the factions of Hébert and Danton they inevitably undermined their own base of support in the sections, in the Paris Commune, in the political clubs, and among the public at large. Thus, just as the Hébertistes depended on the moderates for their political and physical existence, so too the revolutionary government depended on the factions for that mass support without which no "single will" could be effective.

Furthermore, if the French Revolution can teach us anything about the uprisings in Central and Eastern Europe, then surely we can expect analogous factional struggles to appear in the former Eastern bloc. Rifts among the various political parties and groups are becoming sharper—just as they did within the diverse political societies, sections, and institutions created by the French Revolution. Social classes do have economic, political, and cultural differences, and these are bound to find expression, just as they did in 1793 and 1794. Nor can individual prejudices and ambitions be ignored. They played their role in France two centuries ago. They are making their appearance in Eastern and Central Europe today.

It is a pleasure to acknowledge the profound debt I owe to colleagues and friends in completing this work.

James Friguglietti improved the manuscript by numerous suggestions of style and translations from the French. Eric Arnold read an early draft of the manuscript and advised some salutary pruning. Virginia Phillips unlocked the mysteries of the computer and taught me to become reasonably proficient with it. Hildegard Schnuttgen was unremitting in acquiring documents and pamphlets from the Archives Nationales and the Bibliothèque Nationale, as well as interlibrary loans. Marc Bouloiseau and Walter Markov were generous in replying to my questions and encouraged me to continue my research. Mary Bellato performed many chores in helping me prepare the manuscript in its final form.

A two-term residency at the Princeton Institute for Advanced Study provided a stimulating atmosphere and time to finish my research. Robert R. Palmer was helpful in leading me through the labyrinth of Princeton University's Firestone Library and shared his thoughts on the French Revolution with me. Youngstown State University's Graduate Research Council provided financial assistance for microfilm and xeroxed material. I owe much to the late John Hall Stewart, who introduced me to the Hébertistes in one of his imaginative seminars, and to his numerous discussions with me on various problems of the French Revolution.

It is hardly necessary to add that whatever errors of judgment or fact I may have committed in this study are my own. Finally, as in the past, I owe a great debt to my wife, Sophie S. Slavin, whose patience and encouragement helped me complete this work.

ABBREVIATIONS

AN   Archives nationales

AP   Mavidal, M. J., M. E. Laurent, *et al.*, eds. *Archives parlemen-taires de 1787 à 1860: Recueil complet des débats législatifs et politiques des chambres françaises.* Series 1, 90 vols. Paris, 1879–

APP   Archives de la Préfecture de Police

BN   Bibliothèque nationale

B & R   Buchez, P. J. B., and P. C. Roux, eds. *Histoire parlementaire de la Révolution française.* 40 vols. Paris, 1834–38

In the text, dates based on the revolutionary calendar generally are given without the word *year*—for example, 4 Ventôse II instead of 4 Ventôse An II. (The revolutionary year II began on September 22, 1793, and ended on September 21, 1794.)

THE HÉBERTISTES
TO THE GUILLOTINE

INTRODUCTION

On July 14, 1989, the French news magazine *L'Express* published a survey conducted among three hundred high-school teachers of history. The questions posed by the journal focused on how these instructors felt about various episodes and personalities of the French Revolution. One section, entitled "The Barometer of Revolutionaries," asked if they sympathized with eleven prominent figures of the Revolution. Condorcet received the highest positive response—91 percent; Sieyès and Danton each had 72 percent, Robespierre followed with 68 percent, and Marat earned 43 percent. By far the lowest sympathetic response went to Hébert, at only 27 percent. Yet two-thirds of those surveyed, according to the journal, were Robespierristes.[1]

This low opinion of Jacques René Hébert held by history professionals creates a problem for scholars who are interested in examining his role during the Revolution. Some of his biographers tend to stress his virtues and ignore his weaknesses of character. Others ignore his character and focus on his politics—but even there they face controversy: were his politics rooted in firm philosophical and moral principles, or were they opportunistic, based only on expediency?

To add to the dilemma there are the "Hébertistes." It can be argued that in reality they were not *followers* of Hébert at all, as the term implies. They were leaders in their own right, active in the Cordeliers Club and in their individual sections, serving as officers in the Revolutionary army (not to be confused with the regular, professional army), holding important positions in the War Department, or administrating departments in the Paris Commune. Charles Philippe

1. *L'Express* (Paris), July 14, 1989, p. 48. The others named in the survey and their favorable ratings were Saint-Just, 66 percent; Grégoire, 65 percent; Lafayette, 62 percent; Babeuf 59 percent; Mirabeau, 59 percent. Asked whether they regarded Robespierre's role in the Revolution as positive or negative, 64 percent of the respondents replied positive.

Ronsin, François Nicolas Vincent, and Antoine François Momoro were these leaders linked to Hébert, with other militants of secondary importance around them.

The low opinion that modern historians hold of the Hébertistes contrasts with that of their predecessors, the great historians such as Tocqueville and Aulard, who regarded them in a positive light. In examining the opinions of the "classical historians" it becomes obvious that few treat the Hébertistes, in their general histories of the Revolution, with much more than a scholarly aside. Nor are these historians kind to them. Lefebvre alone is generally favorable to the Hébertistes or treats them with sympathy. Heinrich von Sybel, Hippolyte Taine, Auguste Mignet, and Adolphe Thiers execrate and abhor them. Louis Blanc, Alphonse de Lamartine, Jules Michelet, Jean Jaurès, and Albert Mathiez are somewhat less critical of them and their goals.

Alphonse Aulard, who can be classified as a democratic republican, contrasted Hébert's demand for "blood" with Camille Desmoulins' appeal for "clemency." He was convinced that the Hébertistes intended to stage a coup and to decimate the Convention, as charged in their indictment. Still, Aulard admitted that the trial of the Hébertistes "was a mere parody of justice."[2]

Lefebvre, unlike the other historians just cited, understood that "this crisis [the events of March, 1794—by the revolutionary calendar, late Ventôse and early Germinal of the year II] was decisive; in the history of the revolutionary movement the fall of the Hébertistes marked the beginning of the ebb-tide. For the first time since 1789, the government had forestalled the popular movement by suppressing its leaders." Robespierre and his colleagues thought they would remain in contact with the people, but they failed to realize the moral influence of the drama that unfolded that March.

After the Enragés, the Cordeliers society and especially Hébert, through his immensely popular journal, *Le Père Duchesne*, had become the true leaders of the sans-culottes. The survivors of the Hébertistes reproached the Committee of Public Safety for the death of their friends. Who in the crowd was not discouraged to see these patriots struck down as traitors? asks Lefebvre. The economic policy of the Committee now turned toward the prosecution of the war,

2. Alphonse Aulard, *Histoire politique de la Révolution française: Origines et développement de la démocratie et de la république (1789–1804)* (Paris, 1901), 460–61, 462, 463.

not toward satisfying the needs of the people. Could the social policy of the Committee attach the people to the Montagnards (the Jacobin deputies in the Convention)? The answer was, obviously, that it could not.

The Committee of Public Safety thought that by destroying the Dantonistes after the Hébertistes, it would gain the support of the Convention, but it was only fooling itself, wrote Lefebvre. The Convention never forgave the Committee for forcing it to sacrifice its members, and too many empty seats reminded the deputies of a Terror that could strike them as well. Moreover, the Committee had been a mediator between the Convention and the sans-culottes. With the suppression of the popular movement the deputies no longer needed the Committee for this role. They were now free of its tutelage. All that was necessary to destroy it finally was to divide its members against each other, concluded Lefebvre.[3]

The conservative German historian Heinrich von Sybel repudiated the Revolution in language not much different from that of his French counterpart, Hippolyte Taine. In Sybel's eyes the Hébertistes represented "the party of Hôtel de Ville [that is, of the Paris Commune], put together from top to bottom . . . out of disorder and lawlessness." This party, he wrote, wanted to establish "a tumultuous liberty [*eine tumultuarische Freiheit*], a violent equality, a burlesque philosophy, disgusting to every reasonable human being." Robespierre, he held, attained a certain popularity among the middle classes by his opposition to Hébert, but all party feuds were the result of personal ambition and the struggle for power.[4]

Although Taine did not differentiate between Hébertistes and Montagnards, his opinion of Hébert's party can easily be imagined from his characterization of the Jacobins as "amnestied bandits and other gallows birds . . . street strollers and vagabonds, rebels against labor and discipline, the whole of that class . . . which preserves the instinct of savages, and asserts the sovereignty of the people to glut a natural appetite for license, laziness, and ferocity."[5] Taine lumped all factions

3. Georges Lefebvre, *La Révolution française* (Paris, 1951), 375, 376, Vol. XIII of Louis Halphen and Philippe Sagnac, eds., *Peuples et civilisations*, 20 vols. (ongoing).

4. Heinrich von Sybel, *Geschichte der Revolutionzeit von 1789 bis 1795* (3d ed.; Düsseldorf, 1866–70), II, 444, 448, 454 (my translation). See his chapter entitled "Parteikämpfe unter den Jakobinern."

5. Hippolyte Adolphe Taine, *La Révolution* (Paris, 1882), 38, Vol. II of Taine, *Les Origines de France contemporaine* (11th ed.), 6 vols. The quotation is from John Durand's translation, *The French Revolution* (New York, 1931), II, 28.

of the Left together, so he found no need to excoriate the Hébertistes separately from the rest.

Auguste Mignet, too, was convinced that "the municipal faction" (the Hébertistes) represented "democracy without limits." Its twin principles were "political anarchy" and "religious atheism" (*sic*). This party relied on the revolutionary committees in the Parisian sections, in which could be found many foreigners who were agents sent by England to destroy the Republic by pushing it toward anarchy and various extreme measures.[6] In other words, the Hébertistes and the Paris Commune, which they controlled, were really traitors to France and to the Revolution.

In narrating the disputes between the factions, Adolphe Thiers's account is far more balanced than the recitals of von Sybel or Mignet. Still, he believed that Ronsin and Vincent were "madmen" who wanted to govern France by means of a dictator (a "grand judge")—who was to be the mayor of Paris, Jean Nicolas Pache—plus the guillotine. Thiers quotes Louis Antoine Saint-Just, a member of the Committee of Public Safety and a well-known terrorist, with approval: "One of these factions [the Hébertistes] wants to transform liberty into an orgy, the other [the Dantonistes, also known as the Indulgents] to prostitute it."[7]

Surprisingly, Jean Jaurès accepted the charges that the government leveled against the arrested leaders of the Cordeliers Club, namely, that they plotted to dissolve the Convention, starve Paris, massacre prisoners, and set up a "grand judge"—all in order to reestablish royalty. Even more astonishing is his endorsement of the Jacobins' attack on popular societies. His reasoning was that if the sectional societies had instead become affiliated with the Jacobins, they could have transformed the Jacobin "spirit" into a Cordeliers one and "Hébertisme would have gained great force." Jaurès was also convinced that Ronsin wanted to expand the numbers of the Revolutionary army (which he commanded) in order to use it against the Convention. Thus, Jaurès concluded, the Hébertistes were preparing "a kind of military coup d'état . . . which would have dishonored, bloodied, and ruined France."[8]

6. Auguste Mignet, *Histoire de la Révolution française depuis 1789 jusqu'en 1814* (2d ed.; Paris, 1869), II, 30–31.

7. Adolphe Thiers, *Histoire de la Révolution française* (3d ed.; Paris, 1845), V, 332, 337, 346.

8. Jean Jaurès, *Histoire socialiste de la Révolution française*, ed. Albert Mathiez (Paris, 1924; rpr. with notes by Albert Soboul, New York, 1973), VI, 406–407, 410, 415.

Louis Blanc was no more sympathetic to the Cordeliers than was Jaurès. He strongly defended Robespierre against the Hébertistes and believed the slanders of government-inspired witnesses that, while in prison, Ronsin and Vincent indulged in orgies and banquets. He found Anacharsis Cloots alone worthy of compassion and thought Cloots was linked to the Hébertistes only by their common hatred of priests. Blanc was convinced that Hébert aimed to establish the Paris Commune as the government of France, and through it become the ruler of the country. Although he presented a good summary of the factional fight that developed and remained critical of the so-called moderates or Indulgents, Blanc praised Robespierre's policy of maintaining the Terror. Moreover, he was convinced that the Hébertistes not only dreamed of an insurrection but were preparing it. Thus, though he considered their trial to be "a parody of justice," he also believed that the Hébertistes deserved their fate.[9]

Compared with Blanc's history, Lamartine's recital is far more imaginative, but it must be viewed with distrust because the author does not cite his sources. Lamartine quotes Robespierre, who had dined, allegedly, at Hébert's home, as saying that he favored a triumvirate of Danton, Hébert, and himself. Assuming such a dinner took place, it is difficult to believe that Robespierre would have expressed a sentiment so foreign to his political outlook—certainly not to Hébert. Lamartine was convinced that the government had to strike at Hébert or be annihilated by him. The illness of Robespierre and Georges Couthon encouraged the Hébertistes to risk all, he wrote, and had the Hébertistes succeeded, Jean Marie Collot d'Herbois would have embraced the victorious faction.[10]

Jules Michelet, too, was sure that the Hébertistes meant to stage an insurrection by using an expanded Revolutionary army of 100,000 men under Ronsin, who then would have become a military dictator. Although Michelet believed that the Hébertistes meant to starve Paris and to massacre the prisoners, as the public prosecutor charged, he repudiated the accusation that they were royalists.[11]

Mathiez, as is well known, stoutly defended Robespierre's policy

9. Louis Blanc, *Histoire de la Révolution française* (2d ed.; Paris, 1869–70), IX, 485, 471–73. Blanc gave a clear summary of the dispute between the factions, *ibid.*, 223–34, 293–303.

10. Alphonse de Lamartine, *Histoire des Girondins* (Brussels, 1847), VII, 284, 289, 291.

11. Jules Michelet, *Histoire de la Révolution française,* ed. Gerard Walter (Paris, 1961), II, 768–69.

and condemned both the Hébertistes and their opponents the Dantonistes. He argued that the struggle between these factions threatened to destroy the government that alone could consolidate the Revolution. Had the Hébertistes the slightest "political sense," he wrote, they would have rallied around the Committees. Since, however, they had no social program to compete with the government's proposed confiscation of condemned counterrevolutionaries' property and its distribution among the patriotic poor, they were only interested in satisfying their "ambitions and grudges." Furthermore, the Cordeliers were convinced they could carry out a successful insurrection that would place them in power (Mathiez cites fraudulent testimony of witnesses as if it were true); thus, the committees of Public Safety and of General Security had to strike "the ultras in self-defense."[12]

Since in this work I often cite the opinions of Albert Soboul and Daniel Guérin, who examined the Hébertistes/Cordeliers in some detail, it is best to leave comments on their approach to the text itself. Readers can gauge for themselves the important contribution these two historians made to the study of Hébertisme. It is hardly necessary to add that I have benefited much from their insight. At the same time I have modified, and occasionally rejected, their opinions on certain events and individuals. Guérin, for example, saw the sans-culottes as resembling "pre-proletarians" of our own time, and tried to apply Trotsky's theory of "uneven and combined development" to the French Revolution. Trotsky sought to explain the leap from czarism to a "proletarian dictatorship," thereby skipping over the stage of capitalism and "bourgeois democracy," by his theory.[13] Whatever application it might have for the Russian Revolution, it can hardly explain the French Revolution.

Soboul, on the other hand, thought that the Revolution could have been saved by attaching the sans-culottes to it, something that the Hébertistes might have been able to do. Specifically, this could have been done, he wrote, by repressing the moderates, maintaining the Terror, and rapidly executing the measures passed in Ventôse—that is, by distributing the confiscated property of suspects and émigrés. There is much truth in what Soboul says, but questions arise: For one,

12. Albert Mathiez, *La Révolution française* (11th ed.; Paris, 1951), III, 135–37, 148–49, 150, 151, 153, 156.

13. Daniel Guérin, *La Lutte de classes sous la première république: Bourgeois et "bras nus," 1793–1797* (Paris, 1946).

did the sans-culottes possess the knowledge and experience to cultivate the soil and transform themselves into successful farmers? For another, would not the repression of those who were truly moderate in their politics and outlook (not necessarily the Indulgents) have further alienated many from the revolutionary government? If so, this added mass of opponents, together with the commercial classes and with modest holders of landed properties, combined with the bourgeoisie proper, would have made it extremely difficult for the government to maintain itself. Continuing the Terror would scarcely have provided bread and meat for the sans-culottes and their families. It was this lack of the essentials of life that caused so much discontent among them, after all. Furthermore, as long as the war continued, scarcity and high prices were its inevitable consequences.[14]

The historians cited above agree that Hébert would have made his peace with the central authorities had he been offered the position of minister of the interior. In other words, he would have been willing to betray his principles for a mess of pottage. The fact that he was personally ambitious should not be held against him; all politicians are ambitious. But the great leaders of popular movements are too jealous of their historic role to sacrifice their movements for a ministerial post, and if all there was to Hébertisme were demagogy, personal ambition, or vengeance, there would be no problem in condemning it. The essential question, therefore, concerns the extent to which the Hébertistes/Cordeliers promoted, defended, and expressed the aspirations and interests of the sans-culottes. It makes little difference whether they spoke for what some historians call the "plebeians," or the "*bras nus*," or the "*patriotes prononcés*," as opposed to the bourgeois elements of the French Republic. The question remains: to what extent did they support and extend the mass participation of common people in the political process?

Perhaps it would be better to say that the Hébertistes/Cordeliers *refracted*, rather than *reflected*, the interests of the sans-culottes. Political parties, as is well known, often distort the aspirations of their constituents. Nevertheless, in profound social crises, revolutionaries often apply a policy of "critical support" to a regime even if it distorts the ideals of its people.

The Soviet historian Alfred Manfred argued that although the exe-

---

14. Albert Soboul, *Les Sans-Culottes parisiens en l'an II: Mouvement populaire et gouvernement révolutionnaire, 2 juin 1793–9 thermidor an II* (Paris, 1958), 738.

cution of the Hébertistes weakened the Jacobin regime, that regime's intrinsic nature remained the same: essentially a "democratic and revolutionary dictatorship." Like many other Soviet historians he sees the French Revolution as "a total complex" with contradictions among social classes and groups. He does not believe that the essential conflict of the period was between the sans-culottes and the revolutionary government (Soboul's thesis). The Jacobins represented not only the bourgeoisie but other classes as well. They did more to solve the agrarian problem within a month after the insurrection against the Girondins than had been done in all the years previous to May 13, 1793, he writes. Thus, he argues, the Jacobin dictatorship was "a bloc of the democratic middle and petty bourgeoisie, of the peasantry and of the urban *plebeians*, or to revert to the same, of sans-culottes."[15]

This attempt to apply the formula of the Russian Revolution to France (ignoring for the moment the differences between "a bloc of the proletariat and peasantry"—Lenin's early concept—and "a dictatorship of the proletariat supported by the peasantry," as seen by Trotsky) does not help to define the role of the factions in the French Revolution. More exactly, it leaves open the question whether Hébertisme was progressive as against the revolutionary government of France in 1793 and 1794.

If the Hébertistes encouraged mass participation and initiative of common men and women in the sectional assemblies, in popular societies, in the Paris Commune, and in political demonstrations, then it can be argued that Hébertisme was, indeed, progressive. This does not mean, of course, that every such act was rational, tolerant, or democratic. Still, despite their verbal extremism, the Hébertistes constantly appealed to the sans-culottes to introduce a more democratic policy, to champion a social program of benefit to them and to their allies, to limit the power of the propertied or of the new bureaucracy, or to create a new institution. In general they helped educate politically and give dignity to the ordinary people of their day. It is in this sense that they deserve a sympathetic examination from the historian.

15. Alfred Manfred, "La Nature du pouvoir Jacobin," *La Pensée*, CL (April, 1970), 62–83. Manfred writes that "the logic" of events forced the Jacobins to impose the Terror to defend the historic interests of the bourgeoisie, and that after executing the Hébertistes they struck against "the Right," the Dantonistes; *ibid.*, 78, 79–80.

1

Hébert and His *Père Duchesne*

The man who gave his name to the party, Jacques René Hébert, was born November 15, 1757, in Alençon, a large town in northwestern France. He was the son of a jeweler, Jacques Hébert, who as a magistrate and successful businessman had become a notable of the city. The family had established itself in Dauphiné by 1685, when the grandfather—also named Jacques—having completed his apprenticeship as a jeweler, received a license to open his own shop. His son, our subject's father, after establishing himself as a master jeweler, bought a small fief in 1734, thus becoming a bourgeois of Alençon. At age sixty he married (for the second time). The bride, Marguerite Beunaiche de La Houdrie, was twenty-nine. She bore four children, of whom Jacques René was the second.[1]

Hébert's father died at age seventy-four, when Jacques René was but eleven. The boy's education was taken over by his mother, who decided that he should attend the college of Alençon, rather than be apprenticed to his uncle, also in the jewelry trade. After graduation Hébert was employed as a clerk to a *procureur* (public prosecutor). He became involved with a widow, was sued for slandering a physician, lost the case, and was fined 1,000 livres (1779), a sum that ruined the family financially. As a result he left Alençon for Rouen, and shortly thereafter went on to Paris. While trying to establish himself he suffered poverty and even hunger. Some friends, including a writer and a hairdresser, helped him to live. In 1786 he took a modest job in the Varieties Theater as a *contrôleur de contremarques* (in charge of free admission tickets). Finally, when he was down to the one garment on

1. Louis Duval, "Hébert chez lui," *La Révolution française*, XII (1886), 961–81; Gérard Walter, *Hébert et le "Père Duchesne" (1757–1794)*, ed. J. B. Janin ([Dijon], 1946), 11–12, 13.

JAQUES RÉNE HÉBERT.

Né en 1759 à Alençon Dép. de l'Orne.

Substitut du Proc. de la Com. de Paris,

Rédacteur du Journal dit le Père Duchêne.

decapité le 4. Germinal l'an 2.me

Paris Rue du Théâtre Français. N.º 4.

Hébert dit le « Père Duchesne ».

Two contemporary portraits of Jacques René Hébert reveal a considerable difference of opinion between the artists as to their subject's appearance.

his back, he called upon a physician acquaintance, who obtained employment for him editing an obscure work.[2]

2. Duval, "Hébert chez lui," XII, 980–81, XIII (1887), 45–46, 49–50, 52–53; Louis Jacob, *Hébert Le Père Duchesne: Chef des sans-culottes* (Paris, 1960), 22–37, *passim*; Alexandre Tuetey, *Répertoire général des sources manuscrits de l'histoire de Paris pendant la Révolution française* (Paris, 1890–1914), XI, i–ii.

In 1790 Hébert published a pamphlet, *Petit carême de l'abbé Maury*, and found his profession. His *Père Duchesne*, which became more popular than Marat's journal, probably appeared by the end of the year.[3] Hébert possessed an understanding of counterrevolutionary intrigues and shrewdly predicted the course of events. Like others, he was at first a mild monarchist, spoke of Louis XVI as representing the sovereign nation, broke with Lafayette, and reflected an anti-clerical bias, especially against the higher clergy. What made his journal so popular, however, was his talent in addressing the sans-culottes in their own language. No one used the language of the street in a more effective way. His "great joy" or his "great anger" moved thousands of his readers to embrace or denounce an individual or a proposal.[4]

Hébert settled in section Bonne-Nouvelle on rue Neuve de l'Egalité (on the Right Bank, north of the Seine) and soon plunged into the political life of the capital. He met an ex-nun, Marie Marguerite Fran-çoise Goupil, in a popular club, Société fraternelle des deux sexes, which gathered in the Jacobin Club's premises. Marie Goupil had de-cided in June of 1790 to give up her religious vows and turn to secular affairs. She was young, witty, and knew how to prepare a good meal. Hébert married her, and on February 7, 1793, she gave birth to a girl. If we can believe a visitor to Hébert's home, the ex-nun seems never to have lost her religious feelings. She was quoted by him as saying, "I am, monsieur, very devoted to Christianity." On the table was an engraving by Titian showing Jesus with two of his disciples. Under-neath, Hébert had written: "The sans-culotte Jesus supping with two

3. Eugene Hatin, *Histoire politique et litteraire de la presse en France* . . . (Geneva, 1967), VI, 487–88. The issues were not numbered until January, 1791, and began to carry Hébert's signature with No. 131. Hatin traces the origin of the title *Père Duchesne* and the role of Hébert's predecessor, Lemaire, who revived it; *ibid.*, 452–59, 466–69. Walter, *Hébert et le "Père Duchesne,"* 45, 48, thinks Hébert probably began publishing the journal in June or July of 1790. During the last days of 1790 three other *Père Duchesne*s were being published in Paris.

4. For the ideology of *Père Duchesne*, see Jacques Guilhaumou, "L'Idéologie du Père Duchesne: Les Forces adjuvantes (14 juillet–6 septembre 1793)," *Le Mouvement social*, LXXXV (October–December, 1973), 81–116, and Nicos Poulantzas, *Political Power and Social Classes* (London, 1973), 173–80.

Ferdinand Brunot, the great lexicographer, termed Hébert "the Homer of filth"; cited by Gérard Walter in Michelet, *Histoire*, II, "Table analytique," No. 1442. See also Duval, "Hébert chez lui," XIII, 53–54; Jacob, *Hébert Le Père Duchesne*, 42–66, *passim*; Tuetey, *Répertoire général*, XI, ii; and Paul Lafargue, "La Langue française avant et après la Révolution," in Lafargue, *Marxisme et linguistique* (Paris, 1977), 109–12.

of his disciples in the chateau of a former nobleman." Mme Hébert called it one of her husband's "bad jokes."[5]

By January, 1791, Hébert was raising his voice against the division of society into so-called active and passive citizens and had changed his attitude toward both the king and the National Assembly. He charged: "You have destroyed the aristocracy of nobles and of clergy and you have created one a thousand times more hateful, that of wealth." He had by then evolved from a moderate monarchist to a democratic republican. By March, 1791, he had probably joined the Cordeliers Club, and after Louis' flight to Varennes, Hébert became a strong republican.[6]

His growing involvement in politics won him a seat in the electoral college, where he represented his section. After the massacre of the Champ de Mars, Hébert became prudent but assailed the high property requirement (*marc d'argent*) for deputies and campaigned for the election to the Legislative Assembly of "good deputies" like Maximilien Robespierre (currently excluded by the "self-denying" ordinance passed May 16, 1791, by the Legislative Assembly's forerunner, the Constituent Assembly), and the future mayor of Paris Jérôme Pétion. He was arrested on March 5, 1792, for attacking "Mme Veto" (Marie Antoinette), but was quickly released.

In 1792 Hébert was thirty-five years old, sole owner and publisher of the *Père Duchesne*, which played a role in mobilizing the fédérés (national guardsmen from the departments of France) and section-

---

5. Duval, "Hébert chez lui," XIII, 58, cites Dufriches-Desgenettes, *Souvenirs du XVIIIe siècle au commencement du XIXe*, Tome II, pp. 237–54. It seems that Desgenettes had helped Hébert when he was poor, for when he came to visit the Héberts in their home, Hébert immediately took out 100 francs in gold and gave it to his visitor with many thanks. *Ibid.;* Tuetey, *Répertoire général*, XI, ii.

G. Tridon, an admirer of Hébert, in his *Les Hébertistes: La Commune de Paris de 1793* (Paris, 1871), 50, cites a source entitled *Hommes célèbres de la Révolution*, by Lairtullier, that described Hébert as "a very handsome man, of an open countenance, lively, and benevolent." His manners were elegant, the description goes on, and his wife presided over an epicurean table, although she herself was one of the more spiritual women of her time. Hébert's apartment was decorated in good taste with paintings of the masters.

6. Jacob, *Hébert Le Père Duchesne*, 65; Jacques Guilhaumou, "'Moment actuel' et processus discursif: Le 'Père Duchesne' d'Hébert et le 'publiciste de la république française' de Jacques Roux (14 juillet–6 septembre 1793)," *Bulletin du centre d'analyse du discours*, III (1975), 148; Michael Sonenscher, "The *Sans-Culottes* of the Year II: Rethinking the Language of Labour in Revolutionary France," *Social History*, IX (October, 1984), 301–28; William H. Sewell, Jr., *Work and Revolution in France: The Language of Labor from the Old Regime to 1848* (Cambridge, Eng., 1980), 3.

Hébert had a strong hand in orchestrating the events that led up to the overthrow of the king in the *journée* of August 10, 1792.

naires in the antimonarchist demonstration of June 20, 1792. The following month he was elected president of the Cordeliers, which adopted a radical political program—suspension of the king, replacement of Louis' agents by a commission, and several measures to broaden democratic procedures. Hébert advised his readers: "See to it that Monsieur Veto be reduced to zero; yes, f——, if nature has intended him to make locks, let him forge them from morning till night, provided that they do not become shackles to crush us."[7]

During the night of August 9–10, Hébert sat as a commissioner to the Commune when it directed the overthrow of the king, an action

7. Tuetey, *Répertoire général*, XI, iii; *Père Duchesne*, No. 162. I have chosen not to offer a full translation of the most notorious French vulgarism, which Hébert employed abundantly in his journal as characteristic of sans-culotte speech. In all but a few occurrences herein, the approximate (but not exact) meaning is "f——k it"; where variations exist, I have indicated their nature.

he described in a brochure written shortly afterward. The following month, during the tragic days of the September Massacres, the Commune dispatched him with others to halt these killings, a mission that failed. Shortly thereafter he published another pamphlet on the executions in Abbaye prison.[8] On September 12 the electoral assembly of Paris decided that deputies elected to the new legislature, the Convention, should undergo a careful scrutiny (*scrutin épuratoire*) with the intent of "purging" those deemed unworthy to take their seats. Hébert protested that since most electors were at the front, the sections were composed of only Feuillants (conservatives—specifically, those who had left the Jacobin Club as being too radical) and patriots who did not dare lift their heads. The next day he persuaded the Commune to adopt his motion to prepare a poster in defense of the elected deputies of Paris, a poster whose contents he drafted himself. The following week he protested against newcomers on the Commune's *Comité de surveillance* as strangers to the work of the municipal police, and obtained their recall. Among these newly elected representatives to the General Council was Jean Paul Marat. In December, 1792, Pierre Gaspard Chaumette was elected *procureur* of the Commune, with Hébert as second alternate. Thus, he was a member of the Commune of August 10, an elector of Paris, a member of the Commune known as "provisional," an alternate to the *procureur*, and finally, an alternate to the national agent, the representative of the central authorities.[9]

As a "passive citizen" in 1790, Hébert could not join the Jacobin Club. After the insurrection of August 10, 1792, this distinction was formally dropped (it was already unenforceable by the spring of that year), and both Hébert and Chaumette became members. During the trial of Louis, after first denying the need to execute him, Hébert changed his position and argued that people with kings at their head could not be free. As commissioner to the Temple, where Louis and his family had been imprisoned, Hébert used his position to describe the life of the royal prisoners to his readers. When the Convention voted to execute the king, Hébert went with Dominique Joseph Garat,

8. Jacques René Hébert, *Massacre des prisonniers d'Orléans* (Paris, n.d.), in Lb 39 10881, BN; Hébert, "Great detail of execution of all the conspirators and brigands of abbaye Saint-Germain . . . ," in Maurice Tourneux, *Bibliographie de l'histoire de Paris pendant la Révolution française* (1890; rpr. Paris, 1968), I, No. 3465.

9. Tuetey, *Répertoire général*, XI, iii; Jacob, *Hébert Le Père Duchesne*, 126.

the minister of the interior, and Pierre Henri Lebrun, the Girondin minister of foreign affairs, to inform Louis of the verdict. He described the king's dignified behavior honestly and sympathetically, writing that "the king was firm and devout to the last moment." But when a motion was introduced in the Commune to describe Louis' last minutes, Hébert opposed it, claiming that it would make Louis an object of pity, thus, a martyr.[10]

From September, 1792, until June, 1793, Hébert kept repeating: "Our most deadly enemies are the Brissotins," referring to the adherents of Jacques Pierre Brissot de Warville, a leading Girondin who had done much to push France into war with the Habsburg monarchy in 1792.[11] At the same time he was suspicious of General Charles François Dumouriez after Dumouriez's early victories in Belgium in that war. "A nation becomes enslaved when its warriors take up other things than fighting," Hébert wrote. He was especially unsparing of Jean Marie Roland, the minister of the interior, calling him "le cornard Roland" (the horned Roland) and "cocu" (cuckold), and his wife "la reine Coco," all referring to the well-known fact that Mme Roland was not the most faithful of spouses. In a more serious vein, he continued to warn against the Girondin proposal to defend the Convention against the rising insurrectionary forces by an independent departmental army under Girondin control.

Despite Hébert's antagonism to the Girondins he was not unwilling to help individuals linked to them—if the following incident reveals more than a temporary aberration. According to an author of *souvenirs* named Dufriche-Desgenettes, who had loaned money to Hébert during the latter's period of poverty and who was visiting him, the following incident took place: A knock on the door signaled the arrival of a disheveled man who complained to Hébert that he had come three times to see him but had not found him at home. Hébert assured him that he had not forgotten his affair and

---

10. Jacob, *Hébert Le Père Duchesne*, 132. But after Louis' execution Hébert thundered ferociously that both the former "tyrant's" widow and his offspring ought to be destroyed. Tuetey wrote that Hébert enjoyed creating discomfort for the royal family; *Répertoire général*, XI, iv.

11. Jacques Pierre Brissot de Warville (1754–1793) was the publisher of the pro-Girondin journal *Patriote français,* and a leading member of the Girondins. He was an ardent advocate of war against Austria in the spring of 1792 and an opponent of Robespierre and the Paris Commune. His influence ended with the arrest of the leading Girondins after the insurrection of May 31–June 2, 1793.

that he intended to take it up again at the Cordeliers Club the same evening. It turned out that the man was desperate for the post of concierge in a prison. Hébert again assured him that he would speak that same evening to Danton and to Louis Legendre—both influential deputies who could fill positions in the local government—then invited the man to dine with him. The visitor refused but asked for a glass of wine, with which he toasted the company, and then left. Desgenettes revealed that the man was the nephew of a leading Girondin, Charles Eléonor Dufriche Valazé, who came from Hébert's hometown of Alençon. Evidently, as a fellow townsman he had come to Hébert for help, and whether for neighborly or compassionate reasons, Hébert was willing to intervene in his behalf. Desgenettes added that despite the style of his journal, Hébert himself was quite polite.[12]

Hébert seemed ambivalent on how to treat profiteering in the retail trade. After the outburst of February 25, 1793, when a movement begun by desperate laundresses ended with hungry men and women pillaging stores and shops and setting their own prices on food and goods, Hébert defended the shopkeepers. They were not to blame for what speculators and profiteers were doing, he wrote. The result of such action as that of February 25 would only lead to empty shelves and inadequate supplies, he predicted, and he joined Robespierre, Marat, and Chaumette in blaming the food riots on the policy of the Girondins in refusing to regulate prices.

After General Dumouriez deserted to the Austrians, the Girondins arrested Marat in the hope of breaking the Jacobin/sans-culotte offensive against them (which had gained fresh fuel from the fact that it was the Girondins who had promoted and supported Dumouriez up to his moment of treachery). Hébert immediately took up Marat's defense and on April 15, 1793, called for the expulsion of twenty-two leading Girondins from the Convention. Shortly thereafter he called for disarming suspects and creating "a sans-culotte army paid for by the nation which will exterminate the counterrevolution." (The Commune adopted this demand, and it eventually became a rallying point in the successful sans-culotte demonstration of September 4 and 5, 1793.) When the Evêché assembly—the extralegal body that launched the insurrection of May 31, against the Girondins—was formed, consisting of delegates representing thirty-three of the more radical sec-

12. Duval, "Hébert chez lui," XIII, 59.

tions, some with unlimited powers, Hébert defended it as necessary to assure supplies for the capital. The Committee of Twelve, created by the Convention on Bertrand Barère's motion with the aim of nullifying the coming insurrection, arrested Hébert, subjected him to a seven-hour interrogation, and imprisoned him.[13]

From prison Hébert published No. 240 of the *Père Duchesne*, demanding the punishment of "traitors." The Cordeliers Club passed a motion to free him forcibly. The police spy Dutard wrote that the Convention must find means to free him honorably or face the prospect of civil war. By this time great excitement was growing in the sections and a turbulent discussion agitated the Convention. As a result, Hébert was freed on May 27, 1793, and the Committee of Twelve was temporarily shelved. He continued to agitate for an insurrection, in contrast to Chaumette, who still opposed taking illegal measures (much later Pierre François Réal, the first alternate to the *procureur*, testified that Hébert "was the sole municipal officer resolute enough to make an attempt against the integrity of the national representation"). "Citizens," Hébert appealed, "remain on guard!" (*restez debout*).[14]

The successful insurrection against the Girondins beginning May 31 raised Hébert's prestige to new heights. After the king was overthrown on August 10, 1792, the Paris Commune had attempted unsuccessfully to organize a kind of universal commune of all the departments. Now Hébert revived the plan to launch a correspondence with the 44,000 communes of France. The *Affiches de la Commune* was intended to rival the Convention's *Bulletin*. The Montagnard leaders, who had gained power following the May 31 insurrection and had no intention of sharing it with the Paris Commune, viewed this move suspiciously. The Federalist Revolt, breaking out in the summer of 1793, ended the scheme, but Hébert's challenge to the Convention was not forgotten. Months later, after Hébert's final arrest, Louis Roux, a former official of the municipality, testified (March 20, 1794) that "Hébert and Chaumette attempted to usurp the national author-

13. Jacob, *Hébert Le Père Duchesne*, 155, reproduces part of the interrogation from *J-R Hébert, substitut du procureur de la Commune, à ses concitoyens*, in Lc 41 4754, BN.

14. Jacob, *Hébert Le Père Duchesne*, 163; Walter, *Hébert et le "Père Duchesne,"* 110–30, *passim*; Tuetey, *Répertoire général*, XI, iv–v. Jacob differs with Walter on Hébert's role in the insurrection. Hébert was more cautious than Jacob indicates. See Morris Slavin, *The Making of an Insurrection: Parisian Sections and the Gironde* (Cambridge, Mass., 1986), 95n24, 99.

ity in order to concentrate it in the Commune, which they hoped to dominate."[15]

Hébert's drive to make the Paris Commune a rival to the Convention may have arisen at least partly out of his failure to win appointment as a minister. There seems little doubt that after the resignation of Garat as minister of the interior, Hébert vied for his post. Danton, however, had his own candidate for this position. Jules François Paré had been his fellow student at the college of Troyes and was employed by Danton as his master clerk. From his post of secretary to the Legislative Assembly's Executive Council (predecessor to the Committee of Public Safety and led by Danton), Paré was promoted through Danton's influence to become minister of the interior on August 20, 1793. From this date on, Hébert became an opponent not only of Danton but of the Robespierristes as well.[16]

In the conflict that followed, Hébert clashed with Danton and accused him of abandoning the sans-culottes. When on August 26 Danton asked him to retract the accusations, Hébert maintained that his criticism was not directed at Danton alone but included the whole Committee of Public Safety. Danton had fallen short of commitments expected of him by patriots, he declared, and the old Committee had impeded the efforts of Mayor Pache to supply Paris with bread. Danton took the floor and declared that he had had the minister of interior set aside 10 million livres for supplying Paris. He invited his accusers to examine his fortune, which was 40,000 livres—not 14 million, as was charged. Danton concluded by congratulating himself for having been born a sans-culotte and for having the necessary physical energy to earn his living.[17] The duel between the two continued, but Hébert's criticism of Danton was obviously not disinterested.

By the fall of the year the dispute between Hébert and Danton led to the suspension of the *Père Duchesne*'s distribution among the troops at the front. On October 19, 1793, Hébert complained that the *Comité de salut public* of the Paris Department had stopped his journal from circulating in the department on the pretext that he had slandered the

15. Jacob, *Hébert Le Père Duchesne*, 171–72. This charge was to be repeated at Hébert's trial.

16. Soboul, *Sans-Culottes*, 149.

17. Alphonse Aulard, *La Société des Jacobins: Recueil de documents pour l'histoire du club des Jacobins de Paris* (Paris, 1889–97), V, 378–79, 380. Georges Lefebvre concluded that Danton did enrich himself in Belgium; see "Sur Danton," in Lefebvre, *Etudes sur la Revolution française* (Paris, 1963), 53–107.

authorities. In addition, the committee had sent an agent, a former clerk of the criminal court, to Hébert's native town in order to ferret out embarrassing facts about his private life. One member of the committee cited a passage from the *Père Duchesne* that accused the authorities of behaving like vultures instead of working "like ants."[18]

Hébert heartily denied the charges against him. "If the administrators, in general, valued the administrated, things would go well and the Republic would be saved," he declared. Denying criminal behavior on his part he cried: "They pretend that I had vilified the constituted authorities; I who constantly preach respect for the good magistrates of the people! I who never recommend anything but a religious observance of the laws!" When Louis Pierre Dufourny, a Dantoniste and opponent of Hébert, asked him who was responsible for this attack on him, Hébert named a committee employee behind whom, he said, was Danton.[19]

A member of the department's surveillance committee defended himself by citing the offensive passage from the *Père Duchesne*. Dufourny followed declaring, surprisingly, that the authorities ought not to consider themselves reproached by this statement. This turnabout by Danton's colleague might have resulted from a simple recognition that there was, indeed, nothing slanderous in this passage—or it could have been from prudence, since Hébert was still too popular to attack directly. Dufourny possibly knew of the letter signed by three representatives-on-mission to the Army of the North complaining that Hébert's journal had not been received by the troops for three weeks and urging that its suspension be lifted immediately. In any case, several Jacobins joined in Hébert's defense. One member commented that Hébert's journal had a great beneficial effect on the 300,000 soldiers who read it, and thus was worthy of continued subsidy and support. Antoine François Momoro, president of the Cordeliers and staunch supporter of Hébert, declared that the *Père Duchesne* performed good service, and demanded redress for its publisher. Amidst applause, his suggestion was adopted in the form of a resolution. Another Jacobin, Sentex, moved that the issue of the jour-

18. *Père Duchesne*, No. 297. Hébert also wrote that the French were fighting like cats and dogs when they should be united like brothers.

19. Tuetey, *Répertoire général*, V, 473. Hébert declared that the employee's name was Fabricius, known as Leroi, who had revealed to a number of friends that Danton was doing all possible to destroy Hébert.

nal in question be sent to all popular societies in order to strike at "fanaticism." The society ordered that this be done.[20]

The "fanaticism" referred to by Sentex was that alleged against the Catholic church. All revolutionaries combated the Church for allegiance to the new order. As the conflict sharpened, many turned their backs on traditional religion and adopted a secular philosophy instead. Others became atheists. Did Hébert's assault on Catholicism lead him to atheism? This charge was raised against him at his trial, but there is little evidence to support it. It is true that he promoted the dechristianization movement of the Paris Commune in the fall of 1793, together with Chaumette, when many churches were closed down. Still, the worship of the Supreme Being, inaugurated by Robespierre in a famous festival (June 8, 1793), was directed against both Catholicism and atheism. Essentially, it sought to promote a form of deism, a practice Hébert accepted. Hébert maintained that "all religions are good when they inspire love of humanity, respect for the law, peace, and concord," and he saw Jesus as "the founder of all popular societies." The Evangel was the best of books, he wrote, and he looked upon Jesus as a sans-culotte, as we have seen. It is true that he favored a secular education for the young, but he honored the deist Rousseau, rather than the skeptic Voltaire. Moreover, he was tolerant of those who insisted on worshiping their "God of clay."[21]

Of course, Hébert attacked the Church as supporter of the counter-

20. For the resolution, see *ibid.*, 477–78 (October 24, 1793). The three representatives-on-mission who wrote the letter (on August 23, 1793) were Delbrel, Letourneur, and Chales; *ibid.*, X, No. 2219. A citizen-soldier from Metz, Dolivet, complained, however, that Hébert was slandering General Custine and blamed "le parti de Pache" for protecting "the rogues"; *ibid.*, X, No. 2218.

21. *Père Duchesne*, No. 335, in which he added that Jesus was a "good republican who made war on the rich and the priests; in one word, f——, there never existed a better Jacobin." Hébert spoke of a "God of flour." On 21 Frimaire II (December 11, 1793) in the Jacobin Club he denied "formally" the charge of atheism, insisting that the "maxims" of the Bible should be followed in order "to be a perfect Jacobin"; Aulard, *Jacobins*, V, 552–53. Aulard was convinced that Hébert wrote nothing on religion that Rousseau would not have approved. He cited Nos. 307, 310, and 311 of the *Père Duchesne*, in which Hébert attacked priests who had disfigured the Evangel, praised highly the Festival of Reason in Notre Dame, and quoted his wife as saying that God did not place human beings on earth to be tormented but to be happy. Reason, for Hébert, was nothing but "an emanation of God," Aulard wrote. See Alphonse Aulard, *Le Culte de la raison et le culte de l'Etre suprême (1793–1794)* (2d ed.; Paris, 1904), 82–83, 84, 85.

revolution, but it should be noted that Dantonistes such as François Chabot, Claude Basire, Jacques Alexis Thuriot, and Fabre d'Eglantine organized the cult of Reason before the Hébertistes launched their dechristianization movement, and that three days after the adoption of the new calendar Thuriot called for a religion of patriotism to replace traditional religion. Some historians hold that the *Père Duchesne* was mild in its indictment of Catholicism compared with several of the Girondin journals. On the other hand, the police spy Rolin reported on 1 Ventôse II (February 22, 1794) that people criticized Hébert for returning to the theme of defrocked priests. He seemed to enjoy this topic, Rolin quoted an unnamed person as saying. "After forcing them to unfrock themselves, he seeks to make them detestable for having been his dupes," concluded Hébert's critic.[22]

The conflict over religious practices soon led to political differences as well. By late fall of 1793 two distinct parties had formed: the one supported Hébert, the other Camille Desmoulins. The latter had launched a journal, *Le Vieux Cordelier*, championing "moderation" and, eventually, attacking the Terror and the revolutionary organs created by the government to enforce it. Since Hébert and the Cordeliers Club were on the opposite side, Desmoulins used all his journalistic skill to undermine their position and goals among the public. In his issue No. 5 he accused Hébert of profiting immorally from the subsidy that the government provided the *Père Duchesne*. According to his charge, Hébert had received 135,000 livres from the national treasury on June 2, 1793, and after expenses had pocketed 43,184 livres.[23]

Hébert replied in his No. 332 that Desmoulins published 100,000 copies at twenty sous per day, whereas he, Hébert, sold his paper at

22. Pierre Caron, *Paris pendant la Terreur: Rapports des agents secrets du ministre de l'intérieur* (Paris, 1910–64), IV, 218–19. Edgar Quinet argued that the revolutionaries never attempted to overthrow Catholicism because they were too frightened by "the altars of the past," and that Hébert and Chaumette surrendered to the old religion just as the Jacobins had done; Edgar Quinet, *La Révolution* (Paris, 1865), II, 149. François Furet commented that "Quinet deplored not the dechristianization movement but that Robespierre and the Jacobins put an end to it. In fact, Quinet thought that this movement inspired by the Hébertistes was a new, spontaneous kind of religion, that conformed to the spirit of Christianity"; François Furet, *La Gauche et la Révolution française au milieu du XIXe siècle: Edgar Quinet et le question de Jacobinisme* (Paris, 1986), 65–66.

23. *Le Vieux Cordelier*, No. 5, in *Collection des mémoires relatifs à la Révolution française*, LII (Paris, 1825).

two sous a copy. Desmoulins called him a rich man because in June he supposedly had made 90,000 livres for the 900,000 copies sold. But Desmoulins forgot to deduct the cost of more than 15,000 livres in expenses for the presses, type, paper, cost of wood and candles, pay for the workingmen employed, night bonuses, and rent increases. Of the profits that remained, Hébert had to give half to his partner. Finally, Hébert wrote, he had deposited his own half in a voluntary loan to the government. "It is this that Camille calls robbing the Republic," he concluded.

On 18 Nivôse (January 7, 1794) the police spy Latour-Lamontagne reported that people believed the two antagonists were wasting time and damaging the Republic by their personal quarrels. As a result, the Jacobins were ignoring the larger interests of the country by taking part in this fracas. The following day, the police observer Bacon described how people reacted to Hébert's reply to Desmoulins posted on the walls. The well-dressed gentlemen smiled as they read it. The sans-culottes, who remained a long time in reading, kept a gloomy silence, and all those whom he watched scratched their heads as they left. Added to this was the din created over Desmoulins' accusation that Hébert had stolen free passes at the Varieties Theater when he was employed there. Several Jacobins promised to examine the affair, wrote Charmont, another police spy, that same day.[24]

The conflicting reports of the spies make it difficult to know whether Hébert or Desmoulins had more supporters. Pourvoyeur, for example, wrote that "Camille Desmoulins has the esteem of the people," that they regarded Hébert as "an intriguer," and that all agreed in hoping Hébert's and Chaumette's party would not win out. Béraud reported that he had overheard five of six women coming out of the Jacobins complain that laws were being executed badly since the Convention did nothing for starving mothers and wives of defenders while giving 100,000 to 125,000 livres to Hébert, "who wants to lull us with his b[ougre] . . . of a *Père Duchesne*." After some discussion these citizens retired, "but with anger in their hearts," Béraud noted on January 8. The next day Latour-Lamontagne reported that Hébert's reply to Desmoulins had raised the spirits of his followers and that people were saying Hébert was certainly a patriot and would triumph over his persecutors. Some saw a similarity to the

24. Caron, *Paris pendant la Terreur*, II, 223–24, 238, 240.

Brissotin persecution of Hébert; others thought it would be a good idea to keep subscribers to Desmoulins' journal under surveillance. On the same day, however, Charmont stated just the opposite: "No one believes in his patriotism." Dugas added that people were getting tired of this dispute and were waiting for Robespierre to clarify things.[25]

But the quarrel and interest in it continued, according to other observers. Pourvoyeur reported (January 8), that the public was preoccupied with the dispute. On January 7 he reiterated what he had written on December 27, 1793: that "public opinion is wholly in favor of Camille Desmoulins." People said openly that Hébert was an intriguer who sought to undermine the true patriots. Some repeated the charge of Desmoulins against him, that he had not discharged with honor his earlier post at the Varieties Theater. They contrasted Marat's journal with Hébert's to the detriment of the latter, and swore they would no longer buy it, wrote Pourvoyeur. Mercier agreed that "Hébert is today the subject of conversation" and that people had lost confidence in him. Monic also agreed that this conflict was the subject of all conversation. "The good citizens are afflicted . . . [and] the aristocracy begins to raise its head as boldly as ever," he warned. He concluded by declaring that one thing was certain: "Everywhere the citizens argue for or against Camille and others, as well as for Hébert." Bacon added that in almost all neighborhoods that he visited, especially those inhabited by workers, people were interested in their "Père Duchesne" (Hébert himself was by now often called by this name). Why did Desmoulins accuse Hébert of stealing? asked a limonadier. A customer replied, "Be patient, we still do not know who the true patriots are at present."[26] This mood of skepticism was to work in favor of the revolutionary government.

Two days later, on 21 Nivôse (January 10, 1794), Letassey overheard someone say that "Camille Desmoulins seeks to inculpate the Père Duchesne [Hébert] for trying to wash himself clean, but he will not succeed; he [Hébert] is known as a true sans-culotte republican." An interlocutor replied that after Desmoulins washed himself they

25. *Ibid.*, 40, 229–30, and 257 for Pourvoyeur; 239 for Béraud; 247–48 for Latour-Lamontagne; 265 for Charmont; 267 and 282–83 for Dugas. All of these reports were written in the two weeks of 7 Nivôse (December 27, 1793) to 21 Nivôse (January 10, 1794).

26. *Ibid.*, 229–30, 257, 254, 256, 238.

would see, for he was inculpated everywhere. The next day Latour-Lamontagne heard a citizen exclaim indignantly, after readying Hébert's No. 332 (in which Hébert accused Desmoulins of playing Pitt's game with his friends who wanted to undermine the sans-culottes and their generals): "By what right does a private individual condemn to death a representative of the people. . . . I'm surprised that no one puts a rein to this disorder." Another added that at the last session of the Jacobins an individual had cried out for guillotining the Dantoniste Fabre d'Eglantine, a leading opponent of the Cordeliers, but that "wise Robespierre" had moved to have this person expelled from the society; in light of this event, the speaker was surprised that Hébert dared to use the same kind of language. Others demanded that this kind of individual combat cease and that the opponents occupy themselves with things of consequence for the country. A week later, 29 Nivôse (January 18, 1794), Charmont reported that in the café Conti Desmoulins had the reputation of being another Marat, and that he did well to denounce Hébert, who was an intriguer. But in the café du Rendez-Vous it was just the opposite sentiment—Camille was reviled and Hébert was revered. The spy Dugas added on 1 Pluviôse (January 20, 1794) that Hébert was "paralyzed," since he had not succeeded in having Desmoulins expelled from the Jacobins (Robespierre had come to Desmoulins' defense). The next day Dugas revealed that people were saying that the *Père Duchesne* was only repeating itself and that it was losing readers every day.[27]

In addition to his conflict with Desmoulins, Hébert carried on an unceasing war against his implacable enemy Pierre Philippeaux, deputy from the Sarthe Department. The dispute between the two embraced differences on how to conduct the campaign against the monarchist counterrevolution in the Vendée and, especially, whom to place in charge of the armed force—professional officers of the Old Regime or the newly appointed commanders risen from the ranks of the sans-culottes. The Hébertistes supported former noncommissioned officers of the regular army who had been promoted to high command (this issue is discussed more fully in chapter 3). The sup-

27. *Ibid.*, 289, 306–307; III, 22, 58, 72–73. Fabre d'Eglantine (Philippe François Nazaire Fabre) played an important role during the Revolution. He had literary talents but he also profited personally through dishonest deals and was executed for his part in the Indies Company affair. Robespierre thought Fabre was Danton's evil genius. Michelet, *Histoire*, II, 1394–95.

porters of Philippeaux, dubbed by Hébert "Philippotins," were members of or closely linked to the Dantonistes. They opposed the harsh measures of the Terror not because they had compassion for its victims—most of the latter were sans-culottes and their champions on the Left—but because they wanted to "freeze" the Revolution. In short, they wanted to enjoy their newly won wealth, offices, and power. There is no indication that they would have been any more tolerant of their opponents than the latter were of them. Although they called themselves "moderates" (modérés), it should be remembered that if they were willing to forgive counterrevolutionaries or their friends, they were implacably opposed to doing the same for those on their Left.

Hébert always accused the "Philippotins" of hiding behind the mask of patriotism; he did so, for example, in No. 332 of the Père Duchesne, alluded to by Latour-Lamontagne. He called them "sans-culottes of the new brand," who had made their way into the sections' popular societies in order to set one group of patriots against the other. Behind them stood Pitt, Hébert asserted.

Among the leading Dantonistes was a former butcher, now deputy to the Convention from Paris, Louis Legendre. He had played an important part in helping to destroy the Girondins in late spring of 1793. By the fall he had run afoul of some leading Hébertistes, including Hébert himself, who attacked him for supposedly encouraging the counterrevolution in Rouen. Hébert alleged that the public spirit there was bad because the merchants, who were essentially "counterrevolutionary," controlled affairs in the town. The only reason the city had not joined the Federalists was that, unlike the Midi, it supplied Paris with food and other necessities, hence needed the capital as a market. Furthermore, Hébert changed Legendre with "stupidity and malice" against a popular society.[28]

Legendre wrote to the Jacobins of his intention to demand an explanation from Hébert. He had written to the Committee of Public Safety: "Nature, which gave me a violent temperament, at the same time gave me a sensitive soul," and he placarded Paris complaining of being slandered by Hébert. Latour-Lamontagne reported that this

28. Aulard, Jacobins, V, 628; Réimpression de l'ancien Moniteur depuis la réunion des Etats-Generaux, jusqu'au Consulat (mai 1789–novembre 1799) (Paris, 1840–45) [hereinafter cited as Moniteur], XVIII, No. 59 (November 17, 1793), 453.

quarrel was the topic of all conversation, and Dugas revealed that the date for the confrontation between the two had been set in the Jacobins. Both Charmont and Rolin wrote that Hébert had lost the love of patriots for slandering a representative of the people. Béraud agreed that Hébert was regarded as "a vile slanderer" everywhere.[29] It seems that Legendre was getting the better of Hébert when Momoro stepped in and suggested that the quarrel end, as only the aristocrats benefited by it. Legendre opposed ending the matter, but the Jacobins ruled against him. When, however, Momoro proposed that the two antagonists embrace, Legendre firmly refused, declaring that one could not reasonably ask Brutus to embrace Caesar.

From that time on, Hébert stopped attending the sessions of the Jacobin Club and transferred his activities to the Cordeliers. Nor was he heard in the Commune, where Chaumette held forth. It seems that for a time he became more prudent and transferred his attention to the crowned heads of Europe rather than to the political struggles of parties. Still, he did not forget his old enemies the "Philippotins" or Camille Desmoulins. The latter had been expelled from the Jacobins on 21 Nivôse (January 10, 1794), after having Nos. 3 and 5 of *Le Vieux Cordelier* read at previous sessions and having been attacked by Robespierre and Collot, among others, for his moderation. Although it was agreed that Desmoulins had played a progressive role during the early days of the Revolution, his continuing attacks on the Convention, its Committees, and the Terror under the guise that he was discussing Tacitus' *History of the Roman Principate* finally led to his repudiation by the leading Jacobins. Among the charges against him was his warm defense of Philippeaux. Robespierre mocked Desmoulins' enthusiasm for the latter and declared that he had read only one or two issues of *Le Vieux Cordelier*. Yet he appeared to oppose the expulsion of Desmoulins (after it had already taken place, as Dufourny observed) by demanding that the club concern itself with "intrigues" in general, rather than the actions of a particular individual. After a heated discussion the Jacobins reaffirmed Desmoulins' exclusion. Hébert, however, failed to profit from this action because the club was still convinced that the Republic was menaced equally by

29. Caron, *Paris pendant la Terreur*, III, 140, 174, 161–62, 186, 189; Walter, *Hébert et le "Père Duchesne,"* 192; *Moniteur*, XVIII, No. 74 (December 4, 1793), 572, wherein Legendre wrote a letter from Evreux (2 Frimaire), requesting a hearing from the Jacobins on Hébert's charges against him.

both the moderates (called "citrarevolutionaries") and by the Hébertistes (dubbed "ultrarevolutionaries").[30]

The Cordeliers, instead of adopting a more prudent course under the menace that they faced from the authorities and the Jacobins, did just the opposite. On 28 or 29 Nivôse (January 17 or 18, 1794) the society passed a resolution that declared Robespierre the "leader of the moderate party." It is difficult to account for this politically dangerous action. The Cordeliers' leaders knew, naturally, of Robespierre's collaboration with Danton, of his early support of Desmoulins, of his hand in keeping Ronsin and Vincent in prison (discussed in Chapter 3), and of his denunciation of the dechristianization movement. Still, they should have realized that such a pronouncement was bound to make needless enemies and to lose support among the great mass of sans-culottes, who regarded Robespierre with immense reverence and respect.

Rolin revealed on 29 Nivôse (January 1, 1794) that this resolution caused much grumbling in the cafés he visited. The following day Charmont overheard a conversation in a café: "Do you know [asked one of the patrons] that the older Robespierre is regarded by a large part of the Cordeliers as the chief of *moderantisme*, and that he does not enjoy the confidence accorded to him formerly? Yes, replied the other, because you have believed blindly in Hébert as well as in the others of his stamp; but be careful that Camille Desmoulins does not expose it at once in one of his numbers." This exchange proved that people were trying to create a split between the two societies, added the police spy.

The same day (January 19) Rolin reported there was a "common rumor" that the Cordeliers were at loggerheads with the Jacobins; the malevolent rejoiced because of it, but true friends of liberty were distressed. People were saying that the Cordeliers adopted a resolution that regards Robespierre as chief of the moderate party, Rolin noted, but he quoted "a venerable old man who seemed an excellent patriot" as saying, "I don't know if citizen Robespierre is the chief of the party, but in such a case I would have been fooled like many others." Two days later, 2 Pluviôse (January 21, 1794), Le Harivel, another police spy, admitted that the resolution of the Cordeliers had aroused some

30. Aulard, *Jacobins*, V, 590–608 (sessions of 16, 18, 19, 21 Nivôse II [January 5, 7, 8, 10, 1794]); *Moniteur*, XIX, No. 115 (January 14, 1794) [session of Jacobins on 21 Nivôse and of Cordeliers on 22 Nivôse], 198–200.

diverse reflections in his mind. Are we dupes enough to believe that when the Cordeliers slander the Convention they are still attached to it? he asked. We shall not be fooled or fall into its trap, he affirmed.[31]

Thus, the reaction to the Cordeliers resolution aroused near-universal hostility. Leaders of the club should have taken cognizance of this reaction. Had they done so, they might have avoided a far more serious confrontation with the revolutionary government in Ventôse (February 19 to March 20), a confrontation that proved fatal to the Cordeliers.

By the time the economic crisis of Ventôse arrived, one that sharpened differences among all parties, Hébert had taken a bolder position than his criticism of the rioters in February, 1793, seemed to indicate. He began to attack the rich, profiteers, and large merchants for sacrificing the interests of the country in order to promote their own. Until the end of February, 1794, he had opposed the "agrarian law," that is, the redistribution of the land. Now he began to favor the seizure of all products of the soil and their distribution by the government, even proposing to confiscate large estates and to divide them into small plots. Furthermore, he demanded that the sale of national estates be done in small portions.[32]

One of Hébert's biographers, Louis Jacob, declares that Hébert, though a strong nationalist and patriot, opposed a war of conquest and hoped to see "a great Convention" of European states.[33] This assertion is questionable, for in the *Père Duchesne* No. 297, after attacking the English for their allegedly uncivilized behavior at Toulon, Hébert concluded that "in this war, either France or England must perish." Moreover, Dugas on 6 Pluviôse (January 25, 1794) reported that Hébert had urged "the brave defenders of the Republic" to carry "steel and fire" to Germany, Holland, and other lands. However, Dugas added that people were saying that such an attitude did not accord with the principle consecrated by the Convention, "Paix

---

31. Caron, *Paris pendant la Terreur*, III, 33, 38, 48–49, 79–80. Walter states that no journal dared publish the resolution of the Cordeliers, but that it could be known from the reports of the police observers; *Hébert et le Père Duchesne*," 193 n 1. The citations from those reports leave little doubt that such a resolution was, indeed, adopted. Robespierre replied to the attacks on him in his speech of 17 Pluviôse II (February 5, 1794), which Palmer calls "the most memorable of all his addresses"; R. R. Palmer, *Twelve Who Ruled: The Year of the Terror in the French Revolution* (Princeton, 1941), 272.

32. Jacob, *Hébert Le Père Duchesne*, 300–301.

33. *Ibid.*, 301.

aux chaumières, guerre aux tyrans" (Peace to the cottages, war on tyrants). Only by observing this principle, and not in massacring and burning peaceful inhabitants, could the French establish liberty quickly in all countries that they penetrated, Dugas quoted Hébert's critics.[34] The Dantonistes regarded the Hébertistes' program as sheer anarchy; the Robespierristes were frightened by it. Momoro, in reply, attacked "the clever system" of his enemies, which he saw as aimed at "the best patriots," who had destroyed the Brissotins but were now accused of being in the pay of Pitt. Among his opponents he saw Robespierre, whom he accused in an indirect way of inventing the term "ultrarevolutionary, in order to destroy the Friends of the People."[35] Hébert wrote that he, too, had been called an "ultra," a term widely applied by Desmoulins to the best patriots. Among the latter, he noted, were two judges of the Revolutionary Tribunal whom the deputy Moise Bayle had rescued from the slanders of the *Vieux Cordelier* by proving their patriotism.[36]

Thus the rift between the parties continued to grow wider and the accusations against opponents became more strident. It was well known that Robespierre had rescued Danton from the attacks on him by various individuals, not only by the Hébertistes. He also had encouraged Desmoulins in his early efforts by agreeing to read the first two or three issues of his journal; however, Desmoulins' open repudiation of the Terror had forced Robespierre to reject him and his politics. Robespierre's not-so-subtle opposition to releasing Ronsin and Vincent from prison encouraged the Hébertistes to regard him as their enemy. But among the sans-culottes of Paris, Robespierre still remained the most popular revolutionary figure of all. Here was a contradiction difficult for his opponents to resolve. How could the Hébertistes speak for the sans-culottes and at the same time attack their idol? Yet if they kept quiet, it would only strengthen the Indulgents and place their own existence into question. Here again they faced an irresoluble paradox.

Hébert's political position vis-à-vis the ruling Committees was even more paradoxical. It is true that, as some of his biographers hold, he spoke for the sans-culottes. But the latter lacked a consistent policy, which may partly explain why Hébert blew both hot and cold. It is

34. Caron, *Paris pendant la Terreur*, III, 140.
35. Jacob, *Hébert Le Père Duchesne*, 305.
36. *Père Duchesne*, No. 353.

possible that his sad experience with the law in Alençon and the financial ruin that his condemnation brought upon his family opened his heart to the desperate plight of the sans-culottes. His poverty and suffering, made even keener because of his fall from a relatively comfortable middle-class position, could have strengthened his sympathy for the *petites gens*. The emotional outbursts that punctuate his attacks on the perceived enemies of the sans-culottes in the *Père Duchesne* are consistent and seem to be sincere—although there is no way of measuring this sincerity. Still, it would have been difficult to dissimulate only in order to curry favor with his readers.

Once he had discovered the talent within himself of sounding like a true sans-culotte, the desire and need to be successful in his craft made him a captive of sans-culotte prejudice and suspicion. When the interests of the more radical sectionnaires clashed with the goals of the Convention and its Committees, Hébert had either to retreat and modify his politics—which he tried to do on various occasions, as will be seen—or to continue championing the sans-culottes against the government. The former were divided in their politics, of course, so that defending a policy that appealed to one part of the group alienated Hébert from another portion. Nor did the sans-culottes constitute a homogeneous social class. Not only were some sympathetic to Danton and Legendre, but in their vast majority they chose Robespierre and the Jacobins over Hébert and the Cordeliers. The police reports of this period make clear this divided sentiment even among Hébert's own readers.

In addition to the politics of "class," to the extent that the word can be applied, there was Hébert's ambition to become minister of the interior. To oppose the Convention and the Great Committees because he had lost out to Danton's friend Paré was unprincipled. Here his role becomes doubly paradoxical—and dangerous. The heated dispute with Desmoulins must have not only tired the readers of both journals but aroused the wrath of the Committees as well. The more perceptive sans-culottes and Cordeliers must have been aware of this factor. This, too, made Hébert's position as spokesman for the sans-culottes paradoxical.

Furthermore, his painting Jesus as "the best sans-culotte" was in contradiction to shutting down the churches where the same Jesus was worshiped. Whether Hébert was a deist, as some historians claim, or an atheist, as others insist, his action as an official of the Paris Commune was that of a dechristianizer. Between the latter practice and the belief in a Supreme Being was an unbridgeable gulf. Robespierre and his supporters in the Committee of Public Safety were aware of the politics that these different beliefs implied. Hébert was to pay dearly for challenging the powers of heaven and of the new secular authorities who spoke in heaven's name.

2

Food and Politics

The three national assemblies of France could boast of many achievements. Not one, however, could be proud of its record in feeding the population of the towns since the Revolution began. Foreign war, through both the conflict itself and the consequent rise in prices, aggravated the shortage of necessities. By the end of 1793 more than a million men had been drafted into the armed forces, thus depriving the agricultural sector of an important part of its labor force. Along with the men went the workhorses, now engaged in military transport or cavalry. Furthermore, the vastly enlarged military levy consumed food, clothing, and footwear at a rate not experienced since the last wars of Louis XIV and Louis XV.

The shortages of goods and the consequent rising prices for available products of soil and shop were aggravated by the financial policy of the national legislatures. The steady decline of the *assignat*—a form of interest-bearing bond backed by lands confiscated from the Church—discouraged farmers from exchanging their products for this paper money.[1] The confiscated lands, transformed into national estates that should have been used to support the assignats issued, had instead been exchanged by the government for these same falling notes.[2] The seized properties of émigrés and suspects, objects of speculation and profiteering, could not stabilize the assignat any more than could those of the church, since the amount of assignats issued was out of all proportion to the value of what was confiscated. Normal expenses of government, now raised to extraordinary heights

1. An assignat worth 100 livres in late 1789 had dropped in value to 41 livres in February, 1794, to 38 in March, to 37 in April. Pierre Caron, *Tableaux de dépréciation du papier-monnaie* (Paris, 1909), 109.

2. Seymour E. Harris, *The Assignats* (Cambridge, Mass., 1930); Camille Bloch, *La Monnaie et la papier-monnaie* (Paris, 1912).

Assignats and other forms of paper money that proliferated in revolutionary France, plummeting in value from the moment they went into circulation.

by demands of the war, inflated the currency still further. The financial difficulties were thus rooted in both the economic crisis and in the desperate measures adopted by the revolutionary government. In turn, the financial problem undermined production, and thus the health of the economy.

A popular society that presumed to speak for the sans-culottes, as did the Cordeliers Club, had to be aware of the food crisis. The Enragés had been among the first to grapple with the problem of shortages and the consequent speculation in the necessities of life. Their agitation had found ready support in the poorer sections of Paris as well as in other towns. The general wage/price regulation known as the *maximum*, adopted by the reluctant Convention on September 29, 1793, was largely their work. With the arrest in late summer and early fall of 1793 of their spokesmen Jacques Roux, Jean Varlet, Théophile Leclerc, and of the two leaders of the Société des républicaines révolutionnaires, Claire Lacombe and Pauline Léon, the Cordeliers became the undisputed leaders of the popular movement.[3]

Hébert's attacks on profiteers and hoarders therefore found a ready support among the hungry sans-culottes. Paraphrasing the latter's disillusion with the Revolution, he wrote: "We no longer believe anyone. . . . They steal from us, plunder us as in the past; we no longer have either money or provisions. There is no bread f—— at any price . . . we are without work. . . . For four years now we have suffered. What have we gained from the Revolution?"[4] Whatever truth there was in this protest, Hébert and his supporters in the Cordeliers could turn the sans-culottes' discontent into an attack on the revolutionary government.

That this possibility was present almost from the beginning of the agitation for a price ceiling on bread and other necessities may be seen in the way the Jacobin leaders rejected petitions for the *maximum*. When, for example, representatives of several Parisian sections presented their demands, the deputies of the Paris Department protested that their duty as representatives of the people had nothing to do with giving people bread "like to lowly animals in a pasture."[5] On February 22, 1793, they turned down a delegation of women who had come to plead with the Jacobins to discuss the problem of shortages and high prices. Edward Louis Alexis Dubois-Crancé declared it was first necessary to establish liberty, and Jeanbon Saint-André pronounced that the problem of provisions "was not on the order of the day."[6]

The sans-culottes, as consumers, demanded and finally received the passage of two laws to ameliorate their condition. The first was a stringent decree punishing speculators, profiteers, and hoarders.[7] The second, replacing the first, was the *maximum*, which set price ceilings on necessities of life such as bread, wine and beer (urban

3. Albert Mathiez, *La Vie chère et le mouvement social sous la Terreur* (Paris, 1927), esp. Pt. 2, "Les Enragés et la Vie Chère"; Slavin, *Making of an Insurrection*, chap. 8, "The Enragés and the Insurrection," 127–41.

4. *Père Duchesne*, No. 233.

5. B&R, XXIV, 287–88. This response was signed by Robespierre, Danton, Collot d'Herbois, Billaud-Varenne, Desmoulins, and others. Marat, too, was among the signers.

6. Aulard, *Jacobins*, V, 37–38.

7. See Henri Calvet, *L'Accaparement à Paris sous la Terreur: Essai sur l'application de la loi du 26 juillet 1793* (Paris, 1933).

water was often unpalatable, if not outright dangerous), soap, candles, and so on.[8] Neither measure satisfied the needs of the sans-culottes. The law against profiteering could not be enforced because juries, often composed of merchants and other men of property, were reluctant to condemn their fellow businessmen. The *maximum*, in turn, was badly drafted and was often unfair to those engaged in commerce.[9]

Theoretically, the sans-culottes should have been better off under the *maximum* than in the past because the new law set the prices of commodities at their average 1790 levels plus one-third, whereas wages were set at their average 1790 levels plus one-half. One problem was that too often the cost of transportation was ignored or underrated. The costs of raw materials and of production (because of increases in the price of land, tools, animals, and so on) had also risen far above the levels of 1790. In addition, where merchants or their agents dominated the administration, this law was either ignored or was weakly enforced. On top of all this, farmers were discouraged from bringing their produce to market if all they could get for it were depreciating assignats—not to mention the possibility of being stopped en route and having their goods distributed at prices set by rioting and desperate consumers, if not simply seized and spread among the rioters. Finally, there was an insoluble contradiction between an economic system based on laissez-faire and an attempt to regulate it by price controls and by a direct intervention of the state in market relations.

By the winter months of early 1794 the markets, bakeries, and butcher shops were besieged by long lines of hungry women, often with crying children, frustrated by empty stalls. "Misery is at its highest point," warned Hébert. Siret, a police spy, agreed, writing that "the suffering is extreme."[10] In faubourg Saint-Antoine, people pillaged a wagon train on the road to Vincennes, some paying what they

8. See Pierre Caron, *Le Commerce des céréals* (Paris, 1907); Fernand Gerbaux and Charles Schmidt, *Procès-verbaux des comités d'agriculture et de commerce . . .* (Paris, 1908); Georges Lefebvre, *Documents relatifs à l'histoire des subsistances dans le district de Bergues . . .* (Lille, 1914–21); Georges Afanassiev, *Le Commerce des céréals en France au dix-huitième siècle,* trans. under the direction of Paul Boyer (Paris, 1894).

9. Mathiez, *Vie chère,* esp. Pt. 2, chap. 3, pp. 162–87.

10. *Père Duchesne,* No. 289; *Rapports de Grivel et Siret, commissaires parisiens du conseil exécutif provisoire sur les substances et le maximum . . .* (Paris, 1908), 5 Ventôse II (February 23, 1794), 185.

pleased for the supplies seized, others paying nothing at all. Siret's colleague, the police observer Grivel, blamed the popular societies for these outbreaks because they allegedly "inflamed the spirits" by violently attacking the inhabitants of the countryside, the merchants of Paris, and even part of the National Convention as being responsible for the shortages and high prices.[11]

As for remedies, Hébert proposed that the sans-culottes "rise up" and take hold of all property holders, especially the big profiteering farmers, and "threaten them with hanging . . . if shortages continue. Soon enough, f——, wheat will become abundant in the markets, and we will be able to live, f——."[12] Grivel overheard two men in a café complaining that shortages of food were growing worse. One suggested that guillotining a few butchers and grocers would set a good example, that before the *maximum* the shops were full because the owners could charge what they pleased. The second agreed that there were profiteers, "vampires who suck the blood of the people," but he tried to make his partner understand that it was the state of agriculture, rather than the *maximum*, that was responsible for the shortages.[13] Yet a few weeks later Grivel was convinced that enemies of the Republic were creating disturbances in the markets in order "to aggravate the discontent of the people."[14]

Beef was among the rarest of foods. The number of cattle slaughtered by one butcher declined from the average of ten a week to two, and this despite the willingness of people to pay above the *maximum*. The general decline of religious observance that had prohibited the consumption of meat on Fridays and during Lent, as well as the increase of population and the consumption of beef by the armies of France, reduced supplies further. Yet if one surrendered the pleasure of eating beef he had to substitute other comestibles, say eggs. The production of eggs depends on chickens, however, which feed on grain.[15]

One result of the shortages was the seizure of food products by various municipalities, which in turn threatened to disrupt all commerce and to starve the capital in the bargain. Grivel suggested the introduction of ration cards for meat. The General Council of the

11. *Rapports de Grivel et Siret*, 185, 8 Ventôse II (February 26, 1794).
12. *Père Duchesne*, No. 289.
13. *Rapports de Grivel et Siret*, 170, 2 Ventôse II (February 20, 1794).
14. *Ibid.*, 209–10, 19 Ventôse II (March 9, 1794).
15. *Ibid.*, 175, 177–81, 3 Ventôse II (March 21, 1794).

Paris Commune, after hearing the report of its Administration of Provisions, adopted a number of regulations to provide meat for the sick and mothers nursing infants.[16] It hoped to diminish the large crowds before butcher shops and the struggle of women for a piece of meat, as recounted by the police spy Breton. His colleague Charmont revealed that measures were being taken to prevent crowds from gathering before these establishments.[17] Siret pointed out how unfair local regulations were that prohibited the purchase of certain commodities such as wine in one commune although it was consumed in another. This led to a kind of isolation, "a species of federalism," that was undermining the republic and destroying the ideal of fraternity and equality. In general, Siret admitted, it was difficult to reconcile the interests of town and country.[18]

Shortages of beef also reduced the supply of tallow available for candles and soap. If such conditions continued, warned Grivel, half of France would go to bed in the dark and not rise until daybreak. Needless to say, this would result in a great loss of working hours for artisans and laborers. Four years earlier, in 1790, some five million pounds of tallow came from Russia and Ireland. This supply was no longer available. Thus, laundresses had less soap, and they too needed to work by candlelight. Grivel suggested that the government make an effort to buy fat from Russia through the intervention of the French consuls in Denmark and Sweden as well as in Tuscany and Geneva. By using the Rhone to import goods, France could avoid the intervention of enemy navies. Finally, he admitted that in any case the government would have to pay above the *maximum* and use its gold and silver for purchases abroad.[19]

Discontent among workers also grew as prices began to outrace wages. Lack of raw materials, or the shrinking of markets, caused unemployment. Gilders and sculptors, revealed Béraud, were complaining that there was no work, and those employed could no longer afford to eat in inns and restaurants. A meal that formerly cost ten sous had now risen to fifteen, wrote the police observer Prévost. Many working people were far worse off, having nothing at all to eat

16. *Ibid.*, 166, 1 Ventôse II (February 19, 1794); *Moniteur*, XIX, No. 170 (March 10, 1794), 655.
17. Caron, *Paris pendant la Terreur*, IV, 210, 201.
18. *Rapports de Grivel et Siret*, 173–75, 2 Ventôse II (February 20, 1794).
19. *Ibid.*, 217–19, 28 Ventôse II (March 18, 1794).

for lunch, Charmont reported. The Commune should reflect on these shortages, he added, because they could provoke demonstrations.[20]

On 5 Ventôse, Prévost admitted that although workers were well paid, the price of food had risen so high that their wages could not keep up.[21] Agitators in shops for the spinning of cotton (*ateliers de filature de coton*) sought the support of Hébert's *Père Duchesne*, as well as of the popular society of section Marat. "The sans-culottes considered Hébert and the decided patriots as their natural defenders," wrote Soboul. They presented petitions and tried to unite different shops in a common front.[22] Their insubordination forced the resignation of an administrator of a shop, but his complaints must have led to a number of arrests, including that of a woman named Janison, who was declared innocent by the Revolutionary Tribunal.[23] The same discontent manifested itself among journeymen masons and carpenters, who threatened to strike if their wages were not raised.[24]

Thus shortages and high prices, coupled with inadequate wages, mobilized the sans-culottes. General assemblies, popular societies, revolutionary committees, and other sectional organizations made these problems the first order of business. After hearing Barère's report, the Convention decreed on 18 Nivôse II (January 7, 1794) that all towns blockaded by enemy troops were to pool their food and goods, which were to be distributed according to need. The goods sequestered were to be paid for by the national government.[25] Two months later section Marchés resolved that the Commune proclaim the capital to be under siege, in line with Barère's report.[26]

Everywhere the concern of the sans-culottes was how to provision Paris. The popular society of section Gravilliers resolved that its revolutionary committee be authorized to search the houses of the rich and those whose proprietors had left for the country. Women were

20. Caron, *Paris pendant la Terreur*, IV, 200, 218, 227.
21. *Ibid.*, 303.
22. Soboul, *Sans-Culottes*, 684–85; Tuetey, *Répertoire général*, XI, Nos. 60–62.
23. Henri Wallon, *Histoire du tribunal révolutionnaire de Paris* (Paris, 1880–82), IV, 495. She signed herself "fame Janison."
24. See Report of Perrière, 14 Ventôse II (March 4, 1794), in Caron, *Paris pendant la Terreur*, V, 79.
25. *Moniteur*, XIX, No. 108 (January 7, 1794), 144.
26. Report of Bacon, 6 Ventôse II (March 16, 1794), in Caron, *Paris pendant la Terreur*, IV, 307.

especially numerous in these assemblies.[27] The police spy Hanriot (no known relation to François Hanriot, commander of the National Guard in Paris) related that hungry men and women spent three to four hours at the doors of butcher shops without being certain that anything was still available to buy. His colleague Monic wrote that the city's main market, Les Halles, had no vegetables, butter, or eggs. Others cursed the *maximum* as being responsible for shortages, according to Charmont. On rue Rohan the armed force had to be called out to save a charcuterie from destruction by desperate crowds, and a fruit seller's stand near Porte Saint-Denis was sacked because its owner was, allegedly, a profiteer.[28]

Hunger and frustration aggravated the sans-culottes' feeling that it was the rich who were responsible for their plight. Pourvoyeur on 3 Ventôse (February 21, 1794) reported overhearing a number of persons state that "large fortunes were always the source of crime, that it was they who were causing our misfortune, and are still causing it. The aristocrats have no use for the sans-culottes, but to achieve their ruin." Members of the popular society of section Droits de l'Homme complained that wealthy prisoners were fed meat, and asked who needed these aristocrats. "Shouldn't all these scoundrels who starve Paris be guillotined?"[29] The popular society of section Gardes-Françaises resented "the rich egoists" who had everything while the sans-culottes "could not obtain enough to feed their families." Pourvoyeur quoted "the people" he overheard complaining that they had eaten no meat for three weeks and that "it was time . . . that the national ax strike the farmers and the big merchants, who alone are responsible for the ills that we suffer at present."[30]

These threats and complaints obviously grew out of the frustrations and hunger that the sans-culottes and their families shared. The danger was not only that counterrevolutionaries could take advantage of this feeling but that the government would find scapegoats to turn away the popular anger from itself. The reports of police observers throughout the month of Ventôse (February 19–March 20) carry a

27. Bacon mentioned also the popular societies of sections Homme Armé, Faubourg Montmartre, and Bonne-Nouvelle. Some persons criticized hospitals that ordered twice as much meat as their patients could consume. *Ibid.*, 308.

28. *Ibid.*, 231, 238, 258, 268.

29. *Ibid.*, 262, 340.

30. *Ibid.*, 238; Caron, *Paris pendant la Terreur*, IV, 261.

common grievance—the sans-culottes of the capital simply lacked the essentials of life.

Charmont recounted on 4 Ventôse that the guard had to be called out at several chandlers. The same day Latour-Lamontagne admitted that "one could say . . . that Paris is already prey to the horrors of famine." He was surprised that people still abided by the law and respected property. The following day Bacon cited some women in a numerous assembly of section Lombards who exclaimed that all butchers were scoundrels. They were wildly applauded. But in a café on rue Charenton some declared that they could not go back because they had come too far "to knuckle under. But if it's necessary to eat nothing but bread, we'll have to get used to it."[31] Thus, despite the suffering and the complaints, there was a great reservoir of patriotism and self-sacrifice, sentiments the revolutionary government could exploit.

Still, patriotic feelings could not satisfy empty stomachs. On 5 Ventôse (February 23) Charmont quoted people in cafés as speaking of nothing but the terrible misery they felt, saying that it was better to die under the guillotine than from hunger. Dugas recounted that mackerel and salted herring were being sold for very high prices. Le Harivel wrote that "some women cried because there was nothing to be had in the markets." The same day, Grivel warned that because of shortages the public suspected "that the Commune could see a hunger insurrection against the Convention without displeasure"— a dangerous rumor, as Chaumette, the head of the Commune, was to discover.[32]

The next day, 6 Ventôse, Dugas noted that butter was totally lacking, that eggs had been "pillaged," and that Les Halles had never been so empty. The police spy Perrière witnessed desperate women going through the market with their empty baskets, and Pourvoyeur agreed that the same thing could be said of the markets of faubourg Saint-Marcel. Two days later the popular assembly of section Droits de l'Homme passed a resolution to stop supplying "wealthy prisoners" with meat. Charmont reported that "the doors of butchers' [shops] were being obstructed" and that women were complaining of having to wait in queues to buy a chicken at 3 A.M. On 9 Ventôse,

31. Caron, *Paris pendant la Terreur*, IV, 270–71, 274, 289–90, 292.
32. *Ibid.*, 293, 294, 300–301, 295.

Bacon reported a riot in Les Halles. According to Grivel, the price of bread doubled or tripled in a month.[33]

During these trying times Hébert was praising the Convention and urging its deputies to continue "to earn the blessings" of the sans-culottes, but at the same time urging them to assure the necessities of life. In his journal No. 341, he attacked "the merchants who f—— the *maximum*, and who engross . . . all the goods." Grocers "who rob the Sans-Culottes," wine merchants "who poison with their adulterated drink," butchers who short-weight meat by adding bones, and shoe-makers who use cardboard for soles instead of leather—all these and more came under his criticism. He was happy that "little by little the virtue of Saint Guillotine will deliver us from all these devourers of human flesh." Yet before one can be free one must eat, he wrote. Farmers had forgotten that their freedom from the exactions of the Old Regime was due to the towns, which gave them this gift. What would they do with all their products if there were no towns to consume them? "I love the cultivators of the soil who nourish the earth by their sweat," Hébert assured his readers. But did not the sans-culottes deserve recognition for manufacturing things from the stuff of the earth and for defending the Republic? He continued: "All men who work are equal before the law; it ought to protect all. The inhabitants of the countryside have no more right to starve their brothers of the towns, than the latter to destroy their fields, and to fatten themselves on the blood of the cultivators. We make up only one family now; the rich should share with the poor; the strong should aid the weak . . . all good republicans should join hands, f——, and they should unite like brothers."[34]

This moral exhortation was no solution to the problem of shortages, of course, which may explain why Hébert thundered so violently against those who would not or could not be "brothers" to the sans-culottes. In urging the Convention to enforce its laws and the sans-culottes to remain firm, he proposed that should the first sign of shortages appear, a decree ought to be adopted that "the rich, the merchants, the big farmers and all those who are recognized to be starvers of the people, should be condemned to go hungry; soon enough the abundance would return, f——."

33. *Ibid.*, 312, 316, 319, 340, 344, 364, 368. See also the reports of Pourvoyer for 9 Ventôse and of Charmont for 10 Ventôse, *ibid.*, 376, 388.
34. *Père Duchesne*, Nos. 337, 341.

Shortly thereafter Hébert attacked retailers, not only "the rich": "I shall no more spare the seller of carrots than the big wholesale merchant," he wrote, "for, f——, I see a league formed of all those who sell against those who buy, and I find as much dishonesty in the small shops as in the large stores."[35] Those who sold above the *maximum*, however, would soon be converted by the guillotine as the Revolutionary army—a special armed force raised to requisition food and to crush the counterrevolution—approached. For goods to reappear, Hébert insisted, all that was necessary was to punish the profiteers. But this, too, depended on the administration being staffed by sans-culottes.[36]

A few issues later Hébert expressed "great joy" in learning how "the brave defenders of the country" not only shed their blood but were willing to sacrifice their meat ration for the people back home. He assured the soldiers that the sans-culottes were no less self-sacrificing and were ready to give their all for the republic.[37] Thus, like the sans-culottes, Hébert reflected contradictory opinions—from appealing to the rich to help the poor because all were brothers in the Republic, to calling for the guillotining of the wealthy because being rich was a crime.[38]

The revolutionary government was aware of the complaints in the sections and the popular societies. Why, then, did it fail to satisfy the demands of the sans-culottes? A partial answer lies in its concern with the war almost to the exclusion of other matters. National defense and internal security were far more important to the Committee of Public Safety and the Convention than supplying the markets. Not that it was unable to do so in the short run: when it became politically expedient to do it, the government found means to restock the markets. In the long run, however, it was subject to the same economic forces as afflicted the sans-culottes and the whole nation. Meanwhile, it had a powerful weapon in mobilizing public opinion—patriotism. By emphasizing the need to sacrifice for the country and by involving the sans-culottes in helping to defend the nation, the revolutionary

35. *Ibid.*, No. 345. Hébert uses the expression "marchand de carottes" in a double meaning as both a merchant of carrots and as one who tricks another out of his money.
36. *Ibid.*, No. 345.
37. *Ibid.*, No. 352.
38. See Soboul's remarks on "diverse social currents" among the sections of Paris and the inability of the sans-culottes to hammer out a coherent political or economic program. Soboul, *Sans-Culottes*, 689–90.

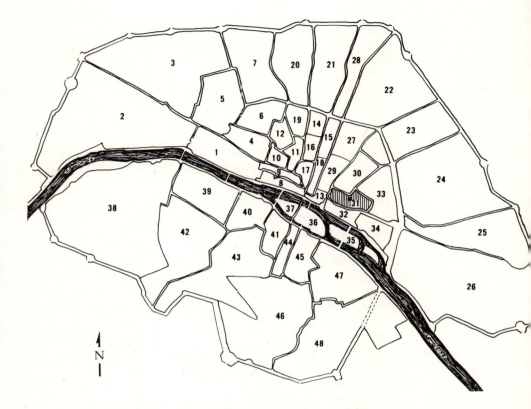

The sections of Paris. The first names given in the key are those of 1790–1791; later names are in parentheses.

KEY

1. Tuileries
2. Champs Elysées
3. Roule (République)
4. Palais Royal (Butte des Moulins; Montagne)
5. Place Vendôme (Piques)
6. Bibliothèque (1792; Lepeletier)
7. Grange Batelière (Mirabeau; Mont Blanc)
8. Louvre (Muséum)
9. Oratoire (Gardes-Françaises)
10. Halle au blé
11. Postes (Contrat Social)
12. Place Louis XIV (Mail; Guillaume Tell)
13. Fontaine Montmorency (Molière et la Fontaine; Brutus)
14. Bonne Nouvelle
15. Ponceau (Amis de la Patrie)
16. Mauconseil (Bon-Conseil)
17. Marchés Des Innocents (Halles; Marchés)
18. Lombards
19. Arcis
20. Faubourg Montmartre (Fbg. Mont-Marat)
21. Poissonnière
22. Bondy
23. Temple
24. Popincourt
25. Montreuil
26. Quinze Vingts
27. Gravilliers
28. Faubourg Saint-Denis (Fbg.-du-Nord)
29. Beaubourg (Réunion)
30. Enfants Rouges (Marais; Homme Armé)
31. Roi de Sicile (Droits de l'Homme)
32. Hôtel de Ville (Maison Commune; Fidélité)
33. Place Royale (Fédérés; Indivisibilité)
34. Arsenal
35. Ile Saint-Louis (Fraternité)
36. Notre Dame (Cité; Raison)
37. Henri IV (Pont Neuf; Révolutionnaire)
38. Invalides
39. Fontaine de Grenelle
40. Quatre Nations (Unité)
41. Théâtre-Français (Marseille; Marat)
42. Croix Rouge (Bonnet Rouge; Bonnet de la Liberté; Ouest)
43. Luxembourg (Mutius Scaevola)
44. Thermes de Julien (Beaurepaire; Chalier; Régénérée; Thermes)
45. Sainte-Geneviève (Panthéon-Français)
46. Observatoire
47. Jardin des Plantes (Sans-Culottes)
48. Gobelins (Lazowski; Finistère)

government hoped to keep the discontent with economic conditions under control. One means of involving the sans-culottes in this effort was to encourage them to deposit saltpeter, often right in the hall of the Convention and to the applause of the deputies.

Saltpeter can be dug up from the soil or from heaps of decaying organic matter. Mixed with lime and other such alkaline substances, it forms nitrates. Nitrates, in turn, can be made into gunpowder. Encouraged by the Convention and its committees, the sections established saltpeter commissions and began to present the results of their work to the deputies. A delegation of section Quinze-Vingts, for example, offered the Convention twelve hundred pounds of unrefined saltpeter at its session of 12 Ventôse. Bacon had reported on 1 Ventôse on a "very numerous assembly" in section Droits de l'Homme that discussed the delivery of saltpeter to the Convention. He also noted that several spoke on the women defenders of the country who were members of the section, and concluded that public spirit was very high. Positive appeals to patriotism were not, of course, the government's only means of encouraging loyalty. Other and harsher weapons were available—for example, the delivery or refusal to deliver civic cards (*certificats de civisme*) that attested to residents' patriotism; there were also periodic purges and censurings of the general assemblies.[39] Yet if some of the more militant sans-culottes, members of the Cordeliers Club, were critical of the government, the overwhelming mass were strongly attached to the Convention and its Great Committees. Above all they admired Robespierre. The latter was ill from 16 to 26 Pluviôse (February 4–14) and was unable to attend the meetings of the Committee of Public Safety. He appeared once or twice in the Jacobin Club to defend the deputies of the Center against their opponents, and only once in the Convention. He resumed his functions for a few days but then took to his bed again from 1 to 23 Ventôse (February 19–March 13).[40]

Robespierre's illness became a cause of concern for many sans-culottes and others. Bacon observed a group of people near the Jardin des plantes anxiously discussing the leader's ill health. One person was heard to remark that if Robespierre died all would be lost. Bacon added that when the sans-culottes spoke of Robespierre's ailment,

39. *Moniteur*, XIX, No. 163 (March 3, 1794), 604; Caron, *Paris pendant la Terreur*, IV, 197–98; Soboul, *Sans-Culottes*, 692–93.
40. Ernest Hamel, *Histoire de Robespierre* (Paris, 1865–67), III, 412–14.

"the well-to-do" said nothing but one could see on their faces a feeling of satisfaction.[41]

Both Charmont and Dugas reported the same concern of the sans-culottes for the health of Robespierre and his colleague Couthon, who was also sick (some believed that Couthon had been poisoned, others that his illness had been brought on by exhaustion from overwork). "It's incredible how many are interested in them," wrote Charmont, and Dugas noted that "the true friends of our country" were affected by the news. Bacon revealed that in the cafés he visited there was much talk about the illness of the two men, and special concern for Robespierre. The popular society of section Lepeletier sent a commissioner appointed for the purpose of reporting directly on the state of Robespierre's health.[42]

Hébert added his bit to encourage loyalty to the revolutionary government. Urging the sans-culottes to have confidence in the Committee of Public Safety and in the Convention, he pointed out that should the counterrevolution ever triumph, the Conventionnels would be its first victims. Then he italicized the following words of Robespierre: *"If it were possible that the Committee of Public Safety should betray the people, I would denounce it."* Twenty times this committee had saved the republic, wrote Hébert, and it would save it again. Then he exhorted his sans-culotte readers to unite with the Convention because all hope rested with it, just as all its force rested with them.[43] When this same Convention and its committees later arrested Hébert and his comrades, the sans-culottes wavered between their old allies and an institution that Hébert himself had urged them so warmly to support.

Loyalty to the revolutionary government and an exalted patriotism in the sections were not universal, however. Opponents of the Terror, called "moderates," appealed to feelings of humanity in favor of many imprisoned or condemned to the guillotine. Unfortunately,

---

41. Caron, *Paris pendant la Terreur*, IV, 199.

42. *Ibid.*, 203, 204, 224; Popular society of section Lepeletier, in Nouvelle acquisitions françaises (hereinafter cited as Nouv. acq. fr.), 2662, f. 64, BN. Courtois reproduces a number of letters to Robespierre during his illness. The General Council of Marion began its salutation with: "Citoyen Robespierre, legislateur, et père protecteur du bon peuple!"; E. B. Courtois, *Rapport fait au nom de la commission chargée de l'examen des papiers trouvés chez Robespierre et ses complices* (Paris, Nivôse III [December, 1794–January, 1795]), 120–21.

43. *Père Duchesne*, No. 324.

counterrevolutionary sentiments and actions were often masked by moderation. When this kind of camouflage was seen or suspected, the revolutionary committees, as agents of the central authorities, especially the Committee of General Security, denounced it. Denunciations in turn led to confrontations in the sections between the two parties, a process that continued throughout the Revolution. In addition, lack of zeal for a revolutionary action in the past, or failure to adopt new customs or costumes, often led to conflicts between "advanced patriots" and their moderate opponents. Among the moderates were men and women who genuinely despised the Terror on humanitarian grounds.

On 2 Ventôse (February 20), Béraud reported hearing a citizen in the café Saint-Denis complain against the revolutionary committee of section Lombards for arresting more than fifty people "whose patriotism and probity are known" to all. This kind of action, he added, threatened trade and led to riots. The same day Latour-Lamontagne wrote of his indignation at constantly hearing, read "with a type of affectation," a list of those guillotined. Obviously, he emphasized, this was a device that counterrevolutionaries used. Had the editor responsible for publishing this piece been a patriot he would have added the far longer list of those acquitted by the court. Clearly this was an attempt to make the Revolutionary Tribunal odious to all France, he insisted.[44]

Three days later (5 Ventôse) Rolin revealed the bitter complaints, "a thousand times repeated," on the arrest and imprisonment of many good patriots, victims of ambition, cupidity, and jealousy. The police spy added that he was sure people would not be fooled by these charges and would treat their authors as they deserved. Good citizens were ever ready to seize the guilty, he concluded.[45] The sans-culottes, aware of this conflict, could not help but support their revolutionary committees against the moderates. Yet their loyalty to these bodies was of a critical nature because the committees were no longer responsible to the sectionnaires who had created them. Increasingly the political life in the sections came under the control of the revolutionary committees, which meant, ultimately, under the control of the Committee of General Security. The sans-culottes, jealous of their autonomy, opposed this trend.[46]

44. Caron, *Paris pendant la Terreur,* IV, 225, 233.
45. *Ibid.,* 305.
46. Soboul, *Sans-Culottes,* 697.

In section Bondy a dispute broke out between, on one side, the revolutionary committee and the popular society it led, and on the other, the civil committee.[47] Béraud overheard a discussion on disputes in the Convention. One citizen declared that the Committee of General Security did not know how to release the innocent prisoners under its authority because the revolutionary committees made the law. "You are right," replied his companion. "Each committee forms a sect, an areopagus."[48]

In section Réunion the Committee of General Security intervened to settle a bitter dispute between the moderates and their sans-culotte opponents, led by Aristarque Didot, former secretary of the section's general assembly and currently clerk to the *procureur*. Didot was a staunch defender of the sans-culottes. When the assembly had fallen into the hands of the moderates prior to the insurrection of May 31, 1793, he had defended the revolutionary committee against the assembly.[49] By the winter of 1794, however, he had committed certain abuses of power as commissioner of the revolutionary committee, which decided to exclude him on 27 Frimaire (December 17, 1793). On 4 Ventôse (February 22, 1794) he denounced his ex-colleagues to the Committee of General Security for not respecting the rights of the people. "The main aim of enemies of the Republic is to have [us] believe that the people are incapable of governing themselves," he wrote. The next day he attacked the revolutionary committee for establishing a commission to check into the forty-sous subsidy paid to poor sans-culottes for attending the meetings of the general assembly. The inquiry violated the rights of the people, he held.

The committee decided to arrest him, but he appealed this decision to the Committee of General Security, which freed him on 11 Ventôse. Four days later he addressed the general assembly of the section against the revolutionary committee. By doing so, however, he endangered the principle of the revolutionary government under which local organs of government were subordinated to the central authority. In short, he was thereby undermining the control of the Committee of General Security over sectional revolutionary committees. As a result, the Committee ordered him rearrested on 17 Ventôse, together with the president of the section, Louvet du Bois. The Committee

47. *Ibid.*, 697–98.
48. Caron, *Paris pendant la Terreur*, IV, 269.
49. W 11, dos. 529, February 11, 1794, in AN.

held that the law prohibited a general assembly from judging the conduct of its revolutionary committee. Didot was only twenty-five years old at this time, and in addition to being secretary of the assembly, he presided over the commission on saltpeter.[50] This example of the conflict between the revolutionary government and its agents in the sections, on the one hand, and the sectional assemblies on the other, was to be repeated until the assemblies were finally curbed by the Great Committees in the spring of 1794.

For most sans-culottes, however, the greater danger was the counterrevolution, not the usurpation of local powers by the Great Committees. Hébert attacked Desmoulins for writing that every person executed created more enemies for the Republic from among his family and friends. Without the guillotine (that is, without the Terror), Hébert retorted, not a single Jacobin would be left.[51] The conflict between the two men, reflecting as they did two different policies, forms a dramatic story in the rise and destruction of the two factions.

Latour-Lamontagne revealed that it was Danton and Robespierre who had dubbed the faction of Hébert's followers "ultrarevolutionaries," and that members of this group were plotting against the Republic. In fact, people he overheard in a café suspected them of having poisoned Robespierre. Then he quoted an unknown person as asserting that "it is they [the ultrarevolutionaries] who say that Robespierre is a used-up patriot, and who seek to establish an odious and unjust distinction between the patriots of '89 and those of 1793." Odious and unjust it might have been, but the distinction was real, as the conflict between the factions was to prove. Everyone complains of the arrests of the best patriots, went on Latour-Lamontagne's unknown witness, and good citizens who employ their fortune or talents for the good of the people face inquisitorial investigations from these new tyrants. A second unknown party reassured him that the Convention was beginning to open its eyes to the secret designs of

50. Tuetey, *Répertoire général*, X, No. 1916; Albert Soboul and Raymonde Monnier, *Répertoire du personnel sectionnaire parisien en l'an II* (Paris, 1985), 341–42. See also Slavin, *Making of an Insurrection*, 40–41. Didot was freed on 23 Thermidor, Year II (August 10, 1794), but was rearrested on 5 Prairial, Year III (May 25, 1795) during the so-called "hunger insurrection."

51. *Père Duchesne*, No. 328. His headline read: "Sa grande colère contre certain jean-foutres qui veulent recruter tous les brigands et former une nouvelle Vendée en proposant d'ouvrir les prisons et de faire grace aux conspirateurs" (His great anger against certain spineless jackasses who want to recruit all brigands and create a new Vendée in proposing to open all prisons and to pardon the conspirators).

these pretended patriots. There was no time to lose, retorted the first: liberty ran a greater risk in Paris than at the front or in the Vendée.[52]

On 8 Ventôse, Perrière narrated a striking incident: When an employer upbraided her cook for exaggerating the number to be guillotined, a "vigorous patriot" grabbed her young daughter and whipped out a knife as if to kill the child. But the man was only illustrating a lesson: if the enemies of the Republic triumphed, he told the horrified woman, *all* her children would die. His point was made so dramatically, observed Perrière, that the woman understood why a policy of terror was necessary against enemies of the republic.[53]

The conflict between moderates and patriots was even sharper in the popular societies than in the general assemblies, as the sansculottes tended to control the societies, especially the sectional clubs. In the struggle that developed between the Jacobins and the Cordeliers, most of the societies formed after May 31, 1793, supported the Cordeliers because they saw the Jacobins as defenders of the Indulgents or compromisers.[54] At the same time the militants in these societies often proved to be intolerant not only of moderates but even of those who merely could not prove that they had performed some service for the Revolution. One example of this intolerance was reported by Bacon on 4 Ventôse (February 22, 1794): An eighty-five-year-old veteran asked the popular society of section Homme Armé to sponsor him so that he could receive his certificat de civisme. A member cried out that an old person who had done nothing for the Revolution should not persuade the members to grant his request. "If you lose a single moment [of] the revolutionary movement, farewell patriots! Their end approaches," he declared. He was wildly applauded as the society turned down the old veteran's request. It was because of such incidents that some wanted the Convention to pass a uniform law so that "the maneuvers" of revolutionary committees "to take vengeance on certain individuals" could be stopped, wrote Rolin.[55]

The struggle with the moderates encouraged a new purge. The popular society of section Lepeletier named a commission for this purpose and provided for the deposit of all papers with the national

52. Caron, *Paris pendant la Terreur*, IV, 297–98.
53. *Ibid.*, 355–56.
54. See Morris Slavin, *The French Revolution in Miniature: Section Droits de l'Homme, 1789–1795* (Princeton, 1984), 319–43.
55. Caron, *Paris pendant la Terreur*, IV, 266, 287.

agent. The twenty commissioners elected had to give an account of their political biographies since July 14 before being endorsed by the membership.[56] Bacon reported on 13 Ventôse (March 3, 1794) that the popular society of section Bon-Conseil was very numerous as it continued its purge. Of twenty-six applicants, only seven were admitted. A sixty-eight-year-old candidate was rejected because he had addressed the president as "monsieur" (instead of the customary "citoyen") and for having spoken with his head uncovered (that is, he failed to put on the "liberty cap," the Phrygian-style *bonnet rouge* worn by sans-culottes and other revolutionaries); the women made an uproar but nothing helped. A fan maker known as a good patriot was also rejected after being challenged by the president. One rejected candidate declared, "Farewell, my friends, keep your censure, I shall censure myself," as noise and laughter followed him. Women were heard to remark that things could not go on like this; it was all trickery.[57]

The Société fraternelle des deux sexes / Défenseurs de la Constitution adopted a regulation on 10 Ventôse not to admit any "priest, noble, banker, or agent of the Exchange."[58] The moderates, on the other hand, appealed to humanity against their opponents, as the following incident illustrates. Three members of section Faubourg Montmartre naïvely admitted that in the demonstration of June 20, 1792, against the king, they had not known which party to support. The revolutionary committee of the section arrested them and, in a declaration to the general assembly, pronounced that moderates had done more damage than the aristocrats. The committee argued that the appeal to humanity only divided the patriots and that revolutionary measures were terrible only to a man without "a soul, without love of country, in short for the moderates."[59] In the same section on

56. Popular society of section Lepeletier, in Nouv. acq. fr., 2662, f. 63, BN. According to its minutes of 4 Ventôse (February 22, 1794), the society was founded in 1790. On 7 Ventôse the society heard a petition of section Indivisibilité regarding the sequestration of properties of imprisoned persons, but took no action on it; *ibid.*, f. 72. A total of eighty-nine members were admitted, thirty-eight postponed, and forty-six rejected; Soboul, *Sans-Culottes*, 701 n 67.

57. Caron, *Paris pendant la Terreur*, V, 43: "Tout se fait ici par compère et par commère."

58. Soboul, *Sans-Culottes*, 701 n 68.

59. *Soutien aux patriotes, guerre aux modérés: Discours prononcé de Quintidi de la première decade Ventôse, à l'Assemblée générale du F.B. Montmartre* (Paris, 5 Ventôse), 4, in Lb 40 1818, BN. "But these cowardly moderates, who do not dare show their faces, are frightened by revolutionary measures"; *ibid.*, 7.

11 Ventôse, Camus, a member of its revolutionary committee, favored the expulsion not only of the moderates and enemies of the Revolution but of all who had done nothing for it, whose "false pity"—their hypocritical sympathy for victims of the Terror—he attacked. "The generosity, the indulgence toward these cowardly beings should be a crime," he declared. Furthermore, in praising the role of popular societies, where "a weak man fortifies and instructs himself," he argued that it was essential to purge them of moderates.[60] It should be noted that the question "What have you done for the Revolution?" was not unusual during an interrogation of prospective members.[61]

In section Lombards a commissioner of the *Administration de l'habillement*, despite the fact that he had his certificate of civic conduct signed by the ten members of the revolutionary committee, and although presented by eight citizens as an honest man and a true republican, was rejected by the popular society of the section. The reason given was that he had "launched a diatribe" against a citizen who had insulted him (Bacon calls this citizen "a hypocrite"). The many women present called the candidate "one of the best patriots." Two hours of disorder followed his rejection as he left the hall in tears.[62]

A similar incident occurred in the popular society of section Bon-Conseil on 23 Ventôse. A carpenter named Léonard, who had been elected three times captain of his company and was soon to be made *assesseur* to the justice of the peace by his fellow citizens, was rejected as "a bit feebleminded." A great tumult broke out as a result. In leaving the hall, the captain was heard to exclaim: "How can it be that I, a patriot of July 14, am treated this way?" The women indignantly accused "these fellows" in the society of being false patriots in rejecting "an excellent republican in order to divide us." Upon leaving the hall Bacon overheard six women discussing the incident. One of them declared: "People are saying that a row is being prepared. Really, one could kick the backsides of these club members, for they create devilish enemies by expelling good patriots with their purges."[63]

The patriots responsible for the arbitrary nature of these refusals

---

60. *Discours prononcé par C. Camus à la Société populaire de la section Constante du faubourg Montmartre* (Paris, 11 Ventôse), in Lb 40 2438, BN. The section published 500 copies of this address, signed by Georges, president, and Buirette, secretary.

61. See section Faubourg du Nord, n.d., in AA/266, f. 194, APP. Among other questions were: "What are your means of support? What was your worth before 1789? What is your actual worth today? Do you have a certificate of *civisme?*"

62. Caron, *Paris pendant la Terreur*, V, 44.

63. *Ibid.*, 267–68.

to admit candidates undermined their own popularity among ordinary citizens. Too often such refusals meant that civic cards would be withheld from applicants turned down by the popular societies. Latour-Lamontagne revealed on 1 Ventôse the grievance of a citizen who complained that after making many sacrifices for the Revolution he still could not find a job because the revolutionary committee of his section would not give him a civic card unless he was enrolled in a popular society. "I made . . . all kinds of advances to enter the [club] of my section, but a powerful cabal, led by the revolutionary committee itself, always rejected me," he was quoted. Latour-Lamontagne observed that many committees acted the same way. Although he pointed out that there was no law that prevented people from obtaining civic cards who were not members of these societies, he admitted that this type of action gave popular societies too much influence and destroyed the jurisdiction of the general assemblies. The latter were being deserted while intriguers were making the societies centers of public affairs in order to control the sections more easily, he thought.[64]

This kind of behavior also undermined the position of the Cordeliers Club, with which many of the popular societies were affiliated. At the same time, it made easier the ultimate victory of the Jacobins over the Cordeliers. There were enough grievances, obviously, that could be exploited by the former, grievances that would make more than one good republican sectionnaire withhold his support from the Cordeliers. On 7 Ventôse (February 25, 1794), for example, according to Rolin, the Jacobins expelled four hundred affiliated fraternal societies. Many of the public seemed to approve of this action because they were opposed to these societies on principle. Rolin shrewdly observed that people were saying that the Cordeliers had become alienated from the Jacobins, and that soon only one society would exist. Furthermore, he quoted an unnamed observer who saw the Cordeliers as being divided, with only its minority favoring the Jacobins. Two days later Rolin wrote that some people were convinced the Cordeliers would destroy the Jacobins because the majority of sectional societies were for the Cordeliers.[65] Just the opposite happened, of course, but many were becoming conscious of the differences between the two organizations. On 2 Ventôse, Rolin had noted

64. *Ibid.*, IV, 208.
65. *Ibid.*, IV, 322, 360–61.

hearing that citizens of the popular societies in Paris "were up in arms against the Jacobin Society." [66] Although he believed that this report was disseminated by malicious people, it was certainly not without foundation.

The unceasing hostility of the Jacobins to the sectional societies impelled a number of them to demonstrate that they were truly popular societies open to all. As early as 9 Brumaire (November 9, 1793), Robespierre had attacked the sectional societies as insufficiently patriotic. "Today," he declared, "all royalists are republicans, all Brissotins are Montagnards." On 6 Nivôse (December 26, 1793) he praised the Jacobin society and its affiliates. "The so-called popular societies multiplying ad infinitum since May 31 are bastard societies and do not merit this sacred name," he charged. [67]

By the spring of 1794 many popular societies were to dissolve themselves under this pressure from the Jacobins. Meanwhile, section Poissonnière assured the Commune that its doors were open to all republicans. [68] The Club électoral, sitting in the Evêché (the archbishop's palace), published a circular on 7 Ventôse assuring its readers that the club accepted affiliates only if their membership was not restricted to one section but was open to everyone. It was a reflection, once again, of the antagonism between the patriots of '89 and those of '93. [69]

If, as many historians argue, the Jacobins reflected the historic interests of the bourgeoisie, the Cordeliers Club defended the interests of the sans-culottes. In addition to these class conflicts, there were differences on matters of principle, from how to conduct the war to how to use the Terror. Nor should the rivalries between individuals or between institutions—between the revolutionary committees and the general assemblies, for example, or between the popular societies and the Jacobin Club—be minimized.

66. *Ibid.*, IV, 245.

67. Aulard, *Jacobins*, V, 503–504, 19 Brumaire (November 9, 1793), and 578–81; *Journal de la Montagne*, Nos. 45 and 46, 8 and 9 Nivôse (December 28, 29, 1793), 356–58 and 363–64; *Moniteur*, XIX, No. 101 (December 31, 1793), 86–87 (session of 6 Nivôse). For an interesting discussion of this subject in which the Jacobin Saintexte (sometimes spelled Sentex) defended the role of these popular societies against Couthon, Dufourny, and even Hébert, see *Moniteur*, XIX, No. 132 (January 31, 1794), 337–38.

68. *Journal de la Montagne*, No. 105 (February 26, 1794), 835.

69. Soboul, *Sans-Culottes*, 703. "Les membres composant la société populaire du Club séant à la salle électorale, à tous les zélés partisans de la Révolution," in AD XVI 70, AN.

"The Jacobins formed the republican organization, harsh, cold, negative, daughter of Fate and of circumstance; but the Cordeliers [organization] expressed élan and initiative. Always it is found at the head of great movements of the Revolution," wrote an admirer of the Paris Commune.[70] Police observers were aware of these growing differences, and commented on them. On 9 Pluviôse (January 28, 1794) Le Harivel wrote: "People talk much about the coming dissolution of the popular societies. The Committees of Public Safety and of General Security have, they say, important reasons to provoke this dissolution: *it is the only way to concentrate authority in one and a single point.*"[71]

On 19 Pluviôse (February 7) Grivel revealed an important schism between the two organizations. François Nicolas Vincent, secretary for the Department of War, and a leading Cordelier, had proposed to the club an address to the Convention asking it to apportion some of the authority held by the revolutionary committees to the popular societies of the sections. This resolution was adopted by a majority of the Cordeliers, who then decided to circulate it among other organizations for their support. Grivel drew the following important conclusion from this proposal:

> Thus, here are two societies absolutely contrary in their opinion, in their views, in their resolutions. The one [the Cordeliers] wants the suppression of revolutionary committees, and the other [the Jacobins] the suppression of all sectional clubs. The latter finds a radical vice in the bizarre regulations of these diverse societies and a federalist attribute in their territorial denomination. They are reproached for continually exceeding the bounds to which they should confine themselves, of arrogating the right to judge the validity of certificates of civic conduct, of influencing the elections, of deciding the share of contributions, of determining even the arrest and the imprisonment of citizens.[72]

The Convention and its committees could hardly allow their authority to be undermined; nor could their supporters in the Jacobin Club. Nevertheless, the danger of recruiting support for such a venture was still present so long as the Cordeliers retained their influence. Moreover, here was proof yet again that the sans-culottes in the popular societies, and especially their more militant and politically conscious members who sat in the Cordeliers, opposed the centralizing policies of the government. For since the failure of the Commune

70. Tridon, *Hébertistes*, 43. Tridon was a member of the Paris Commune of 1871.
71. Caron, *Paris pendant la Terreur*, III, 194, my emphasis.
72. *Ibid.*, 369–70.

to control the sections on 14 Frimaire (December 4, 1793), the militants had steadily lost influence in them.[73]

Efforts at reconciliation between the two societies failed to resolve their differences. On 8 Ventôse a delegation of Cordeliers arrived at the Jacobins to swear fraternal unity.[74] Two days later, however, Béraud revealed that this action had not been inspired "by love." People in the café he frequented were heard to remark that the Cordeliers hoped to persuade the Jacobins to abandon Desmoulins, a sharp critic of Hébert. Another added that the majority in the Cordeliers was not entirely in favor of Vincent. A third critic declared that all popular societies acted the same way: all were led by former aristocrats who now "vomit flames of civic conduct" in order to monopolize their (privileged) positions.[75] Thus the breach between the two clubs grew ever wider.

Certainly shortages led to short tempers as well. Hunger and scarcity of essential commodities made the sans-culottes and other consumers restless and dissatisfied. Sacrifices for the country, offerings of saltpeter, participation in the political life of the sections—all had their limitations. Factional fighting and divisions among patriots when the country was still at war appeared irresponsible. It was doubly so to criticize the Committees and to create doubt in the minds of the public. The prestige of Robespierre was at an all-time high; hence an attack on him or on the Jacobin Club, whose spokesman he was in the eyes of many, appeared little short of treason.

Yet the Cordeliers and other popular societies, the sections, and the Commune had interests of their own. Could they surrender their independence and give up their role as defenders of *sans-culottisme* to the revolutionary government? For a long time they had looked upon the deputies of the Convention as their mandatories, their proxies. But the Conventionnels were more than that, and they had no intention of surrendering to the *clubbistes* or their allies. The question remained: how long could this unstable equilibrium last?

73. B&R, XXX, 306, 309. With the creation of national agents by the Convention, the power of the Paris Commune was much diminished.

74. *Journal de la Montagne*, No. 108 (March 1, 1794), 860.

75. Caron, *Paris pendant la Terreur*, IV, 347, 385 (reports of Dugas and Béraud). On 18 Ventôse (March 8, 1794) Rolin wrote that two parties existed within the Jacobin Club, one of which was ready to arrest Robespierre, Danton, Legendre, and others. He warned that people were fearful of a civil war; *ibid.*, V, 144.

3

The Vendée Campaign and Factional Conflicts

If the differences between the Cordeliers and the Jacobins were profound, those between the Indulgents and the Cordeliers were far deeper. In addition to the usual clashes of personality—and these must not be minimized—the views of Danton, Desmoulins, Philippeaux, François Louis Bourdon de l'Oise, and others were in direct conflict with those of Hébert, Ronsin, Vincent, Momoro, and their adherents in the Cordeliers.[1] While the more radical sans-culottes insisted that the Terror must not be modified—that, if anything, it should be intensified—their "moderate" enemies favored dismantling it by releasing persons imprisoned for counterrevolutionary crimes, real or alleged (it should be added that there is no indication that had the *moderates* been in power, they would have been indulgent toward their enemies). In early 1794 an unceasing, bitter war existed between the Cordeliers and the "Philippotins," as Hébert derisively called them.

A year before, in March, 1793, the crisis in the Vendée had already shaped the battle lines between the two parties. The Vendée, as a map of France makes clear, is a maritime department in western France bordering on the Atlantic Ocean. Because of its violent opposition to the Republic and to the draft of its men into the army, the department revolted several times. A civil war broke out in the region between peasants, led by royalists and priests, and the troops of the Convention. As a result of this conflict, the department's very name became synonymous with counterrevolution. To quell the revolt the Convention had to carry on a vicious war, in which many a military reputation was destroyed. Conflict on how to suppress the uprising began shortly after the treason of General Dumouriez forced important changes in the Department of War (Dumouriez, having suffered a disastrous defeat at Neerwinden on March 18, 1793, made a treach-

---

1. These men are discussed below and their biographies sketched.

erous peace with the Austrians whereby he agreed to march on Paris; his soldiers refused to follow him, and he crossed over to the enemy on April 5). Jean Baptiste Noël Bouchotte, sympathetic to the sans-culottes and a staunch republican, had replaced Pierre Beurnonville as minister of war. In staffing his ministry he surrounded himself with many supporters of Jean Nicolas Pache, the mayor of Paris and a resolute Montagnard. Among this group was the Cordeliers' Vincent, appointed as general secretary of the War Department. It was an important position because it enabled Vincent to staff his office with sympathizers of the Cordeliers and to remove his opponents.

As his first adjutant, Bouchotte employed Ronsin, the future commander of the Revolutionary army. On May 9, 1793, the Provisional Executive Council (predecessor to the Committee of Public Safety) sent Ronsin to Tours to take charge of operations against the Vendéens.

Charles Philippe Ronsin, son of a cooper, was born at Soissons on December 1, 1751. He attended college until age seventeen, then enrolled in a regiment of infantry in 1768 and remained in the army until 1772. Since he could not rise above the grade of sergeant under the Old Regime, being a commoner, he left for Paris. There he began writing plays, one of which was read before the company of the Comédie-Française but never produced. He wrote others—with little success, although he published them—and translated poetry.[2]

On July 11, 1789, Ronsin was elected captain of the bourgeois guard of his district, and in August he published a pamphlet against Marie Antoinette, whom he called "an Austrian Messalina." Yet like many revolutionaries he praised Louis as the best of monarchs. At the Festival of the Federation (July 14, 1790), his comedy in verse *La Fête de la Liberté; ou, Le Dîner des patriotes*, whose subject was the reconciliation of the privileged classes with the people, reflected his new politics. His tragedy in five acts *Arétaphile; ou, La Révolution de Cyrène* was performed on June 23, 1792. Among the lines that brought applause were those spoken to the tyrant: "Without you, the people are everything, and you are nothing without them"—another reflection of his new political thinking.

Shortly thereafter Ronsin joined the Jacobins and the Cordeliers. On August 11, 1792, after the overthrow of the monarchy, he took the

2. General Herlaut, *Le Général rouge Ronsin (1751–1794), la Vendée, l'armée révolutionnaire parisienne* (Paris, n.d.), 3–13, *passim*; Tuetey, *Répertoire général*, XI, x.

oath of loyalty to the nation before Momoro, future president of the Cordeliers Club, and at the moment presiding over section Théâtre-Français. Soon afterward he was appointed as one of thirty commissioners to the army to organize the defense of the Seine-et-Marne Department. He seems to have succeeded in all missions, showed courage and firmness, and participated in a number of battles. Pache then offered him the post of commissioner to France's Army of Belgium, but he replied that he hoped to obtain a higher post, as director (*commissaire-ordonnateur des guerres*), not as a mere commissioner.[3]

As commissioner of the Executive Council, Ronsin proceeded to Belgium and was present in November, 1792, at the battle of Jemappes, although he never claimed that he fought there. Shortly thereafter a dispute broke out between Dumouriez and the Convention over control of army supplies, something that the general wanted in order to make himself independent of civil control. The government had no intentions of granting such powers to him, however, and arrested Dumouriez's two administrators. As a result, Ronsin became chief director of supplies.

Upon assuming the new post Ronsin found that the French army lacked almost everything. He took heroic measures to raise money and supplies, and confiscated Crown and Church properties (which Dumouriez had refused to do, under the pretext that he did not know anything but military matters). When the French were forced to evacuate Belgium, General Claude Vezu was surprised to find warehouses full of clothing and boots that the army thought it did not have. It appears that Ronsin was good at raising supplies but lacked the organizational skills needed to transfer them from depots to the front.[4]

Ronsin's arrival in the Vendée failed to provide the unity of com-

3. Herlaut, *Ronsin*, 15–21, *passim*; Tuetey, *Répertoire général*, XI, x–xi.
4. Vezu, called "Jean Bart," accused Ronsin of sabotage and betrayal in his testimony of March 15, 1794. A captain, Henri Vrie, testified that he was surprised to find food and clothing in the warehouses of Liège, but he blamed this on poor organization by Ronsin, whom he did not know personally. Further witnesses included Paul Chaix, former Spanish consul at Ostend; Alexandre Sagniel, a négociant of Paris present at Liège; and Nicholas Michel Jolivet, an administrator of military transport. Others also testified against Ronsin as incompetent and given to orgies. Tuetey, *Répertoire général*, X, Nos. 2271, 2272, 2275, 2279, 2291. Much of this testimony is suspect, since it was given at the time of Ronsin's final arrest, when a number of witnesses must have been under pressure (self-imposed, perhaps) to please the government; Herlaut, *Ronsin*, 28–29, 35–36, 46, 51; Tuetey, *Répertoire général*, XI, xi.

mand so necessary for republican arms. The confusion between the powers exercised by the representatives-on-mission—deputies of the Convention sent by it to the armies and departments with supreme powers to reorganize and oversee them—and their rivals, the agents of the Executive Council, was aggravated by division in the general staff of the army, among individual generals, and within the ranks of the representatives themselves. The chaos that resulted from this division contributed powerfully to the rout that the republicans suffered on June 9, 1793, at Saumur.

Ronsin's military adviser, General Alexandre Berthier, favored a simultaneous attack on the rebels, rather than marching against them by dividing the republican forces. The plan itself arose partly from Ronsin's criticism, upon his arrival, that the army lacked a general plan of campaign and a centralized command. Ronsin was ready to assume command, but Danton's appointee, General Armand Louis Biron, took over instead. Just how ready he was to make war is questionable, since he asked to negotiate with the rebels before launching his campaign.

The disaster at Saumur forced the republican army to reorganize its general staff. Ronsin tried to explain the reasons for the defeat, but the Committee of Public Safety was not convinced and ordered him back to Tours. Meanwhile, General Biron complained to Bouchotte that agents of the Executive Council were preaching indiscipline and defiance of authority. He requested, therefore, command of another army. One of the representatives-on-mission, Pierre René Choudieu, accused Biron of inactivity, however, and lauded Ronsin's merits. Choudieu's colleagues, representatives Bourdon de l'Oise and Jean François Marie Goupilleau de Fontenay, on the other hand, opposed Bouchotte and Ronsin, insisting on their dismissal. To aggravate the situation, the Vendéens occupied Angers and threatened Nantes.

A military commission, composed of representatives-on-mission and the generals, split on how best to defend the city. Goupilleau de Fontenay departed for Paris to argue before the Committee of Public Safety that Biron, who had refused to carry out the plan of the commission, was the best general available. Choudieu presented a different picture. On July 1 he refuted the arguments of Goupilleau and Biron and warmly defended Ronsin, his agents, and Berthier. The outbreak of the Federalist Revolt against Paris helped persuade the Committee in favor of Choudieu and the military commission's plan of operations. Thus, the Committee had reversed itself. On June 29,

1793, the republican armies repelled the Vendéens at Nantes. Within four days Ronsin was promoted from captain to chief of squadron, then to adjutant general, and finally to general of brigade.[5]

The successful defense of Nantes did not end the disputes in republican ranks. One revolved around the arrest of a lieutenant colonel by the name of Jean Rossignol, a true sans-culotte in origin. He was born on November 7, 1756, the last of five children. His father, a transport agent, died when Jean was nine; his mother was a postwoman or merchant's agent. He attended a parish school, got into mischief, then decided to apprentice himself to a jeweler. At age fourteen he left his bourgeois master for Bordeaux, where he found employment with a merchant-jeweler. He was dismissed after a week and migrated to La Rochelle, where he worked for two months before being dismissed for wounding a fellow worker in a fight, typical of a pattern that he pursued for some years. Shortly after that episode he returned to Paris.[6]

The young Rossignol worked for a time, then decided to enlist in the army. He became a private in the Roussillon Infantry regiment, stationed at Dunquerque (1775). After a number of brawls and duels, he quarreled with his captain for not giving him leave. As a result he was placed under guard and was saved from a court martial and probable hanging only because the chaplain and the captain's wife intervened in his favor. Rossignol was sentenced to six months in prison but was released after less than a month. He continued to quarrel and fight; on leave in Paris he "drew the sword" seven times in six months. Returning to his regiment, which was about to embark for the West Indies from the port of Brest, he fell ill and did not sail with his comrades but remained in Brest, where he was badly wounded in a fight with sailors. It took him six months to recover, but he was chronically troubled by his wound. Then more duels and wounds confined him to the hospital, where he was operated on twice and, as a result, exempted from sailing to the West Indies.[7]

Rossignol wrote that like other soldiers, he was forced to smuggle salt in order to raise money. He continued to get into scraps and had to sell all his goods for debts that, he insisted, he did not owe. To add to his discomfiture, his colonel was a religious bigot who made his

---

5. Herlaut, *Ronsin*, 73–80, 87–96, 97–100; Tuetey, *Répertoire général*, XI, xiii–xiv.
6. Victor Barrucand, ed., *La Vie véritable du citoyen Jean Rossignol (1759–1802)* (Paris, 1896), 1–5, *passim*.
7. *Ibid.*, 20–32, 33–42, 43–52, *passim*.

men pray morning and evening, and attend regimental mass on Sunday. Soldiers from other regiments teased Rossignol's comrades as "Capuchins." Eventually, Rossignol left the army in disgust.[8]

When the Revolution broke out, Rossignol admitted, he knew nothing of politics or revolutions. It was not long, however, before the excitement in the streets converted him to the cause of the Third Estate. He witnessed the pillage of the house of a wealthy wallpaper manufacturer named Réveillon, who was rumored to be planning to lower his workers' wages. Rossignol also saw the killing of rioters by the Gardes-Françaises, and was present when Swiss mercenary troops fired on people who were throwing bricks at them from windows. The hatred of the Gardes-Françaises by the inhabitants of faubourg Saint-Antoine was so great that none of the soldiers dared patrol the neighborhood.

On July 12, 1789, as Rossignol went out to drink with some friends, he heard that the barriers were being burned down. Crowds in the street were crying "Long live the Third Estate!" Rossignol and his comrades fraternized with them. The following morning on rue Saint-Honoré he joined a large crowd armed with all kinds of weapons. As he listened to various speakers in the Palais Royal he began to understand and to appreciate their message. Meanwhile, the people tried to obtain more weapons but failed.[9]

On July 14 Rossignol tried to persuade a platoon of Gardes-Françaises to follow him to the Bastille. He failed but went there himself and participated in the attack. In his *Vie véritable* he described the fight: Shortly after 2:30 P.M. two companies of Gardes-Françaises arrived and began firing on the Swiss guarding the fortress. Children carried cannonballs and women carried gunpowder. Someone waved a white kerchief from the fortress. When the crowd surged forward thinking the Swiss had surrendered, a volley struck them as the defenders continued shooting. The crowd brought up a cannon and began to fire again. When the Swiss finally decided to surrender, Rossignol opposed their request because of the treacherous firing on the crowd. The drawbridge was lowered, however, and the crowd surged forward, crushing a number of unfortunates. Rossignol was sick for two weeks as a result of this action, probably because an old wound or his operation still gave him trouble. In summarizing this experi-

8. *Ibid.*, 53–61, 62–64.
9. *Ibid.*, 70–72, 73–75.

The siege of the Bastille. Jean Rossignol, who was there, claimed that only six hundred people carried out the attack. At least two of them, François Desfieux and Pierre Dubuisson, were later condemned with Hébert as counterrevolutionaries.

ence he maintained that there were no more than 600 people among the "conquerors of the Bastille," despite the official figure of 863. He added that the rich and undeserving were decorated, whereas only the sans-culottes deserved recognition because they alone were in the place of danger.[10]

Rossignol continued to give an interesting account of the Revolution as he saw it. As a grenadier in the newly organized National Guard (he does not tell us what rank he held), he was present when the guard followed the famous march of women to Versailles on October 5 and 6, 1789, and later he described the clash with the king's

10. *Ibid.*, 77–79, 80–90, *passim*.

guard there, which ended only when the royal family appeared on the balcony, to be taken the next morning to Paris. Rossignol championed the principle of equality in the guard, demanding that the troops receive the same food as officers and that grenadiers be paid the same amount as volunteers. At the Ecole Militaire he opposed the promotion of unworthy officers—who then laid a trap for him by writing a letter that they made appear to be his, directed against the men. He was able to persuade the soldiers of his innocence, however, when the officers refused to show them the original.

Shortly thereafter Rossignol left the school and enrolled in the battalion of his section on August 20, 1791. It seems that he held the rank of sergeant until August 10. Once again he clashed with his commanding officer, one Hullin. When the Paris Commune appointed a commission to investigate his charges against Hullin, it ruled against him and he was hooted down in the General Council.[11]

On March 23, 1793, the Provisional Executive Council ordered Rossignol to depart for the Vendée. He was now a captain of gendarmerie, 35th Division, and quickly rose to become a lieutenant colonel. A number of disasters to the republican forces elevated him to the rank of general, an indication of the paucity of professional officers during this period of the Revolution. A fellow general named Louis Marie Turreau wrote that Rossignol's appointment struck fear into the Vendéens because they knew that this republican general would not compromise. Furthermore, Turreau thought, the appointment of a plebeian raised the morale of the republican armies.

The appointment of Ronsin as commanding general of the newly created Revolutionary army, launched to combat the counterrevolution in the interior, opened the way for Rossignol's further promotion. This institution, for which militants had been agitating for some time, was authorized by the Convention after the successful mass demonstration of the sans-culottes on September 4 and 5, 1793. The post of commanding general in the Vendée was now open, and Ronsin recommended Rossignol for it. The latter was "brave, frank, loyal, and disinterested," wrote Turreau, but he lacked the talent to command an army. Rossignol himself recognized this shortcoming and refused the offer, but pressure from his colleagues and subordinates finally induced him to accept.[12]

11. *Ibid.*, 92–97, 98–112, 113–17, 118–22, 127–30.
12. Barrucand, *ibid.*, 199n–200n, cites Turreau's *Mémoire pour servir à l'histoire de la guerre de Vendée.*

Although Momoro, as commissioner of the Provisional Executive Council, had called for republican commanders, the promotion of such lowly men as Ronsin and Rossignol to positions of command sowed division among the other generals. Many older officers resented serving under them because of their sans-culotte origin; some others simply judged them as professionally incapable of command. General Talbot, for example, called Ronsin "a braggart, a spy, a jealous and dangerous person."[13]

The representatives-on-mission expressed the same division of opinion. Philippeaux, Bourdon de l'Oise, and the two Goupilleaus (de Fontanay and de Montaigu) bitterly opposed the promotions. On the other hand, Choudieu, Joseph Etienne Richard, and Pierre Bourbotte supported the elevation of Ronsin and Rossignol and defended them warmly before the Committee of Public Safety and the Convention. Choudieu, for example, realized that "it was quite a shock" to have an "obscure plebeian" replace "a grand seigneur" like General Biron. But he also knew that Ronsin's chief of staff, Berthier—the future chief of staff under Napoleon—could be relied on to give his commander the best professional advice. Thus, with a good plan of campaign, there was no reason why Ronsin and Rossignol could not command successfully.

The dispute over strategy and tactics became sharper over the employment of professional soldiers. When the city of Mainz surrendered to the Prussians in the spring of 1793, the articles of capitulation stated that the troops of the French garrison could not be used against the Coalition (England, Austria, Prussia, Russia, Spain, and lesser powers) for one year. Here was a battle-hardened force that could be sent to the Vendée. The question was, under whose command would it be employed?

Philippeaux asked Rossignol for two battalions of the Mainz troops, and Rossignol complied. But when two days later he asked for another two, Rossignol refused, arguing that such a move would break the line established by his forces. Reacting angrily to this refusal, Philippeaux accused the sans-culotte general of wanting to sacrifice Nantes.[14] Rossignol then appealed to Choudieu, who came to

13. Herlaut, *Ronsin*, 113. Talbot was shocked to find that Ronsin had appointed an actor, Grammont, as adjutant general, thus placing the man on a level with Talbot himself: "Here he is, on the same footing as me. What a pity!"

14. *Réponse de Philippeaux à tous les défenseurs officieux des bourreaux de nos frères dans la Vendée, avec l'acte solennel d'accusation, fait à la séance du 18 nivôse, suivie de trois lettres*

his defense. For example, Philippeaux had boasted to the Convention that "Everything has changed since my arrival in this place," but Choudieu declared that Philippeaux had not once appeared at the head of the columns he should have led, which meant that he had never fought at all. Adding irony to his observation, Choudieu wrote that it was good to have a conquering Caesar among them, and that he only waited for Philippeaux to tell all of his exploits.[15]

As for the military plan itself, Ronsin and Rossignol, supported by Choudieu, favored massing their forces and using the Mainz troops in one blow aimed at the heart of the Vendéen army. Philippeaux urged instead the division of forces by marching them in a circuitous route between Saumur and Nantes. Such a march, it was observed, would take them some fifty miles out of the way instead of striking directly at the Vendéens, who were a mere ten miles distant.

The council of war was split because both the representatives and the generals were given the vote on what plan to follow. Choudieu remarked that only Lazare Carnot and Claude Antoine Prieur de la Côte d'Or knew anything about military matters, yet Philippeaux had persuaded the Committee of Public Safety to endorse his plan. General Jacques Menou, with map in hand, demonstrated how a direct

---

écrites à sa femme, de la prison (Paris, l'an III), in Lb 41 1040 B, BN. This ninety-seven-page brochure was published by Philippeaux's widow after his execution. In it, Philippeaux calls Choudieu's report to the Convention "this monstrous diatribe" and an apology for Ronsin, whom he dubs "a rogue and a gallows bird" (pp. 23, 25–26). He insists that he alone was responsible for saving Angers (37–38) and replies at length (57–78) to the charges against him. His last three letters to his wife (93–97), written from Luxembourg prison on March 31 and April 1 and 2, 1794, are quite moving.

15. *Pierre Choudieu à ses concitoyens et à ses collègues* ([Paris], n.d.), in Le 39 64 bis, BN. This is Choudieu and Richard's report to the Convention on what transpired in the Vendée; it is signed by Choudieu alone. Choudieu began by writing that he had hesitated for a long time to reply to Philippeaux because the dispute between them could encourage enemies of the Republic, but that his silence had emboldened Philippeaux to redouble his attacks on Choudieu, Richard, and others; hence his determination to reply.

Choudieu organized his text into twenty-six charges made by Philippeaux, with a reply to each accusation. He treats Philippeaux's boast to the Convention with irony: "'Everything has changed since my arrival in this place,' he wrote modestly to the National Convention, on his way through Angers" (*ibid.*, 3). Choudieu insists that Philippeaux never left Nantes when the military action was going on during the summer and fall of 1793, and he warmly supports Ronsin and Rossignol throughout his narrative (both sans-culotte generals fought Philippeaux's plan to divide the army into separate striking forces).

attack was superior to any other route, and Antoine Joseph Santerre, the former "Bastille conqueror" and commander of the National Guard, likened the Philippeaux plan to the treason of a Dumouriez. The council was evenly divided, and in order to break the deadlock Rossignol gave up his vote. The result was that Philippeaux carried the day and assured the defeat of the republican forces. Napoleon wrote later that it was difficult to conceive of a more absurd plan: "This huge deployment of forces, well led, could have overthrown like a furious torrent the weak obstacles opposed to its march," he declared.

The separate columns were defeated and the republicans fell back on Rennes. Rossignol, who had been wounded and thus could not direct the operations, told the hastily summoned council of war that the defeat was due to the refusal of the generals to carry out their orders, as well as to their individual ambitions. He offered his resignation, but the representatives present refused to accept it. Prieur de la Côte d'Or then informed the generals that Rossignol enjoyed the full support of the Committee of Public Safety no matter how many defeats he suffered, and he warned them not to undermine this trust, as they would be held responsible for any defeats. Rossignol was now named commander in chief of all three armies: Brest, the West, and Cherbourg.

Differences of strategy and an unwillingness to accept service under a sans-culotte commander help to account for the disputes among the military and the representatives-on-mission, but a more personal and more tangible reason also existed. Goupilleau de Montaigu and his cousin Goupilleau de Fontenay owned considerable properties in the region under attack. The Convention decree of August 1, 1793, endorsed the destruction of property as a weapon of war against the internal enemy. When Fontenay asked Rossignol if he intended to carry out the decree and was told that he did, the representative immediately contacted both his cousin Montaigu and his friend Bourdon de l'Oise. The three deputies then decided to suspend Rossignol (at this time still only commander of the 35th Division) under the pretext that he had tolerated pillage and had comported himself in a manner that, "far from inspiring confidence, had rendered him unworthy." Fontenay and Bourdon even attempted to arrest him on the pillaging charge. Faced with this threat, Rossignol left for Tours, then Paris. There he reported to the Committee of Public Safety, whose members agreed to let him appear before the Convention the next day, August 28, 1793.[16] The session, presided over by Robespierre, ended in complete vindication of Rossignol—and thus also of Ronsin. This dramatic reversal owed much to the efforts of the representative-on-mission Pierre Bourbotte.

Like Rossignol, Bourbotte had fled to Paris under duress from Bourdon de l'Oise and the two Goupilleaus. Speaking in the name of his colleagues Choudieu, Richard, Antoine Michet, and Philippe Antoine Merlin (*dit* de Douai), he reminded the Convention that Rossignol had originally refused the command of the armies and had agreed to serve only after being promised help and in order to avoid betrayal by others who might have accepted the job. Bourbotte next attacked Bourdon, the Goupilleaus, and their ally General Tuncq, charging that when he himself had asked them whether they intended to carry out the plan of campaign agreed to by the Committee of Public Safety, they not only told him that they would refuse but also threatened to kill anyone, including him, who did follow such a plan. At that point, Bourbotte said, he had whipped out two pistols and vowed to shoot anyone who tried to arrest him. He had been allowed to depart but was given no escort and almost fell into the hands of Vendéen insurgents.

After this recital a deputy in the hall shouted, "It is easy to see that Bourbotte wanted to destroy the rebels, and the Goupilleau[s] to save their properties." When Jean Lambert Tallien, the future Thermidorian, demanded that Rossignol be restored to his command and was asked, "What has he done to become a general?" Tallien replied that he had fought more than fifty battles as chief of the 35th Division, had reorganized his troops, had taken over the command of a wounded general, and had repaired the injustice done by Biron. The result was that the Convention recalled Bourdon and Goupilleau de Fontenay and repealed the leave of de Montaigu. Rossignol entered amidst applause and was given the honors of the session. On the next day he departed for the army.[17]

It is easy to imagine the enmity that such a bitter dispute left be-

16. *Ibid., passim;* Barrucand, ed., *Rossignol,* 202–204, 225–31, 247–49, 250; Herlaut, *Ronsin,* 128, 131–36, 141, 143–44, 147–48. In a "Mémoire justificatif," reedited in 1795, Rossignol defended himself against various accusations of Bourdon de l'Oise, who "attacks a man in the morning, then praises him in the evening," and quoted Legendre on Bourdon, that the color of his hair changed from morning to evening ("rouge le matin et gris le soir"); Barrucand, ed., *Rossignol,* 286n2.

17. Barrucand, ed., *Rossignol,* 206–209, 213–15, 217–19, 222.

hind. On September 11, 1793, Bourdon tried to explain to the Jacobins his motives for trying to arrest Rossignol. He asked that his deposition to the Committee of Public Safety be examined by a committee of the club, rather than in public. Brushing aside Bourdon's argument, Robespierre replied that Rossignol was a victim of intrigue: he had been persecuted by those who had properties in the Vendée to defend and those who did not want republicans at the head of French armies. When Bourdon asked if Robespierre was willing to testify formally to these allegations, a tumult broke out and Bourdon was attacked as a slanderer by Hébert, who added that Bourdon's charges against Rossignol should convince all that the sans-culotte general was a good republican.[18] Thus, the seeds of conflict between the Cordeliers and their "moderate" opponents had been planted in the Vendée months before the crisis of Ventôse.

The *journée* of September 4 and 5, 1793, begun by sans-culottes in a march on the Hôtel de Ville to demand bread, quickly found support among the Parisian sections. Their spokesmen, in turn, convinced the Convention to establish a Revolutionary army, which would requisition foodstuffs in the countryside. It was a major concession to the sans-culottes.[19] The Provisional Executive Council was authorized to appoint the army's general staff, subject to confirmation by the Committee of Public Safety. On September 17 Bouchotte submitted a list of officers for the newly created army. The Committee of Public Safety confirmed all the candidates except Ronsin; the Committee intended to appoint the commander of the Paris National Guard, François Hanriot, whom they trusted to do their bidding,

18. Aulard, *Jacobins*, V, 398–402. Bourdon claimed that the reason for the defeats suffered by the republican forces was Rossignol's failure to march with his own force on Fontenay while the other two armies converged on the town. This assertion was denied by many members present at the session. Danton, like Robespierre, praised Rossignol highly, but when a motion was made to expel Bourdon, Robespierre had it tabled.

After the arrest of the Hébertistes, Rossignol was imprisoned and not released for fifteen and a half months—until 15 Thermidor. He was arrested again by the Directory in May, 1796, but acquitted shortly thereafter. In September, 1800, he was rearrested and deported to the island of Mahé in the Indian Ocean. From there he was again deported to Anjouan in the Comoro Islands (between Madagascar and East Africa), where after a desperate struggle to survive, he died on 8 Floréal, Year X (April 28, 1802). Barrucand, ed., *Rossignol*, 264–76, 336–41, 349–59, 369–76.

19. B&R, XXIX, 26–29, 37–38, 45–46. "This was the high point of the popular movement. The Convention bowed before it for the last time"; Walter Markov, *Maximilien Robespierre, 1758–1794: Beiträge zu seinem 200. Geburtstag* (Berlin, 1958), 194.

rather than Ronsin, whose link to the Cordeliers Club and whose appeal to and support by the sans-culottes made him too independent for their tastes. Ten days later Léonard Bourdon (no relation to Bourdon de l'Oise) demanded that the officers so appointed (or proposed) appear before the Jacobins to prove their patriotism. Among those who appeared was Ronsin, who sought to demonstrate his loyalty to the nation. In heated discussion some Jacobins questioned the competence of several appointees while others, such as Léonard Bourdon, declared that in this post military skill was less essential than devotion to the country.[20]

In defending his conduct of the war in the Vendée, Ronsin criticized that of several generals opposed to him. Philippeaux countered this recital with one of his own. The popular society of Tours then denounced Ronsin and corroborated what Philippeaux had said; in short, the society held Ronsin responsible for the disasters in the Vendée—although, at the same time, the society assured the Jacobins that it really did not know him except through false reports. Despite this opposition, the Cordeliers approached the Jacobins to support Ronsin for commander of the Revolutionary army. As a result of this pressure the Executive Council invested Ronsin officially with the post on October 2, 1793. Because of Hanriot's opposition to any armed force in Paris not subordinate to him, Article 2 of the newly adopted regulations for the Revolutionary army provided that, when in the capital, the army was to be under his command.[21]

On October 29 Ronsin presented the Revolutionary army to the Convention. He was then at the height of his power; however, the attacks on him by the "moderates" and personal enemies continued. Philippeaux cited his alleged affluence and extravagance. While generals of combat divisions were earning 20,000 livres a year, Ronsin's salary was double that. Even Chaumette fulminated against the officers of this force for wearing golden epaulets and for riding horses that should have been used only for dragging the "ambulatory" guillotine and baggage.[22]

On November 25, 1793, Ronsin entered Lyon (named Ville-Affranchie after its surrender) with two thousand troops to punish

---

20. Herlaut, *Ronsin*, 160–62; Aulard, *Jacobins*, V, 426.

21. Tuetey, *Répertoire général*, XI, xv–xvi; Herlaut, *Ronsin*, 164. The Convention adopted Barère's motion to place the Revolutionary army under the same discipline as the regular army (October 30, 1793); Herlaut, *Ronsin*, 169.

22. Tuetey, *Répertoire général*, XI, xvi; Herlaut, *Ronsin*, 174.

the rebels there who had challenged the Convention. Amidst a heavy silence and palpable fear in the crowds who watched this force march in, the general prepared the instruments of punishment wielded by Collot d'Herbois and Joseph Fouché. The bloody executions that followed not only created irreconcilable enemies of the Republic but gave ammunition to the Indulgents as well. The latter launched an attack on the Committee of Public Safety by denouncing the minister of war—Bouchotte—and his commissioners. Philippeaux blamed them for the defeats in the Vendée, and Desmoulins asked what Ronsin had done to deserve his post. "Much intrigue, much thievery, much lying," was how he characterized Ronsin's actions. In addition, he called Ronsin's supporters "tainted patriots," and "ultrarevolutionaries with mustaches in red caps." [23]

On December 17, 1793, the Convention finally acted. Among the charges launched against Ronsin and Vincent were that their posters were stirring up the people and giving ammunition to counterrevolutionaries. One of these posters carried Ronsin's letter from Lyon, in which he boasted that the guillotine and the "fusillades" (mass shootings) had already done away with four hundred rebels and promised that another four hundred would be executed soon. "We must make the bloody Rhone, on its way down to the sea, roll up on its banks the corpses of the cowards who have killed our brothers, while the thunderbolt, which should exterminate them in a moment, will carry the terror throughout the departments where the seed of rebellion has been sowed," he wrote in mixed metaphors. Given this kind of provocation, the Indulgents through their spokesman, Fabre d'Eglantine, demanded the arrest of Ronsin, Vincent, and Maillard. The Convention agreed, and that same day the Committee of General Security ordered and carried out the arrests. [24]

On 18 Nivôse (January 7, 1794), the police spy Mercier reported that people were preoccupied with the charges against Ronsin, Vincent, and Stanislas Marie Maillard, one of the "Bastille conquerors" and a leader in the march on Versailles on October 5 and 6, 1789. Furthermore, it seems that Desmoulins' attacks on Hébert had convinced many that the radical journalist was not the patriot he appeared. The same day, Bacon seconded these observations. He heard

23. Herlaut, *Ronsin*, 182; *Le Vieux Cordelier*, No. 4.
24. Vincent and Ronsin, 27 Frimaire (December 17, 1794), in dos. 2, F7 4775 48, AN; Herlaut, *Ronsin*, 184.

talk in cafés about Rossignol, Ronsin, Vincent, Chaumette, and Hébert as described by Philippeaux and Desmoulins. But in some cafés, the police observer admitted, Hébert and Ronsin had their partisans. A citizen commented that all should suspend judgment until the Convention settled matters, which brought agreement from the patrons as they changed the topic of conversation.[25] It seems that whether the Cordeliers leaders were praised or reviled, as revealed in the police reports, often depended on the neighborhood where the café was situated.

Who was Vincent and what was his role in this dispute? François Nicolas Vincent, general secretary of the Department of War, was born in Paris in 1767, the son of a concierge in Parisian prisons. He had been poor during his early days, employed as a clerk by a *procureur* for five years before the Revolution and during its first years. The Revolution introduced him to politics, and he became active in his section. He soon joined the Cordeliers, linking his fortunes to its president, Momoro. In 1792 he became an elector of his section, Théâtre-Français (the future Mutius Scaevola). On August 10 he was elected to the General Council, and as commissioner he was charged with examining storage depots. Shortly thereafter he was employed to examine the administrative operations and the accounts of a military school, a task he discharged satisfactorily for Pache, then minister of war. As a result, he was promoted in October, 1792, to the office dealing with the discharge of troops.[26]

On February 27, 1793, he solicited the position of commissioner of war in one of the divisions, having high recommendations for the post. The following day the Executive Council appointed him to the army of the Corsican patriot Pascal Paoli, but Vincent refused to leave Paris. Pierre de Beurnonville, who had replaced Pache as minister of war, made Vincent commissioner at Versailles, in charge of inspecting stores of army uniforms. The same day he was appointed extraordi-

25. Caron, *Paris pendant la Terreur*, II, 228, 218. Bacon witnessed an interesting incident on the street. A "petit bon-homme" hawking his papers was shouting, "Great denunciation against the minister of war, who has given money to Père Duchesne to let the wives of patriots languish and die of hunger!" Two men approached him and said: "You lie, you don't know what you're talking about. You're a fool, a tramp, and undoubtedly are being paid to slander the true patriots." Then they kicked him and tore up his journals. A passerby gave him fifteen sous, admonishing him not to cry and to become a patriot.

26. Tuetey, *Répertoire général*, X, No. 2337; XI, xx.

nary commissioner of war before the troops of a lieutenant general named Barruyer. When Bouchotte became minister of war, he appointed Vincent to the important post of secretary general of the Department of War, the post he held until his final arrest.

Vincent pursued the goal of purging "the antique and dusty bureaucracy" in the Department of War, substituting active patriots in their stead. His letter to the revolutionary committee of section Gardes-Françaises, in requesting information on a candidate for a post (Jean Joseph Halle), reveals his determination to employ only patriots, not those who hid under this term. "I do not have to tell you, brothers and friends, that since the death of the tyrant, many intriguers and rogues have *popularized* themselves, the better to hide their maneuvers," he wrote. Then he named a number of men, popular in the past, who allegedly were disguised partisans of royalty. "Moderates, politicians, and speculators . . . , in general all those who have shown themselves detractors of popular societies and of all measures tending to consolidate the Revolution and the indivisibility of our republican government on the basis of equality"—none of these should be employed, he insisted.[27]

At a dinner given by Pache with the assistance of his son-in-law, François Xavier Audouin, where Hanriot, Ronsin, the Jacobin deputy Louis Legendre, and Servan Baudouin Boulanger, aide-de-camp to Hanriot, were present, Vincent revealed "the violence of his character and the intemperance of his language," according to the archivist Alexandre Tuetey. In greeting Legendre, Vincent is supposed to have said, "I embrace you for your past and not for the present, for I do not recognize you as the same Legendre, so strong from 1789 until 1792." This remark was to be cited against him at his trial. Legendre, obviously angry, replied that "it was possible that a madman like Vincent took a wise man for a moderate."[28]

It would have been better for Vincent had he retreated somewhat, but in the conversation around the dinner table he persisted in baiting the deputy. When he asked Legendre if he wore his deputy's uniform on mission, the latter replied that he did when he met the local constituted authorities. Vincent then remarked that he intended to dress

27. F7 4738, AN, reproduced in Tuetey, *Répertoire général*, XI, xxii–xxiii. Vincent's letter to Phulpin, justice of the peace and president of section Arcis, in which he replies favorably on employing a "père de famille," is also reproduced *ibid.*, xxiii.

28. Testimony of Mathias Halm in W 77, pl. 379, AN (Halm, of 3d Battalion, Revolutionary army, residing in section Grenelle was present at the dinner). Also partly in Tuetey, *Répertoire général*, X, No. 2338, and XI, xxiii.

a mannequin in the outfit of a deputy and place it in the Tuileries in order to teach the people that while the deputies preached the virtue of simplicity of manners, they were outfitting themselves in a style to create fear among the simple and to impose on them. Legendre angrily replied that should Vincent do so, he would throw him under the mannequin and break both Vincent's and the dummy's legs. Pache tried to intervene at this point by advising Vincent to listen to Legendre—after all, he pointed out, both shared the same politics. The insults exchanged, however, had angered the two men, and upon leaving Legendre warned Vincent that although he regarded him as a brother, if he persisted in his thoughtless remarks, he would break both his arms. Vincent only laughed "sardonically." Legendre then heard Ronsin remark that "if Vincent were different from what he is, he would be worth nothing under the circumstances." Upon entering the mayor's office Legendre was congratulated by Pache for his handling of Vincent. Finally, Legendre turned to Bouchotte, whom he found in the room, and cautioned him: "I like to think that Vincent is only a madman; it's for you to watch him, and if he does not change his behavior, you ought to show him the door of your office, or he will compromise you."[29]

Bouchotte took this advice and wrote Vincent shortly thereafter that although he did not doubt his patriotism, he wondered if Vincent had the maturity to fill the important post he held. Consequently, he asked him if there were another position he might want in which his patriotism could be utilized. After the condemnation of the Hébertistes, Bouchotte wrote Robespierre explaining why he had employed Vincent. The letter was probably motivated half by fear and half by a genuine need to defend his past.

Not all in the Department of War had the same high regard for the secretary general as Bouchotte, however. An employee named Dupont accused Vincent of converting the department into an anticivic bureau where "incompetence, harshness, and ignorance" reigned, adding that the secretary general was "an enemy of work." Dupont further charged that Vincent denounced everyone only to enhance his own status and that he was guilty of bribery and of misappropriating the enormous funds at his disposal. A former assistant head of the department, Marat Guédon, also accused him of accepting bribes.[30]

29. Tuetey, *Répertoire général*, XI, xxiv; Herlaut, *Ronsin*, 242–43.
30. Tuetey, *Répertoire général*, X, Nos. 2307, 2312.

There is no evidence of bribery in Vincent's case, if we can believe the testimony of the police who examined his private papers.[31] His defense of incompetent generals, on the other hand, undermined his credibility. The commission to investigate causes of the defeats in the Vendée was established by the Convention on 1 Brumaire (October 22, 1793). As secretary general of the War Department, Vincent was implicated, of course, in the criticism of those officers whom he still supported. On 7 Brumaire (October 28) Vincent threatened Philippeaux at a dinner to which both had been invited: "I have denounced you to the Cordeliers; we will make short work of your Commission, and we will bring down the deputies who, like you, dare criticize the conduct of generals invested with our confidence."[32] It is hardly necessary to comment that whatever his motives were, it was ill advised for a young employee of the War Department to condemn the Convention's commission in advance of its report and to insult and threaten one of the Convention's own deputies.

On 27 Frimaire II (December 17, 1793), Vincent was arrested in his apartment on the rue Grange Batelière and five boxes of his papers were seized. According to the police report, he and his wife occupied two small rooms on the third floor, hardly the affluent surroundings he was charged with enjoying by some of his enemies. Upon arriving at the Luxembourg prison, Vincent composed a number of letters to the Committee of General Security and to the Convention demanding his release and attacking his political enemies. He was ardently supported in this attempt by his friends in other sections and in several popular societies.[33] His appeals attacking Fabre d'Eglantine were widely placarded throughout Paris. His presence in the Luxembourg

31. Procès-verbal of Joseph Faure and Louis François Beffara, commissioners of police of section Mont Blanc, 17 Pluviôse II (February 5, 1794), in F7 4775, 48, AN. Not only was there nothing suspicious, they wrote, "but on the contrary the major portion of these papers prove the patriotism and civic conduct of citizen Vincent."

32. Philippeaux, représentant du peuple, à ses collègues et à ses concitoyens, 6 Nivôse, an II, in AD XVIIIa 55, AN, cited by Tuetey, *Répertoire général*, XI, xxv.

33. Warrant of arrest from the Committee of General Security issued to the revolutionary committee of Mont Blanc, 27 Frimaire II (December 17, 1793); Procès-verbal of Joseph Nicolas Cohendet, commissioner of police of faubourg Montmartre; Letter attacking "Phillipon," Bourdon de l'Oise, "Deglantine," and "camille des moulins" and defending Vincent and Ronsin and threatening to march with faubourg Saint-Antoine to defend them, undated and unsigned; Resolution of general assembly of Homme Armé expressing confidence in innocence of Vincent and Ronsin, 5 Pluviôse II (December 24, 1793); all in F7 4775 48, AN.

terrified a number of noble prisoners, it was alleged; meanwhile, numerous delegations from popular societies and revolutionary committees of sections, as well as individuals, continued to visit him in prison. Hébert defended him in the Jacobin Club, praising his warm patriotism, revealing that when things did not go well Vincent often raged and called even Hébert a Feuillant. Marat, declared Hébert, also had complete confidence in him.[34]

The Convention considered the affair on 23 Nivôse (January 12, 1794) and found that no proof against Vincent existed but did nothing about it for the time being. On 6 Pluviôse (January 25, 1794), Vincent wrote again complaining that he had not been heard and that he was a victim of Fabre d'Eglantine's malice; he invoked Article 31 of the Rights of Man, which stated that crimes of the people's representatives—meaning Fabre d'Eglantine—"must never go unpunished." The same day he complained to Marc Guillaume Alexis Vadier, a powerful member of the Committee of General Security, that although he had served the popular cause from the beginning of the Revolution, he was oppressed just as under the reign of "the tyrant," and he demanded to be tried. On 12 Pluviôse (January 31, 1794), sections Mutius Scaevola, Bonnet Rouge, Unité, and Marat denounced his imprisonment and demanded that he and Ronsin be tried before the Revolutionary Tribunal. Two days later Jean Henri Voulland, a member of the Committee of General Security, demanded Vincent's release. Danton supported the motion. Although Bourdon de l'Oise, Legendre, and Philippeaux objected, the Convention ordered Vincent and Ronsin released that same day (February 2).[35] Vincent was received by numerous delegations and with music as he left the prison. The following day the Committee General Security authorized the revolutionary committee of Mutius Scaevola to remove the seals on his papers.

Ronsin's protests and accusations had also been placarded throughout the city during his imprisonment. Counter to his efforts, as early as 30 Frimaire (December 20, 1793) a petition was presented to the

---

34. Aulard, *Jacobins*, V 572.

35. See the order to release Vincent, 14 Pluviôse (February 2, 1794), AF II* 294, fols. 77, 78, 80, in F7 4775 48, AN. This police file on Vincent contains a description of the papers seized in his apartment, Vincent's letter to Vadier, his petition to the Convention, and the petition of sections Mutius Scaevola, Bonnet Rouge, Unité, and Marat for his release. The sections' petition carries many individual signatures. See also Tuetey, *Répertoire général*, XI, Nos. 2314, 2315, 2317.

Convention to stop the punishment of Lyon. Besides its negative implications for Ronsin, the document was an indirect denunciation of Collot d'Herbois and Joseph Fouché, the representatives-on-mission, who were in charge of the repression. Aware of the groundswell that would give rise to this petition, Collot had departed for Paris on December 16. Five days later he addressed the Convention, defending the role of the Revolutionary army and that of its commander, Ronsin. In concluding his remarks Collot asked the approval of the Convention for the measures taken in Lyon and for an investigation into the motives for Ronsin's arrest. The Convention agreed—they applauded Collot—and thus stopped any attempts to show Lyon the "pity" sought by the petition.[36]

Collot also reported to the Jacobins, at Hébert's request, on his mission to Lyon. He warmly defended Ronsin, calling him an "ardent friend of liberty . . . and a true and outspoken Jacobin" who had undergone great danger in the Vendée and in Lyon. He then asked the members to reiterate their continued confidence in Ronsin, which those present immediately gave. Hébert also spoke in Ronsin's favor and launched a sharp attack on Philippeaux and Fabre d'Eglantine, concluding with the demand that Jean Baptiste Amar of the Committee of General Security report on the famous conspiracy of the Indies Company, a massive financial scandal to which a number of Indulgents were closely linked. Furthermore, he demanded the expulsion of Desmoulins, Bourdon de l'Oise, Philippeaux, and Fabre d'Eglantine. An extract of the proceedings was sent to Ronsin and Vincent, and a petition for their release was presented to the Convention and to its police committee. The following day (3 Nivôse—December 23, 1793) the Jacobins sent a delegation to the Convention for the same purpose.[37]

While Hébert defended the arrested men in his issue No. 326—wherein he also called Collot d'Herbois "a giant"—the sections too

36. Herlaut, *Ronsin*, 185, 188–89. Collot brought pressure on the Convention by parading the remains of the martyred Jacobin Marie Joseph Chalier and of the soldiers who had died fighting against the federalists of Lyon. Crowds of mourners and sympathizers turned out. The response discouraged the campaign for clemency; Jacob, *Hébert Le Père Duchesne*, 271.

37. Aulard, *Jacobins*, V, 571, 572–73; Herlaut, *Ronsin*, 190–91. On the Indies Company affair, see Albert Mathiez, *Un Procès de corruption sous la Terreur: L'Affaire de la compagnie des Indes* (Paris, 1920).

were in ferment demanding the prisoners' release.[38] Section Quinze-Vingts on December 26 presented a "fierce" petition for their freedom to the Jacobins. Robespierre promptly denounced this petition as "the work of Pitt," his favorite term of abuse. He argued that since the Convention had already decided to investigate the arrests, "justice" should take its course. But despite Robespierre's effort to dampen it, the agitation in the sections did not diminish. Two days later the spokesman of Quinze-Vingts warned the Convention that the sans-culottes of faubourg Saint-Antoine were ready to march on "the traitors who mock sans-culottisme, just as they marched against the crowned tyrant on August 10." The next day (9 Nivôse—December 29) a delegation of Cordeliers went to the two Committees but was not received.[39]

Two days later a delegation from the electoral college of Paris joined the demand for Ronsin's and Vincent's release. The Convention refused to receive them, under the pretext that since the college had no rights of deliberation, it could not present its views. Since both Ronsin and Vincent were members of this institution, the Convention's decision was directed against them. On January 2 Latour-Lamontagne reported that people were constantly talking about Vincent and the others struck by the same decree. At the same time, they were complaining against Fabre d'Eglantine, Desmoulins, and others as being "more dangerous than Brissot and his companions." An individual in the café de Foy declared it was infamous that the best patriots, who had rendered such great service to the Revolution,

38. "The giant has appeared, and all the dwarfs who plagued the best patriots have returned a hundred feet underground." Collot had spoken to the Committee of Public Safety, to the Convention, and to the Jacobins, and had confounded the intriguers who wanted to arm the patriots against each other, divide the Mountain, and recall the toads of the Marais; the patriots were once again in control, Hébert assured his readers. *Père Duchesne*, No. 326.

39. The petition, in F7 4775 48, AN, underscored the well-known Article 34 of the Rights of Man, which begins: "There is oppression of the social corps, when a single one of its members is oppressed" and was signed by Momoro and a fellow Cordelier, Louis Barthélemy Chenaux, future president of the society. Although the petition carries the date of 29 Pluviôse, that is obviously incorrect, since Vincent was released two weeks prior to this date.

On the Cordeliers delegation, see Tuetey, *Répertoire général*, X, No. 2322. Tuetey, *ibid.*, No. 2318 (14 Pluviôse), notes that the delegation was ineffective in obtaining the release of the prisoners.

were being persecuted. Faubourg Saint-Antoine was stirring as it demanded Vincent's release, the man said, and he predicted that the people would not allow this oppression of patriots to go on much longer. The next day Latour-Lamontagne repeated his observations—that there was a ferment over the arrest of Vincent and Maillard.[40]

The Convention too became a scene of conflict between the enemies and defenders of Ronsin and Rossignol. On 18 Nivôse (January 7, 1794) Philippeaux, in twenty-six separate articles, brought formal charges against the sans-culotte commanders. Choudieu counterattacked by declaring that if Philippeaux "is not crazy, he is the greatest impostor," and called him "a liar" for describing Rossignol as a coward.[41] A few days later the Cordeliers branded Philippeaux "a slanderer and an intriguer."

During their imprisonment Vincent and Ronsin were visited by Hanriot, Boulanger, Albert Mazuel (commander of the cavalry squadron in the Revolutionary army), Momoro, and more than a hundred individual Jacobins and Cordeliers. It seems that the two men had unlimited freedom within the prison and that Ronsin, at least, dined rather well. Some fellow prisoners who later testified against him accused him of participating in "orgies." One witness, Louis Claude Cezeron, reported an alleged statement of Ronsin's to one of the Hébertistes, François Desfieux. "I want," Ronsin supposedly said, "the Revolution to reach a point that when I cross Pont-Neuf, if I should encounter a whore who pleases me, I can tuck up her skirt and f——— [her] publicly." On a more serious note, Ronsin is said to have added that the Committee of Public Safety must be changed because it was "gangrened," and that when he and Vincent were released they would guillotine aplenty.

Other witnesses testified that Ronsin and his companions lodged and dined together, nor would they admit others in their circle. Ronsin was also accused of having received visits from two Austrian bankers, the Frey brothers, who were involved in the Indies Company scandal. Furthermore, Ronsin was overheard to oppose Robes-

40. *Moniteur*, XIX, No. 103 (January 2, 1794), 104; Caron, *Paris pendant la Terreur*, II, 138–39, 155. On 19 Nivôse (January 8, 1794) Charmont revealed that everyone was talking about the fight between Philippeaux and the generals of the Vendée, and that many favored Philippeaux because they did not think he would risk his head just to denounce Ronsin and the others; Caron, *Paris pendant la Terreur*, II, 240.

41. *Moniteur*, XIX, No. 109 (January 8, 1794), 153–55.

pierre and to frighten the concierge and his wife during their rounds. If true, Ronsin must have enjoyed a good bit of freedom as a prisoner, something to which other witnesses testified.[42]

How much of this testimony was ruled by fear of the revolutionary government, how much was anxiety to please the authorities, and how much was personal resentment and antagonism to Ronsin is difficult to assess. That the prisoner enjoyed an unusual amount of freedom during his captivity was due partly to his status and partly to the awareness that there were still forces on the outside who were pressing for his release. Nevertheless, it must be remembered that Ronsin and Vincent had been jailed for some six weeks. With all their power and prestige, and despite the fact that Ronsin, at least, had been warmly supported by Collot d'Herbois and other deputies, they had not been able to win over the Convention to their cause. This failure was a harbinger of things to come. Could they prepare a defense should they be under attack again? It was obvious that their enemies would not retreat. A more important question was whether the revolutionary government could allow this kind of continuous factional dispute to interrupt its concern with the war effort and the serious economic crisis it was facing.

The release of Ronsin and Vincent, on February 2, became the talk of the town.[43] Dugas reported that it was the subject of discussion in all cafés and neighborhoods: "Many of their partisans, who did not dare for some time to pronounce themselves quite openly on their account, have burst with joy at this news."[44] Public opinion, if we accept the many contradictory accounts of the police spies, seems to have been divided. Evidently the situation was still fluid. Furthermore, it is clear that whether a police observer recounted opposition or support for the Hébertistes depended largely on the neighborhood of the cafés he frequented. Those sections whose inhabitants favored Ronsin and Vincent would express themselves openly—except during the more frequently occurring times when fear restrained them. In contradistinction to these sections were those that, above all, were

---

42. Tuetey, *Répertoire général*, X, Nos. 2273, 2283, 2285, 2295, 2300.

43. Order to release Vincent, 14 Pluviôse (February 2, 1794), AF II* 294, fols. 77, 78; Tuetey, *Répertoire général*, X, No. 1603. The following day (15 Pluviôse), the revolutionary committee of section Mutius Scaevola lifted the seals from Vincent's papers and effects. The revolutionary committee of section Mont Blanc did the same for Ronsin.

44. Caron, *Paris pendant la Terreur*, III, 283.

loyal to the regularly constituted authorities. Their citizens would hear praise of Philippeaux and Desmoulins and condemnation of Vincent and Ronsin with open satisfaction.

On February 11, Momoro, as president of the Cordeliers, proposed to a Jacobin named Delcloche, who was on the club's membership committee, that he submit Vincent's name to the society. Delcloche did so, but Louis Pierre Dufourny, a leading Dantoniste, charged both Momoro and Delcloche with bias in favor of Vincent, and had the motion postponed. The result was that Vincent was never admitted into the Jacobin Club, an act that rankled not only him but also his supporters in the Cordeliers. Vincent never forgave the slight and sought vengeance against the moderates among the Jacobins. Momoro was indignant and attacked "the scoundrels [who] by means of the mask of virtue and of popularity, which they have never deserved, seek to destroy the true sans-culottes, the friends of equality." The following day at a session of the Cordeliers, several members spoke out against the maneuvers of Dufourny. Hébert denounced "enemies of equality who . . . pompously" called his party "ultrarevolutionaries" and "must be punished." Another member declared, "Vincent is a good Cordelier; this is as good as being a good Jacobin, if not much better." [45]

The refusal of the Jacobins to admit Vincent possibly undermined his reputation among the public, because as Pourvoyeur noted on February 18, "In general all individuals expelled [or not admitted, presumably] from the Society of Jacobins have lost the confidence of the public." The police spy specifically noted that neither Vincent nor Ronsin—especially Vincent—enjoyed a good reputation among the people. [46] This assertion should be assessed with some skepticism. There were many patriots, as we have seen, who admired them; others agreed with Hébert that even if Vincent was no Jacobin, he was still a good patriot. [47]

45. Aulard, *Jacobins*, V, 651; B&R, XXXI, 295–96. An attempt was made to reconcile Dufourny with Vincent when both were appointed editors of an address by the Club central des sociétés populaires, but Dufourny refused to serve; B&R, XXXI, 297; Walter, *Hébert et le "Père Duchesne,"* 196–97.

46. Caron, *Paris pendant la Terreur*, IV, 217. After the final arrest of the Hébertistes, the Jacobins recalled that Delcloche had introduced Vincent to the society and promptly expelled him; Aulard, *Jacobins*, VI, 3–4.

47. The Jacobins were not unanimous in their opposition to Vincent. On October 8, 1793, Pierre Louis Bentabole, the deputy from Colmar, charged Vincent with abusing

Some evidence exists that the Committee of Public Safety wanted Ronsin and Vincent to quit Paris. Saint-Just met with Vincent and offered him the post of *commissaire-ordonnateur* to the Army of the North, the most important of the French armies. To Ronsin he offered the command of any army he wanted. Both men refused because accepting would have meant a step down from their current positions. It is possible, also, that by agreeing to Saint-Just's offer they would have surrendered their important political roles. They did promise, allegedly, to calm their agitation in the capital.[48]

Other sources, however, quote the two as taking the offensive against Saint-Just and accusing him of a desire "to manage the Center." Why hadn't the seventy-three Girondins been judged? they asked. If there was famine, they protested, it was not due to their agitation but because the government had perverted the law. Finally, they warned Saint-Just that if he (and the Committees) continued to pursue them, the government would lose the patriots of the city. "'And if we should die or be proscribed,'" they prophesied, "'you will perish!'" Saint-Just supposedly asked whether they would agree to go once the imprisoned patriots were released; "'I, to the Army of the North,' said Vincent. 'I, wherever it pleases you,' replied Ronsin."[49] This scenario smacks too much of hindsight. Besides, why would Saint-Just have offered such a deal to Ronsin and Vincent unless the Committee felt threatened? But if so, it was essential to de-

---

his confidence. When Vincent tried to reply, he was hooted down. On the other hand, when the Jacobins heard attacks on the Indulgents (December 21, 1793) they passed a resolution of "amitié fraternelle" in favor of Vincent and Ronsin. Couthon had reported their arrest four days previously. Aulard, *Jacobins*, V, 450, 563, 572–73.

48. Pierre François Tissot, *Histoire complète de la Révolution française* (Paris, 1834–36), V, 106. Tissot is convinced that the government did not want to destroy Vincent, Hébert, or Ronsin. "If the confreres did not accept [the offer] they seemed convinced [nevertheless] of the necessity of unity, and promised to calm [their agitation]." This interview was held, allegedly, in the first days of Ventôse. But "the conspirators were not converted," wrote Tissot, and instead of calming the agitation, they breathed new fire into it.

Tissot's history cannot be dismissed out of hand. The author was active in various administrative capacities during the Revolution (he was born in 1768 and died in 1854), wrote literary works, and was elected to the French Academy in 1833. See the article on him by H. Monin in *La Grande Encyclopédie*, XXXI, 119.

49. Herlaut, *Ronsin*, 213, citing Tissot, as above. According to Georges Avenel, *Anacharsis Cloots: L'Orateur du genre humain* (Paris, 1865), II, 374–75, Ronsin and Vincent told Saint-Just (whom Avenel calls "a monster") that they did not want to be "managed." Some of this testimony must be taken with a grain of salt.

stroy, rather than treat with them. If, on the other hand, the government really tried to reach an agreement with the Cordeliers leaders, the latter certainly misunderstood their own influence and position and paid a bitter price for this misunderstanding.

On February 21, Jean Baptiste Carrier, the terrorist responsible for the mass drownings of the condemned in Nantes, in addressing the Jacobins, warmly defended Ronsin, Rossignol, and Santerre, the militant of faubourg Saint-Antoine. In contrast to their patriotism he exposed "the cowardly behavior of Philippeaux," who allegedly hid when the fighting began, unlike his colleague, René Levasseur; besides, Philippeaux deserved no credence, since he knew nothing of military operations. Philippeaux, he concluded, was no counterrevolutionary; he was just plain crazy. Collot d'Herbois seconded Carrier's report. Both spokesmen agreed that General François Joseph Westermann, an opponent of Rossignol, was brave enough, but they questioned his devotion to the Revolution. Collot reminded the Jacobins that it was the soldier who won battles, not only the general. Moreover, there was a danger in praising generals, he warned. "Let Westermann study Rossignol," he urged. "Then he can win again our esteem." [50] That a professional military man of the highest rank should have to learn from a former common soldier must have rankled the Westermanns and their supporters.

Hébert, too, denounced in the *Père Duchesne* "a new faction of moderates, of Feuillants, of aristocrats called Phelipotins [*sic*] subsidized by England." The Philippotins came from a certain canton in Normandy where *huissiers, avocats,* and *procureurs* swarmed under the Old Regime, he continued. "Phelipotin" (Philippeaux) was born of the devil, he went on, and at an early age learned how to argue on either side of a question, having been taught by his father to carry two faces: one for the sans-culottes as "a rabid patriot," the other for his and his father's friends, the aristocrats. In the Vendée he had supported generals like Biron, Dubayet, and Tuncq, who wanted to ruin the Republic. Philippeaux was joined by Bourdon of the Vendée, Fabre d'Eglantine, and "the renegade Camille" (Desmoulins). [51]

50. *Moniteur,* XIX, No. 159 (February 27, 1794), 571; Aulard, *Jacobins,* V, 659–60; Caron, *Paris pendant la Terreur,* IV, 253.

51. *Père Duchesne,* No. 330. Philippeaux accused Hébert of poisoning the minds of the troops with his journal. Hébert replied that he never betrayed the sans-culottes and that it was by order of the Committee of Public Safety, through Bouchotte, that his journal was distributed among the soldiers of the country's armies.

In the next issue, Hébert denied that he was head of a party. But if his party was the one that exposed traitors and had been the victim of the Committee of Twelve (a committee staffed largely by Girondins and their allies before their overthrow in the insurrection of May 31, 1793), then he was happy to be head of such a party. "For the past two years I have not stopped telling the sans-culottes that they should not expect their salvation from anyone but themselves; because it is only for themselves that they have made the revolution, and not to give themselves new masters."[52]

This encouragement of independence was a double threat, whether Hébert realized it or not. The economic interests of the sans-culottes were in opposition to those of the propertied. Urban commercial classes and their dependents believed in laissez-faire and the free exchange of the market, not a controlled economy with its regulations and restrictions of price, allocation of raw materials, and strict supervision of trade and commerce. The Jacobins and the Montagnards shared this conviction. But more than this: they adhered to a policy of centralization and strict control from above—not always successful, of course, but transmitted and implemented by their proxies, by their representatives-on-mission, and by their national agents. The encouragement of sans-culottes to pursue their own, independent policy endangered that "single will" toward which Robespierre and his colleagues strove.

Both the Jacobins and the Cordeliers desired the unity of all patriots, but this goal was difficult to reach because the Jacobins were unwilling to break with their moderate allies. The Cordeliers, on the other hand, were ready to suppress all moderates. The Jacobins themselves were not united on this matter. For while Robespierre was still cooperating with Danton and Camille Desmoulins, who were urging a policy of clemency, Collot d'Herbois replied to all those who thought that such a policy could be both revolutionary and at the same time "accommodating and many-sided": they were "partisans of a false humanity," he declared as he defended the arrest of suspects and promised that the Mountain would not yield.[53]

Collot added to this pronouncement a call for unity of all patriots and proposed a festival to celebrate this theme. He was followed by the appearance of a delegation from the Cordeliers, whose spokes-

52. *Ibid.*, Nos. 331, 333.
53. *Moniteur*, XIX, No. 162 (March 2, 1794), 589.

man declared that the Jacobins and his organization would always be united, and further denounced "the enemies of the Revolution" who would divide them. The delegation then took an oath that the Cordeliers would always be Jacobins, to the wild applause of all present. The president of the Jacobin Club gave a fraternal accolade to the delegation, and all seemed happy with the outcome.[54]

But two days later, on February 28, the police observer Béraud reported overhearing people in a café say that although they agreed there should be brotherly love between the Cordeliers and Jacobins, the real reason why this demarche of the Cordeliers was undertaken was in the hope that the Jacobins would abandon Camille Desmoulins and others like him. Vincent, Béraud added, had ridiculed the Jacobins and accused Desmoulins of various crimes.[55] It was difficult to compromise the two clubs' differences, as the Cordeliers had adopted a resolution passed by a popular society, the Défenseurs des Droits de l'Homme, sitting in the former cathedral of Notre Dame (now the Temple of Reason), section Maison Commune. The resolution had declared that Fabre d'Eglantine, Philippeaux, Bourdon de l'Oise, and Camille Desmoulins were traitors and, as such, unworthy to sit in the Convention.

The motivation that triggered this adoption was linked to an arrest of a "patriot," Marchand, a retailer of wine, on February 28. He had denounced the national agent of the Paris Department, Louis Marie Lulier, for having suggested, allegedly, the dissolution of the Convention in the general assembly of Bon-Conseil and for recommending that people find "virtuous representatives worthy of the French nation." Lulier appealed to the assembly and pointed to his revolutionary past. The numerous gathering (nine hundred people filled the hall), after a heated discussion, supported him against Marchand, recognized him as a true patriot, and recommended that Marchand, whom it called a slanderer, be turned over to the Revolutionary Tribunal.[56]

Marchand was expelled from the section's revolutionary committee

54. Ibid.; Aulard, Jacobins, V, 666.
55. Caron, Paris pendant la Terreur, IV, 385. Two days before, Dugas reported that all good Jacobins desired unity with the Cordeliers. Ibid., IV, 347.
56. Extrait du registre des délibérations de la Section de Bon-Conseil (Paris, 10 Ventôse), in LB 40 1727, BN. The certificate of civic conduct given to Lulier (sometimes spelled Lhuillier) was signed by Garnier, president, and Deperthe, secretary.

and its popular society, then arrested. The Cordeliers, in turn, protested this attack on the liberty of a patriot. Louis Barthélemy Chenaux, the club's secretary, spoke out firmly in Marchand's defense. Where would we be, he asked, if we were arrested for daring to express our feelings in denouncing factions? Marchand had conducted himself as a true republican when he expressed himself in this matter.[57]

The sectional society of Marat, which had taken its name from his sobriquet "l'ami du peuple," also reaffirmed the Terror. Momoro presided over the society with the aim of unmasking the "moderates," whom his partisans therein often attacked. On February 27 the society adopted a resolution that began by strongly reaffirming its devotion to the principles of the Mountain and continued: "Considering that members of a society that has taken for its patron Marat the apostle and martyr of liberty . . . cannot maintain silence on the maneuvers that slacken the pace of the revolution; that certain individuals have attempted to give a dangerous direction to public spirit. . . ; that the Cordeliers Club . . . has declared that the cabal of Philippotins had lost the confidence of the true Sans-Culottes . . , the society of Amis-du-Peuple will never diminish its energy in affirming the Republic and crushing its enemies."[58] Nevertheless, the clash between the Cordeliers and section Bon-Conseil boded ill for the unity of the sans-culottes in opposition to the revolutionary government.

Whatever abstract right Marchand had to criticize the national agent—and it is inconceivable that Lulier actually suggested dissolving the Convention—once the Cordeliers Club came to the wine seller's defense it opened a serious breach between itself and the central authorities. Such a public dispute was bound to alarm the Committees.

It is interesting to note, also, that Collot d'Herbois seems to have

57. Caron, *Paris pendant la Terreur*, IV, 382–83; F7 4774 27 and D XLII 11, AN, cited by Soboul, *Sans-Culottes*, 706 n 88; *Moniteur*, XIX, No. 167 (March 7, 1794), 629; Soboul and Monnier, *Répertoire de personnel sectionnaire*, 198. The revolutionary committee of the Paris Department reaffirmed Marchand's arrest on 29 Ventôse (March 19, 1794) and called him a "very hot-headed and turbulent man." This was after the arrest of the Hébertistes. Marchand was freed on 10 Messidor II (June 28, 1794). Mathiez, *Vie chère*, 546.

58. *Liberté, égalité. Société républicaine de l'ami du peuple* (Paris, 9 Ventôse), in Lb 40 2194, BN; signed by Auge, vice-president, and Degeorges and Ducroquet, secretaries.

been playing an intricate game. He appeared as an ally of the Cordeliers in his uncompromising assault on the moderates. Yet within a
few days he would lead the Jacobins against the Hébertistes and act
as spokesman of the central authorities. The position of the Cordeliers vis-à-vis both the government and the sans-culottes was becoming uncomfortable.

4

Another Insurrection?

On 8 Ventôse (February 26, 1794), Saint-Just delivered an important address that justified the Terror and promised to compensate the sans-culottes for their sacrifices in defending the Republic. This was to be done by confiscating the wealth of the Republic's enemies and transferring it to the patriotic poor. Saint-Just added that despite the complaints of some, in comparison with other governments the revolutionaries of France were moderate. Citing the figure of three hundred "villains" executed by the Revolutionary Tribunal in one year, he insisted that this was smaller than the toll exacted by almost any other government. Everything depended on the firmness of measures taken by France, he affirmed as he excoriated the "moderates." In conclusion he declared:

> In effect, the force of events may produce results which we scarcely comprehend. Wealth remains in the hands of numerous enemies of the Revolution. Want makes people who work dependent on their enemies. Do you suppose a state can exist if social relations are based on the enemies of that form of government? Those who make revolutions by halves do nothing but dig their own graves. The Revolution leads us to recognize this principle, that those who have proven themselves to be enemies of their own country cannot be property holders in it. . . . You should recognize this principle, that only those people have rights in our country who have cooperated to keep it free. . . . The property of patriots is sacred, but the property of conspirators belongs to the needy.

The Convention then decreed that its Committee of General Security be authorized to free all patriots wrongfully imprisoned and that the property of enemies be seized for the benefit of the Republic.[1]

1. Saint-Albin Berville and Jean François Barrière, eds., *Collection des mémoires relatifs à la Révolution française* . . . (Paris, 1828), 190–204, Vol. LVIII of Berville and Barrière, eds., *Débats de la Convention nationale*, 2d ser., 65 vols.; *Moniteur*, XIX, No. 159 (February 27, 1794), 565–69; B & R, XXI, 298–311.

Five days later, on March 3, Saint-Just proclaimed that "happiness is a new idea in Europe" and proposed that the municipalities of France prepare a list of their poor. They were to be indemnified with the confiscated property of their enemies as defined in his address of 8 Ventôse. The Committee of Public Safety would decide on how best to satisfy the indigent.[2]

Article 3 of the Convention's decree provided that those imprisoned since May 1, 1789, would be reexamined and if proved to be patriots, released. Collot d'Herbois, addressing the Jacobins, hailed this provision as proof that the Convention had not succumbed to the pressure of the Indulgents and that the imprisoned Hébertistes would be freed. "They will find themselves once more in their true element; they are going to plunge again into the Revolution, to go forth with new vigor," he exclaimed. The spokesman of the Cordeliers delegation that had arrived to fraternize with the Jacobins applauded this statement and denied that there was disunity between the two organizations. He was given the fraternal embrace amidst general rejoicing.[3]

Was the government serious in proposing the program of confiscation and indemnification? Mathiez was convinced that the Convention was about to undertake a major restructuring of the property relations in France, "a vast transfer of property from one political class to another . . . , a social program," and other such revolutionary measures. He was surprised that those in whose favor this decree was passed did not understand it.[4] Gérard Walter thought that nothing of a concrete nature was proposed by the Committee of Public Safety; they would await the completion of documentation on the matter and "make a report," and that was all.[5] Daniel Guérin called it "a demagogic maneuver," a kind of charity with no intention of redistributing the estates of the suspects.[6] Soboul wrote that it was designed to blunt the sans-culottes offensive against the moderates and to quiet their immediate demands. Furthermore, he was convinced that it did

---

2. Berville and Barrière, eds., *Collection des mémoires relatifs à la Révolution française* . . . , 204–206; *Moniteur*, XIX, No. 164 (March 4, 1794), 611; *AP*, LXXXVI, 13 Ventôse II, 22–23; B&R, XXXI, 311–13, in 4 articles.

3. Aulard, *Jacobins*, V, 664–66, 8 Ventôse; B&R, XXXI, 322.

4. Mathiez, *Révolution française*, III, 149.

5. Gérard Walter, *Histoire de la Terreur, 1793–1794* (Paris, 1937), 208.

6. Guérin, *Lutte de classes*, II, 95–98.

not fool the patriots because it offered no solution to the problem of shortages and high prices.[7]

The idea of confiscating property for the benefit of society was not new. Montesquieu, Rousseau, and Gabriel Bonnot de Mably had discussed its history. Mably favored an "agrarian law" limiting the amount of land held by individuals, and he argued that small plots were cultivated better than large ones. He was convinced that well-being could be found only in "the community of property."[8] A number of cahiers had urged that a limit be placed on the amount of land a seigneur could own. Brissot thought that if a man needed only 40 écus to live on but had 200,000 he was guilty of theft. Since the "Supreme Being" had given the land to all men, "exclusive" possession of it was "a true crime against nature," he wrote. Moreover, unlike animals and savages, only "social man" extends his ownership far beyond his needs and then has the audacity to call his property "sacred."[9]

Claude Fauchet, founder of the Cercle Social, a utopian reform society, advocated "an agrarian law" and defended the right of every man to a piece of land. Jacques Roux favored distributing among the sans-culottes and their widows the confiscated property of "émigrés, federalists, and deputies who had abandoned their posts and betrayed the nation."[10] Hébert, too, in his issue No. 247, advocated the confiscation and distribution of property among "the republican soldiers" in any department that received the Girondin "traitors" Buzot, Pétion, Barbaroux, and others. In No. 280 he wrote that anyone who refused to serve in the armed forces of France had no right to hold property in the Republic, and in No. 289 he demanded the confiscation of land belonging to any proprietor who had failed to furnish a quantity of grain to the Republic proportional to the yield of his land.

7. Soboul, *Sans-Culottes*, 710.

8. Gabriel Bonnot de Mably, *De la législation; ou, Principes des loix* (Lausanne, 1777), I, 70, 152–53. "Why do we allow a Seigneur of a village or of a community to become the sole proprietor? This depopulates a country, multiplies within it the vices of wealth and of poverty," Mably declared; *ibid.*, 155.

9. J. P. Brissot de Warville, *Sur la propriété et sur le vol* (1780; rpr. Brussels, 1872), 62–63, 64, 95.

10. *La Bouche de Fer* (Claude Fauchet's "Sixth Discourse") in Lc 2 317, BN; *Le Publiciste de la République française* (published by Jacques Roux), No. 263, in Lc 2 227, BN. See also R. B. Rose, "The 'Red Scare' of the 1790s: The French Revolution and the 'Agrarian Law,'" *Past and Present*, CIII (May, 1984), 114–30.

The fields so confiscated were to be distributed among the sans-culottes.

On October 23, 1793, Pierre Gaspard Chaumette, the *procureur* of the Paris Commune, proposed to the General Council that the Convention be asked to allow "republicans" to take possession of "lands occupied by enemies of public affairs." Hanriot complained that nothing had been done for the sans-culottes who had liberated Lyon, and he proposed that "houses, lands, everything ought to be divided among those who had vanquished these scoundrels." Certain Montagnards also shared this sentiment. Marc Antoine Baudot, a zealous Montagnard, advocated that the Jacobins excite the sans-culottes of the departments to strike at the rich and the aristocrats. "We must assure the sans-culottes of all the property they seize from them by force," he declared.[11] On 7 Pluviôse (January 26, 1794) Couthon intended to propose the confiscation of property of former nobles, priests, bankers, agents of the Exchange, farmers-general, parents of émigrés, and others declared suspect by the law of September 17, 1793. Although he never gave his report, the growing food crisis during the winter of 1794 again revived the proposals to confiscate property.[12]

A week before Saint-Just's report, Le Breton, a police spy, wrote that the decision to confiscate the property of suspects had a great effect. People were saying that once peace was made, this property would be given to soldiers who served at the front, with each one receiving a portion of the land to cultivate. Some said this was the "agrarian law"; others insisted that the troops deserved the property as compensation for having preserved liberty. A day later Hanriot

11. *Moniteur*, XVIII, No. 34 (October 25, 1793), 197; and No. 40 (October 31, 1793), 294. On 12 Prairial III (May 31, 1795), a letter was read before the Convention from the Jacobins of Sédan, penned, evidently, during the summer of 1793, to their colleagues in Paris. It advocated the confiscation of real and personal property of the wealthy residents in any town who were held responsible for instigating a revolt against the Convention. Half of this confiscated property was to be divided among the sans-culottes engaged in suppressing the revolt; the other half was to be appropriated by the Republic. But times had changed, and a Thermidorian in the Convention now denounced the letter as "this atrocious petition." *Ibid.*, XXIV, No. 256 (June 4, 1795), 594. For Baudot, see Aulard, *Jacobins*, V, 308.

12. Soboul, *Sans-Culottes*, 713, writes that these confiscations were proposed by the bourgeois leaders, but that the "advanced patriots" favored compensation rather than confiscation.

revealed that he had heard a citizen in a café praise the Convention for its wise decision to confiscate the property of enemies, and that the man was loudly applauded for it. Dugas reported the same sentiment as being prevalent in the Jacobins, and the feeling was widely shared by many people, according to Pourvoyeur, Charmont, and Latour-Lamontagne.[13]

That the Convention's decree had an effect on the sections of Paris may be seen in their petitions on the confiscation of property. Indivisibilité submitted a resolution drafted on 30 Pluviôse (February 18, 1794). Modeled on one that section Fontaine-de-Grenelle had proposed as early as 8 Frimaire (November 28, 1793), it demanded the limitation of public funds spent on suspects to three livres a day, the municipalization of the section's butchery, and the rationing of meat to one-half pound a day for each person. The resolution attacked merchants and suggested that two commissioners be placed in bakeries and in butcher shops to supervise the sale and distribution of bread and meat.[14]

The idea of confiscation to indemnify patriots spread to popular societies as well.[15] Thus, Saint-Just's reports of 8 and 13 Ventôse were not exceptional. The government knew how to make propaganda out of them, but there was nothing new in the venture, for both utopians and revolutionaries favored it.[16] Despite popular satisfaction with

13. Caron, *Paris pendant la Terreur*, IV, 210, 230–31, 247–48, 356, 366–67, 371. "The patriots, people say, are now assured of sleeping [undisturbed] in their beds," Dugas wrote, *ibid.*, 247–48. Rolin reported (10 Ventôse) on a motion allegedly made by Barère regarding the confiscation of property, but which Barère in fact never made, says Caron, *ibid.*, 380n1. Evidently, the expectations aroused by the Convention's decree unleashed a host of rumors.

14. *La Section de l'Indivisibilité à la Convention nationale* (Paris, 30 Pluviôse II), 8 pp., in Lb 40 1891, BN. The section blamed the police for giving special protection to the imprisoned. Essentially the resolution was a plea for food, in eight articles. The general assembly published 1,200 copies of this brochure and circulated it among the constituted authorities. It was signed by Devanciat, president, and Delaterre, secretary. *Journal de Paris*, No. 422 (February 26, 1794), 1706–1708.

15. Popular society of Lepeletier, 4 Ventôse (February 22, 1794) and 14 Ventôse (March 4, 1794, the latter date being when the proposal of section Indivisibilité to confiscate the property of the imprisoned was read), in Nouv. acq. fr., 2662, fols. 63, 72, BN.

16. *Moniteur*, XIX, No. 159 (February 27, 1794), 565, and No. 164 (March 4, 1794), 611. Soboul wrote that confiscation of property was a weapon used by the bourgeoisie against its aristocratic enemies; *Sans-Culottes*, 715.

Saint-Just's report and the decree of the Convention, little was said on how to implement the resolution of 13 Ventôse. It was destined to remain a dead letter.

Still, Hébert congratulated the Convention on its decrees in his No. 350. At the same time he continued to demand justice against "the scoundrels." Nor did he think that the promise of confiscation and indemnity was enough. He persisted in demanding work for all citizens, aid for the aged and the infirm, and public education for all. ("Organize promptly public education," he urged; "this will be your masterpiece; because, f——, without education, there is no liberty, f——.")[17]

The decrees of the Convention could not resolve the immediate crisis. Shortages and the consequent hunger persisted. Seditious placards aggravated the discontent of many sans-culottes and at the same time, encouraged the Cordeliers to take what they hoped would be decisive action. Rumors of another September massacre in the prisons and of another uprising similar to that of May 31 persisted. Talk of eating cats and dogs as a way of easing the hunger was heard in the sectional assembly of Marchés. A member of its revolutionary committee even seriously proposed to kill and eat the prisoners held in the capital's jails.[18] In section Arsenal the second in command of its armed force, a former member of its revolutionary committee, was arrested for threatening to hang government officials and the "moderates" because of persistent shortages.[19]

Various people testified that a number of Montagnards were to be killed beginning with "the warmest patriots," such as Robespierre and Barère.[20] The idea of another insurrection similar to that of May 31 was closely linked to the rumor of prison massacres and probably originated in some popular societies. An employee in the Department of War, Jean Louis Toutin, declared that as a member of the Société des défenseurs he heard six members speak of an insurrection, and that he thought the day for the uprising had been set for 14 Ventôse (March 4, 1794). After a session of the club, several members visited a wine shop, where Toutin heard one of them say to the

17. *Père Duchesne*, No. 350.
18. Tuetey, *Répertoire général*, XI, Nos. 60–71.
19. Dos. Vincenot, in F7 4775 48, AN, cited by Soboul, *Sans-Culottes*, 718n119.
20. Tuetey, *Répertoire général*, X, Nos. 2194–96, testimony of femme Haquin, Dubarran, Voulland, and Cholet, 3–5 Ventôse (February 21–23, 1794).

owner, "We're counting on you as a solid [member]." To which the latter is said to have replied, "I will always be that which I have been." Once the group walked outside and were asked the objective of the coming insurrection, one replied that it would be a second May 31 in order to demand that the Convention punish the traitors responsible for the shortages. When the questioner stated that he would be away until the thirteenth, Forin du Havre, who seemed to be the leader of the group, replied, "Very well, but you should arrive at the moment of action and hear from afar the sound of cannon; furthermore, wherever you are, your presence will always be useful."[21] Others, in the societies Hommes révolutionnaires du dix août and Club électoral de l'Evêché, quoted a man known as Brutus, who spoke of insurrection and the need to purge fifty thousand conservatives of various stripes.[22]

The government, naturally, was disquieted by these rumors. An anonymous letter written on 9 Nivôse (December 29, 1793), but conveniently found at La Halle on the morning of 12 Ventôse (March 2, 1794) by a police commissioner, called on women to gather ten to twelve thousand of their sex and march on the Convention to dissolve it. The reason for this action was the famine that had persisted for the last two months, its author wrote, and he called for a "leader" to replace the seven hundred "kings and thieves."[23] The same day, Pilon, the inspector of vegetables in the market, transmitted to the public prosecutor, Antoine Quentin Fouquier-Tinville, another anonymous letter, this one directed at the women merchants. It blamed the Commune for the shortages resulting from the policy of requisitions imposed on the farmers and called on the women to demand peace from the Convention.[24]

Members of the revolutionary committee of section Marchés were familiar with the contents of these letters but knew nothing of their

21. *Ibid.*, XI, No. 53, 28 Ventôse (March 18, 1794).
22. *Ibid.*, XI, No. 56, testimony of René Descoing, Jacot Villeneuve, Pierre André (who limited himself to speak of Vincent's influence in the section), and Guillaume Laloumet, 29 Ventôse (March 19, 1794).
23. *Ibid.*, No. 2. The phrase "qu'il soit nommé un chef au lieu de 700 roy[s] et voleurs" is from W 77, plaq. 6, AN, cited by Soboul, *Sans-Culottes*, 720n123. Jean Crehant of the revolutionary committee of section Marchés testified that he knew the phrase from the letter as "it is better to have a king than seven hundred hangmen"; Tuetey, *Répertoire général*, XI, No. 8.
24. Tuetey, *Répertoire général*, XI, No. 7.

origin or their authors. They were convinced, however, that profiteering in food was a deliberate policy of the rich against the poor. One member, Esprit Rougier, a jeweler, complained that the wealthy citizens sent their servants to market to buy up supplies so as to produce shortages. He added that provisions arriving in Paris were being hidden by the rich after being bought up, then were sold to "aristocrats" in order to deny them to the sans-culottes. Another member testified on the extremely high price of meat.[25] Some of the placards protesting the current state of affairs evidently expressed the opposition of merchants to the *maximum*. But the popular prejudices evoked by members of the revolutionary committee were endangering the civil peace and could only disturb the authorities. Furthermore, the tense atmosphere they reflect made the anonymous posters doubly dangerous. Anyone who spoke of insurrection, let alone called for one, must have been a threat to the revolutionary government.

By the middle of Ventôse (early March), the crisis had reached its height. Shortages and high prices were impelling the sans-culottes to move. Some were impatient with the authorities; others attacked the moderates. At the head of these committed sans-culottes were the Cordeliers. They hoped to rid themselves of the moderates and, once again, as on September 4 and 5, 1793, to force the government to do their bidding. But the government had no intention of bowing before this pressure. At the session of 16 Ventôse (March 6, 1794), Barère, borrowing the arguments of Robespierre, blamed the agitation over shortages on "foreign conspiracies." Responsible for this agitation stood Pitt and his spies, he declared as he denounced "incendiary posters" and "seditious provocations"; moreover, the conspiracy sought to save the rich enemies of the Revolution. Thus he linked the "agitators" both to wealthy counterrevolutionaries and to the royalists of Europe. Tallien followed Barère and revealed an anonymous letter that called for a "chief." He insisted that measures be taken not only against the royalists but against the agitators. It was essential, he declared, for people to understand that those who called for an uprising wanted to reestablish royalty: "They will see that these men, despite their pantaloons and clogs, are nothing but aristocrats." The Convention charged the public prosecutor with taking measures against agitators, pamphleteers, and placarders and ordered the revo-

25. *Ibid.*, Nos. 8, 9, testimony of Jacques Duvallet, a shoemaker; Jean Crehant, a printer; Dominique Michel, another shoemaker; and Rougier, the jeweler.

lutionary committees of the sections to discover the authors of the conspiracy.[26]

Was there a conspiracy against the government? Certainly talk of insurrection was heard, but no organized plot to overthrow the Convention and its Committees existed. Before the fall of the monarchy on August 10, 1792, or the expulsion of the Girondins on June 2, 1793, the Parisian sections and their Commune, the Evêché assembly and its Comité des Neuf, various popular societies, and individual militants had shared a general plan on how to stage an insurrection. Both actions succeeded because there was a large mass movement influenced or directed by committed men and women with clearly defined goals. Not the slightest evidence of such a "conspiracy" or any such preparation by the Cordeliers or their leaders exists. Threats and demands for the execution of "traitors," attacks on the "Philippotins," denunciations of "moderates"—none of these amounted to a concerted effort to replace the existing government. Most important of all, perhaps, no coherent social or economic program to satisfy the hungry sans-culottes was ever launched by the Cordeliers. The dramatic session of the club on 14 Ventôse (March 4, 1794) bears this out.

Two days earlier Ronsin had proclaimed from the podium of the club the necessity of an insurrection. According to the witnesses present, both Hébert and the member called Brutus opposed him. They declared that all that was needed was to send a delegation to the Convention asking for the "punishment" of the sixty (sic; actually there were seventy-three) Girondins held in prison and the leaders of the "moderates"—that is, Philippeaux, Bourdon de l'Oise, and Desmoulins. This disagreement, publicly expressed by the leaders of the society, reflects the irresponsibility of the Cordeliers. Could such a division of opinion have been possible if a serious uprising were being planned? That there was confusion even in Ronsin's own mind as to what he meant by an "insurrection" can be seen in the deposition of a witness, Jean Brochet. After Hébert's objection, Ronsin returned to the tribune and "explained" that he did not mean a general insurrection; rather, it was to be aimed at the leaders of the "moderates."[27]

26. Berville and Barrière, eds., *Collection des mémoires relatifs à la Révolution française*, 206–208, 210–12, 214–15, 216–17, 218.

27. Tuetey, *Répertoire général*, XI, No. 44, testimony of Edme Philippe Jarry, a courier of the War Department; No. 21, declaration of Jean Etienne Brochet; No. 36, declaration of Marie Jeanne Elisabeth Brocard Jolly, femme Metrasse, a seedswoman (grainier) and inspector of military relay stations; *ibid.*, X, No. 2522, deposition of Anne

This was going to be the formula of retreat for the Hébertistes after their disastrous session two days later.

On the evening of 14 Ventôse many important individuals came to the session. Among them were patriots and activists from the large provincial towns, officers of the Revolutionary army, and wives of militants, seeking bread for their children. The wives of Hébert, Ronsin, and Vincent also attended, together with Albertine Marat, the "martyr's" sister. The club's leaders revealed that plans had been made to publish a journal with Marat's old title, *L'Ami du peuple*. It was to be issued under the responsibility and guarantee of the entire society, rather than a board of editors. The journal was to contain "useful information and denunciations against the public functionaries and especially against the unfaithful mandatories of the people."

The decision to publish the journal in the name of the whole society meant that the opinions expressed would not be signed by individuals; the authors would remain anonymous. This policy moved Albertine Marat to write indignantly to the leaders of the society attacking Hébert's cowardice and those who had designated themselves as her brother's "successors." "Is life then worth so much that it ought to be preserved at the price of cowardice?" she asked. "It is in defying death, it is in viewing it calmly, that one is worthy of liberty," she lectured the Cordeliers editors, who nevertheless persisted in their decision.

After some discussion the assembly decided to veil the plaque containing the Rights of Man "until the people shall have recovered their sacred rights . . . by the destruction of the [moderate] faction." This act challenged the authorities and would soon be harshly denounced by all supporters of the Committees, including some who were sympathetic to the Cordeliers.[28] Vincent then denounced Lulier, the *procureur-général-syndic* of the Paris Department; Dufourny, president of the department's directory; Philippeaux; and others. This

---

Marguerite Evrard, femme Soulard, who quoted Brutus: "*What! an insurrection? Why an insurrection? No, we don't need an insurrection.*" Jacob writes that the word *insurrection* was first used by Ronsin on 7 Ventôse, not on 12 Ventôse as Mathiez and Walter thought; *Hébert Le Père Duchesne*, 309n2.

28. On January 23, 1794, the popular society of Sédan had veiled its Droits de l'Homme in protest against the first arrest of Ronsin and Vincent (plus two of its own patriots). Albert Mathiez, "Les Droits de l'Homme voilés au club de Sédan en pluviôse," *Annales historiques de la Révolution française*, III (1926), 495.

Nº. 243. (*)

L'AMI DU PEUPLE,

PAR LE CLUB DES CORDELIERS,

SOCIÉTÉ

DES DROITS DE L'HOMME ET DU CITOYEN.

Reprise du journal de Marat par le club des Cordeliers. — Nouveaux conspirateurs à démasquer. — Engagement contracté par le club des Cordeliers de poursuivre les scélérats, à quelque poste qu'ils soient. — Avis au peuple pour consolider la liberté. — Union intime des Jacobins avec les Cordeliers. — Leur résolution de sauver ensemble la république et de terrasser tous les scélérats.

LE club des Cordeliers, justement alarmé des dangers nouveaux qui menacent la république, convaincu de la nécessité d'éclairer le peuple sur les

<hr />

(*) Ce Nº. fait suite au dernier Nº. de Marat, 242.

A

The Cordeliers' short-lived revival of Marat's former journal, *L'Ami du peuple*.

faction of "moderates," he declared, was more to be feared than that of Brissot.

Vincent was followed by Carrier, dubbed by Michelet "missionary of the Terror," who confessed that upon his return from Nantes he had been startled by talk of a new "moderation" and by the new faces he saw among the deputies of the Mountain. They wanted to turn back the Revolution, he warned. "They don't want the guillotine because they sense that they [themselves] are worthy of it." Then he declared: "Cordeliers! you want to publish a Marateste paper. I applaude your idea and your enterprise. But this dike against those who want to swamp the Republic is indeed a feeble resistance. The insurrection, a holy insurrection, that's how you should resist the scoundrels!" This conclusion met wild applause.[29]

Hébert followed Carrier. Why have Chabot and Fabre not been punished? he asked (François Chabot was heavily implicated in the Indies Company scandal), and replied to his oratorical question by declaring that it was because Amar, a leading member of the Committee of General Security, was interested in saving the remnant of the Brissotin faction. The ambitious were more to be feared than the thieves, he proclaimed. They hide behind the curtain, but it is they who have "closed the mouths of the patriots in the popular societies." Then, throwing off all restraint, and encouraged by his listeners, he declared that he would name those responsible. Boulanger, the second in command of the Parisian armed force, shouted, "Père Duchesne, speak, and fear nothing." Momoro agreed: "Speak, we will defend you." Vincent added: "I have carried in my pocket an issue of the *Père Duchesne*, written four months ago. In comparing its truthful tone to that of today, I would have believed that Père Duchesne is dead."

Spurred on, Hébert admitted that he had been forced to adopt a prudent tone because of the heavy attacks made against him. Recalling that he had been refused the floor "in a well-known society" three or four times, he then made a fatal allusion to Robespierre: after Desmoulins had been expelled from the Jacobins "by the patriots,"

29. *Moniteur*, XIX, No. 167 (March 7, 1794), 629–30; B&R, XXXI, 325–26; Adolphe Schmidt, *Tableaux de la Révolution française* (Leipzig, 1869), II, 146; Walter, *Hébert et le "Père Duchesne,"* 197–98.

Avenel writes that the session is distorted in the *Moniteur*; Avenel, *Cloots*, II, 386 n 1. He is critical of the Cordeliers because they are men "of propaganda and the word," and trust in the power of the word; *ibid.*, 382.

he said, "one man, misled no doubt . . . I do not know how to qualify it otherwise, found the nerve to have him reinstated, despite the will of the people, who had expressed themselves clearly on this trai-tor."[30] This criticism of Robespierre, although couched in mild terms, sealed Hébert's doom. All his future attempts to repudiate these re-marks proved fruitless.

The next day, many journals carried the account of the proceedings in the Cordeliers Club. The general public was astonished to read an open appeal to insurrection, a ringing defiance of the government, its ministers, the Committee of Public Safety, and Robespierre himself, this "misled man" who had saved "the traitor Desmoulins." Most bewildering were the words of the two main speakers, Carrier and Hébert. Rumors and false reports had amplified their remarks beyond what they had uttered. Nor should it be forgotten that Carrier was at odds with Robespierre over Carrier's conduct in Nantes. He was wait-ing to justify himself before his colleagues in the Convention, but his call for a "holy insurrection" must have compromised him in their eyes. As for Hébert, people said upon reading his remarks that he was a doomed man, who had called for his own execution.[31]

It is obvious that the Cordeliers proclaimed only political goals of the insurrection, not the social demands, rooted in shortages, of the sans-culottes. They were attempting to use the social malaise caused by shortages for their own ambitions. But even if we accept their will to power, they failed miserably to prepare the insurrection. They did not even "make revolutions by halves," to paraphrase Saint-Just. It was all talk—in contrast to their forthright actions of August 10, 1792, and May 31, 1793.[32]

On 16 Ventôse (March 6, 1794), the police spy Grivel observed: "It appears to me that Vincent, Hébert, Momoro who lead the Corde-liers, have combined their interests and their efforts to employ this society in order to realize their ambitious plans . . . and to serve their particular passions." Recalling Hébert's desire to become minister of the interior and his attacks on Paré for blocking him, Grivel noted also his hatred of Danton and Robespierre for supporting Paré, al-though he did not dare strike at them openly. Nor could Hébert for-

30. *Moniteur*, XIX, No. 167 (March 7, 1794), 629–31; B&R, XXXI, 327–30.

31. Walter, *Hébert et le "Père Duchesne,"* 205.

32. Soboul wrote that the policy of the Cordeliers was "motivated primarily by spite and ambition," and that even their "political goals" were not really political. *Sans-Culottes*, 726.

give Desmoulins for criticizing the subsidy given his journal. Vincent was no less ambitious, Grivel continued, and he had never forgiven those responsible for his arrest. As for Momoro, he enjoyed credit by supporting the other two. All three were made bold only because the Convention acted so mildly against them, he continued. Thus, "They believed themselves so strong . . . they raised their heads daringly; they provoked, they attacked openly and impudently."[33] This was not a bad analysis, although whether the Convention failed to act out of weakness is doubtful, considering the earlier arrest of Ronsin and Vincent. Moreover, the Committees surely recognized the danger from the Right once this opposition on the Left was eliminated.

Some members of the Cordeliers greeted Hébert's call for an insurrection enthusiastically, but they were few. Among them was Jean Baptiste Ancard, who was to perish with the others. Witnesses testified that until recently Ancard had had no visible means of existence but that he now was seen frequenting cafés, where he "slandered the representatives of the people and sang the praises of Hébert." After Hébert's call for insurrection Ancard allegedly shouted, "Long live the Republic!" Other witnesses declared that after the arrest of Ronsin and Hébert, Ancard stated that the Cordeliers should take a clear stand on what party they supported. Still others heard him boast that "the cabal" would be finished soon and that in three weeks some eighty thousand heads would fall. Finally, when Ancard was asked the purpose of the insurrection, he replied that he meant "a September 2," that is, a prison massacre.[34] The Cordelier member called Brutus, an employee in the Hôtel de Ville, who had repudiated Ronsin's March 2 call for an insurrection, now declared: "We need a[nother] May 31; there are 105 rogue deputies we ought to kick out."[35] Thus

33. Caron, *Paris pendant la Terreur*, V, 109–10.

34. Tuetey, *Répertoire général*, X, Nos. 2524, 2526, 2520. The witnesses were Pierre Jean Rousseau; Marie Madeleine Guérin, femme Lafrette; Josephine Belledame, a grocery clerk; and Claude Tessier.

35. *Ibid.*, XI, No. 48, testimony of René Charles Mercereau, age thirty-six, a justice of the peace; and Nos. 2529 and 2530, testimony of Nicolas Pigeot, occupation unknown, and Louis François Barrois, a bookseller of the section.

Avenel writes indignantly that the day following the session of 14 Ventôse rumors of insurrection as preached by Hébert and Vincent had made their way everywhere: "And on the morrow, at daybreak, muscadins, deserters, negrophobe colonials, ruined speculators, buzzed the news in the cafés; [the news] spread, and from the cafés reached the shops, [till] it struck the ears of the merchants of the *maximum*, who howled like suspects." Avenel, *Cloots*, II, 389.

no one knew precisely what kind of insurrection the Cordeliers leaders wanted, against whom it was to be launched, or what its purpose was.

The limited and largely symbolic meaning of this debate may be clearly seen in the action of the radical section Marat. When Frédéric Pierre Ducroquet, its commissioner on profiteering, demanded veiling the Rights of Man and the dispatch of a delegation to the Commune to protest its lack of action on shortages, the general assembly held that his reasons were insufficient. Ducroquet then replied that they should declare themselves to be in a state of insurrection. Denis Etienne Laurent, a member of the General Council, opposed Ducroquet's motion and wanted it referred to the municipality. Others in the section demanded a mass march on the Commune until supplies were assured. But when a citizen named Rougevin asked against whom the insurrection was aimed, a tumult broke out.

Obviously the section was split between those who wanted an uprising, even if they were unclear on its goals and victims, and those who remained loyal to the constituted authorities, both local and national. A member of the assembly, Jacques Louis Frédéric Wouarmé (often Warmé), municipal officer and secretary of the section, declared that the people had already made three insurrections that had proved profitable to public affairs. There was no need for another, he implied; and he opposed veiling the Rights of Man. Momoro, who presided over the assembly and had applauded Ducroquet's motion, decided to end the discussion, which was beginning to grow more heated, by putting the motion before the body. When it passed, about half the members left the hall, leaving behind only the "forty-sous people"—that is, the very poor who were subsidized to attend the meetings of the sectional assembly. According to a participant, Louis Nicolas Deloche, the "patriots" in the assembly kept quiet because they did not want to aggravate things and to arouse the forty-sous people against them.[36] Here was a new label for "patriots"!

36. Tuetey, *Répertoire général*, X, Nos. 2366, 2531 (wherein Jacques Thomas testifies that there were many "mutterings" against the idea of a fourth uprising), 2532 (in which Etienne Nicolas Fabre, an homme de lettres, asserts that Ducroquet used the word *violer* for *voiler* the Rights of Man).

Edme Philippe Jarry, a courrier for the War Department, quoted Vincent as demanding a purge of moderates and described his altercation with a woman who disapproved of Hébert's conduct. Vincent wanted her expelled; she had been paid, he said, to injure Hébert. She retorted: "Yes, rascal, I have been paid by you to applaud

In order to focus the attention of the assembly on the proposed march to the Commune set for the next day, Momoro acted arbitrarily by blocking a report on profiteering that had been scheduled beforehand. He accused a notary named Pierre Jacques Guespereau of being "an aristocrat" and was quoted as saying, "Here is how some people, by making trivial motions, want to bury the larger objectives in deliberation." He thus forced the discussion back on the motion to march to the Commune. Some accused Momoro of treating the wealthy as villains and of encouraging the ferment in the section over shortages, so that property owners felt threatened.[37]

These threats of marching on the Commune, coupled with the irresponsible statements on the need for yet another insurrection, forced the government to act. On 16 Ventôse (March 6, 1794), Barère obtained a decree from the Convention charging the public prosecutor to inform it on the authors of leaflets and pamphlets being distributed in the markets, and enjoining the Committee of Public Safety to present a report to the Convention on means to protect the government. Did the revolutionary government have anything to fear? Did not the Committee of Public Safety realize that all these excursions and alarms were nothing but wind? There is little question that counterrevolutionary elements were beginning to take advantage of the agitation launched by the Cordeliers. In addition to posters denouncing Desmoulins and Philippeaux, Montagnards on mission were also attacked. Exaggerated rumors of famine were also being spread. Some women were heard to cry, "If the Commune does not want us to become prostitutes, let it feed us!" The Convention itself was split between supporters and opponents of the Cordeliers. When Carrier entered the premises of the Committee of Public Safety, Barère exclaimed: "Damned fool! You're the reason why we can't arrest Hébert, Momoro and the others."[38]

On 16 Ventôse (March 6, 1794) the members of section Marat did indeed appear en masse in the Commune. They had resolved to "rise" because their enemies were still enjoying the fruits of profiteering while they themselves were left without the necessities of life.

---

you" (Oui, polisson, je suis payée par toi pour te claquer). Ancard moved to expel her, and she left amidst the applause of Hébert's feminine supporters. *Ibid.*, XI, No. 44.

37. *Ibid.*, X, Nos. 2368, 2367, declarations of Bathélemy Damour and Marie Lesage.

38. *Moniteur*, XIX, No. 167 (March 7, 1794), 635; for Barère's decree. His exclamation is from *Catalogue Charavay*, cited in Avenel, *Cloots*, II, 390–91, 392n1.

Hence they had veiled the Rights of Man until subsistence and liberty had been assured and the enemies of the people had been punished, they declared. The president of the General Council, Jean Jacques Lubin, replied that the Commune was aware of the problem, and he adroitly turned their complaints about shortages against "the Court of St. James" and Berlin. The Convention and its Committee of Public Safety were dealing with the problem while the Committee of General Security was confiscating the property of suspects, Lubin reminded them. This surely was not the time to demonstrate against the authorities, he admonished, and he assured them that their magistrates were still the same men who had made the revolutions of August 10 and May 31. The national agent followed and pointed out how dangerous it was to adopt such measures at a time when France was at war. Like Lubin, he referred to Saint-Just's "excellent report." Chaumette then had five harmless measures adopted that, essentially, asked the Administration of Provisions to report on what it was doing to supply Paris and, at the same time, to request the Convention to redouble its efforts to provide food for the capital, which it should regard "as a town at war in a state of siege."[39]

Thus, the demonstration failed in its objectives. The section was too easily appeased by paper resolutions, and the "uprising" to assure supplies gained nothing. Even the section's revolutionary committee was unclear on the meaning of the word *insurrection*. Most of its members knew nothing of the subversive placards and complained only of shortages. One of them, François Joseph Genetz, defined the insurrection as taking "measures so that the poor be not always victims of the egoism of the rich and that Paris, finally, have food."[40] This, needless to say, was hardly an insurrectionary objective.

Mathiez thought that the Cordeliers' appeal "fell into the void."[41] But as we have seen, there was no appeal. Neither the Cordeliers nor section Marat had any plan for action. The other sections went about the business of gathering saltpeter and concerned themselves with

39. Tuetey, *Répertoire général*, XI, Nos. 19, 25, 26; *Moniteur*, XIX, No. 169 (March 9, 1794), 645–46; Buchez and Roux, eds., *Histoire parlementaire*, XXXI, 331. Deloche testified that only sixty or seventy individuals from section Marat came to the Commune; Tuetey, *Répertoire général*, X, No. 2366.

40. Tuetey, *Répertoire général*, XI, No. 20. Louis Robert Edme Goust, an architect and member of the revolutionary committee, testified how a discussion on the necessity for an insurrection ended in mere conversation.

41. Mathiez, *Révolution française*, III, 154.

provisions. On 15 Ventôse—the day after the Cordeliers' "insurrection" meeting and the day before the march on the Commune—Momoro himself appeared at the head of a numerous delegation of section Marat bearing large loaves of saltpeter amidst the roll of drums and loud acclamations by the Convention's deputies. His declaration that section Marat had "inexhaustible sources of moral saltpeter" was greeted with lively applause and was inserted in the *Bulletin*.

Georges Avenel is sarcastic in describing this scene. Has section Marat risen? No, he replies, it is Momoro heading a delegation to the Convention bearing saltpeter.[42] Bacon reported on the numerous assemblies of sections Amis de la Patrie, Contrat Social, Lombards, Maison Commune, and Arsenal—all of them discussing shortages and the need for saltpeter. In Contrat Social a shoemaker was applauded for demanding thirty-six men every day to dig saltpeter (he wanted this task to fall as punishment on the "dandies who . . . feared dirtying their dainty, white hands").[43] None of this, obviously, reflected hostility to the government, least of all the action of Momoro and section Marat.

Nevertheless, the continuing discussion on the need for another May 31 agitated public opinion. True, there was confusion on the goals of this new insurrection, and some continued to demand the unity of all good republicans. No doubt those who were aware of the discussion in the Cordeliers Club were somewhat bewildered. But this discussion, added to the problem of shortages, threatened the stability of society and the revolutionary government. All observers on 15, 16, and 17 Ventôse agreed on the gravity of the food crisis and the danger of gatherings in the street with their potential for violence, and Saint-Just and Carnot signed a decree ordering Mayor Pache to report periodically on the state of public feeling in Paris.[44]

During the night of 15–16 Ventôse (March 5–6, 1794), in section Indivisibilité, Robespierre, Prieur, Robert Lindet, and Barère were described on posters in such terms as "cannibal, deceiver of the people, always a fool and stupid, thief, assassin," and so on.[45] One poster

42. *Moniteur*, XIX, No. 168 (March 8, 1794), 640–41; Avenel, *Cloots*, II, 391.

43. Caron, *Paris pendant la Terreur*, V, 84–85, 86.

44. Alphonse Aulard, *Recueil des actes du Comité de salut public avec la correspondance officielle des représentants en mission et le registre du conseil exécutif provisoire* (Paris, 1889–1951), XI, 522; Soboul, *Sans-Culottes*, 732.

45. Tuetey, *Répertoire général*, XI, Nos. 3, 10.

appealed: "Sans-culotte, it is time. Beat the general alarm and sound the tocsin. Arm yourself, and be quick about it, because you can see that they are pushing you to your last breath. Believe me, it is better to die defending your country than to die of the hunger into which the politicians want to plunge you."[46] The discontent with the new *maximum* on wages made this appeal doubly dangerous.

It was in order to combat this subversive attack on the Convention that Barère charged the public prosecutor to locate the source of the posters, whose authors were "more dangerous than émigrés and fugitive aristocrats."[47] At the same time the Committee of Public Safety faced a dilemma: if it acted severely against the Cordeliers, this would encourage and strengthen the Indulgents (Danton and his supporters) on their right. Moreover, two members of the Committee—Collot d'Herbois and Jean Nicolas Billaud-Varenne—owed their positions on it to "Hébertisme," that is, to the sans-culottes. Both had been elected after the militant demonstrations of the sections on September 4 and 5, 1793. The Montagnards could hardly cut their links to the sans-culottes, on whom they, like the Hébertistes, relied. The war was still not won; the zeal and devotion of the sans-culottes were needed to bring it to a successful end. Besides, if the Montagnards liquidated "Hébertisme," the question of strengthening the Indulgents again arose. For the time being, if the government could calm the agitation over shortages, it would cut the ground from under the Cordeliers' popular appeal. The fact that the Committee of Public Safety relied on repression, rather than acting on the problem of provisions, reveals the evolution of the Committee. For the first time its members felt strong enough to risk alienating themselves from the sans-culottes.[48]

It is also possible that the Committee of Public Safety felt more

46. *Ibid.*, Nos. 6, 4; the text is given in Introduction, lxxvii.
47. *Moniteur*, XIX, No. 167 (March 7, 1794), 635.
48. Soboul, *Sans-Culottes*, 734; Guérin, *Lutte de classes*, II, 108. The possibility of the government's reaching some sort of secret accommodation with the Hébertistes, the Indulgents, or both is raised interestingly but unreliably in J. B. Fortescue, *The Manuscripts of J. B. Fortesque, Esq., Preserved at Dropmore* (London, 1892–1927), II, 541–42, 548–49, containing a series of "Bulletins" allegedly written by the comte d'Antraigues and transmitted through the British consul in Geneva to the British foreign secretary, William Wyndham Grenville, and purporting to describe several improbable meetings, including ones between Barère and Danton, Robespierre and Sieyès, and various Hébertistes and members of the Committee of Public Safety. Few historians place any faith in these "Bulletins" today.

confident in preparing its strike against the Cordeliers because of the reports by various police observers that there was much opposition by the sans-culottes to another insurrection. One of them overheard people saying in the Tuileries that Hébert and his friends deserved the guillotine for preaching insurrection. In addition, "the actions of Hébert, Ronsin, and Vincent have lowered them in public opinion." People were also saying that Hébert was repeating himself in his journal, although they did agree that some good patriots were being slandered, as he wrote.[49]

Meanwhile, Desmoulins continued his attacks on the Hébertistes; indeed, now that Hébert, Vincent, and Momoro were supposedly preaching insurrection, he redoubled his efforts. What would have happened to Philippeaux, Bourdon de l'Oise, and himself, he asked, if they had imitated their enemies and had preached insurrection against Bouchotte and Vincent? Would they not have been guillotined? Where, then, was the equality of the law?[50]

The revolutionary government was about to act "impartially" and to demonstrate to Desmoulins that it believed in "the equality of the law" by striking at both the Hébertistes *and* the Dantonistes. The Committees did not intend to allow the agitation by the Cordeliers to continue. At the same time, they could not let Desmoulins and his friends take advantage of the situation and end the Terror. If the offer of Saint-Just to Ronsin and Vincent was made in good faith, the Cordeliers made no effort to test it. This, too, was a fatal mistake on their part. Perhaps they did not yet realize the danger in which they stood. If not, they must at least have felt forebodings when a new blow was struck against them: their abandonment by their friend Collot d'Herbois.

49. Schmidt, *Tableaux de la Révolution,* II, 150, 23 Ventôse (March 13, 1794).

50. *Vieux Cordelier,* No. 6. In this issue Desmoulins makes an interesting point, writing that in England it was the aristocrats, led by Pitt, who wanted to continue the war, whereas in France it was the patriots and the revolutionaries who demanded that it continue, whereas the moderates and the Feuillants wanted peace. Throughout the journal, Desmoulins keeps citing Robespierre as the wise and perceptive statesman. It is obvious he hides behind Robespierre in order to reinforce his own arguments. At the same time, his writings reflect an implacable hatred of the Hébertistes.

5

Jacobins Versus Cordeliers

The threat of insurrection expressed in the Cordeliers Club on 14 Ventôse menaced the government, the Montagnards, and the Jacobins. Police reports indicate, however, that few sans-culottes would have supported such a move against the revolutionary government. The sections and the Paris Commune remained hostile to the possibility. In addition, it is questionable if the Cordeliers leaders were committed to an uprising. They took no steps to organize one and were only too eager to repudiate the fatal session of 14 Ventôse. Still, the government could not dismiss the threat.

At this critical juncture, a trump card turned up in Collot d'Herbois. Like Carrier, Collot was closely linked to the Cordeliers. He had been installed on the Committee of Public Safety following the sans-culotte demonstrations of September 4 and 5, 1793, and Hébert had praised him as a "giant." Collot had resorted to "fusillades" (mass shootings of prisoners) in Lyon, just as Carrier had employed the notorious "noyades" (mass drownings) in Nantes. The Cordeliers, being partisans of terror tactics against counterrevolutionaries or those deemed to be such, naturally supported the policies of Collot and Carrier. The Committee of Public Safety, too, had encouraged its representatives-on-mission to adopt terrorist measures in order to crush the Federalist Revolt in the summer and early fall of 1793. Now, however, as it sought to impose a monolithic policy on France—an effort that necessitated striking at the Hébertistes on the one hand and at the Indulgents on the other—the government began to separate itself from the former "terrorists" whom it had supported against the counterrevolution. Carrier had been recalled, and Collot felt menaced by the arrests of Ronsin and other Cordeliers.[1]

1. See Guérin's discussion on the centralizing and bureaucratic policies of the revolutionary government as it began to deprive the local authorities of taking independent measures in conflict with the Convention and its two Committees: *Lutte de classes*, II,

If the Committee of Public Safety could recruit a sympathizer of the Cordeliers like Collot to persuade the club to join the Jacobins in support of the government, it would be an important victory. The victory was achieved: Collot did decide to embrace the government's policy and break with his former allies. As to why he did so, we can only speculate. Perhaps he realized the weakness of the Cordeliers or simply believed that the club's policy was endangering that unity which alone could triumph against the foreign coalition and the internal counterrevolution. Nor can the possibility be dismissed that criticism of his policy in Lyon was endangering his future position. No documents exist to prove this, of course, but his sudden abandonment of the Cordeliers could have had personal, as well as political, motives.

In any case, Collot did abandon the Cordeliers. On 16 Ventôse, just two days after the Cordeliers session in which calls for insurrection had sounded, he rose in the Jacobin Society to demand that the Jacobins deal with the danger that threatened them. Calling attention to the absence on mission of several members of the Committee of Public Safety and the illness of Robespierre and Couthon, he emphasized the gravity of the situation in the capital, where the "intrigues" of France's enemies were rife. Collot declared that although he respected the Cordeliers, the club's members were being misled as in the past when Jacques Rooux had seduced them into opposing the adoption of the new Constitution because it did not proscribe speculation and hoarding. Now a group of ambitious men wanted to make insurrections in order to profit from them. What have they done for public affairs? he demanded. He proposed sending a delegation to the Cordeliers to explain to them that they had been misled by "intriguers."[2] Obviously he hoped to separate the rank and file of the Cordeliers from the leaders.

12–57, *passim*. Mathiez, *Révolution française*, III, 129, writes that Collot felt threatened after the arrest of "his agent Ronsin" and other Hébertistes.

2. *Journal de la Montagne*, Nos. 115–16 (March 8, 9, 1794), 915–16, 921–22. Among his other remarks, Collot charged "an insurrection because two men have suffered, because a physician had not cured them, during the time they were ill! . . . Anathema on those who demand an insurrection!"

It is possible that Collot was involved in the plot of the Hébertistes, "which if successful might conceivably make him master of the Republic" (Palmer, *Twelve Who Ruled*, 282). Meanwhile, while attacking the Cordeliers leaders, he said nothing about Carrier's equally great threat in calling for an insurrection.

Momoro replied immediately that Collot was mistaken. For one thing, the Declaration of the Rights of Man had been veiled at the Cordeliers Club for a month prior to the session of two days ago, as could be demonstrated by the club's minutes. Moreover, this had happened at a time when the Jacobins, too, were struggling "against oppression." Collot retorted that according to a number of journals, the ark had been veiled only during the past few days. Furthermore, the time of oppression had passed; unlike the days when, before the insurrection of May 31, the voice of patriotism had been stifled, now only individual differences remained in the Convention. Popular decrees meet no difficulty today, he assured his opponents, and he blamed the popular societies of the sections for the "intrigue" under discussion. When Momoro objected to this accusation against the Cordeliers, Collot replied that he was not blaming them but, rather, the sectional societies that were inciting people to march on the Convention—a reference to section Marat. The Cordeliers were linked to these societies despite themselves, he declared.

These remarks persuaded the Jacobins to send a delegation to their sister organization with Collot as its spokesman. It was a wise choice. Collot, after all, was linked to the sectionnaires whose pressure on the Convention during the dramatic demonstration of September 4 and 5, 1793, had helped propel him onto the Committee of Public Safety. In addition, he was an orator and an actor, talents that were to prove useful in persuading the Cordeliers to reverse their course. Had Robespierre, Saint-Just, or some other member of the Committee been chosen as the envoy to the Cordeliers, no one could have been certain of the club's response. With Collot, the chances for success were enhanced.

Carrier, it will be recalled, had spoken in favor of "a holy insurrection" at the Cordeliers meeting of 14 Ventôse. Now, at the Jacobins, he wished to "explain" that session. He was preceded, however, by a Jacobin named Renaudin, a juror of the Revolutionary Tribunal, who must have spoken for many of his fellow club members: "They want insurrections! Fine! Let them show themselves and we shall see who will triumph, we or they." Carrier then attempted to prove that no one had spoken of an insurrection "except in case of being forced by circumstances," and pledged his head "if anyone had made a motion against the Convention." He admitted that some people wanted to divide the Jacobins from the Cordeliers, but emphasized that it was against the "moderates" that the threat of an insurrection had been uttered. Furthermore, although some Cordeliers had denounced the writings of Philippeaux, and others had spoken against the factions in the Convention, none had used the word *insurrection* in the traditional sense.

Several Cordeliers present supported Carrier and complained that Hébert's speech had been distorted in the press. All repeated that the threat of insurrection had been used only in a conditional sense—that is, should "patriots" ever be oppressed by a faction arising on the ruins of the Republic, only then might an insurrection become necessary. Hébert himself sought to retreat from his damaging remarks of 14 Ventôse by blaming the journalists for misinterpreting them. In No. 354 of the *Père Duchesne* he threatened the Feuillants and moderates with the unity of Jacobins and Cordeliers "in a final insurrection against the traitors." The damage, however, had been done, and no ingenious explanation could erase the threat of insurrection that had been uttered. The police spy Dugas reported that there was much talk in the cafés about the session of the Cordeliers. Hébert, Vincent, Momoro, and others were being called "English patriots," and people were especially angry with Hébert for having attacked Robespierre.[3]

The following day, March 7, Collot arrived with the Jacobin delegation in the Cordeliers Club. They were received in bad humor. Vincent moved that the seven or eight Jacobins be placed to the left of the president so that they would not trouble the order of business and impede the deliberations of the society. A delegation from section Mutius Scaevola was given the floor first by Momoro, who presided over the session. This was a deliberate slight to Collot and his supporters. There was also confusion whether the procès-verbal of the 14 Ventôse session had been adopted or rejected.

After many objections were heard to reading the previous minutes as submitting to Jacobin censorship, Collot finally was allowed to take the floor. He stammered, saying that the Cordeliers should not be so upset just because two of their members (Vincent and Ronsin) had suffered imprisonment. Some shouted that this was not the issue, that it was a matter of principle. But before long Collot, employing his theatrical skills and gift of oratory, won over his audience. Even Momoro was seen to shed tears, and in his reply he swore that the

3. *Moniteur*, XIX, No. 169 (March 9, 1794), 646–48; Aulard, *Jacobins*, V, 671–74; B&R, XXXI, 331–32; Walter, *Hébert et le "Père Duchesne,"* 206–207; Soboul, *Sans-Culottes*, 731–35; Caron, *Paris pendant la Terreur*, V, 107.

Cordeliers would support the Rights of Man together with the Jacobins, whom he invited to visit them often.

Not everyone was convinced by Collot, however: Mme Hébert, according to a woman who sat next to her, characterized him as "a comedian, an intriguer." All through his speech she kept saying, "It's a show; doesn't it seem he is playing a comedy?" When those around her protested, she accused them of being bribed by the Jacobins and stated that the Cordeliers could not compete with them because they were not "millionaires." When Collot was applauded, Mme Hébert insisted that unlike his role, which was treacherous, that of the Cordeliers was sincere.[4]

Nevertheless, Collot's appeal was powerful enough to win over the majority of the Cordeliers to his side: "You have pronounced the word 'insurrection.' Under what circumstances does one speak of revolt? At a time when Pitt and Coburg are hovering like birds of prey over France; when it is being announced in all the courts of Europe that the Jacobins and the Cordeliers are ready to join in fight to the death." When he finished there were shouts of "bravo," and caps were thrown into the air as the assembly applauded his moving oration.

Hébert's quibble that by "insurrection" he meant only the unity of the two societies against their common enemies convinced no one, and in any case was no reply to Collot's patriotic appeal. The result of this session was that in a burst of enthusiasm the Cordeliers tore the veil from the Rights of Man and gave it to the Jacobin delegation as a gesture of fraternal unity. But when Collot asked to see the original minutes of the Cordeliers' session of 14 Ventôse, Momoro evasively replied that it was being edited because a number of amendments had not been included and some inaccuracies had to be corrected.[5]

Collot reported to the Jacobins that he had been received fraternally, and he showed the veil that had draped the Rights of Man.

4. Tuetey, *Répertoire général*, X, No. 2362, wherein Momoro swears the Cordeliers will never degenerate and will "clamp on" to the edifice of the Republic together with the Jacobins; *ibid.*, XI, Nos. 43 and 36, testimony of François Farjaire, a clockmaker, and of Marie Jeanne Elisabeth Brocard Jolly, femme Metrasse, a seedswoman (grainier) and inspector of military relay stations; Avenel, *Cloots*, II, 401–402.

5. *Moniteur*, XIX, No. 171 (March 11, 1794), 663–64; B&R, XXXI, 334; Amable Guillaume Prosper Brugière, baron de Barante, *Histoire de la Convention nationale* (1851–53; rpr. New York, 1976), IV, 125; Tuetey, *Répertoire général*, X, no. 2372, declaration of J. B. Loys of section Bon-Conseil.

Even so, he exhorted his audience not to listen to "the insidious spokesmen who say that the whole republic is suffering," which he labeled "the usual language of the aristocracy." Furthermore, he warned against the perfidy of a small number of individuals" who were opposed to the unity of the two organizations.[6]

Who were these perfidious individuals? They were the unreconciled leaders of the Cordeliers. Collot, after all, had said nothing about "the moderates," nor had he mentioned the food crisis. Vincent still demanded to know why "the Brissotins" had not yet been punished, why a report on "the conspiracy" had not yet been made, and he concluded that there existed "a dangerous faction" that should have been arrested long ago. And Ronsin, on the same day that Collot addressed the Cordeliers, had warned them to be on guard against the "hypocrites of humanity" operating under the guise of "clemency, of humanity, of moral virtues." Then, without naming him, he attacked Robespierre in discussing the term *ultra-revolutionary*. It was, Ronsin said, a word that had set back public opinion for two years, a word that had served as a pretext for the new factionalists to oppress the most devoted patriots—a word, finally, that might have had a less sinister influence if it had not come from the mouth of this Montagnard who so many times had thundered against the vile supporters of tyranny. Ronsin then attacked Philippeaux and his moderate friends, who undermined patriots "not out of regard for various individuals who have been their first victims, but because in arresting in its course the revolutionary torrent, they have killed the public spirit." This speech was published by the Cordeliers and was placarded on the walls of many buildings.[7]

Vincent and Ronsin had partisans in the Cordeliers who rejected Collot's appeal, and there were others in sections like Brutus and Finistère, and in the popular Society Lazowski. These groups did not approve of the retractions that Hébert and Momoro had made, and they continued to adopt fiery resolutions against "hidden royalists, moderates, and indulgents." A spokesman for Society Lazowski, Guillaume Boulland, demanded to "free" the Revolutionary army and to judge summarily "the profiteers."[8] On 22 Ventôse (March 12,

6. *Journal de la Montagne*, No. 118 (March 11, 1794), 937–39.

7. *Moniteur*, XIX, No. 172 (March 12, 1794), 670; Aulard, *Jacobins*, V, 677; B&R, XXXI, 335; Tuetey, *Répertoire général*, X, No. 2263.

8. Boulland (sometimes Bouland) was a leader of section Finistère, thirty-seven years of age, with a distinguished and long revolutionary career. He was arrested after the demonstration of June 20, 1792, became an elector in 1792, and was elected substi-

1794), Hébert, evidently once again pressured by Vincent's attacks against the new "Cromwellistes," declaimed against Barère. At the same time Momoro complained of being interrogated by a judge of the Revolutionary Tribunal about the incendiary posters, the threat of insurrection, and "the artificial famine." He revealed that the public prosecutor wanted to know which members of section Marat had initiated the action to veil the Rights of Man. Momoro reported also that he had questioned the judge of the court, in turn, after the latter had interrogated him. He was indignant that patriots had to be subjected to these judicial inquiries while "disguised royalists" remained unpunished.[9]

On 19 Ventôse (March 9, 1794), Boucheseiche made an important observation on the Cordeliers Club: "The composition of the galleries was not the same as in the preceding session. The majority of the spectators was made up of regulars, all quite discontented with the applause given two days before to the speech of Collot d'Herbois. Before the session they expressed their regret that the Declaration of Rights was stripped of the veil that covered it. Such was the feeling of the galleries." Boucheseiche then turned to the remarks of Vincent and pointed out that the latter sought to diminish the effect of Collot's oratory. Without naming Danton, Vincent stated that some day it must be revealed why "a certain person had worked for the Executive Power, etc., and that [some] wished that the [threat of the] guillotine

---

tute judge and, then, to the court of the 2d arrondissement. He was denounced on 11 Floréal (May 30, 1794) for having defended "Momoro, Vincent, and the others." Arrested some time later, he was released after Robespierre's fall; he was denounced again in 1795 but escaped further arrest. Bouland supported the idea that an insurrection was essential and attacked "property," according to some of his colleagues on the revolutionary committee. He was accused of being a partisan of both Hébert and Robespierre, of being a *septembriseur* (that is, a participant in the September Massacres of prisoners) and a terrorist, of being a member of Monsieur's guard (Monsieur was Louis' brother), of being a "leveler" (that is, of favoring equality of wealth or property), and of creating a party (faction) in the section. Richard Cobb, "Note sur Guillaume Bouland de la section du Finistère," *Annales historiques de la Révolution française*, XXII (1950), 152–55; Soboul and Monnier, *Répertoire de personnel sectionnaire*, 526–27.

9. Delegates from section Finistère and from Society Lazowski demanded that the Revolutionary army be unleashed against profiteers. *Moniteur*, XIX, No. 172 (March 10, 1794), 672; Caron, *Paris pendant la Terreur*, V, 248; Mathiez, *Vie chère*, 554–55. Mathiez believed, however, that "Momoro, Hébert, Ronsin himself, in succession, made due apology, proclaiming that people had misled the Committee of Public Safety and the Jacobins on their real feelings." This is doubtful. Ronsin made no such apology, and Momoro had the courage, as seen above, to interrogate the Revolutionary Tribunal when it sought to question him.

would prevent him [Vincent] from saying these things." The police spy added, "The satisfaction of his colleagues and of the galleries proved to him that they shared his sentiments."[10]

Thus, a kind of "left wing," to use Guérin's term, existed in the Cordeliers, led by Vincent and Ronsin. This group was not taken in by the sentiments of unity expressed by Hébert and Momoro and by the Jacobins. Nor would they retreat from their links to the popular societies of the sections whom Collot had blamed for the threats to the duly constituted authorities. Few would have forgotten that Collot d'Herbois owed his own appointment on the Committee to the sans-culottes. He was, in a sense, the Montagnard's link to the mass of artisans, working people, small shopkeepers, and journeymen who made up the sans-culotterie of the capital. Vincent felt that they had a right to expect something more from Collot than a defense of what the Cordeliers called "a system of pernicious moderation."

A few days later, on 21 Ventôse (March 11, 1794), the Cordeliers finally sent a delegation to the Jacobins. The latter had waited in vain for it since Collot's visit. According to Latour-Lamontagne, people speculated that one reason for the delay may have been the Cordeliers' preoccupation with editing "new minutes." The Cordeliers had decided against an address to the Jacobins as being undignified, agreeing instead on "a very simple and firm resolution." The spokesman of the delegation insisted that "spiteful journalists" had deliberately distorted and perverted the Cordeliers session of 14 Ventôse. Now amity and fraternity were renewed amidst enthusiastic cries of "Long live the Republic!"[11] But beneath this superficial harmony no real reconciliation existed.

Hébert vacillated from one issue of his journal to another. In No. 354 he congratulated the Jacobins and the Cordeliers on their amity, but in his next number he wrote: "There is no longer room to retreat, f——; the Revolution must complete itself. . . . One step back would ruin the Republic."[12] Yet he had nothing concrete to propose, nothing that could have mobilized the sans-culottes around a program that, at a minimum, would have provided their pound of bread.

10. Caron, *Paris pendant la Terreur*, V, 175. Guérin, *Lutte de classes* II, 103, asks if Vincent meant Danton alone, or if he included Robespierre in his remarks.
11. Caron, *Paris pendant la Terreur*, V, 185 (report of Latour-Lamontagne, 19 Ventôse) and 224 (report of Dugas, 21 Ventôse). The next day Dugas revealed that sections Brutus and La Montagne had denounced "the seditious" who had preached insurrection and had veiled the Rights of Man; *ibid.*, 251–52.
12. *Père Duchesne*, No. 354.

Nor should it be forgotten that however militant and uncompromising the avant-garde of the Cordeliers was, it was certainly not the majority of the club. The police observer Grivel interviewed a member of the Cordeliers who attended the session at which Collot spoke. Grivel had seen this member at a previous meeting, and from the man's remarks judged him to be one who knew something of the politics in dispute. The man admitted that he was pleased with Collot's address, was happy to see the veil removed from the Rights of Man, and thought that his fellow members had accepted the union with the Jacobins. And what about those who had spoken of insurrection? asked Grivel. I can assure you, the man replied, that these people were very embarrassed. Things had not turned out as they had hoped; public opinion was not in their favor. They blamed "the perfidious journalists" for misinterpreting their use of the word *insurrection*, but Hébert's explanation had caused much grumbling. Wasn't it odd that Hébert tried to persuade his hearers that they did not hear what they heard and that he did not say what he had said? Wasn't it strange that the word *insurrection* turned out to mean "unity"? Whom would Hébert persuade of this? The anonymous observer was confident that no one had faith in Hébert, or in Vincent or Ronsin. The past disturbs these three, and the future frightens them. In this respect, I agree with them! They are not wrong, he concluded.[13] Thus spoke this anonymous observer who expressed the views of the political Center.

If the Cordeliers had its right and left wings, many members repudiated both. The anonymous member who spoke to Grivel rejected both the demagogy of Hébert and the radicalism of Ronsin and Vincent. One reason could have been simple loyalty to the revolutionary government and an attachment to Robespierre. But whatever the reasons for rejecting the call to insurrection, clearly the Cordeliers Club was divided in its own loyalties.

Collot's success was limited, however; the Cordeliers did not surrender their objective, nor had he been able to separate the rank and file from the leaders. The Great Committees understood this and began to prepare an end to Hébertisme. The police observers reported this change clearly. Dugas spoke of "certain factious [men] who inject trouble into the two societies" and who wanted to monopolize the top positions in the government. Bacon reported that citizens in the galleries spoke openly about the need to arrest Hébert, Vincent, Ron-

13. Caron, *Paris pendant la Terreur*, V, 179–81.

sin, and Momoro. Hébert, they said, was a villain, for "no one but a villain would call on the people to rise up, at the critical time we are in." Prévost and Charmont warned against a "general insurrection," which all citizens ought to fear, and that "the Hébertistes did not accept their defeat" and "would not yield one iota." Jarousseau also agreed that Vincent was seen as planning a counterrevolution. People were assured, however, that Hébert and a part of his "clique" would be arrested soon. Meanwhile, Fouquier-Tinville was authorized to hire as many agents as he needed to foil the "plot" being prepared.[14]

While rumors of plots and approaching arrests were being discussed publicly, the food crisis continued to aggravate the situation. The General Council reported that beef was in shorter supply than ever and that fewer cattle were being slaughtered than before. The Commune proposed, therefore, to ration meat by distributing the amount available to the sections according to population. The Administration of Provisions suggested that with the approach of spring, the gardens of former aristocrats, émigrés, and others be used for planting vegetables. There were shortages of butter also; it was reported that women had to stand in line two to three hours under a hot sun just to get one-quarter of a pound.

The observer Perrière noted that people were also violently jealous of the rich—who he said were themselves responsible for this feeling because of their behavior. According to Pourvoyeur, there was talk that one guillotine was not enough, since counterrevolutionaries were trying to starve Paris. As for foreigners and nobles, "they could not but betray us," it was agreed, and "it was necessary to throw them out completely and not to have any confidence in them at all." Bacon revealed that in section Droits de l'Homme a numerous assembly, after a long debate on shortages, appointed commissioners to tell the Commune how concerned they were and to suggest that it issue ration cards good only for the merchants who signed them. On 22 Ventôse (March 12, 1794), Rolin revealed the complaints against commissioners of civil committees who presided over the distribution of meat and other necessities: The commissioners were charged with having an understanding with certain wholesale merchants to supply them with what they wanted. Butchers in section Gardes-Françaises were allegedly being insulted because they did not comply with these officials' desires.

14. *Ibid.*, 152, 148, 143, 177, 203, 209; *Moniteur*, XIX, No. 170 (March 10, 1794), 659.

Posters calling for an insurrection were still showing up every day. One such call seemed to have come from section Marat. Another, on rue Montmartre, called on the French to rise and annihilate their enemies, at the same time freeing the imprisoned patriots. A portion of this placard was covered by a poster of the Cordeliers declaring that Desmoulins, Philippeaux, Fabre d'Eglantine, and Bourdon de l'Oise had forfeited the people's confidence. A commissioner on hoarding in section Panthéon was quoted as saying that another insurrection was essential and that there were over one hundred "maggoty" deputies in the Convention who should be imprisoned.[15]

On March 12, workers in a plate-glass factory complained before the Commune that they were being maligned, having been accused of wanting to stir up trouble. The president assured them that the citizens of faubourg Saint-Antoine were known for their patriotism and that "the conquerors of the Bastille" would not do anything prejudicial to public affairs.[16] Yet shortages and high prices could easily be exploited, and the patriotism of the workers was no proof against disaffection caused by hunger. This, too, contributed to the tense atmosphere in the capital.

Prévost had revealed on March 9 that house searches were going on in section La Montagne, and that those who had supplies for more than three days saw them confiscated, while those with two sets of clothes had to surrender one. Two days earlier he had written that there were many foreigners and counterrevolutionaries in the capital and that to avoid an insurrection some people in faubourg Saint-Germain wanted to arm the citizens. Charmont repeated this observation two days later and added that popular societies were getting ready to follow the Cordeliers blindly.[17]

On March 11 a certain Ducastel declared the need for three thousand cartridges, and the captain of a battalion in the Revolutionary army reportedly chimed in that his men were going "to dislodge the

15. *Moniteur*, XIX, No. 170 (March 10, 1794), 655; Tuetey, *Répertoire général*, XI, lxxvii–lxxviii and Nos. 5 and 11; Caron, *Paris pendant la Terreur*, V, 189–90 (Perrière on 19 Ventôse), 192 (Pourvoyeur on 19 Ventôse), 214 (Bacon on 21 Ventôse), 262 (Rolin); Tuetey, *Répertoire général*, XI, No. 32, testimony of Mathieu Koenig, 26 Ventôse. A Pierre Crossnier testified that he had heard expressions from a crowd reading a poster: "Yes, it's high time that we rose up en masse"; Caron, *Paris pendant la Terreur*, V, 189–90 (Perrière).

16. *Moniteur*, XIX, No. 178 (March 18, 1794), 718.

17. Caron, *Paris pendant la Terreur*, V, 194, 143, 177.

sparrows," designating some sixty deputies. The following day Jean Baptiste Balestier, the commissioner of section Contrat Social, affirmed the need for an insurrection. The same desire was expressed by two citizens overheard by Rolin in the Garden of the Revolution.[18]

Thus rumors and reports of a contemplated insurrection were continuing. At the same time the influence of the Cordeliers was still great enough to cause uneasiness in governmental circles. An indication of this fact can be seen in an incident involving a woman named Moreau, arrested by the revolutionary committee of section Observatoire for having created trouble in a line outside a butcher's stall. Longpré, paymaster of the Administration for Clothing, protested this arrest to the police of the Commune. Upon their refusal to release Moreau, he threatened to "trumpet" the arrest at the Cordeliers. He was promptly arrested himself (he was acquitted by the Revolutionary Tribunal the following month).[19]

The Cordeliers leaders were encouraged by the agitation but, again, did nothing to organize the movement of opposition to the government. Hébert wrote duplicitously in his No. 354 that "the *jean-foutres* who wanted to set the Jacobins on the Cordeliers like a dog on a cat have only struck water with their sword," and blamed Pitt, the "moderates," Feuillants, and royalists for attempting to disrupt the unity of the two organizations. Then came the saving phrase that "the Jacobins and Cordeliers, always united with the Convention," would rise together in a final insurrection against their enemies.

The Cordeliers session of 19 Ventôse (March 9) was in the same spirit. Boucheseiche revealed that Momoro declared the reason why the minutes of the previous two sessions had not yet been published was because they were being edited for accuracy—that they lacked "the usual vigorous character of the Cordeliers." Hébert, Vincent, and Momoro were applauded by the gathering, which was made up of those who had been critical of Collot's discourse two days earlier, wrote the police observer. Moreover, this audience expressed regret

18. Plaq. 7, p. 379, in W 77, AN, cited by Soboul, *Sans-Culottes*, 742n52; Caron, *Paris pendant la Terreur*, V, 265.

19. Dos. 669, in W 344, AN, cited by Soboul, *Sans-Culottes*, 742–43n54. Anne Claudine Moreau, femme Trousset, was a journeyman carpenter. Much later (May 20, 1795) she was accused of having made seditious proposals and was remitted before the police court. There is no record of the court's verdict. Soboul and Monnier, *Répertoire de personnel sectionnaire*, 511. It was unusual for a woman to be accepted as an apprentice in the trades.

that the veil had been removed from the Rights of Man. A resolution, unanimously adopted, declared that they had veiled the document in the first place because of persecution of true patriots.

Grivel revealed in his report of March 12 that Collot had dropped certain significant phrases in his address to the Jacobins four days earlier. After saying that most Cordeliers wanted to unite with their sister club, Collot added that

> nevertheless we could sense certain obstacles. . . . We sensed that at first our opinion was not generally acceptable to the Cordeliers, but as we professed our principles, a general sentiment rallied them around us. . . . Let us not listen to some insidious spokesmen, who in order to avenge a personal injury, tell us that humanity is outraged and want all to suffer for their own satisfaction. . . . We must tell them that there cannot be two forms of patriotism; that tomorrow's opinion must be that of yesterday; that in revolution there can be neither yesterday nor tomorrow, that all days are the same.[20]

Grivel added that the Jacobins understood well enough the motives behind the veiling of the Rights of Man and did not fool themselves about those who were meditating an insurrection. Second, the Cordeliers themselves understood the error into which they had been led and were doing everything they could to give a favorable impression to their conduct and expressions. But, added Grivel, "they lack force; they dissimulate." They no longer had the influence in the popular societies that they had enjoyed formerly. The warning to those Cordeliers who had sat on their hands when Collot addressed them was clear. The Jacobins, meaning the revolutionary government, would not allow them to place "obstacles" in the path of the one, true patriotism, which must be the same for all.

After Momoro read the newly edited version of the minutes, which received universal applause from those present, Hébert again denounced the "slanders" against the club, vigorously denying that it wanted to dissolve the Convention. Once again he reaffirmed the unity of the two societies and attacked "the domineering and high powers," that is, the two Committees. Yet he asked the society to disavow the "insinuation" by journalists that he had spoken against Robespierre. The Cordeliers gladly gave him this assurance. Hébert was followed by Vincent, who denounced the "Cromwellistes" for wanting to establish "a pernicious system of moderantism." A secre-

20. Caron, *Paris pendant la Terreur*, V, 253–54; Soboul, *Sans-Culottes*, 743–44.

tary read a summary of the Cordeliers activities since the insurrection of May 31. The document amounted to a vigorous defense of the club, explaining what had led it to veil the Rights of Man, and was obviously directed against the government and Robespierre. It ended with the declaration that the Cordeliers would not retreat an inch. Rolin stated categorically that the peace between the two societies could not last and that the Cordeliers would not give up until they had thrown out all the ministers except Bouchotte.[21]

Meanwhile, the club had sent out letters to its affiliates urging them to follow the mother society's lead and remove the veils from their Rights of Man. These letters were being seized by the authorities in preparation for the trial. As a further preparatory measure, Hanriot was ordered to mobilize his armed force. On March 9, the same day Momoro presented the edited minutes before the Cordeliers, Hanriot concentrated 1,200 troops and 400 cannoneers at the former Palais Royal and "carried off 130 foppish schemers and deserters, all very fat and chubby."[22] In addition to removing a few potential troublemakers, the show of force was of course meant to discourage anyone else who might be considering "insurrection."

To add to the Cordeliers' difficulties, Hébert was accused of hoarding. A large package was seen to arrive at his home; the contents turned out to be twenty-four pounds of salt pork. It seems to have been a gift from one of his comrades, who had received it from his

21. *Moniteur*, XIX, No. 172 (March 12, 1794), 671; Tuetey, *Répertoire général*, XI, No. 28, testimony of femme Chenié; Caron, *Paris pendant la Terreur*, V, 242; Soboul, *Sans-Culottes*, 744–45.

During the session of 22 Ventôse (not mentioned by the *Moniteur*, says Schmidt), a member by name of Monin (or Moynin), aide-de-camp of Hanriot, criticized what he called "the faction" in the Convention that had existed even before the insurrection of May 31. He revealed that François Chabot (later to be executed for his role in the Indies Company plot) and Léonard Bourdon (a shady deputy and future Thermidorian) had threatened the Comité central révolutionnaire, which directed the uprising of May 31, with the armed forces of the departments if a single deputy were touched. In short, Chabot and Bourdon opposed the insurrection. Hébert attested to the truth of this recital. Schmidt, *Tableaux de la Révolution*, II, No. 202, pp. 146–47; Caron, *Paris pendant la Terreur*, V, 245–47. The implication of this affair is discussed in Slavin, *Making of an Insurrection*, 145–46.

22. Avenel, *Cloots*, II, 405–406. Avenel writes that Fouquier-Tinville could not find a single royalist or counterrevolutionary placard. Finally, someone had pity on him and posted a brief note written in ink, which the public prosecutor found and brought to Barère. But the police observers, as seen above, reported many such posters.

parents and sent it on to Hébert. Someone reported the arrival of the package to the revolutionary committee of Hébert's section, Bonne-Nouvelle, and suggested that the premises of his publication be searched. Hébert insisted that the commissioner who discovered the pork distribute it among the poor. It is possible that upon receiving the package Hébert neglected, or simply lacked the time, to report this gift. Nor can the possibility be excluded that his enemies or agents of the Committee of General Security sent the package, then informed the revolutionary committee to search his premises, in an effort to destroy his popularity. In a short time rumors spread that he was a hoarder. The revolutionary committee of his section, together with the popular society, gave him a certificate testifying that the pork had been meant for the poor. Nothing seemed to help, however, and soon the amount of meat that he allegedly had hoarded was five hundred pounds.[23]

To scotch these rumors Hébert placarded the walls of the capital with his justification. After reciting the events, he attached the statement of the revolutionary committee and that of the popular society. He then proceeded to deny the "calumny" that he headed a counter-revolutionary party, that he had veiled the Rights of Man, and that he had called for an insurrection. Hébert added that he was accused of denouncing "a patriot" (Robespierre) for whom he in fact had the highest respect. It was true, he admitted, that a veil had been placed over the Rights of Man, but this was done at a time when the best patriots had been arrested. Nor had he been present when the act was committed—although, he hastened to add, he did not repudiate it. Moreover, far from being an attack on the Convention, the veiling had been accompanied by measures for the support of that body, which a new system of moderation had tended to paralyze.

Journalists had distorted the session and the discourse of the Cordeliers members, Hébert added; in truth, the club had supported him and continued to give him its confidence. He had refused lucrative posts and had no other ambition than to serve liberty and good principles, he assured his readers. For four years he had been the butt of royalists and other enemies of the people. Today he was being re-

23. *Père Duchesne*, No. 354; Walter, *Hébert et le "Père Duchesne,"* 208; Soboul, *Sans-Culottes*, 745. A letter from a Grosley (headquarters of the Revolutionary army) complained to Hébert that it was better he should write to his friends than to hoard twenty-four pounds of pork. Tuetey, *Répertoire général*, X, No. 2236.

proached with the same slanders used by the "Austrian Committee" and the "Comité des Douze" (that is, the royalists and the Girondins)—but their reign happily had passed, and no patriot would now be punished with impunity.[24]

Boucheseiche reported that the public read this "Réponse" attentively. Hébert's supporters were overheard saying it was too bad he was not a minister; if he had been a member of the Executive Council things would have gone a lot better. All members except the minister of war, they added, were "Philippotins." A number of women agreed. But Le Harivel on March 11 commented: "If Père Duchesne, say [some] citizens, in reading his supposed justification, believes that he has washed himself off from the stain newly imprinted on his forehead, he is fooling himself rudely."[25] This proved to be an accurate evaluation of Hébert's situation.

The appearance of the new *Ami du peuple,* aimed at the "unfaithful mandatories of the people," gave the impression to both the government and the public that the Cordeliers were engaged in a systematic propaganda campaign. Actually only two issues appeared, Nos. 243 and 244, so numbered because Marat's last issue had been No. 242. The decision to publish the journal had been taken on 2 Ventôse (February 20, 1794), as we have seen. On 19 Ventôse the first number appeared. It affirmed the principles of Marat, attacked moderation and indulgence (which, the editors charged, had made their appearance even among the Jacobins), denounced unfaithful mandatories, and made only one implicit reference to an insurrection. The editors gave credit to the vigilance of the government against counterrevolutionary activity but asserted that this vigilance came to pass only after the Cordeliers had alerted the authorities. The journal attacked all despotism and promised "to put the people on guard against all decrees that were the fruit of intrigue, of passion, or of the spirit of domination." It threatened to strike "most particularly the unfaithful mandatories" and declared its indignation against false patriots and

24. *Réponse de J. R. Hébert, auteur du "Père Duchesne," à une atroce calomnie,* in Lb 41 4809, BN. The statement of Bonne-Nouvelle's revolutionary committee is reproduced in Tuetey, *Répertoire général,* X, No. 2242. Dugas' report of 22 Ventôse (March 12, 1794), summarizes Hébert's response, in Caron, *Paris pendant la Terreur,* V, 252.

25. Caron, *Paris pendant la Terreur,* V, 217–18, 231. Harivel added: "What a dazzling act of patriotism he has demonstrated to his fellow citizens, in awarding the poor the product of his hoarding!" Schmidt, *Tableaux de la Révolution,* II, No. 202, p. 144.

"the ambitious." The editors ended their appeal by promising to continue to pursue the people's enemies and to destroy the moderate faction.[26]

Le Breton reported on the day No. 243 came out that he overheard one person remarking, upon hearing a hawker announcing the sale of the new journal in the Tuileries, "May it please God to resurrect the poor man [Marat]; he would have ended soon all these quarrels." Another declared that considering the state of the country, only unity and harmony could preserve liberty. The police agent added that people seemed to agree with this sentiment. The journal did not call for an insurrection, but it threatened the government by its attack on unfaithful representatives and its campaign to win over public opinion.[27] All this gave further ammunition to the Committees against the Cordeliers.

That many of the Jacobins did not take seriously the expressions of unity with the Cordeliers may be seen in Dufourny's provocative assertion that the protestations of the Cordeliers were not enough. What did they think of sectional societies? was his question. This was what must be discussed, he insisted, to the warm applause of the Jacobins, who adopted his proposal.[28] Police spies noted that people were convinced that unity between the two popular societies had not been established. Some predicted that either Hébert or the minister of interior would perish; others saw the party's split infecting the individual sections, and feared a civil war.[29]

On March 12 the Cordeliers heard Chenaux's report on their dele-

26. *L'Ami du peuple*, No. 243, 19 Ventôse II (March 9, 1794), in W 77, plaq. 5, p. 334, AN. In a footnote on the leading page the editors stated, "This No. [243] follows the last No. of Marat, 242." A précis of its contents began with "Reprise de journal de Marat par le club des Cordeliers" and ended with "Leur resolution de sauver ensemble [with the Jacobins] la république et de terrasser les scélérats."

Soboul, in *Sans-Culottes*, 747 n 1, points out the gap between the journal's first appearance and that of the prospectus, which seems to have confused some historians and observers; he dates the first issue as of 19 Ventôse (March 9, 1794). (The lead page of No. 243 has "Le 28 Ventôse" written in ink on its surface, which probably means the issue was examined on that date.)

27. Caron, *Paris pendant la Terreur*, 187, 205; Schmidt, *Tableaux de la Révolution*, II, No. 202, p. 146.

28. *Journal de la Montagne*, No. 121 (March 14, 1794), 961; *Moniteur*, XIX, No. 177 (March 17, 1794), 711; Buchez and Roux, eds., *Histoire parlementaire*, XXXI, 335–36. All for the session of the Jacobins, 22 Ventôse.

29. Schmidt, *Tableaux de la Révolution*, II, No. 201, p. 143.

gation's visit to the Jacobins, where, he confessed, they had experienced "an unfavorable moment."[30] Momoro read the second number of the new *Ami du peuple*, containing Ronsin's "hypocrites of humanity" speech that he had placarded throughout the city. Under the guise of reviving Marat's portrait of a patriotic informer of Brissotins, the lead article spoke of "a new coalition, less bold in its language [than the former Brissotins], but no less hypocritical, no less perfidious in its schemes."[31] Albertine Marat's letter, published in the same number and reproaching the Cordeliers for not signing the articles published under their individual names, aroused a long discussion. She accused them of cowardice, as we have seen, and contrasted their behavior with that of her brother, who, she wrote, always signed his work, even in the stormiest of times. It was finally decided to continue publishing the journal under the sponsorship of the whole society, rather than under individual responsibility.[32]

The session continued and turned to a discussion of attacks on patriots and details of the *journées* of August 10 and May 31. The need for continued surveillance was agreed upon. Hébert was applauded for demanding "to tear away the veil" behind which unnamed persons were persecuting the patriots who had saved the Republic. The members then decided to present to the Convention an address outlining the club's activities since May 31; responsibility for the address fell to a commission established three days before and composed of Hébert, Momoro, Ronsin, and Chenaux.

Delegates from section Marat's popular society, Amis du peuple, complained that they had been subpoenaed to appear before the Revolutionary Tribunal. The section had named a commission to ask the Convention to annul its law of 16 Ventôse (introduced by Barère), which aimed at discouraging antigovernment activity like the veiling of the Rights of Man, placarding the city, and other such subversive acts. There was much opposition to lifting the veil in some sections, especially in that of Champs-Elysées. Jean Baptiste Lubin, president of the general assembly, asked the protesters to have patience because he was sure that in a few days there would be a purge in the Conven-

30. Louis Barthélemy Chenaux was a member of the General Council and secretary of the Cordeliers. He was a lawyer by profession. Chenaux was to be acquitted in the trial of the Hébertistes. Caron, *Paris pendant la Terreur*, V, 248n2.

31. *L'Ami du peuple*, No. 244, 17 Ventôse, an II (the date of the Ronsin article as originally published), in Lc 2 227, bis, BN.

32. *Ibid.*; Caron, *Paris pendant la Terreur*, V, 244–45.

tion of those who opposed the insurrection of May 31—that is, of the moderates. Others thought that Fouquier-Tinville was preparing the moderates' arrest, but after one of the delegates was interrogated by the public prosecutor he protested angrily to his comrades: "We have been duped! It is we who are accused!"[33]

Momoro assured the society's delegates that their interrogation was directed at learning about the subversive posters discovered in Les Halles and that he, too, had been examined by the Tribunal, adding that he had, in turn, questioned the interrogators, asking them if they intended to prosecute the most devoted patriots. Still, he insisted that it was the moderate faction that sought to divide the Jacobins and the Cordeliers, that blamed the Cordeliers for causing famine in Paris, and that was plotting against section Marat and its president (himself). A wave of panic seized the Cordeliers who had not known about these subpoenas. It was then that Hébert asked and received confirmation from the club that he had never spoken against Robespierre during the session of 14 Ventôse.[34] It was a naïve effort to undo the damage. In less than forty-eight hours he was to be arrested.

The last issue of the *Père Duchesne*, No. 355, sharply attacked the moderates for opposing revolutionary decrees aimed at "aristocrats and conspirators." It advised republicans to carry out the laws of the *maximum* and the confiscation of suspects' property. Once again Hébert blamed the "moderates" for "staying the hand of the people" from finishing off the "traitors," and for thereby encouraging a civil war. These "new Brissotins," he wrote, were undermining the government in order to seize control of it and to create their own Committees: "Those who preach moderantism are your greatest enemies." The sans-culottes must rally against the conspirators and never allow the Republic to take a single step backward, he concluded.[35]

33. See Avenel, *Cloots*, II, 412, citing *Catalogue Charavay*, 411 n 1, for Lubin's remarks. Avenel is sarcastic, calling Robespierre "the incorruptible Myopic (short-sighted person), the god of moral government."

34. *Ibid.*; Schmidt, *Tableaux de la Révolution*, II, 147–48; Tuetey, *Répertoire général*, X, No. 2360; Soboul, *Sans-Culottes*, 749–50. Soboul says that Momoro knew better than to cite the decree of 16 Ventôse as an explanation for the interrogations undergone by members of section Marat. Furthermore, he interprets Boucheseiche's report on Momoro as embarrassing to Momoro because of his attempts to avoid answering the Tribunal by putting questions, in turn, to its members.

35. Hébert concluded his appeal: "Jurons donc, f . . . , la mort des modérés, comme celle des royalistes et des aristocrates. De l'union, du courage, de la conscience, et tous

"Between the moderates' resistance and the popular movement, the Committees of the government, prisoners of their contradictions, did not dare to choose, conscious as they were that this choice risked the destruction of the fragile social equilibrium upon which their action rested," wrote Soboul. Concerned as the government was with national defense, it contented itself with denouncing both factions. But it could not postpone the confrontation after the offensive of the Cordeliers in mid-Ventôse.[36]

During the night of March 10, Fouquier-Tinville reported to the Committee of Public Safety, where Billaud-Varenne, Saint-Just, Barère, and the ailing Robespierre awaited him. He was told to prepare charges against Hébert, Vincent, Ronsin, and Momoro. "What!" he exclaimed in surprise. "The Parisian authorities, the war office, the department, the sans-culotte army, the Commune, in one word, the Revolution?" Who said anything about Pache, Hanriot, or Lhuillier (Lulier)? replied the Committee: "We're talking about the Hébertistes." When Fouquier objected that there was no evidence against them, Saint-Just ordered: "Amalgamate." Now the prosecutor understood, but when he demanded written orders, Billaud-Varenne answered for the Committee that such an order could not be given in writing. Fouquier insisted, however, that he would have to wait for Saint-Just's report before proceeding—to which Saint-Just impatiently agreed.[37]

Evidently the Committee of Public Safety had decided to arrest the four Hébertistes as a way of balancing the four Indulgents (Chabot, Fabre d'Eglantine, Jean Julien of Toulouse, and Joseph Delaunay) involved in the scandal of the Indies Company. As described in Desmoulins' journal, Fouquier was told to invent a story of Vincent's meeting the Dutch banker de Kock and to employ Hanriot to arrest him. Apparently Hanriot was less than willing to do this, but the Committee had a secret weapon. It seems that Hanriot had been outlawed by the Girondin-led Convention on May 31, just prior to the successful insurrection. "This decree had never been reported," the

---

nos ennemis seront à *quia*, f . . . " (Let us swear, then, f——, to the death of moderates, like that of royalists and aristocrats. Unity, courage, firmness, and all our enemies will be reduced to nothingness, f——). *Père Duchesne*, No. 355.

36. Soboul, *Sans-Culottes*, 751–52.

37. Avenel, *Cloots*, II, 413 and, citing the *Procès de Fouquier*, 413n1. The letter to Fouquier-Tinville summoning him to the Committee on 23 Ventôse is in Tuetey, *Répertoire général*, X, No. 2210.

Committee told him "calmly." Hanriot had to submit, and Fouquier was powerless to resist the orders of the Committee of Public Safety even if he had desired to do so.[38]

The following day, without waiting for Saint-Just's report, Fouquier launched proceedings against the insurgents of section Marat for their demarche in the Commune on March 6. There is some evidence that Bonaparte was offered Hanriot's command but refused it.[39]

When Momoro accused Fouquier of attacking the Cordeliers, Fouquier admitted it was true. Yet the Cordeliers did nothing to mobilize support. They were repudiated in the Jacobins, even though the presidents of both clubs had exchanged a fraternal embrace. The members of various popular societies did not want to hear Hébert's justification on the charge of hoarding. In short, the Cordeliers seemed to be demoralized and paralyzed.

Saint-Just gave his report on "the foreign conspiracy" in the midst of profound attention "often interrupted by the most lively applause." He began by accusing "the pretenders to the name of Marat" of being hypocrites playing a false game of patriotism, and of being in the pay of foreign powers. "Whoever conspires must dissimulate," he declared. Thus, "One must not judge either by deeds or by words" (how, then, were they to be judged, one wonders). At the same time he attacked the Indulgents as contributing to the same goal of destroying the Republic. One claims the revolution is complete, the other that it has not reached its high point, he charged. Among his proposals adopted by the Convention was the death penalty for anyone attacking the security and dignity of the Convention. The Convention also gave a broad definition of *traitors*, including under this heading "corrupters of public opinion" and those who prevented "necessities from arriving in Paris"—charges that were to be leveled at the Hébertistes during their trial.[40]

The Cordeliers had no reply to Saint-Just's charges except to appeal to the conscience of the governing committees. But Saint-Just un-

38. Avenel, *Cloots*, II, 415–16, says that Hanriot swore vengeance even though he could not resist at the moment. Fouquier-Tinville informed the Convention of the arrests of Ronsin, Vincent, Hébert, Momoro, Ducroquet, General Laumur, and "Knoff" (de Kock); *Moniteur*, XIX, No. 176 (March 16, 1794), 706.

39. Avenel, *Cloots*, cites the *Mémoires* of Lucien Bonaparte for this statement, 417n1.

40. Aulard, *Jacobins*, V, 682. AP, LXXXVI, 434–42; B&R, XXXI, 336–58; Barante, *Histoire de la Convention nationale*, IV, 127–28.

loosed a campaign of slander aimed at destroying them totally. The government used a journal called *Le Sappeur Sans-Culotte* to counter Hébert's *Père Duchesne* and mixed accusations and threats with promises in order to confuse and undermine the support of the Cordeliers leaders. For a brief time it appeared that the Indulgents would take advantage of this turn of events, and even the royalists rallied. But the government struck back at the Dantonistes. It interrogated Legendre on 25 Ventôse (March 15, 1794) and issued an arrest warrant the following day for Chabot and his friends implicated in the Indies Company affair. On March 17 it struck against Marie Jean Hérault de Sechelles (a "moderate" member of the Committee of Public Safety) and arrested Chaumette as well.

After Fouquier-Tinville informed the Convention (March 15) that he had ordered the arrests of Vincent, Hébert, Momoro, and Ronsin, Robespierre rose to denounce the Cordeliers by contrasting the "old" club with the current one, thus undermining its leadership further.[41] Furthermore, he appealed to "all good citizens" to rally around the Convention. "All the factions ought to perish by the same blow," he declared, and he called on the sectionnaires to "stifle the voice of spokesmen, mercenaries subsidized by the coalition of [foreign] powers." Couthon followed by attacking "the conspirators" under the guise of wanting to place "morality, justice, and virtue" on the Convention's agenda. Conspirators can be recognized by their physiognomy, Couthon assured his audience. All of them have a haggard eye, a dismayed appearance, a hangdog look, and so on.

Barère added that the "conspiracy" had been traced to the armies as well and that some three hundred witnesses had already been heard, all pointing to a foreign plot. Then he asked: "What should one think in seeing these men of large mustaches, with long sabers, insulting good citizens, and, especially, the representatives of the people, and staring at them as if to say: If you dare open your mouth to utter a single word, I'll exterminate you? This is what I've seen with my own eyes. (Several voices: That's right, we've seen it also.)"[42] At

41. Robespierre called for an extraordinary session of the Jacobins (on the morrow), to discuss "a frightful plot against the Convention and against the Jacobins." Couthon followed him and declared that "those who believe themselves to be more patriotic than a Jacobin of '89 are aristocrats." Aulard, *Jacobins*, V, 681.

42. Berville and Barrière, eds., *Collection des mémoires relatifs à la Revolution française*, 218–20, 223; *AP*, LXXXVI, 490; *Journal de la Montagne*, No. 120 (March 13, 1794), 989; B&R, XXXI, 358–59; Barante, *Histoire de la Convention nationale*, IV, 133–35; *AP*, LXXXVI, 500–503 and "Pièces Annexes," 512, for Couthon's report.

LE SAPPEUR
SANS-CULOTTE.

GRANDE COLÈRE
DU PEUPLE,

Contre l'infâme PÈRE DUCHESNE et ses complices, qui vouloient faire sortir de leur cage les Louveteaux du Temple, donner la clef des champs à tous les conspirateurs détenus dans Paris, égorger les membres de la Convention Nationale, et proclamer pour roi le fils du tyran Capet.

C'EN est fait ; le jour de la vérité est enfin arrivé, le Peuple ne sera plus duppe de ses sacrés

A

The government lent support to *Le Sappeur Sans-Culotte*, a sheet that crudely parodied Hébert and his *Père Duchesne*.

the same time Fouquier and René François Dumas, the judge who was to preside at the trial of the accused Hébertistes, were told to quash any charges against Pache, Hanriot, and others who could be separated from the Cordeliers.[43]

What was Robespierre's personal role in destroying the Cordeliers? He had recovered his health by March 9 and was back at his post in the Committee. His spy in the Cordeliers, a man named Gravier, a juror on the Revolutionary Tribunal, had written to him that "they [Hébertistes] have profited by your illness to prepare their plots. I know that they fear your health which can uncover their perfidious conspiracy and their insurrection." One Souberbielle, a surgeon and an intimate of Robespierre's, reported to him that he had overheard Ronsin declare there was only one way to save the Republic, and that was to destroy all its enemies. Ronsin allegedly added that the Jacobins were getting soft and were supporting the Indulgents. The cartloads of the condemned on their way to the guillotine were arousing pity in the public even for enemies of the people. There was only one way out, Souberbielle quoted Ronsin as saying, and that was to finish with all enemies by one quick blow and then to bring an end to the revolutionary government. Robespierre, "with trembling lips," is said to have replied to all this: "Eh! what! always more blood! The Revolutionary Tribunal hasn't shed enough?" Then, after calming down, he declared: "It has been a long time since I've attacked them [the Hébertistes], for it's always me that people place in the breach. All right! I shall dedicate myself yet again. I have sacrificed my life for the people; I shall continue to the very end."[44]

Robespierre did continue "to the very end," of course—an end that embraced his own faction and himself. Before this happened, however, the sans-culotte movement, as expressed by the Cordeliers, also came to an end. In light of what happened during the tragic days of Ventôse, it is surprising how naïve the Hébertistes were in misreading the signs that led to their arrest. Some three hundred witnesses were being interrogated by the public prosecutor in prepara-

43. Avenel, *Cloots*, II, 425, 435–36, 437–38, 440–41; Barante, *Histoire de la Convention nationale*, IV, 129, 130–31. Avenel describes Saint-Just as giving his report "coldly, impassively, governmentally." As for the Cordeliers' appeal to the "conscience" of the government, Avenel holds that the politics of the latter could only tolerate those "whose consciences were mute."

44. Herlaut, *Ronsin*, 225–26, citing Léonard Gallois, *L'Histoire de la Convention nationale* (1835), VI, 266, 267.

tion for the coming trial of the Cordeliers leaders, and the latter still had not made a forthright repudiation of their fatal session of 14 Ventôse. They were still vacillating and straining to give an impossible explanation for having uttered the word *insurrection*.

If their pledge to Saint-Just to tone down their attacks on the moderates was sincere, this was surely the time to redeem it. Suppose Ronsin and Vincent had come forward and agreed to accept whatever posts the Committee of Public Safety had been ready to give them— assuming that Saint-Just had actually made such an offer—would this have changed the situation? It is possible, providing their opponents also had been willing to bring the factional dispute to an end. The Committee of Public Safety might have been appeased—for the moment, at least. Barring such a concession, it was inevitable that the Convention and its Committees would not allow, and could not allow, the disruption of political life to continue.

As for Robespierre's role in the suppression of the Cordeliers, it is doubtful that he could have forgiven Hébert's attack on his politics. Robespierre's politics, after all, were those of the Convention. The charge of "moderation" against him was, thus, more than a personal accusation. Once the fatal words had been spoken by Hébert, the pressure of public opinion condemning him made it convenient and relatively easy for the government to suppress him and his faction. Here again the Cordeliers leaders exhibited an inexcusable naïveté. Still, an unresolved question was whether the Commune and some of the sections would be firm in supporting the government or rally to the Cordeliers and their imprisoned spokesmen. For despite everything, the Commune's members must have recognized that the arrest of the Cordeliers leaders threatened them as well.

6

The Arrests and the Sans-Culottes

The arrest of the Hébertistes astounded the public. Yet a few days before the government acted, irrefutable proof existed that the Convention enjoyed overwhelming support in the sections and popular societies of Paris. A police action taken by the deputies against their alleged enemies was bound, therefore, to find firm support in the popular movement. Except for section Marat, no assembly endorsed the tentative initiative of the Cordeliers. On the contrary, the continuous offerings of saltpeter and warm resolutions of support presented by the sections—including section Marat—assured the Convention of the sans-culottes' loyalty.

This loyalty can be demonstrated by following the actions, proposals, and decisions of the sections and popular societies. The popular society of section Lepeletier, for example, resolved on 17 Ventôse (March 7, 1794), to go en masse to the Convention and pledge its support against all enemies. Three days later section Arsenal deposited 1,700 pounds of saltpeter, an "emblem of its zeal." Then came section Brutus, whose spokesman denounced moderation as "counterrevolution" and at the same time condemned "false patriots and intriguers" who wanted to rise against the government—an obvious allusion to the Cordeliers.[1]

Numerous sectional assemblies witnessed attacks on former signers of conservative petitions as well as on "egoists and royalists." Whistles and shouts interrupted moderate spokesmen, and there were demands that only sans-culottes be elected to civil committees. In Gravilliers some two thousand persons assembled in the former

---

1. Section Arsenal, in C 290, pl. 990, p. 16, AN; *Section de Brutus. Adresse à la Convention Nationale* (Paris, March 10, 1974), in Lb 40 1755, BN. The spokesman for section Brutus declared, "It is time that the tree of moderantisme, which sought to carry out a counterrevolution by a humane policy, be cut down to its very roots." The delegation deposited two thousand pounds of saltpeter; *Moniteur*, XIX, No. 171 (March 11, 1794), 667.

church, St. Nicolas des Champs, where Jacques Roux had preached shortly after arriving in Paris, and now renamed a Temple of Reason; sentiment in favor of the Mountain was strong. In some sections patriotic hymns were sung. In the popular society of section Guillaume Tell a spokesman declaimed energetically against Hébert. The society went on record as disapproving Hébert's "counterrevolutionary diatribe." Dugas revealed that people had applauded several sections for denouncing the Cordeliers, and said he hoped that others would follow their example.[2] Bacon concluded that all Paris was tranquil and gay.

Despite Bacon's evaluation, other police reports reveal that bitter divisions existed in some sections. One dangerous rumor blamed Chaumette and Hébert for causing shortages in order to profit from the discontent, and then using this discontent to launch their insurrection. Some sections sent delegations to the Convention demanding that the guilty be punished and voicing indignation at the call for an insurrection by the Cordeliers. In section Homme Armé there was a dispute as to whether the *Père Duchesne* should be read. Some favored it, but others objected that its language was not fit for the young to hear—meaning, no doubt, that Hébert's political language was unfit for some adults to hear as well. Jarousseau, the police spy who reported this debate, concluded that it proved "there were two parties" in the section. "The worst thing is that each section has people that it prefers, so that one is for Hébert, the other for Danton, still another for the Cordeliers, another for the Jacobins," wrote Rolin on March 11, 1794.

Two days later Bacon revealed that the popular society of section Amis de la Patrie was "very numerous" as it enthusiastically applauded Saint-Just's report on the Hébertistes. In the society of section Bon-Conseil, after the rejection for membership of a carpenter named Léonard, criticism of clubbistes for their arrogant behavior was heard. This complaint was similar to the one the Jacobins had leveled against affiliates of the Cordeliers. In the popular society of section Droits de l'Homme a numerous gathering criticized a wine merchant for sending his product to Lille, thus depriving his own customers. He justified his action, however, in light of "the bad

---

2. Section Faubourg du Nord to the National Convention, in C 295, pl. 991, p. 3, AN; Caron, *Paris pendant la Terreur*, V, 197–98, 199, 200, 251; Soboul and Monnier, *Répertoire de personnel sectionnaire*, 388.

news" that an insurrection would take place in the capital.[3] Thus, despite the support manifested by the sections and popular societies for the Convention, there was uneasiness, evidently, that an uprising could still break out.

Certain proposals made in several sections and popular societies could have disquieted other merchants, as well as the government. A delegation from section Finistère and one from the popular society of section Lazowski, after presenting their contribution of saltpeter to the Convention, demanded that the Revolutionary army be unleashed against profiteers.[4] A spokesman from Bonne-Nouvelle, after praising the Convention for destroying "the noble and priestly aristocracy," proposed that the government crush "the mercantile aristocracy," whom together with "the rich" he blamed for shortages. The general assembly then resolved to exclude merchants from all public posts and ordered all citizens to buy from retailers only.[5] The popular society of section Observatoire, Vertus républicaines, demanded price controls on chicken, meat, and game, while that of section Mont Blanc wanted supervision of butchers to prevent the wealthier citizens from buying up the meat. Mont Blanc also endorsed the proposal to use the Revolutionary army to provision Paris.[6] On March 12 the popular society of section République decided to annul the certificates of civic conduct of all priests and merchants. Obviously the "civil peace," which the government and the Jacobins promoted, was in danger of being disrupted.

There was enough discontent caused by shortages to be exploited

3. Caron, *Paris pendant la Terreur*, V, 224, 225, 242, 267–68, 269; *AP*, LXXXVI, 321–22; *Moniteur*, XIX, No. 172 (March 14, 1794), 685. Section Montagne resolved that it would not "rise" unless called on by "the sacred Mountain." Under the present circumstances, stated its spokesman, an insurrection would benefit only aristocrats, nobles, suspects, and intriguers.

4. *AP*, LXXXVI, 294; *Moniteur*, XIX, No. 172 (March 12, 1794), 672. Among other sections presenting saltpeter to the Convention and testifying to their support were sections Montreuil, Bonnet Rouge, Réunion, Popincourt, and Indivisibilité. Soboul, *Sans-Culottes*, 753.

5. See *Maurin, employé au départment des affaires etrangères, à ses concitoyens* (Paris, n.d), in AD I 55, AN. Maurin was accused of making the motion adopted by section Bonne-Nouvelle and of his alleged influence on and by Hébert. As a result he was expelled from the Jacobins.

6. *Moniteur*, XIX, No. 176 (March 16, 1794), 706. But *AP*, LXXXVI, 498, reports that the resolution was greeted by protests and was rejected. See *Moniteur*, XIX, No. 172 (March 12, 1794), 669, for the popular societies in sections Observatoire and Mont Blanc.

and linked to political demands by a determined revolutionary party. The Cordeliers made no effort, however, to win over the sections by sending agitators and spokesmen into their assemblies or popular societies. Needless to say, even had this been done it would not have guaranteed their success. The Great Committees had the prestige, the finances, the control of revolutionary committees in the sections, and the means to stock the markets (as they were to do after the arrest of the Cordeliers). Given the political sentiments of the sans-culottes in the sections, it is doubtful if the Cordeliers' delegates would have been allowed to speak. In any case, the Cordeliers were isolated and vulnerable to the attack launched against them.[7]

The support of local authorities and the sections encouraged the government, finally, to strike at the Cordeliers. On March 6, Fouquier-Tinville spoke of conspiracy to subvert the Convention, showing as evidence two posters he had removed that morning.[8] On March 9 Hanriot exhorted his comrades to be vigilant against "those who want anarchy and the dissolution of society," an obvious reference to the Cordeliers. The committee of surveillance of the Paris Department also warned citizens against incendiary placards calling for insurrection. "Those who talk of insurrection are traitors who want to destroy Liberty by your own hands," it proclaimed.[9] Any placard calling for insurrection could easily have been "amalgamated" with a royalist poster.

The growing pressure against the Hébertistes persuaded Bouchotte to ask Vincent to resign from the War Department. The minister of war praised Vincent's zeal but told him bluntly that his imprudence made it necessary for him to seek other employment. Bouchotte added that he was willing to support him in another position where his patriotism could be useful.[10] Nevertheless, Vincent's removal from a key position would have weakened the Cordeliers had they pressed for an uprising. Their arrests during the night and early morning hours of March 14 made Bouchotte's request academic. Clearly, the Committee of Public Safety also enjoyed the support of

7. Soboul, *Sans-Culottes*, 757, points out that while the Cordeliers were stressing the politics of the crisis, the sans-culottes emphasized the effort to obtain provisions. Thus there was an absence of liaison between the two parties, which put the Cordeliers in a hazardous position vis-à-vis the government.

8. *Moniteur*, XIX, No. 170 (March 10, 1794), 659.

9. Tuetey, *Répertoire général*, X, Nos. 1929, 1956.

10. Tuetey, *Répertoire général*, X, No. 2325.

the Convention. When Couthon reported that the time had arrived to change the membership of the Committee, the Convention voted unanimously to renew its powers and composition.[11]

Although the vast majority were not about to challenge the government authorities, many Parisians refused to believe the newspaper hawkers as they shouted out the charges against the Cordeliers. Le Harivel reported on March 14 that a hawker who announced the arrest of "Père Duchesne" was taken into custody by an unknown supporter of the Hébertistes, who accused him of disseminating false news. But when the man tried to bring up the newspaper vendor before the revolutionary committee of section Montagne, he was himself arrested and taken to the guardhouse, "to the great satisfaction" of the onlookers, who had gathered in great number, wrote the police observer. Bacon recounted the same day that near the café Conti a group was discussing Hébert's arrest when a young national guardsman interrupted to say that the act had astonished many, especially the patriots. "If this continues, farewell to Liberty, and all is f—ked." Everyone immediately retired without a word.[12] Elsewhere, there were those who felt certain that Hébert and his comrades would be released after a trial. A gendarme quoted his lieutenant, a member of the Cordeliers, as saying that Hébert "will walk out with the greatest glory possible." The gendarme too was sure that Hébert would be released.[13]

The same day Pourvoyeur depicted a feeling that was becoming quite common among the crowds discussing the affair—the mistrust of individuals who mentioned or displayed their patriotism. People were especially astonished at the arrest of Chaumette. Someone recalled that Pétion, the Girondin former mayor of Paris, had also "fooled the people." As for Hébert, anyone who preached insurrection was a dangerous man, another said. Contradicting what his own colleagues had reported, Pourvoyeur observed that in general, Hébert had never been perceived as an intriguer or a dubious individual. The spy added that people were also astonished at Momoro's arrest because he had always been regarded as a patriot.[14]

Bacon's March 14 report mentioned a gardener who expressed an-

11. *Moniteur*, XIX, No. 174 (March 14, 1794), 686.
12. Caron, *Paris pendant la Terreur*, V, 300–301, 288.
13. Tuetey, *Répertoire général*, XI, No. 43. Antoine Edmond Bertier was the gendarme who cited the remarks of Lieutenant Caillet.
14. Caron, *Paris pendant la Terreur*, V, 305, 306.

ger at the arrest of Vincent; a woman responded that one should not trust "false patriots" but only the Convention, that without the latter the Republic was "finished." She told him to read Saint-Just's report and he would "tremble at the plot of these scoundrels." Bacon stated that the crowd approved her remarks and shouted "Long live the Convention!" before dispersing. But Le Breton, the same day, revealed that whereas one group expressed its dislike of Hébert, another declared that the reason he was detested was that he had enlightened the people on their true interests. "However," Le Breton admitted, "for the moment the majority does not hold this view."[15] The following day he reported that in a cabaret the wives of "the little people, I want to say, of the true sans-culottes," spoke of "Père Duchesne's" arrest. One decried the betrayal of Hébert and asked what would become of them when they were betrayed by people they trusted. Another responded that after this new discovery of treason they should trust only the Convention because it spared no one.[16]

While some sectional societies and individual sans-culottes were anxious, wondering what would happen to their confreres, many others were completely disoriented. "Is it possible," asked a sans-culotte, "that a patriot like Père Duchesne farts on our hand?"[17] The police spy Hanriot reported on March 15 that Hébert's arrest had brought joy to all Paris. People had begun to realize, he wrote, that in a revolution individuals must not be idolized, and that he who appeared to support the cause most ardently was only "an aristocrat in his heart." Furthermore, Hanriot overheard a man declare that he was not surprised at Hébert's arrest, since his journal proved he was an "ultrarevolutionary" who, in denouncing profiteers, had only discouraged supplies from reaching Paris so as to mount an insurrection.

Two days later Bacon revealed that the popular societies and general assemblies of sections Réunion, Indivisibilité, and Arsenal, as well as faubourg Saint-Antoine, were all anti-Hébertiste and pro-Convention. But in a café of bourg l'Egalité, outside Paris, a laborer told his two companions that "the imprisonment of 'Père Duchesne' has astounded everyone." More revealing was the report of Prévost (27 Ventôse), who overheard the following statement: "They say also

15. *Ibid.*, 287–88, 300.
16. *Ibid.*, 311.
17. Cited by Soboul, *Sans-Culottes*, 762, no reference given.

that if Marat were still alive at this moment he would have been indicted and perhaps guillotined, because he cried out often in favor of
the people, and that he was no less than a second Père Duchesne,
that is to say, Hébert." The next day Le Harivel heard the same kind
of conviction expressed by unknown spokesmen: "Marat is now regarded as the chief of the conspiracy just discovered. He was, people
say, in the public arena, one of the warmest partisans of the Cordeliers Club, of which he was the founder. He had always supported
Hébert, Momoro, Vincent, and Ronsin, and it is the latter who honored him so greatly." [18]

Thus, although much of the public looked to the Convention and
its Committees to lead the way, some individuals and groups realized
the danger posed by the arrests. A refugee from Liège asked whether
the imprisoned Cordeliers were guilty or simply victims "of a plot."
"There would no longer be time to denounce the mistake when it was
recognized," the man warned, and "yet if they were innocent, what
greater satisfaction could there be for our enemies than to see them
perish!" [19] Many who did not challenge the charges leveled against
the imprisoned Cordeliers by Saint-Just nevertheless were not convinced that the Hébertistes were traitors and assassins.

Fouquier-Tinville, meanwhile, was "amalgamating." He informed
the Convention that the Dutch banker de Kock had been imprisoned
in the Conciergerie. He added that he had learned that Ronsin, Hébert, their wives, and many others had met daily in a certain house,
thereby arousing the suspicions of the surveillance committee. Testimony was being taken regarding the proposed insurrection in the
Cordeliers, he wrote; he asked for more agents. [20] The Committees
authorized him to hire as many assistants as necessary, but fearing a
sharp reaction to the arrests, also instructed Mayor Pache to take all
precautions necessary. [21] The Committee of General Security warned
the revolutionary committees of the sections to be vigilant and alert. [22]

---

18. Caron, *Paris pendant la Terreur*, V, 321, 322, 358, 360, 373, 391.

19. W 345, plaq. 676, p. 15, AN, cited by Soboul, *Sans-Culottes*, 763.

20. Fouquier-Tinville to the Committee of Public Safety regarding De Koff [sic],
March 15, 1794, in F7 4435, plaq. 7, p. 19, AN.

21. Aulard, *Actes du Comité de salut public*, XI, 690. The Committee ordered Pache to
report the same evening on the steps taken "to suppress the efforts of the malevolent."

22. Committee of General Security to revolutionary committees of the sections,
March 24, 1794, in AF II* 286, AN. The Committee of General Security asked the revolutionary committees to report daily everything that appeared of interest to them.

These precautions proved quite unnecessary because whatever the sentiments of their supporters, no one made an effort to demonstrate in favor of the imprisoned Cordeliers.

The extraordinary session of March 14 in the Jacobins, which met on Robespierre's call, heard Billaud-Varenne sharply denounce the Cordeliers' appeal for an insurrection. He accused Ronsin of being an agent of foreign powers, informing the enemies of France in Frankfurt of the approaching insurrection.[23] This charge was fabricated out of whole cloth. An unnamed person also accused Boulanger, the second-in-command, for his remarks in the Cordeliers Club on March 4 supporting Hébert: "Père Duchesne, fear nothing, we shall ourselves be the Pères Duchesne who will strike." At this point Robespierre recognized the danger of tarring patriots and supporters of the government with the same brush used against the Cordeliers. He quickly warned against this step.[24]

On March 16 Amar reported for the Committee of General Security on the arrests of François Chabot, Claude Basire, Joseph Delaunay, Jean Julien of Toulouse, and Fabre d'Eglantine—all involved in the Indies Company scandal. Both Robespierre and Billaud-Varenne spoke in favor of amending the report to state that the "conspirators" wanted to defame the Convention. Robespierre argued that only individuals were corrupt, not the Convention itself, a declaration incorporated in the amendment and adopted by the legislators with Amar's compliance.[25] The Montagnard leaders realized the danger of falling victim to the attack of the Indulgents on the Convention under the guise of striking at the "ultras"; indeed, a movement had already begun aimed at verbally assaulting the militants in the sections and the most devoted patriots who had nothing to do with the Cordeliers' demarche. The arrests in the Indies Company case were a signal that the government would not permit the Indulgents to use the fall of the Hébertistes as ammunition in a revived counteroffensive.

23. *Journal de la Montagne*, No. 123 (March 16, 1794), 986–87.

24. *Moniteur*, XIX, No. 178 (March 18, 1794), 719; Aulard, *Jacobins*, V, 683. Soboul, *Sans-Culottes*, 764n16, points out that, curiously enough, no one attacked Carrier, whose role on March 4 in the Cordeliers Club was far more important than that of Boulanger.

25. *Moniteur*, XIX, No. 178 (March 18, 1794), 723–24; *AP*, LXXXVI, 557, and "Discours non prononcé de Robespierre sur l'affaire Chabot," in "Pièces Annexes," 561–65. Among the sections present in the Convention were Bon-Conseil, Lepeletier, Mont Blanc, Panthéon-Français, Halle-au-Blé, Maison Commune, and Gravilliers. The last deposited its gift of saltpeter. *Journal de la Montagne*, No. 124 (March 17, 1794), 1007.

Both Guérin and Soboul are convinced that Mathiez was wrong when he wrote that the Cordeliers leaders were arrested "in the midst of general indifference."[26] The women who had been devoted to Hébert were especially upset. Boucheseiche had reported on March 4 that as they left the hall of the Cordeliers they were overheard exclaiming, "We will have our patriots in spite of the scoundrels who accuse them, and if it becomes necessary for the women to mix in, we shall." Pourvoyeur added on March 12 that Hébert enjoyed much support among women, and Rolin repeated the same observation on March 24 (4 Germinal). After the Hébertistes were executed Bacon reported that in a café frequented by "charcoal-burners, carters and others of the same class," he heard patrons disapprove of the "indignant" conduct of the executioner.[27]

Some evidence exists that Collot d'Herboise and Billaud-Varenne were also involved with the Hébertistes. Addressing the Jacobins April 12, Collot claimed that "the conspirators" had threatened to assassinate those members of the Convention who stood in their way; on the other hand, they promised satisfaction to members who went along with them. He declared that "they sought to try out some terrible proposals . . . they promised them some high posts if they consented to carry out the projects of our enemies."[28] Charmont cited a court official named Villeneuve, who on March 26 said that when Billaud was told of the arrests he protested that he knew nothing of this conspiracy: "that having learned of this upon his arrival [in Paris], his arms fell from astonishment."[29] Obviously, if Billaud-Varenne were suspected of having links with the Cordeliers, he would not have been informed of the Committees' plan to arrest the suspects. The following day, March 27, in a café de la Société, a man declared that the arrest of Collot had been confirmed at the Tuileries.[30]

Did the original charges given to Fouquier-Tinville implicate Mayor Pache? According to the *Procès de Fouquier*, the Committee denied that

26. Mathiez, *Révolution française*, III, 156; Guérin, *Lutte de classes*, II, 112; Soboul, *Sans-Culottes*, 764.

27. Caron, *Paris pendant la Terreur*, V, 293, quoting the women. Pourvoyeur, Rolin, and Bacon are *ibid.*, VI, 42, V, 89, and VI, 118.

28. Aulard, *Jacobins*, VI, 66.

29. Caron, *Paris pendant la Terreur*, VI, 121.

30. *Ibid.*, 140, for Bacon's report. Noting that both Billaud and Collot owed their appointments to Hébertisme, Guérin, *Lutte de classes*, II, 108, comments of the rumors surrounding the two that "where there is smoke there must be fire."

Pache was to be indicted. But some historians and memorialists are convinced that the Committee of Public Safety dropped the charges against him after first agreeing to arrest him along with the Cordeliers leaders. Senart, an agent of the Committee of General Security, wrote that the papers seized in Pache's home were compromising, "but these documents must have been almost immediately destroyed." When the trial of the Hébertistes opened, a police spy cited Westermann's testimony that Pache was slated to be "the grand judge in the conspiracy."[31]

Mme Roland said of Pache that he "assumed the mask of the greatest modesty. . . . Politically, he is the Tartuffe of Molière." He was like a modern bureaucrat in knowing how to appoint his own creatures to the offices he controlled. Although a progressive Jacobin, he was a fierce defender of private property and a resolute adversary of the Enragés, wrote Guérin. Moreover, according to Mme Roland, he was well-off after acquiring national property. Like Claude Emmanuel Dobsent—"the man of May 31"—and Barère, he seems to have enjoyed a mysterious protection. He survived not only the fall of the Hébertistes but the Revolution itself, living on to age seventy-seven in 1823. Guérin believes that "the constant indulgence" shown him was an expression of "the gratitude" owed him by "the bourgeoisie."[32]

The police spy Soulet gave quite a different reason, writing that Pache, Bouchotte, Hanriot, and Santerre were spared in order to "save the other greatly guilty" parties.[33] Later, the deputy Laurent Lecointre reproached Billaud, Collot, and Barère for canceling the order to arrest Pache.[34] Thus, enough evidence existed to have impli-

31. Gabriel Jérôme Senart, *Révélations puisées dans les cartons des comités de salut public et de sûreté générale; ou, Mémoires inédits de Senart* (2d ed.; Paris, 1824), cited by Paul Sainte-Claire Deville, *La Commune de l'An II: Vie et mort d'une assemblée révolutionnaire* (Paris, 1946), 160n2. Deville gives no page reference for his remarks. These and other "revelations" of Senart's cannot be accepted at face value. They are largely self-serving, and in some cases absurd. Senart seeks to place the members of the two Committees in the worst light possible.

Schmidt, *Tableaux de la Révolution,* II, 185.

32. J. F. Barrière, ed., *Mémoires particulières de Mme Rolland* (Paris, 1847), 387, 392, in a section entitled "Portraits et Anecdotes"; Guérin, *Lutte de classes,* II, 107. Gérard Walter, editor of Michelet's *Histoire,* in the section "Personnages," II, 1518–19, also believes that Pache was "seriously compromised" at the trial of the Hébertistes.

33. Caron, *Paris pendant la Terreur,* VI, 138.

34. *Dénonciation faite à la Convention nationale par Laurent Lecointre . . . ,* Article 11 ([Paris], 11 Fructidor II), in Le 38 2175, BN.

cated the mayor with the Cordeliers leaders. Indeed, as head of the municipality he could have been held responsible for the machinations, real or imagined, of the Hébertistes. If, then, he and his associates—Hanriot, Bouchotte, and Santerre—were not indicted, surely one reason was the government's need to retain ties to the sans-culottes. The war had not been won yet, and the Indulgents stood ready to take advantage of the situation, while behind them loomed the real counterrevolutionaries.

Although the public was shocked by the arrests, the sections and popular societies soon fell in line behind the Committees and the Convention. The general assembly of Guillaume Tell, reported by police spies on March 15 as being numerous, applauded the discovery of the "conspiracy."[35] Five days later Bacon reported that as a justice of the peace read a crowd Saint-Just's report, he was followed most attentively, in great silence. Water carriers sitting near the police observer declared that they had been fooled by those who had gained their confidence. Speakers stressed the need for unity as all shouted "Long live the Convention!" Still, Bacon admitted, there was a stormy session as someone accused the revolutionary committee of neglecting to enforce the law against butchers who sold meat to the rich illegally. Another speaker warned the crowd that "these people" were trying to take advantage of the "Hébert affair."

In section Contrat Social the assembly cried "Down with the scoundrels!" against the "conspirators" (although a few days later Bacon reported a more contentious session, in which some citizens were accused of not belonging to the section). In section Lombards similar opposition was manifested against the Hébertistes: some women were overheard saying that they never did have confidence in Hébert; others spoke of "new conspirators" in the section, saying that all would go to the scaffold. The speeches of Saint-Just and of Billaud-Varenne were applauded in section Maison Commune. Bacon added that the public spirit in the section was "revolutionary." In Panthéon-Français the general assembly heard a detailed report of "the conspiracy" amidst cries of indignation. It was reported that partisans of the arrested had gone from door to door soliciting help and that three of them had been jailed. One man urged the arrest of the "intriguers" who were seeking support for Hébert—proof that not everyone had embraced the assembly's enthusiasm for the Convention.

35. Schmidt, *Tableaux de la Révolution*, II, 156–57, 158.

Sections Temple and Muséum also expressed their hatred of "the conspirators," and Fontaine-de-Grenelle swore to stand united against them. Béraud revealed that the general assembly of section Temple applauded not only Saint-Just's report but even his attack on sectional societies. In Mutius Scaevola (Vincent's section) and in section Marat, Béraud added, the sessions were tranquil despite the government's fear of an "uprising." (This was not entirely true, as will be seen.) In Arsenal a gendarme who did not reside in the section was arrested for trying to make an unspecified motion (possibly in favor of the Cordeliers). In a café of this section, it was reported, someone insisted that Marat's portrait had been tossed into the muddy street, while another was sure the Convention was about to remove Marat's body from the Panthéon.

Some women were heard comparing Hébert to Pétion. Few believed Hébert was innocent, reported some police spies, who assured their superiors that the mass of people were quiet. Bacon revealed that in various cafés there were rumors that Santerre was to be arrested and that Hanriot was also compromised in the Hébert affair. People were also heard asking why Ronsin had planned "the operation" without consulting his general staff. Where had he intended to take his battalions? Other spies noted that in a café on rue Saint-Honoré people applauded "the letter" of Fouquier-Tinville to the Committee of Public Safety on the arrest of the Hébertistes. Everywhere, reported one spy, people were indignant because they had been fooled by Hébert and his friends. Now they were demanding vengeance. Some were convinced that "the conspirators" had sown famine and that harsh punishments must be meted out to them in order to end the shortages. Dugas observed the same support for the Convention on March 15 in sections Guillaume Tell, Halle-au-Blé, and Muséum.[36]

On March 16 police spies reported that "the conspiracy" was the subject of all conversation. The general opinion, they wrote, was against the Cordeliers leaders, and many in the populace felt that the guillotine was too good for the accused. All expressed their veneration of the Convention and the Committees. Despite this ferment,

36. Caron, *Paris pendant la Terreur*, V, 309–13, 315, 318–19, 425–26, 427–28, 429. In section Contrat Social a member declared, "We have arrived at the point where the rich must pay [their share], where it's necessary that he who has two plates should give one to him who has none." This was greeted with shouts of "Bravo!" and "Long live the Republic!" *Ibid.*, 310.

Paris was remarkably peaceful, the observers noted. Hanriot was rumored to have dined with the banker de Kock, and soldiers of the Revolutionary army were believed to be circulating in different uniforms. The public accepted the charge that the Hébertistes were responsible for the famine in the city, and that behind them was Pitt. In addition, Momoro was slandered with the accusations that he ate out of silver bowls and that 190,000 livres in specie had been found in his house, proof that he must have been the treasurer of the conspiracy. Although no one had spoken up in the general assemblies of sections Marat and Mutius Scaevola in favor of the Hébertistes the day before, some dozen or fifteen men had been arrested in Marat for proposing to march on the Convention. Popular societies had also come under attack as rumors circulated that their members shared the conspiracy with the Cordeliers. The police spies noted that before March 15 some persons had still defended the imprisoned Cordeliers, but since then they had feared to do so.[37]

On March 17 the cry that the guillotine was too good for the arrested Cordeliers was heard "universally," if one can believe the reports of the police spies. Everyone wanted a prompt judgment of the accused in order to show Europe that the French government was firmly resolved to crush all opposition. Most popular societies decided to renew their oaths of loyalty to the Convention at the next session. There was also talk that many members of civil and revolutionary committees were involved in the conspiracy and that a number of them who had been quite arrogant in the past were now trying to become popular by their new, "cringing conduct."[38] This groundswell against constituted authorities was not allowed to develop, however. The government could not afford to sacrifice its own local supporters and to encourage the Indulgents and counter-revolutionaries.

Béraud revealed on March 20 that lines in front of shops and in Les Halles were not as numerous as before the Hébertistes were arrested. The government had begun to supply the markets temporarily to gain public support and to strengthen its charge that the "conspirators" had caused the shortages. Républicaines révolutionnaires, the women's society founded by Claire Lacombe and Pauline Léon that in 1793

37. Schmidt, *Tableaux de la Révolution*, II, 151–52, 158–59, 160–62; Caron, *Paris pendant la Terreur*, V, 353. The men arrested in section Marat had made too much of a fuss in the general assembly, insisting that their fellow sectionnaires demand the release of "the oppressed" from the Convention.

38. Schmidt, *Tableaux de la Révolution*, II, 163.

had supported the Enragés, now came under attack. Some accused Lacombe of supporting the Cordeliers and declared that if the premises of her club were searched, even if no arms were found, there would surely be plenty of food hidden there. Others remarked that Hébert had sixty pounds of meat hoarded at home and blamed his section's revolutionary committee for testifying that only twenty-four pounds had been found.[39] It was evident that the government's propaganda was having its effect.

The man who was to work as the government's spy in the ranks of the Cordeliers leaders, Jean Baptiste Laboureau, proposed in the assembly of section Marat on March 16 that it furnish two defenders for Momoro; thus he was acting as a provocateur as well. Jean Etienne Brochet, a Jacobin and Cordelier on the section's civil and revolutionary committees, pointed out that such a motion was useless, since the court had appointed defenders for the accused. Wouarmé, a member of the General Council and serving as the section's secretary pro tem, also rose in opposition to the proposal. Although Momoro's supporters applauded Laboureau's rhetoric—such as his declaration that if Momoro's "innocent head fell," his own should fall also—when the vote came the assembly followed Brochet's advice, holding that it had full confidence in "the magistrates of the people"—quite a change from the resolution adopted on March 5, when the body had decided to march on the Convention. Defeated in the general assembly, Laboureau attempted to win over the section's popular society to the idea of appointing two defenders for Momoro. According to a witness, Jacques Thomas, a woodturner by trade, a member of the section's civil committee even heard Laboureau ask if the cannoneers could be relied on; again, he obviously was acting as an agent provocateur.[40]

The Cordeliers Club was helpless before the onslaught of the government. Immediately after the arrest of its leaders on March 14, it met under the provisional president, Louis Barthélemy Chenaux, a

39. Caron, *Paris pendant la Terreur*, V, 429–30.
40. Tuetey, *Répertoire général*, X, Nos. 2366, 2654, 2656; the latter item contains the carpenter André Dumas' testimony about Laboureau's remarks on heads falling. For a sketch of Brochet's revolutionary career, see Soboul and Monnier, *Répertoire de personnel sectionnaire*, 457–58. For information on Wouarmé's membership on the General Council, see Tuetey, *Répertoire général*, XI, No. 25. Because of his service on the Council, Wouarmé may have foreseen the danger of a demonstration before it and the Convention. Another Council member, one Laurent (not mentioned in Soboul and Monnier), stood with Wouarmé in opposing Laboureau's motion in section Marat.

lawyer, elected in the absence of the vice-president, Gobert. Chenaux announced that the Declaration of Rights had been violated anew, and to emphasize this pronouncement asked that the Declaration be read to the assembly. This act of "opposition" showed how impotent the society was now.[41] Its time of glory, when it had helped to overthrow the monarchy and expel the Girondins from the Convention, was over. In a few days its sessions would no longer be worth reporting in the press.

Jean Baptiste Ancard, a leading Cordelier, "listlessly" deplored the fate of his friends (he was to share it in a few days). Saint-Just's report, he declared, would destroy the most devoted patriots. How could the Cordeliers allow Collot d'Herbois to use such language without protest? he asked. Ancard then denounced a member present, Claude Prétot, a *huissier* by profession, who had attacked Hébert publicly as "a villain." A disturbance ensued as Prétot protested his patriotism. Chenaux interrupted him and demanded that he reply to the charge against him. Prétot rose and asked, "Isn't it true that the insurrection has been preached from this tribune?" The assembly cried out with a loud "No!" and he was expelled from the society. Shortly thereafter Prétot was to enjoy his revenge.

Chenaux then declared his astonishment that not a single Cordelier had expressed forcefully his support of the four leaders held in prison. Other speakers noted that a number of members who usually occupied the tribune were absent. "It's in time of crisis that one ought to show the most courage," one asserted. Several members testified that they knew the four as the most ardent patriots, innocent of the charges against them. Some thought of resistance, others of vengeance. When delegates of the fraternal society Amis du peuple, of

41. Details of the meeting as recounted in the following paragraphs are drawn mainly from Caron, *Paris pendant la Terreur*, V, 291–93 (Boucheseiche's report of March 14) and 344–45 (Grivel's report of March 16); *Moniteur*, XIX, No. 179 (March 19, 1794), 726–27; Schmidt, *Tableaux de la Révolution*, II, 153–55; and B&R, XXXI, 359–60. Boucheseiche quoted the women leaving the premises as saying that they would have their patriots despite the scoundrels who attack them, as cited above. He ended his report by stating that the Cordeliers did not believe in the charges leveled against the prisoners.

Tuetey, *Répertoire général*, X, No. 2521. A witness named Julie Capelet testified that she heard Ancard call the two Committees "tyrants," and that a carpenter from Saint Marcel by the name of Gautruche repeated this charge; *ibid.*, No. 2522. Ancard was arrested on March 16 for "provoking destruction of the national representation" and "conspiring against liberty"; *ibid.*, No. 2523.

section Marat, asked what was being done for the prisoners, they were told that the Cordeliers intended to dispatch a delegation to the public prosecutor—not the most militant act, it was seen. The revolutionary society of Hommes Libres, from section La Cité, sent a delegation to express alarm over the arrests and to "solidarize" itself with the Cordeliers. It was given the fraternal embrace by a grateful Chenaux.

Brochet then reported on Billaud-Varenne's slanderous attack in the Jacobins against the four Cordeliers, charging them with plotting to massacre prisoners, as well as the deputies of the Mountain. This recital was received with horror and disbelief. Mathurin Bouin, a justice of the peace, added that "the plotters" were accused of wanting to establish a regent over France. Boucheseiche, who reported this session of the Cordeliers at some length, wrote that the society was astonished. The Cordeliers could not believe in such atrocities and persisted in demanding that the public prosecutor hurry the trial, as they were convinced of their leaders' innocence.

Section Marat was as powerless as the Cordeliers. Rolin reported on March 16 that those in the section who had always opposed Momoro and his supporters found the arrests acceptable. He cited only one person who spoke up in Momoro's defense. But Brochet, who was obviously playing the government's game in the section, "enlightened" the gathering; since the government had appointed defenders for the accused, he said, and since the assembly trusted the magistrates, there was no need for such a measure as sending commissioners to the public prosecutor and the Committee of Public Safety. The meeting passed on to its order of business.[42]

Although the sections fell into line behind the Convention, several harbored staunch supporters of the arrested Cordeliers. That some individuals did speak out against congratulating the deputies for uncovering the "conspiracy" is an indication not only of their personal courage but of the fact that opposition indeed existed, in some sections, weak though it must have been. For instance, Le Harivel revealed on March 20 that in section Tuileries an unnamed citizen dissented from the resolution adopted by the general assembly to demonstrate its support of the Convention. The police spy noted with surprise that this man was not even censured by the assembly.[43]

42. Caron, *Paris pendant la Terreur*, V, 355–56.
43. *Ibid.*, 436.

In section Unité, Jean François Bereytter, a merchant in the paper trade who would be arrested after 9 Thermidor and the Prairial uprising, opposed sending congratulations. Among the charges brought against him in the Year III was his alleged hope to "press in [his] arms Vincent, Hébert, and the others" on the eve of their trial.[44] Guillaume Boulland of Finistère, a leading sans-culotte of the section with a long history of revolutionary activity, an elector of 1792, and member of the popular society Lazowski, also dissented. He was arrested in Floréal, Year II, for having defended Momoro, Vincent, and the others and for urging an insurrection "more terrible" than that of 1792.[45] In section République a motion was made to furnish cartridges and pikes—in order to free the imprisoned Cordeliers, evidently—but no practical steps were taken. René Corbin, a tailor who had participated in all the revolutionary demonstrations, was arrested in Floréal, Year II, as an Hébertiste. He was denounced by Léonard Bourdon on March 18, together with his colleague Victor Maurice Gaudet, also to be arrested in Floréal, Year II, as an Hébertiste. Both men held the office of justice of the peace and remained true to the Cordeliers leaders.[46]

Since the sections were now dominated by their revolutionary committees, with the latter under the control of the Committee of General Security, opposition to the central authorities proved difficult. The deposition of Deloche against Momoro in section Marat is eloquent testimony to this development. The popular societies were relatively freer than the general assemblies, and militants could still be heard because they enjoyed the support of their fellow patriots. Grivel reported on March 17, "One can believe they incite the people to wrest the guilty from the vengeance of the law." Two days later he revealed that friends of "the conspirators" still hoped to save them by winning over the majority of the jury.[47]

In the popular society called "Sans-culottes révolutionnaires du 31 mai," section Chalier, Jacques Montain Lambin, a health officer

44. Soboul and Monnier, *Répertoire de personnel sectionnaire*, 446; Tuetey, *Répertoire général*, XI, No. 63, where Bereytter is accused of staffing the revolutionary committee of the section.

45. Soboul and Monnier, *Répertoire de personnel sectionnaire*, 526–27.

46. *Ibid.*, 63.

47. Caron, *Paris pendant la Terreur*, V, 365, 407. A former *procureur* was asked what would happen to the prisoners. He recalled the experience of Marat, but when someone objected that the comparison was improper he said nothing. Grivel recommended that this man be watched. *Ibid.*, 408–409.

and founder of the club, was arrested on March 18 as a supporter of Chaumette. He had been a member of section Chalier's first revolutionary committee and one of the section's more active revolutionaries. He sported a Jacobin outfit, including the *bonnet rouge*, and boldly announced from the tribune that he knew Momoro was a good patriot. According to a witness, Lambin had also stated that should civil war break out, at least the Sans-culottes révolutionnaires would know their partisans, adding that it was "the aristocrats" who were happy with the arrest of the Cordeliers.[48]

In section Guillaume Tell, a witness later testified, a ferment bubbled up caused by "intriguers" who sought to influence the popular society concerning the innocence of Hébert and his friends. Among these was Jean Mathieu Brichet, an under secretary in the War Department and founder of the section's popular society. In September, 1793, the revolutionary committee had praised him for his firm republicanism and given him "the glorious title of *enragé maratiste.*" He was expelled from the Jacobins after Robespierre denounced him and was arrested on March 18 for defending Hébert.[49]

Boucheseiche reported on March 15 that Hébert's partisans had gone from door to door in section Panthéon-Français asking for support of Hébert and the others. The following day Pourvoyeur admitted that Hébert had a party among various groups who still defended him, and that rumors were circulating of an uprising to be launched by them on the day of his trial.[50] None of this was true. The Cordeliers who had sought to defend their leaders immediately after their arrest, and who had expelled Prétot for attacking Hébert, made a 180-degree turn less than forty-eight hours later. Members who had opposed the leadership of Momoro and his supporters and who had not dared speak up in opposition in the past now regained their voice. When a member demanded that in this time of crisis those who were absent should be expelled, he was opposed and his motion failed. Furthermore, the members now reversed themselves and restored Prétot's membership card, amidst applause. When someone suggested that the membership list of the conservative Sainte-Chapelle Society be read so that the Cordeliers would know their ene-

48. Soboul and Monnier, *Répertoire de personnel sectionnaire*, 491; W 345, pl. 676, p. 45, AN, cited by Soboul, *Sans-Culottes*, 771 n 43.
49. Tuetey, *Répertoire général*, X, No. 2208. The witness was Marie Jeanne Babet Bronchon; Soboul and Monnier, *Répertoire de personnel sectionnaire*, 155. Brichet was executed on July 9, 1794.
50. Caron, *Paris pendant la Terreur*, V, 315, 353, 355, 419.

mies, the suggestion was met with loud objections. Yet this kind of proposal would have been accepted without protest in the past. Now it had become controversial, an indication of how intimidated the Cordeliers had become.

In addition, it was decided that since the Revolutionary Tribunal was to try the imprisoned leaders, the Cordeliers would await the outcome without their usual practice of holding permanent sessions during a crisis. In fact, the club went to extremes and ruled that "the affair" was not to be discussed at all for the present. Finally, the society resolved to elect a new commission of fourteen members to purge the organization. This commission was to be composed of those courageous enough to have met immediately after the Champ de Mars massacre in July, 1791; it was hoped that this would prove that only respected patriots would now rule the society. Brochet's proposal to send four delegates to the Jacobins to assure them that "firm and enlightened patriots" were now at the head of the Cordeliers was enthusiastically decreed. But when someone added that a spokesman should be designated, the members refused, saying that their former spokesmen had undone them.[51] Clearly the Cordeliers Club was no longer the watchdog of the Revolution; it had capitulated wholly to the government, and in doing so had abandoned its leaders to their fate.

Things were no better in section Marat. On the eve of the arrests the section had presented a resolution to the General Council in which it denounced "the system of oppression directed against the most ardent defenders of liberty." It saw with indignation the rights of man violated (making a Freudian slip by writing *voiler* instead of *violer*). The resolution was signed by Momoro as president. The General Council, however, took no action upon it and simply passed on to its next order of business. During the night of March 18 at least thirty militants were arrested. Needless to say, this development made a singular impression. Charmont revealed that the Cordeliers in the section were terribly nervous, afraid of being involved in "the affair."[52]

The following day the section's civil and revolutionary committees admitted the "fateful error" into which they had led the section and

51. *Moniteur*, XIX, No. 180 (March 20, 1794), 735–36; Schmidt, *Tableaux de la Révolution*, II, 163–64. The spirit of the Cordeliers now changed fundamentally, wrote Schmidt, and its sessions became "very dry."

52. *Journal de la Montagne*, No. 125 (March 18, 1794), 1012; Caron, *Paris pendant la Terreur*, V, 384–85.

were now "burning" with desire to express their feelings of pure *ci-visme* and their attachment to the "sacred decrees" of the Convention. Their error, they declared, had been "involuntary," and they now denounced "the false friends of liberty." The president graciously replied that the Convention always distinguished between error and crime. The Convention was satisfied and gave them the honors of the session. On 1 Germinal (March 21, 1794), section Marat's spokesman assured the Convention that the section had never fallen into "that excess with which it is reproached," and that it had recognized immediately its error in veiling the Declaration of Rights.[53]

Possibly the real feelings of the sans-culottes over the arrest of Hébert were not reflected in the warm resolutions of support presented to the Convention. A kind of stupor overcame the majority, but the more politically conscious minority tried to resist. Still, many remembered the triumph of Marat against the Committee of Twelve when he was freed by the Revolutionary Tribunal, so how could they resist the Great Committees now? This feeling of impotence only aggravated their suffering. For their movement to have been effective they would have needed a base in the sections and the latter's active involvement, as in all the great *journées* of the past. But the addresses and resolutions of loyalty presented to the Convention by the sections demonstrated a definitive consolidation of the revolutionary government.[54]

Immediately following the arrest of the Hébertistes the sections began a long procession to the Convention bearing their fiery resolutions of support. No doubt they were intimidated and anxious to express their loyalty. Still, it seems doubtful that fear alone motivated their action. Like many ordinary individuals who had confidence in the deputies and their Committees, the members of the sections, with

53. *AP*, LXXXVI, 673–74, LXXXVII, 52; Tuetey, *Répertoire général*, X, No. 2099; *Moniteur*, XIX, No. 180 (March 20, 1794), 738; *Journal de la Montagne*, No. 127 (March 20, 1794), 1027.

54. Soboul, *Sans-Culottes*, 772, writes that the real feelings of the sans-culottes were not in doubt: these people supported Hébert but were helpless and felt a "painful stupor" at the turn of events; even the more politically conscious of them, although awakened to resistance, could not oppose the Revolutionary Tribunal (which, after all, was their own government). On the other hand, Schmidt, *Tableaux de la Révolution*, II, 165–68, cites police reports of the numerous assemblies in sections Réunion and Arsenal and the talk in cafés and in the street of people convinced that Hébert and his companions were guilty as charged. Everywhere, the police spies noted, one heard demands for the death of Hébert and blessings for the Committee of Public Safety. Thus, if a minority tried to resist, it must have been isolated.

few exceptions, voluntarily sided with the government against the Cordeliers leaders. The bitter feelings of betrayal and the extreme expressions of vengeance against Hébert signified more than fear of the authorities. Police observers noted a universal demand for punishment.

As early as March 15—that is, the day after the arrest of the Hébertistes—the sections began to congratulate the Convention for uncovering the "conspiracy." Some expressed indignation against the "plotters," others demanded a quick trial for the "traitors." Shortly thereafter the sections began to endorse formally the action of the Convention and to call for the prompt execution of the "conspirators." [55]

On March 18 Amis du peuple, the popular society of section Marat, blessed "the immortal work" of the Convention. Still, its members dared ask why they should not have been fooled, since some of the men arrested had "helped us overthrow the royal despotism." [56] The popular societies of other sections, together with the general assemblies, joined the chorus—all congratulating the National Convention. A day later, Mutius Scaevola, Vincent's section, followed, together with still other societies and sections. [57]

On March 18 the president of the General Council, Jean Baptiste Lubin, read the decree of the Committee of Public Safety appointing new national agents in place of Chaumette and Hébert. The Commune dutifully applauded the order and adopted a servile address to be presented to the Convention. Lulier, the national agent of the

55. Tuetey, *Répertoire général*, X, Nos. 2059, 2060, 2061, 2063, 2064, 2065, 2068, 2069; *AP*, LXXXVI, 543–44, 549–52; *Moniteur*, XIX, No. 177 (March 17, 1794), 711–12, 715, 724, for sections Halle-au-Blé, Maison Commune, Panthéon-Français, Mont Blanc, Lepeletier, Arsenal, Bonnet Rouge, and the Société fraternelle des deux sexes of Panthéon-Français (March 15–18); for sections Poissonière and Homme Armé, C 295, plaq. 995, pp. 18, 27, AN; also Tuetey, *Répertoire général*, X, No. 2077, for Homme Armé. Both of the latter two sections brought offerings of saltpeter to the Convention. See also *Société fraternelle des deux sexes du Panthéon-Français*, "Adresse presentée le 27 Ventôse, par cette Société, à la Convention nationale" (in the form of a poster with the response of Rühl, president of the Convention), in Lb 40 2457, BN.

56. C 295, plaq. 995, p. 39, AN, signed by Le Blanc, president, and Degeorges, secretary, of the society. See also Tuetey, *Répertoire général*, X, No. 2072.

57. *AP*, LXXXVI, 627–31, 658, 659, 673; Tuetey, *Répertoire général*, X, Nos. 2096–98; *Journal de la Montagne*, No. 126 (March 19, 1794), 1020. These were the popular societies of sections Chalier, Lazowski, Guillaume Tell, and Unité, together with sections Lombards, Bonne-Nouvelle, Champs-Elysées, Fraternité, Réunion, Muséum, and Guillaume Tell.

Paris Department, like the municipality a bit tardy in bowing before the national authorities, began by apologizing for the late action but assured the Convention that the department had carried out its civic duty.[58]

On March 20 five more sections demonstrated their loyalty to the government. The next day, 1 Germinal, as the trial began, twenty-two sections and popular societies appeared at the bar of the Convention to swear their loyalty. The popular society of section Mutius Scaevola praised the Convention in the most obsequious language and violently denounced "this infamous conspiracy." Many communes and popular societies from various districts and departments that had been silent until now joined those of the capital. Not one challenged the authorities' charge of a "foreign conspiracy." Could the Cordeliers have won over many of these groups if they had launched a propaganda campaign, assuming they had been free to do so? It is more than doubtful. The Convention had by far the greater prestige, and few could have believed it guilty of deliberately concocting a fraud.[59]

A number of sections that had been tardy in congratulating the authorities now appeared and swore allegiance. Whatever sympathy had existed in their assemblies for the Cordeliers, it could not prevent the sections from joining the parade of loyalty to the government. Indeed, it became dangerous not to take part in the chorus of praise for the authorities.[60] A number of addresses viciously demanded

58. *Journal de la Montagne*, No. 127 (March 20, 1794), 1026; *AP*, LXXXVI, 669.

59. *AP*, LXXXVI, 718, 719, 722, 725, and 727 for the popular society of Gardes-Françaises, and sections Faubourg du Nord, Piques, Contrat Social, and Fontaine-de-Grenelle. The last presented saltpeter to the Convention in the form of a mountain at whose summit was an image of Marat. Sections Mont Blanc, Maison Commune, Chalier, and Lombards also deposited gifts of saltpeter. *Ibid.*, 729–30.

On March 21 sections Invalides, Amis de la Patrie, Faubourg Montmartre, Tuileries, République, Chalier, and Temple, plus the society of Les Hommes du 14 juillet added their congratulations; *Ibid.*, LXXXVII, 28, 29, 30–31, 33–34, 34–35, 36. Faubourg Montmartre admitted, however, that "the people are now uneasy, and find themselves without any support after all the heinous crimes [*forfaits*]"; in C 299, plaq. 1045, p. 8, AN.

60. See Tuetey, *Répertoire général*, X, for the following on March 20: No. 2105, section Droits de l'Homme; No. 2109, Unité; no. 2112, Faubourg du Nord; No. 2113, Piques; No. 2116, Contrat Social; No. 2100, popular society of Poissonière; No. 2122, popular society of Gardes-Françaises; No. 2133, Invalides; No. 2137, Faubourg Montmartre; No. 2126, Tuileries; No. 2138, Hommes du 14 juillet; No. 2139, République; no. 2125, Temple and its popular society of Sans-Culottes; No. 2127, Finistère, which gave the excuse that the law limited their meeting to every five days; No. 2128, Obser-

punishment of and vengeance against the imprisoned Cordeliers, denouncing them as "conspirators," and lauded the Convention, its Committees, and the Mountain as "saviors of the country."

The spokesman of section Marat apologized yet again for "having fallen into error." He explained that one part of the section's general assembly had been "despotized" by exaggerated patriotism and popularity, while another part had been compromised by the Terror. The same day (March 21) the section's spokesman also apologized to the Commune. He insisted that the commissioners sent by the section to the General Council (with the section's resolution veiling the Droits de l'Homme) had failed to carry out their mission as defined for them by the assembly. The president of the council replied that people were fundamentally good even though they were sometimes misled, and he invited the "regenerated" section to the honors of the session.[61]

The Cordeliers met again on 26 Ventôse (March 16, 1794), but few members attended, and these did not know what to discuss. The police observer Grivel called it "a council of rats." Chenaux, who had presided at the March 14 session, was absent ("in view of the circumstances," wrote Grivel). There were no papers on the desk and no one took the floor. It was decided that letters addressed to Momoro and Chenaux would be turned over to the public prosecutor. Finally, a member read Saint-Just's report for about an hour without comment. The meeting then adjourned and each individual went his own way.[62]

The next day the Cordeliers met again and, on a motion of Jean Etienne Brochet's, elected four commissioners to invite members of the Convention who were both Cordeliers and Jacobin members to visit "frequently" the sessions of the Cordeliers. It was so ordered. The following day, March 18, the commissioners arrived at the Jaco-

---

vatoire; No. 2130, Homme Armé; No. 2131, Révolutionnaire. And the following on March 21: No. 2134, Amis de la Patrie; No. 2146, Cité; No. 2147, Brutus; No. 2148, Gardes-Françaises; No. 2150, Bondy. On March 23 three popular societies followed; see Nos. 2164–66. See also the *Moniteur*, XX, No. 182 (March 22, 1794), 11–14, for the March 20 session of the Convention.

61. *Moniteur*, XX, No. 183 (March 23, 1794), 20–21; *ibid.*, No. 181 (March 21, 1794), 2; Tuetey, *Répertoire général*, X, No. 2152.

62. Caron, *Paris pendant la Terreur*, V, 388. Grivel's report of March 18 ends with the observation, "This justifies the proverb which says: strike the shepherd and the flock will scatter."

bins to "solidarize" themselves with "the patriots" and to assure the Jacobins that the Cordeliers were working "assiduously" to unmask the "intriguers and traitors" in their midst. Before they could proceed, however, a barrage of denunciations descended upon them.[63] Legendre was the first to take the floor and to warn them that no one would rejoin the Cordeliers until they stopped "slandering the pure patriots," that is, Jacobins like himself. He accused them of remaining silent when one of their members—a clockmaker named Dubois, from section Unité—had dared to say that Vincent was still not guilty, that he had only been accused.[64] Who among you, Legendre went on, opposed the declaration that the Cordeliers should prepare a celebration when the accused are released in triumph?

Dufourny followed, declaring that the true Cordeliers had not committed a crime or veiled the Declaration of Rights. It was all done by a group of "intriguers." Until this group was destroyed, he continued, it was impossible for the Jacobins to recognize the Cordeliers; it would be like expressions of amity between Russia and Turkey. Having been embraced twice by the Jacobins, the Cordeliers would stab them on the third embrace, he warned. "Let us reserve our affections for the true Cordeliers," he urged. Robespierre then launched a violent attack on the Cordeliers, accusing them of wanting the public to believe that the Jacobins had adopted their principles. Those who come here are not the true Cordeliers, he charged, because they threaten the true patriots. Then, linking them to Jacques Roux, he declared that the latter never would have been expelled from their society if not for the initiative of the Jacobins. The Cordeliers, he emphasized, needed a thorough purge, and he concluded by demanding that no correspondence be undertaken by the Jacobins with the Cordeliers until they had been "regenerated." This demand was adopted by acclamation.

Following Robespierre, Tallien charged that the Cordeliers' new

63. The following account of the Cordeliers' cold reception by the Jacobins is drawn from *Journal de la Montagne*, No. 127 (March 20, 1794), 1028–30; *Moniteur*, XX, No. 182 (March 22, 1794), 9–11; and Aulard, *Jacobins*, 699–701. Both the *Moniteur* and Aulard give the date of this session as March 18; the *Journal* gives March 17, which appears to be wrong.

64. Dubois was an administrator of the Paris Department and an elector of 1791 and 1792. He was arrested on the same day Legendre attacked his declaration but released on March 24. He was disarmed but soon rearmed in Floréal, Year III, rearrested on 6 Prairial III (May 25, 1795), and freed and rearmed on 16 Messidor (July 4) of the same year. Soboul and Mounier, *Répertoire de personnel sectionnaire*, 447.

Robespierre, the Cordeliers' fatal nemesis, had himself belonged to the club, as this membership card, signed by Brochet, attests.

president, Chenaux, was an intriguer who had been expelled from the Commune on August 10 (that is, on the eve of the king's overthrow).[65] He, too, demanded that no communication be permitted with the Cordeliers until they had purged themselves. Couthon added the accusation that Ronsin had drafted a list of prisoners to be massacred, and he moved that the Jacobins send out an address to their affiliates on "the abyss" from which all good citizens had just

65. Chenaux was compromised in the Chaumette affair but acquitted on April 13, 1794. He was later denounced by the surveillance committee of the 4th arrondissement as a former president and secretary of the Cordeliers and for having declared that the pillage of February 25, 1793, had "a moral goal." Disarmed in Floréal III and arrested on 5 Prairial III (May 24, 1795), after the so-called hunger insurrection, he was given provisional freedom on 20 Messidor III (July 8, 1795). *Ibid.*, 123.

been saved. Thus spurned, the Cordeliers could do little but complain loudly afterward of their treatment.[66]

On March 16 the Jacobins had heard Couthon's report on the Indies Company. The discussion that followed revealed that although some members were eager to take advantage of the government's suppression of both the Cordeliers and their enemies, Robespierre and his supporters were careful to keep a rein on them. When Léonard Bourdon spoke of the many "aristocrats" in the sections, and especially of their functionaries, who he said should be purged by the Jacobins, Robespierre denounced his proposal. It would destroy the popular societies, deprive the constituted authorities of all influence, and re-create the system against which the people had risen, he warned. This was exactly what Pitt wanted, he declared. Then, recalling Hébert's tirades against commerce as being merely a way of starving the towns, he linked Bourdon to this "same conspiracy" aimed at sowing distrust. Tallien, too, warned against denunciations of old patriots "by patriots of the moment who want to mount on the debris of reputations of old defenders of the peoples' rights."[67]

On March 20 Bourdon de l'Oise asked his fellow deputies why Bouchotte had not yet been arrested and why foreign prisoners were allowed to remain in Paris consuming food at the expense of the native population. This attack on the minister of war was another indication that some opponents of the government were indeed ready to "mount on the ruins" of old patriots' reputations. The Convention was not ready to follow him, however. Meanwhile, Mayor Pache arrived at the head of a delegation from the Commune come to demonstrate their devotion to the legislative body. President Philippe Jacques Rühl responded that although the municipality was slow in expressing its feelings, he nevertheless hoped that they were sincere. Lively applause followed, and it seemed that the Convention was satisfied.[68]

On March 22, with their leaders already on trial, the Cordeliers began a thorough purge as the Jacobins had demanded. Boucheseiche reported that after the secretary read the minutes of the last session

66. Charmont reported on March 20 the complaints of the Cordeliers. Caron, *Paris pendant la Terreur*, 432.

67. *Journal de la Montagne*, No. 126 (March 19, 1794), 1021–22, 1023. Of the "old patriots," Tallien used the phrase "athletes of the rights of the people."

68. *Ibid.*, March 20, 1794, p. 1031.

(March 17), a member declared his surprise there had been no mention of the motion made to hold a banquet after the judgment of the prisoners.[69] A long discussion followed in which Prétot (having been reinstated) and Brochet, the new leader of the club, both took the floor to condemn the past leadership. Prétot called for the thorough purge the Jacobins had demanded. In addition, he moved that the journal published by the society carry the names of individuals, rather than of the whole organization. In this way the "villainy" of one would not implicate the whole membership, he explained (turning Albertine Marat's argument upside down). The applause that followed his proposals was a dramatic indication that the role of the Cordeliers in the Revolution had ended. Brochet also called for a purge. He declared that there had been no freedom of speech under Momoro and Vincent. Rather, the society had been directed by a cabal who set the agenda in advance and designated speakers who would support their proposals; even the wives were placed in the hall where they could effectively applaud these speakers, and on a signal from one of the two leaders, those who disagreed were drowned out with shouts of "Down with the moderate!"

Brochet revealed that there was a list of the old Cordeliers members; they numbered forty-four, of whom four were founders of the club. These four, plus three others, were elected to a purge commission of seven. When someone asked what kind of questions should be put to the members under scrutiny, someone replied that they ought to be the same as the Jacobins asked. Brochet added that the commissioners should look carefully at those who owed their positions to the former Cordeliers leaders. Like Prétot, he was applauded. Obviously the new Cordeliers would do all in their power to please their now more powerful rivals.

Brochet was followed by a member named Rousselin, who stated that the Cordeliers' great error lay in the belief that a difference existed between them and the Jacobins. Only when the two organizations were united did the Cordeliers appear strong. He suggested, therefore, that the club ask the Jacobins to appoint four of their own members to the purge commission. The latter suggestion was too much even for the chastened Cordeliers. But when Rousselin de-

69. Boucheseiche's report is in Caron, *Paris pendant la Terreur*, VI, 23–24. See *Moniteur*, XX, No. 189 (March 29, 1794), 69–70 for the Cordeliers' sessions of March 22 and 24, 1794, described in this and following paragraphs.

manded the exclusion of all accomplices of the "vincentistes, ronsin-istes, momorotistes," he was applauded.[70]

Mathurin Bouin of section Marchés, a worker in the stockings trade, suggested that the society conduct its purge quickly and then inform the Jacobins that it wanted to heal the division between the two organizations. Furthermore, he thought it might be wise to have only one society in each section, rather than the multiple clubs that existed at present. The society took no action on this proposal, how-ever, as it was about to launch its purge.[71]

The purge in the Cordeliers was accompanied by growing attacks of the moderates on the more solid reputations of many revolution-aries in the sections. "The people henceforth will not believe so easily those who say they are its friends," declared section La Cité, and added that it was in the name of Marat that "the vile conspirators" wanted to destroy liberty.[72] Le Harivel revealed on March 29 that dur-ing the session of the Jacobin Club a member of the revolutionary committee from section Tuileries, Bertrand Lacombe, had denounced the administration of police for a tendency "to remove the busts of Chalier" from their pedestals in various public places.[73]

Thus, if we are to believe the police reports, no organized opposi-tion had sprung up to protest the arrests of the Cordeliers leaders. Indeed, it is doubtful that such an opposition could have developed once the Hébertistes had been imprisoned and the charges of Saint-Just had been publicized. There was opposition, but only by a few scattered individuals. Needless to say, it was ineffective. The ardent patriotism of the sans-culottes and their loyal support of the Conven-

70. Rousselin proposed that each member state his worth in writing, so that if he became wealthy one could question him on how he had acquired his wealth. This proposal was adopted. The Rousselin referred to was probably Alexandre Rousselin of section Unité, who played an important role in creating the Revolutionary army of the Aube Department; Soboul and Monnier, *Répertoire de personnel sectionnaire*, 441.

71. Caron, *Paris pendant la Terreur*, VI, 25. Boucheseiche thought that Bouin spoke wisely. For Bouin, see Soboul and Monnier, *Répertoire de personnel sectionnaire*, 203.

72. Section La Cité's address to the Convention, a document of five pages in which the section pledged its support, is in C 299, pl. 1045, p. 32, AN.

73. Caron, *Paris pendant la Terreur*, VI, 191–92. For Bertrand Lacombe, see Soboul and Monnier, *Répertoire de personnel sectionnaire*, 50. Marie Joseph Chalier, 1747–1793, was the leader of the Jacobins in Lyon. His group was defeated by a bloc of Girondins, various moderates, and royalists. He was executed on July 16, 1794, and became a Jacobin martyr. See the recent study by W. D. Edmonds, *Jacobinism and the Revolt of Lyon, 1789–1793* (New York, 1990). See also Morris Slavin, "Théophile Leclerc: An Anti-Jacobin Terrorist," *Historian*, XXXIII (May, 1971), 398–414.

tion and its Committees precluded the possibility of an organized movement in support of the arrested Cordeliers.

In addition to this loyalty and patriotism, the government's use of slander against its opponents had become a fine art. The more militant and experienced Cordeliers members certainly were not taken in by the preposterous charges of Saint-Just and the Jacobins. But the great mass of sans-culottes had no reason to suspect the honesty of their deputies. Whatever opposition still existed to the revolutionary government had been "chilled," to use Saint-Just's word. Certainly chilled was any serious thought of revolt by the Cordeliers. With their suppression, however, the political situation of France itself was transformed.

Attacked by both the government and the moderates, the militants in the sections who still remained true to the old spirit of the Cordeliers were caught in a dilemma. To break with the Mountain was to strengthen the hands of counterrevolutionaries, but to accept the slander and destruction of their leaders was to surrender their own goals and ideals. It was to accept a different kind of revolution from that which they had made in July, 1789, August, 1792, and even May, 1793. Still, what could they do? They could not become "accustomed to . . . treason [of] . . . their best friends," as Perrière wrote on March 18.[74] But neither could they accept the moderate offensive. Between the two choices, support for the Committees seemed the lesser evil. For many, however, there was no choice. They became passive and indifferent. For them the Revolution was over.

74. Caron, *Paris pendant la Terreur*, V, 397.

7

The Hébertistes

The revolutionary careers of Hébertiste leaders and those linked to them, in addition to Hébert, Ronsin, and Vincent, demonstrate their devotion to the sans-culottes and the popular phase of the Revolution. Although neither Jean Pierre Berthold Proly nor Antoine Ignace François Descombes was a member of the Cordeliers Club, the two militants' political principles and their common fate bound them indissolubly to the Hébertistes. Historians find little to differentiate Proly and Descombes from most other champions of the sans-culottes. If there was a difference between them and their colleagues of the Cordeliers, it was that the two had nothing to do with the alleged "plot" against the revolutionary government.

Although differing in origin and occupation, the Hébertistes and those linked to them were equally dedicated to the Revolution. All were active participants in the main *journées*. All held posts of trust—appointive or elective. Unlike some of the Conventionnels and Jacobins who questioned their patriotism, they had risked their lives at the siege of the Bastille, the attack on the Tuileries, or as agents of the central authorities on various fronts or in the Vendée.

True, some of them could be charged with exaggerated and intolerant opinions against their moderate or conservative enemies. Still, it must be admitted that the Revolution itself was, in a sense, an "exaggeration." All six men were egalitarians and democrats by conviction, if not always in practice. Five were still relatively young when they mounted the scaffold. The youngest, Antoine Descombes, was only thirty. The oldest, Jacob Pereyra, was fifty-one.

Perhaps it was their enthusiasm for the Revolution that led these men to oppose the government once they were convinced it had abandoned their common principles. The extreme individualism, personal ambition, and defiance of authority that characterizes them bordered on anarchy, however—sensed by many in whose name they spoke. Surely this extremism was one reason why they failed. All opposed the revolutionary government, pressed though it was by foreign war, internal counterrevolution, growing inflation, and factional struggles.

Antoine François Momoro, president of the Cordeliers Club, exemplifies these men's common devotion to democracy and equality (at least in theory; his behavior when presiding over the general assembly of his section is sufficient proof of the contradiction between his principles and his practice). Unlike the others, however, Momoro's revolutionary activity was demonstrably grounded in theoretical premises that help explain his convictions. This is not to say that his colleagues lacked principles or theoretical knowledge, but unlike him they left no written records of their beliefs.

Born in 1756 of an old Spanish family, Momoro arrived in Paris as a young man, probably in 1780, and became a skilled printer and successful book dealer. In 1785 he published a manual on the history and art of printing. When the Revolution broke out in July, 1789, he was employed as the printer of Desmoulins' journal, *France Libre*.[1] Shortly thereafter he joined the Cordeliers Club and was elected its secretary and editor of its journal. Later he presided over the club as well as the popular society of the section, Amis du peuple, affiliated with the Cordeliers. His political activity made him popular enough to be elected secretary of his section's primary assembly (Théâtre-Français, the future Marat), and then its elector. After the king's unsuccessful flight to Varennes, Momoro joined with the Amis de la vérité (Cercle Social), the popular reform society of Paris, to oppose his reinstatement. Immediately after the massacre of the Champ de Mars he drafted an indignant report that blamed the marquis de Lafayette as responsible for the event. As a result Momoro was imprisoned in the Conciergerie on August 9 or 10, 1791, and was not released until September 15. He was bitter when he left prison, resenting both his arrest and his loss of livelihood.[2]

1. Antoine François Momoro, *Traité élémentaire de l'imprimerie; ou, Le Manuel de l'imprimeur* (Paris, 1796); Tuetey, *Répertoire général*, XI, xxviii.

2. Antoine François Momoro, *Petition à l'Assemblée nationale* (Paris, n.d.), 3 pp., in Ln 27 14429, BN. Momoro asked for compensation as a victim of the events of July 17, 1791—the massacre of the Champ de Mars. Momoro's role in these events is described in Albert Mathiez, *Le Club des Cordeliers pendant la crise de Varennes et le massacre du Champ de Mars* (Paris, 1910), 131–37, 174–79 (Momoro's eloquent and indignant description of the shooting), 225, 286 (the arrests and the searches of Momoro's premises), 302–309 (interrogation of Momoro), and 369 (the indictment by the public prosecutor).

A likeness of Antoine François Momoro from the days when he was still regarded as a hero of the Revolution.

On September 25, 1792, Momoro protested the arbitrary actions of the electoral assembly's president and insisted on free discussion as the only way by which legislators ought to be chosen.[3] An address of July 30, 1792, signed by Danton, Chaumette, and Momoro for section Théâtre-Français, criticized the idea that citizens could be divided into "active" and "passive" categories. "A special class of citizens does not have the option to appropriate the exclusive right to save the country," the three wrote; they urged the "passive" citizens to serve in the National Guard, attend the general assemblies, and in brief, exercise the "rights of sovereignty that belong to the section."[4] That section Théâtre-Français was ready to exercise this sovereignty on its own may be gleaned from its bold statement, made the day after the king fled to Varennes, ordering the battalion of Saint-André des Arts to accept orders only from the Permanent Committee (that is, the special police committee of the municipality), rather than from the staff of the National Guard, now suspect. Furthermore, the section ordered *"the arrest of every aide-de-camp"* who might appear on its territory. This order, too, was signed by Momoro.[5]

After the overthrow of the king, Momoro was elected to the administration of the Paris Department (August 21, 1792) and to its directory (December 29). He was accused of profiting by annulling the decree on sequestration of property belonging to an émigré, but nothing came of the accusation.[6] On May 11, 1793, he was sent to the Vendée as one of the commissioners of the Executive Council. There he became an active and devoted agent of Ronsin. In the dispute between Rossignol and the representatives-on-mission Bourdon de l'Oise and Goupilleau de Fontenay, he supported Rossignol and held the professional generals responsible for the early defeats suffered by the republican forces. In his report to the Convention he noted that the nobles changed their clothes for those of peasants and prayed and

3. The resolution signed by Momoro and others was adopted by the assembly of electors sitting in the Evêché. Among other complaints, it condemned the decisions by a "particular society deliberating behind closed doors," that is, the conservative Club of Sainte-Chapelle. Etienne Charavay, ed., *Assemblée électorale de Paris 18 novembre 1790–15 juin 1791 . . .* (Paris, 1890), II, 512–13.

4. MSS, Nouv. acq. fr., 2684, f. 125, BN, cited by Soboul, *Sans-Culottes*, 506n4.

5. Michelet, *Histoire*, I, 611n1 (emphasis in resolution). The General Council annulled this decree, as it later did the section's July resolution that sought to integrate the passive citizens into the political life of the section.

6. Tuetey, *Répertoire général*, X, No. 2357. Charles Goret, an agent of the Commission of Subsistences, charged that Momoro received 24,000 livres from the former ambassador, Colbert-Maulevrier.

lived with the peasantry, thus gaining their confidence and persuading them that all were fighting for the common religion. After describing several skirmishes and battles, Momoro blamed the defeat at Saumur on the divided command and the failure to pursue the rebels by the Republic's generals when they had the opportunity to do so.

Momoro noted that the war in the Vendée differed markedly from that against the Coalition. In the Vendée the enemy was a whole population "fanaticized by priests" and led by nobles. Women served as spies and peasants had become brave in combat. Furthermore, the Vendéens had three armies numbering 30,000 men each, with 120 pieces of artillery. They possessed stores of grain for the winter. The individual fighter was paid only with food, except for certain nuclei of the rebel army. Priests prayed with the soldiers, and when Momoro analyzed the public morale in the departments he visited, he concluded that "the Republic can no longer allow priests in its midst."[7]

In July, 1793, Momoro became a member of the Council of War (a strategy-planning body made up of generals and representatives-on-mission) and signed the letter sent from Saumur by Ronsin and Rossignol to the Committee of Public Safety, in which they held their opponents responsible for their early defeats. Shortly thereafter he denounced Westermann in a letter to Vincent and demanded that all nobles be expelled from the army. In his report he noted the sharp differences between Rossignol on the one hand and Bourdon de l'Oise and Goupilleau de Fontenay on the other, and he assailed the latter two's removal of Ronsin. Certain strategic towns had been depleted of troops by General Tuncq and the two representatives-on-mission, he claimed, against the express orders of the Convention and General Rossignol. The rebels' supplies were not touched and La Rochelle was needlessly exposed to the enemy. Momoro concluded by demanding the recall of Goupilleau, Bourdon, and Tuncq, and the reinstatement of Ronsin (and, in a separate letter, of Rossignol) by the Committee of Public Safety and the Convention.[8]

In his letter to the Jacobins written from Saumur on August 13,

---

7. Antoine François Momoro, *Rapport sur l'état politique de la Vendée, fait au Comité de salut public de la Convention nationale* . . . (Paris, [October 13, 1793]), in Lb 41 3389, BN.

8. Tuetey, *Répertoire général*, X, No. 2352. Momoro suggested employing the Mayence Army against the Vendéens in his letter *Rapport des évenemens relatifs à la visite faite par le Général en chef Rossignol, des differentes divisions composant l'armée des côtes de la Rochelle* (Paris, n.d.), in Lb 41 3324, BN. For Momoro on Luçon, see his *De Saumur* (Paris, August 13, 1793), in Lb 46 3219, BN.

1793, Momoro described the victory of Luçon, exaggerating the numbers of the enemy. When the Convention dismissed Goupilleau and Bourdon and reinstated Rossignol, Momoro sent a copy of the announcement to the *Journal du soir*, where it was published. Rossignol thanked Momoro and assured him that his sole ambition was to conquer or die for the country.[9] Throughout September and October, Momoro continued to accuse the generals whom he held responsible for pursuing the wrong strategy in the Vendée. He did this in a number of reports to the Jacobins, the Executive Council, and the Cordeliers.

While in the Vendée, Momoro was accompanied by his wife, Marie Françoise Josephine Fournier, whom he had married in 1786. He treated her like a "grande dame," which was resented by his future enemies. One of the latter testified that she made a show of scandalous luxury with her sumptuous furnishings, rich clothes, and beautiful carriage. A few months later Josephine portrayed the goddess of liberty in the cult of Reason celebrated in the former cathedral of Notre Dame. None of this could have endeared Momoro to his political opponents or to the more puritanical Jacobins like Robespierre. That Momoro could afford to indulge the rich tastes of his wife may be believed if we accept the statement of his uncle, a tailor by occupation, that his nephew had always paid his debts and that he was worth some 80,000 livres.[10]

Momoro's social and economic opinions were to the left of the Jacobins—possibly another reason he was condemned. In May, 1793, he examined the question of property rights in connection with his exposition of the need for a *maximum* on grain. Attempting to prove that the regulation was both necessary and workable, he argued that the products of the soil belonged to society, rather than to individual owners. The *maximum*, he wrote, would lower the price of grain, discourage profiteering, establish a just proportion between the market price of the crop and the pay of the worker, encourage respect for property, and develop agriculture, commerce, and the arts. Unlike other supporters of the measure, he favored a sliding scale for adding

9. Aulard, *Jacobins*, V, 352–54; Tuetey, *Répertoire général*, X, Nos. 2353, 2354.

10. Tuetey, *Répertoire général*, X, No. 2370, declaration of Pierre François Sebillotte to Armand Martial Claude Herman, president of the Revolutionary Tribunal (March 16, 1794), and No. 2375.

Josephine was arrested with other wives of the condemned Cordeliers but was released on May 27. On August 25, 1794, she was forced to ask for welfare. Tuetey, *Répertoire général*, XI, xxxiv.

the price of transportation to the total price of grain on the market. To the question of whether the proprietor of a piece of land had the right to the ownership of the products produced on it, Momoro replied: "Not at all. These products are meant for the subsistence of society in exchange for a fair preliminary compensation which is the due price. This compensation must be commensurate with the means of the citizens."[11]

Among his earlier writings was an exposition on the Rights of Man. Unlike the official Declaration, Momoro's Article 2 stated that "social distinctions . . . based on common usefulness, *and that do not injure equality*, shall be accepted by the nation and are revocable at will." Article 27 guaranteed the inviolability of industrial property only. Among his other articles, Article 1 declared that "the Nation assures equally to the citizens the guarantee & inviolability *of what one falsely calls landed property*," but even this guarantee was limited by the law, which would determine such property's ultimate status. Some time later Momoro challenged Sieyès to prove that the juring clergy were of good faith, and he denied that differences existed between them and the nonjurors. When Marat was indicted, Momoro, as president of his section, drafted an appeal to the Convention. It was endorsed by the General Council, which authorized him to circulate the document among the other forty-seven sections for support.[12] In short, Momoro was active politically as speaker, writer, and administrator, ready to risk prison for his principles.

In presiding over the sectional assembly, Momoro imposed silence on his opponents by threatening them with the Revolutionary Tribunal or by refusing to recognize them when they attempted to take the floor. On 15 Ventôse (March 5, 1794), when Ducroquet proposed an insurrection, a citizen Guespereau, in order to turn the discussion away from this dangerous proposal, asked to read a report on provisions. Momoro immediately intervened with a sharp denunciation:

11. Antoine François Momoro, *Opinion de Momoro administrateur et membre du directoire du département de Paris* (Paris, n.d.), in Le 38 2464, BN. Momoro argued also that France produced beyond her needs, hence had no need to import grain from abroad. This was untrue during the period under discussion.

12. Antoine François Momoro, *De la Convention nationale . . . Déclaration des Droits* (Paris, n.d.), in Lb 41 2978, BN (Momoro's emphasis); Momoro, *Réflexions d'un citoyen sur la liberté des cultes religieux, pour servir de réponse à l'opinion de M. l'Abbé Sieyès . . .* ([Paris], 1792), in Ld 4 3556; Momoro, *Section du Théâtre-Français dite de Marseille* (Paris, April 15, 1793), in Lb 40 542, BN.

"This is how some people, by making trivial motions, want to bury the larger objectives in deliberation."[13]

Momoro held more sophisticated political views than his colleagues, partly because he approached theory and the principles that flowed from it in a serious way. On March 7, 1794, replying to the Jacobin delegation, he declared: "We recognize only principles. Men merit no consideration in our eyes when they put principles in danger." His last speech, never given, contained a harsh attack on moderates and those "who betray the confidence of the people." He denounced "the perfidious system of these cowardly men who because they lack vigor make it a crime for those who have it," and he accused them of violating the principles of liberty and equality.[14] Momoro's radical views favoring the consumer and his belief in equality of property won over the poorer sectionnaires, especially the so-called forty-sous people. Thus, he had a ready base for controlling the section. The moderates could do little against him until his arrest reversed the situation.

Momoro was interrogated on March 12 by a judge of the Revolutionary Tribunal in the presence of Fouquier-Tinville. When asked what he knew of incendiary placards and "incidents that arise," he replied that he had no knowledge of them. He did mention that Ducroquet's motion for an insurrection had been adopted unanimously by the general assembly over which he, Momoro, had presided. After his arrest a commissioner of the Committee of General Security and two members of the section's revolutionary committee searched Momoro's premises and sealed them. They confiscated three pistols and a saber but found no suspicious papers. Josephine was to be the guardian of Momoro's effects, but she, too, had been arrested. A summary of Momoro's interrogation was submitted to René François Dumas, president of the Revolutionary Tribunal. When asked if he had plotted against the Republic, Momoro replied that he had not. He chose Gobert as his defense attorney.[15]

If Momoro was both theoretician and activist, another defendant, François Desfieux, was far more of the latter. A wine merchant, he

13. Tuetey, *Répertoire général*, X, No. 2375, testimony of Jean Schmitz, a tailor, and *ibid.*, No. 2368, testimony of Pierre Jacques Guespereau, a former notary, and of Barthélemy Damour, captain of the 1st Company.

14. *Annales historiques*, III, 484–92 (three speeches of Momoro presented by Mathiez).

15. Tuetey, *Répertoire général*, X, Nos. 2363, 2365, 2371, 2373.

was born in Bordeaux in 1755 and came to Paris sometime in July, 1789. According to his memoir written in Sainte-Pélagie prison, Desfieux was already active in the Revolution on July 12, when he urged arming the people against the court. He was among the first to sport the new rosette, a symbol of defiance, and mounted the barricades in the evening. He joined the Gardes-Françaises and fought the king's troops. Later he suggested broadening the enrollment of the National Guard by opening it to "passive" citizens; he also exposed royalist agents in the guard. On July 14 he was a participant in the siege of the Bastille. By October he was back in Bordeaux, where he founded a popular society called Club du café national, whose president he became until his departure for Paris again. In June, 1790, he helped establish a popular club in Toulouse, and from there was sent to Paris to celebrate the Festival of the Federation in July, 1790. He remained in the capital and joined the Cordeliers and the Jacobins, becoming the latter's treasurer and later its vice-president.[16]

Desfieux was active politically throughout 1791 and 1792 and advocated an insurrection against the monarchy. He condemned Bailly and Lafayette for their role in the Nancy affair, which saw the execution of soldiers for objecting to their officers' control of the regimental treasury. He was present at the Champ de Mars during the massacre, and unlike others, he maintained his membership in the Jacobins during its period of repression. By 1792 he resided in section Bibliothèque (later section 1792 and, finally, Lepeletier), and by the summer of that year he was agitating openly for an uprising against the king. The country was in danger, he warned, and he called on the people to destroy "the impure center of the counterrevolution in Paris," that is, the court. The *fédérés* (troops from the various departments) were just waiting for Paris to give the signal, he urged.[17]

After the king was toppled, Desfieux was appointed juror to the newly established Revolutionary Tribunal, became an elector, and as president of his section was asked to give an address upon the installation of the busts of Marat and of Lepeletier. In the second half of October he was back in Bordeaux but was forced to flee the city under

16. "Desfieux détenu dans la prison de Sainte-Pélagie à ses concitoyens," in F7 4672, dos. 2, AN. Desfieux wrote that he respected "the decrees on the subject of the Jews," evidently to show his innate tolerance and respect for the law.

17. *Ibid.*; Aulard, *Jacobins*, III, 472–73, IV, 151. Desfieux was convinced that out of the seven hundred deputies who sat in the National Assembly, a mere forty-five or forty-six were reliable; Aulard, *Jacobins*, IV, 166.

the threats of the local Girondins, whose leaders he had begun attacking shortly after the king's fall.[18]

Desfieux wrote that he was among the first to denounce Dumouriez and (on March 9, 1793) to advocate the removal of suspected officials and to establish a revolutionary tribunal. When Pierre Victurnien Vergniaud, a leading Girondin, attacked him as an apologist for the September Massacres, Desfieux counterattacked, arguing that the Girondin was dangerous to the Republic. The following month Bouchotte sent Desfieux on a mission to Switzerland, but he was forced to cut short his visit because the Girondin journals denounced him as an agent of Marat and Robespierre, sent to foment anarchy. Two weeks before the insurrection of May 31, 1793, Desfieux presided at a Jacobins meeting to which a delegation of volunteers from section Unité was admitted prior to their departure for the Vendée. He asserted that while they were going to fight "the fanatics of the Vendée," the enemy's chiefs (that is, the Girondins) were in Paris, and that "the brigands of the Vendée were only their instruments"—an indication how bitter the factional struggle had become.[19]

When the Girondins were expelled from the Convention after the insurrection of May 31–June 2, 1793, Desfieux was in Basel. He returned to Paris on June 10 and announced that the victory of the "Maratiste party" had raised the value of the assignat. On July 21 he supported Hébert's motion to exclude all nobles from civil and military employment, and the following month demanded that the minister of the interior, Dominique Joseph Garat, give an account of his tenure before being allowed to take another post.[20] On September 8, he reported to the Jacobins the arrest of Jacques Roux and that a commission had been created to take depositions against Roux and his fellow Enragé, Théophile Leclerc.[21] It is doubtful that Desfieux felt sympathy for the two Enragés, despite their concern, common with his own, for the welfare of the sans-culottes and the safety of the Republic.

18. Among the Girondins he attacked were Claude Fauchet and Louis Marie Jacques Norbonne (former minister of war); Aulard, *Jacobins*, IV, 293, 295–303. Desfieux's address is in Proly's dossier in F7 4774 83, AN, which means that it was written by Proly for him. The address must have been given sometime in July, 1793, after the death of Marat. It began: "Marat and Le Pelletier will be forever united in the homage that the French owe their memory."

19. Descombes, F7 4672, AN; Aulard, *Jacobins*, V, 195.

20. Aulard, *Jacobins*, V, 246, 309, 365.

21. *Ibid.*, 392.

Desfieux had made many enemies by his denunciations and personal attacks. As a result he now was accused of being an intriguer and a scoundrel. On October 14, 1793, he was arrested by the revolutionary committee of section Lepeletier; however, he was immediately freed by the intervention of Collot d'Herbois, an indication, perhaps, of the ambivalent role that Collot was playing at this time. Three days later Desfieux reentered the Jacobin Club amidst universal applause and declared that he hoped to continue to serve the Revolution as had great patriots like Marat, Robespierre, and others.[22]

Shortly thereafter he accused Louis Pierre Dufourny, president of the Paris Department's directory, of being responsible for his arrest. Dufourny denied that he had ever given an arrest order for Desfieux, and Collot gave his assurances that this was so. On 3 Brumaire (October 24, 1793) Collot reversed his earlier stance toward Desfieux and launched a bitter attack on him, calling him a scoundrel and, strangely enough, blaming the Jacobins for having defended him. A Jacobin by the name of Sambat, a juror of the Revolutionary Tribunal, revealed that Collot had apologized for having defended Desfieux. Collot had learned, allegedly, that Desfieux's connection to the Belgian banker Pierre Berthold Proly made him suspect. Desfieux replied that since the beginning of the Revolution he had known Proly as a good patriot; he then sought to defend himself further by asserting that his being the first to denounce Dumouriez was the real cause of the charges against him. This claim convinced no one, and on November 21 Robespierre demanded the expulsion of Desfieux and some others—Dubuisson, Proly, and Pereyra. Two days later Desfieux was arrested and imprisoned in Sainte-Pélagie and his effects were sealed. Hébert also denounced him in the Commune, although he did testify to his patriotism. Desfieux asked the revolutionary committee of his section to allow him to retrieve his papers so he could prepare his defense and convince Robespierre he was mistaken.[23]

22. *Moniteur*, XIII, No. 26 (October 17, 1793), 130. Collot addressed the General Council on October 15 complaining that "true patriots . . . should not be treated like aristocrats" and asking the council to inquire of the police why Desfieux had been arrested. See Tuetey, *Répertoire général*, XI, xlvii–xlix, for a summary of his last months before the trial in Ventôse. See also Aulard, *Jacobins*, V, 475–77; Tuetey, *Répertoire général*, X, No. 2456, where Desfieux demands a "rigorous examination of his conduct since the Revolution," and No. 2457, his arrest.

23. Descombes, F7 4672, AN. On October 22 two members of the revolutionary committee of section Lepeletier drafted a report stating that nothing suspicious was

He remained in prison more than two months, occupying the same cell with Ronsin and Pereyra—which ultimately helped to destroy him, since he could more easily be charged as an accomplice of the two. A jeweler named Jean Jacquemier testified he heard Desfieux say that had the revolution of May 31 been carried out as originally planned, there would have been neither a Convention nor any constituted authorities left. Furthermore, he was alleged to have declared, "I want to see things reach the point where a father f——s his daughter at a corner-post and even on the Pont Neuf." The circumstances under which this testimony was given, and the incongruity of mixing a political critique with a piece of vulgarity, deserves some skepticism. On 10 Pluviôse (January 29, 1794), Desfieux composed his letter to the Committee of General Security and soon thereafter was transferred to Saint-Lazare prison. The concierge of Saint-Lazare asked that Desfieux and his accomplices be removed because they were too dangerous to remain under his care. On February 18 Desfieux was taken to the Conciergerie, which he left only to face the guillotine.[24]

Among Desfieux and Ronsin's cellmates was Jacob Pereyra, a dealer in tobacco. Of Portuguese Jewish origin, born in Bayonne in 1743, he established himself in Paris shortly after the start of the Revolution as a "manufacturer" of tobacco. According to his petition for release from prison, Pereyra claimed he was the first to take up

---

found among his papers. Desfieux asked the committee to allow him a change of linen. On December 3 he defended his revolutionary role since July 12, 1789, and emphasized that he had never solicited any post. Desfieux dated his original letter 10 Pluviôse (January 29, 1794), and signed himself as "Jacobin dans l'âme et jusqu'à la mort." Also in Tuetey, *Répertoire général*, X, Nos. 2458–65.

Robespierre's long and extremely harsh attack on Desfieux, Dubuisson, Proly, and Pereyra was given in the Jacobin Club on 1 Frimaire (November 21, 1793); *Moniteur*, XVIII, No. 66 (November 26, 1793), 509. On the following day Chaumette reported to the Commune the expulsion of Desfieux, Dubuisson, and Pereyra, and apologized (with Hébert) for being late to the council meeting because they had to free themselves of the accusations against them initiated by Chabot and Basire, who were involved in the Indies Company scandal; *Moniteur*, XVIII, No. 65 (November 25, 1793), 498.

24. Descombes, F7 4672, AN. A letter to Fouquier-Tinville (March 15) quoted Desfieux, while in prison, as declaring "we need an insurrection." On March 20 Desfieux was brought before Claude Emmanuel Dobsent, judge of the Revolutionary Tribunal, and was given a defense counsel. Also in Tuetey, *Répertoire général*, X, Nos. 2201, 2262, 2466, 2468, 2469. Mathiez incorrectly places Desfieux with the Enragés. He calls him "a suspicious person," and "almost illiterate"; Mathiez, *Révolution française*, II, 202, III, 94.

arms in Bordeaux on July 16, 1789, and that he then engaged in a military campaign at Montauban. Not long afterward he brought his family to Paris, joined the Jacobin Club, and came "under fire" as a participant in the Champ de Mars demonstration. On August 10, 1792, he participated as a cannoneer in the attack on the Tuileries.[25]

The following year Pereyra was elected assessor to the justice of the peace in his section, Bon-Conseil, of which he had become president. He was sent by the Executive Council on a mission to General Dumouriez, whom he exposed upon his return in April, for which he was honored by the Convention. He signed the address of his section demanding a decree of accusation against the leading Girondins and was under arms with his section throughout the three days of the insurrection beginning on May 31, 1793. On June 19 he was sent by the Jacobins as a commissioner to the Committee of Public Safety, where he asked for the exclusion of all noblemen from civil and military posts. When General François Christophe Kellermann wrote the Jacobins claiming to have been dubbed "general of the Jacobins" by his enemies and asking the Parisian club to confirm him in this title, Pereyra not only opposed the request but demanded that Kellermann be stricken from membership. The society adopted his motion without debate.[26]

In Brumaire, Pereyra was sent on a mission to the North by François Louis Michel Deforgue, minister of foreign affairs. He was received enthusiastically by the popular societies of Dunquerque and Lille (November, 1793), but two days after Robespierre's famous speech of November 21 denouncing the antireligious crusade of the Paris Commune and those connected with it, Pereyra was arrested. His papers were sealed and his wife, Rachel, made guardian of them. Some three weeks later his fellow cannoneers protested his arrest and vouched for his republicanism. Despite this testimonial Pereyra remained in Sainte-Pélagie prison. At the end of Ventôse he was trans-

---

25. Tuetey, *Répertoire général*, X, No. 2509, XI, liv. Pereyra was fifty-one at the time of his trial; *Moniteur*, XX, No. 183 (March 23, 1794), 18.

In an address entitled "Au peuple français . . . " the Jacobins wrote that Pereyra was one of three commissioners who had exposed Dumouriez, one of the others being Desfieux, who was characterized as "a citizen of burning patriotism." And when the society resolved to send commissioners to the Committee of Public Safety to inform it of its resolution to retire all ex-nobles from civil and military positions, Pereyra was appointed as one of six commissioners. Aulard, *Jacobins*, V, 158, 267.

26. Tuetey, *Répertoire général*, X, No. 2509; Aulard, *Jacobins*, V, 468.

ferred to Saint-Lazare, where he was interrogated by a judge. Sent to the Conciergerie, he met the fate of his comrades on March 24, 1794.[27]

Among the foreigners in Paris was the banker Pierre Berthold Proly, who had gone to Holland on a mission with Pereyra and Desfieux. He was born in Brussels in 1752, grew up in Nantes, and arrived in Paris in 1783 passing for a natural son of the prince de Kaunitz. Having made a great deal of money in the Indies, he could afford to live like a man of wealth until he lost his fortune in 1789. After that he speculated on the stock exchange with whatever funds he could scrape up but did not do well until he launched a journal, *Le Cosmopolite*. This publication appeared from December 15, 1791, to March 31, 1792. Who funded it? About half of the cost was underwritten by a former counselor of the Cour des Aides named Regnier, but the other half reportedly came from the Austrian court—whose secret agent Proly allegedly was.[28]

Proly joined the Jacobins and began to meet important people. In March, 1793, he was sent to Holland, together with Pereyra and Pierre Dubuisson, as the Jacobins' commissioner and as an agent of the minister of foreign affairs. Their mission was to undermine the Bank of England through the intervention of the Portuguese Jewish bankers in Amsterdam. There is no indication that they accomplished much. Upon their return Proly and his two companions were entrusted with visiting the camp of Dumouriez, who was prepared to crush the Convention and establish a personal dictatorship. They reported this plot, and Proly was personally praised by Pierre Henri Hélène Marie Lebrun, then minister of foreign affairs (April 6, 1793). Later, the three were to be accused of delaying their report. Meanwhile, Proly became more active politically. He established a number of sectional societies and unified them under his control, one possible reason for the government's decision to arrest him.[29]

A decree of arrest was signed on 27 Brumaire (November 17, 1793)

27. F7 4774 67, dos. 2, AN; Tuetey, *Répertoire général*, X, Nos. 2504–2508, 2510, XI, lv.

28. F7 4774 83, dos. 1, AN; Tuetey, *Répertoire général*, X, No. 2446 (Proly's interrogation by the revolutionary committee of section Lepeletier on February 20, 1794), XI, xli; Gérard Walter, "Table Analytique," in Michelet, *Histoire*, II, 1531–32.

29. Tuetey, *Répertoire général*, X, nos. 2451, 2437; Aulard, *Jacobins*, VI, 10. A Jacobin named Briart accused Proly, Pereyra, Dubuisson, and Desfieux of using their patriotism only to mislead the society. One of the accusations launched by Robespierre against Proly on November 21, 1793, was that he had formed some fifty popular societies; *Moniteur*, XVIII, No. 66 (November 26, 1793), 509. See also Tuetey, *Répertoire général*, XI, xliii; Michelet, *Histoire*, II, 1532.

by both Committees against a number of bankers, Proly among them (it should be noted that this was months before the arrests of the Cordeliers, with whom Proly had no relations). The revolutionary committee of Proly's section, not finding him at home, sealed his papers after uncovering nothing suspicious in them. Members of the committee then interrogated his mistress, his valet, and a number of individuals named by the latter who were either acquaintances or who had business relations with him. Desfieux was also interrogated but could tell them nothing. Proly, meanwhile, was hiding and could not be found; it is possible that Hérault de Sechelles, who defended him, might have given him refuge in his own home. Collot was also his friend and shielded him.[30]

On 9 Nivôse (December 25, 1793) the Committee of Public Safety intervened and authorized the revolutionary committee of section Lepeletier once again to arrest Proly, but he managed to hide by changing his sleeping quarters every night. In addition to Proly's friends' hiding him, the six police officers who were combing the city must have been discouraged to know that Collot and Hérault were his powerful supporters.[31]

Using various disguises, Proly avoided capture for four months. He was finally caught on February 18, 1794, and brought in for interrogation. He denied attacking the Convention or the Republic, pointing to his past actions in defending the Revolution and denouncing the Brissotins. He blamed Desmoulins and Fabre d'Eglantine for slandering "pure patriots" by calling them "factious," or "seditious persons." Dufourny expressed his pleasure when he learned that Proly finally had been arrested. Addressing the Jacobins, he charged that the banker had been kept free by intrigue and accused him of being an agent of Austria. Collot—it was obvious that Dufourny was accusing him, too, of this intrigue—mounted a strange defense of the Belgian, replying that although he believed Proly was a scoundrel, still he was a Jacobin and thus deserved his support.[32]

30. Tuetey, *Répertoire général*, X, Nos. 2410–15, 2418 (wherein Proly's domestic, François Bombard, age thirty, names various individuals and is himself arrested until Proly is found), 2423, 2430–32 (interrogations of Proly's acquaintances). A number of the foregoing are in F7 4774, 43, AN.

31. Tuetey, *Répertoire général*, XI, No. 221, X, Nos. 2447, 2448 (also in F7 4774 83, AN). A document dated 11 Nivôse by the Committee of General Security authorizes the revolutionary committee of Lepeletier to take all measures necessary to carry out its order; original in F7 4774 83, AN.

32. Aulard, *Jacobins*, V, 658–59; Tuetey, *Répertoire général*, X, No. 2446, wherein Proly gave a brief sketch of his affairs.

On February 21 the Committee of General Security sent Proly to the Carmes prison, from which he wrote an appeal for help to his friend the deputy Pierre Louis Bentabole. Was it not true, he asked, that he had always been a friend of liberty, and that he had fought aristocrats, Feuillants, and Brissotins? He concluded by blaming Fabre, Desmoulins, and Dufourny for his imprisonment. But Bentabole was in no position to help him even if he wanted to. On March 9, Proly was interrogated by the Committee about his relations with Pereyra and Dubuisson and about their mission to Belgium. Questioned for the last time by Dobsent on March 20, he denied conspiring against the Republic. Like the other prisoners, he was given a defense attorney for the coming trial. But the following day Robespierre launched his virulent attack on the "foreign conspiracy." There was little Proly or his defense counsel could do against the storm raised by the Incorruptible's speech. He was to perish simply because he was a foreigner and a banker.[33]

Sharing the cell in Sainte-Pélagie with Ronsin, Desfieux, and Pereyra was Pierre Ulrich Dubuisson, a "man of letters" and a former commissioner of the Executive Council. He was born in 1746 at Laval, department of Mayenne, the son of a physician. The family left France for one of the colonies but returned before the Revolution. Dubuisson was divorced, the father of two girls aged eleven and four at the time of his arrest. He had written some seven or eight dramas—comedies, comic operas, and tragedies. Dubuisson said that he lived off his plays' earnings, which could not have been much even if one were to add what he made as a stage manager.

Dubuisson took part in the siege of the Bastille, then went to Belgium, where he joined the revolutionary movement against the aristocracy and was imprisoned; he was released in 1790. When the attack on the Tuileries took place on August 10, 1792, he was among the besiegers and was wounded slightly. Shortly thereafter he joined the Jacobins and was elected the club's vice-president during the presidency of Marat. The Jacobins gave him the task of drafting an address against the policy of Brissot and Roland, which he delivered on January 7, 1793. As already mentioned, he was a commissioner with Pereyra and Proly on a mission to Holland in March, 1793, to undermine the Bank of England, and later that same month he accompanied them on the mission to Dumouriez.[34]

33. Tuetey, *Répertoire général*, X, Nos. 2449, 2451, 2453, XI, xliv–xlv.
34. *Ibid.*, X, No. 2651; XI, lxxi–lxxii.

Returning to Paris on March 31, 1793, Dubuisson was arrested with Pereyra and Proly by the Committee of Defense and the Committee of General Security, evidently on suspicion of dealings with Dumouriez.[35] But two days later he read his report to the Jacobins on Dumouriez's treason, a report he had presented earlier to the Convention. After the latter body had approved the report, Dubuisson was elected president of the Jacobins for the period of April 10–22, 1793. Lebrun sent him on a mission to the Army of the Lower Rhine and to Switzerland. Upon his return, he was at Poligny in the Jura Department when he heard of Marat's assassination. He seems to have been so moved that in expressing his sentiments he was arrested by the local authorities, although it is not clear just what the charge was against him. On July 29, 1793, he reappeared in the Jacobins and gave them the details of the fall of Mainz, where he must have been present.

Arrested on a joint charge of the two Committees on November 17, 1793, he was incarcerated in the Sainte-Pélagie. Shortly thereafter, Robespierre denounced him as an "intriguer" and an agent of foreign powers, a charge to which the Incorruptible was beginning to resort against foreign revolutionaries. As a result, Dubuisson was expelled from the Jacobin Club together with his fellow commissioners. Accused of plotting against the Convention, he was quoted as having said, "We need another May 31, but there's no one to lead it." When interrogated by Dobsent on March 20, 1794, he denied having plotted against the Republic, and like the others was given a defense attorney. Ronsin suggested that he abridge his political career from the document he prepared for the surveillance committee of section Montagne, and that he send a copy to his protector Danton. Nothing helped, of course, as his fate had been determined before the trial began.[36]

Since the government was determined to blame the shortages on those it had arrested, what better way to make the accusation seem plausible than to charge those working to supply Paris with this crime? Antoine Ignace François Descombes of section Droits de l'Homme, who had nothing to do with the Cordeliers, was victimized precisely because his heroic efforts to supply Paris fell short of solving the food crisis. Born in Besançon in 1764, he worked as a greengrocer,

---

35. Aulard, *Jacobins*, V, 118. Dubuisson had given his report to the Comité de défense générale.

36. Aulard, *Jacobins*, V, 531; Tuetey, *Répertoire général*, X, No. 2650, XI, lxii–lxiii.

and earned a degree as a master of languages at age nineteen. When the Revolution broke out he was in Marseille but returned to his native town and joined the Jacobins shortly thereafter. In April, 1791, he arrived in Paris. He became active politically, attacked Lafayette, and on June 20, 1792, was arrested for demonstrating against the king. That December he was elected secretary, then president, of his section. The following month he was sent as one of the section's representatives to the General Council, and as a result of his clash with the Girondin Committee of Twelve, was elected commissioner to the revolutionary assembly sitting in the Evêché that launched the insurrection of May 31. Shortly thereafter he was appointed to the Commune's commission that was struggling to organize supplies of grain and flour for the capital.[37]

At first he was sent into the departments of Loiret and Eure-et-Loire, then was assigned to Seine-et-Marne, and finally was limited to the districts of Rozoy and Provins in the latter department. His fellow commissioner Pierre Basse Champeaux worked closely with him as they struggled to supply the hungry Parisians. In August, 1793, the administration of the Commune's Food Commission informed their two agents that Paris was down to a mere 100 sacks of flour a day from the normal requirement of 2,000. To remedy this catastrophic shortfall the two representatives-on-mission authorized Descombes to collect grain by armed force if necessary. As if this supply problem were not enough, Descombes had to beat off the slanders of a personal enemy in the section, a grocer named Chollet.[38]

By October, Descombes had to order the municipal authorities of Provins to requisition transport in order to send flour to the capital. The letters of alarm continued, however. One reason for the persistent shortages was beyond Descombes' ability to solve—the continuing decline of the assignat, the only currency available to him. For the first and only time he considered resigning from his difficult post, once he thought the crisis had passed, but realizing that his departure would only revive the problems, he determined to stay on. On No-

37. The sketch of Descombes is based on his dossier, 1, in F7 4672, AN; on W 94 (a carton that contains Descombes' records as the administrator of provisions in Provins for supplying Paris), AN; and on his brochure *Descombes, electeur, membre du Conseil général* . . . (Paris, n.d.), in Ln 27 5894, BN. See also Slavin, *French Revolution in Miniature,* 251–57.

38. Tuetey, *Répertoire général,* X, Nos. 2556, 2558, 2567, 2593, 2596, 2598, 2566, XI, lxvii–lxviii.

vember 10, 1793, Mayor Pache asked him to take charge of adminis-
tering supplies for the commune, a task that required much correspondence from the center. Descombes agreed, and the following
month was asked to surrender his accounts and supporting documents to the newly established Commission of Food Supply under
the direct supervision of the Committee of Public Safety and its
agents.[39]

While providing supplies for the capital, Descombes was forced to
resort to unpleasant requisitions and demands. No wonder, then,
that he made enemies in his section. Among them were Pierre Carron, commissioner on profiteering, and Philippe Denis Pinet, a captain in the section's armed force who was employed in the post office.
They denounced Descombes to the popular society for dealing leni-
ently with a former judge of the section, Louis Fayel. Carron was
quoted as having said to Descombes, "I'd rather be a Marat than a
traitor Mirabeau like you." This personal fracas was made to order for
the higher authorities in their desire to "amalgamate" the diverse persons to be tried. On December 29 the Committee of General Security
arrested Descombes and sent him to La Force prison. His papers were
examined by members of the section's revolutionary committee before being sealed and placed under the guardianship of his wife,
Jeanne Antoine Bernard. They contained nothing suspicious, of
course; on the contrary, they demonstrated the unflagging attention
that Descombes had paid to his work.[40]

Descombes' wife appealed to the Committee for her husband's release, blaming the aristocrats and the moderates for his imprisonment. His friends defended him heatedly in the general assembly of
the section, and petitions began to arrive from his native Besançon
asking for his release. Descombes' co-worker in Provins also came to
his support. Added to this was a letter from the Administration of
Provisions that recalled "the important services rendered to public
affairs by Descombes," and a resolution in his favor by the general
assembly of section Droits de l'Homme. Even the popular society of
the section, which contained a number of his personal enemies,
asked for his freedom.[41]

Nothing helped, however. It seems that even Descombes' egali-

39. *Ibid.*, X, Nos. 2603, 2606, 2617, XI, lxviii.
40. Descombes, F7 4672, AN; Tuetey, *Répertoire général*, X, Nos. 2620, 2621, 2523.
41. Descombes, F7 4672, AN; Tuetey, *Répertoire général*, X, Nos. 2226, 2632, 2636,
2639.

tarian attitude was held against him, for when the deputy Garnier, of the Aube Department, had once visited Provins, Descombes had declared in the course of a conversation with him, "You are [just] a man, I'm another," which was now interpreted as disrespect. The general assembly of the section was widely attended on March 18, according to Bacon's report. When the revolutionary committee revealed that its members had waited for five hours in the offices of the Committee of General Security without getting a hearing on its petition in favor of Descombes, the assembly exploded in indignation.

Meanwhile, Descombes was being interrogated by Dobsent, now president of the Revolutionary Tribunal. Things took a turn for the worse when Etienne Lasne, commander of the section's battalion, reported Descombes' observation that he did not expect to be released unless there were five or six good patriots in prison like himself, implying a rescue operation. The remark was turned over to the public prosecutor. On 3 Germinal (March 23) François Dupaumier, a former member of the section's revolutionary committee and a jeweler by occupation, confirmed this supposed threat of escape by Descombes. That was all Fouquier-Tinville needed to "amalgamate" him with the Hébertistes. Two days before his condemnation Descombes wrote a letter to his wife expressing the conviction that he would be freed shortly. On 4 Germinal he was guillotined with the others.[42]

The execution of the six "Cordeliers" militants struck not only at the popular movement but at the radical and democratic phase of Jacobinism as well. After all, the political history of these revolutionaries embodied the history of Jacobinism itself—before it had become bureaucratic and safe. Moreover, the Jacobinism they represented was hardly different from that of the Cordeliers. If former presiding officers and spokesmen for the Jacobin Society could be re-

---

42. Descombes, F7 4672, AN; Tuetey, *Répertoire général*, X, Nos. 2226, 2632, 2636, 2639, 2647, XI, lxix–lxxi; Caron, *Paris pendant la Terreur*, V, 376–77.

On 26 Fructidor II (September 12, 1794), Jeanne Antoine Bernard, Descombes' wife, petitioned the Convention to remove the seals from her late husband's effects, as she and her young child had nothing to live on. Moreover, the guardian of these effects was being paid 3 livres a day and this expense had already cost her some 500 livres. The note in the margin reads that the petition was sent to the Committee of Legislation. D III, 240, dos. 4, AN.

Soboul wrote that Descombes earned 1,800 livres a year and that he left behind property worth only 400 livres. Like many other sans-culottes Descombes was not legally married. This was the pretext for the Convention's refusal to help his wife and son. *Sans-Culottes*, 791 n 117.

viled, expelled, and executed, was it not evident that no dissenter from the official policy of the Convention and its Great Committees was safe? But if this were the case, innovations from below would be discouraged and the Jacobins themselves, not only the Cordeliers, would become obedient servants of the government. Thus, the end of the Cordeliers also spelled finis to the earlier, democratic period of Jacobinism.

8

The "Amalgamated" and Reasons of State

If "Terror chills the heart," as Saint-
Just declared, then the wider the Terror, the more potential opponents of the government would it chill. Still, such a policy must be
accepted by Frenchmen and Frenchwomen everywhere. They must
be convinced that the Great Committees were defending their interests by ruthlessly destroying enemies of the people. The sans-culottes
must be persuaded that the patriotism of the Cordeliers was a false
patriotism designed to mislead the people. How better to accomplish
this end than to link counterrevolutionaries, criminals, and other
dubious elements to honest political opponents? In short, by "amalgamating" diverse oppositionists to the government with honest
political dissenters, the sans-culottes could be persuaded that the
Cordeliers deserved to die.

If the Cordeliers leaders constituted a political opposition, few of
those amalgamated with them were motivated by politics alone. Albert Mazuel was an ambitious military officer, Anacharsis Cloots was
a Prussian ex-nobleman, Jean Charles Bourgeois was an engineer,
and Armand Hubert Leclerc was an archivist (the latter two being
linked to Vincent). Jean Baptiste Ancard was a true sans-culotte; Jean
Armand, a student; Michel Laumur, an ex-governor of Pondicherry,
India; Jean Conrad de Kock, a Dutch banker; and Frédéric Pierre
Ducroquet, a wigmaker and hairdresser. There was also a woman,
femme Quétineau, determined to rescue her imprisoned husband.
And there was Jean Baptiste Laboureau, a physician by profession,
now acting as a spy for the government. It was enough to tie these
diverse individuals to the Cordeliers leaders, even if no real knot existed, for the amalgam to work.

Mazuel, for example, was linked to Ronsin because he commanded
a squadron of cavalry in the Revolutionary army. He was never confirmed as chief of the full four squadrons, but he liked to consider
himself as being such and often referred to "his cavalry." Mazuel was

born in the Comté de Nice, the future Villefranche (department of Alpes-Maritimes), in 1766. He worked as a shoemaker, then as a designer or decorator of woven material, or an embroiderer in silk, in Montpellier (department of Hérault) for nine years. The latter occupation brought him in contact with other artisans of the luxury trade, and his close relatives were either small retailers or better-off master workers. Mazuel was never a sans-culotte—except psychologically. Although he was married and had a child, he left his wife at home as he visited or traveled with various of his many mistresses. In short, he was a ladies' man, and after he could afford it he always dressed like a dandy.[1]

Like other ambitious young men, Mazuel found opportunities to advance his political career in the National Guard, which he joined upon the outbreak of the Revolution. Later he was to boast of his struggle against "fanaticism" in Montpellier and of his support of the patriots in southern France. In a brochure aimed at his fellow citizens, he blamed his own persecution on the support he professed for Marat, the Mountain, and the Jacobins.[2] By 1792 his reputation and popularity had carried him to the leadership of the troops from the Hérault Department as they departed for the Festival of the Fédérés in Paris.

In the attack on the Tuileries on August 10, Mazuel distinguished himself brilliantly and as a result became the spokesman for the fédérés. For despite his frivolities, Mazuel possessed courage, knew how to command men under fire, had convictions, and was politically ambitious. As a young provincial he was the more eager to throw himself into the exciting world of the Revolution in the capital. Moreover, he now had a political base as defender of the National Guardsmen.

Mazuel was reported to have been killed in the storming of the Tuileries—an error he hastened to rectify on August 12 in the Jacobin Club, which he had joined some time before (as well as joining the

1. Richard Cobb, *Les Armées révolutionnaires: Instrument de la Terreur dans les départements, avril 1793–floréal An II* (The Hague, 1961–63), I, 131–33, translated into English as *The People's Armies: Instrument of the Terror in the Departments* (New Haven, 1987). On October 12, 1793, Ronsin had to inform his officers that Mazuel was neither chief of the cavalry brigade nor commander of the four squadrons. Guillaume Antoine Grammont, chief of staff of the Revolutionary army, reminded Mazuel of this again shortly thereafter. Cobb, *Armées révolutionnaires*, I, 131n232.

2. Albert Mazuel, *Mazuel à ses concitoyens* ([Paris], Nivôse an II), in WIa, AN, cited by Cobb, *Armées révolutionnaires*, I, 133n245.

Cordeliers). A week later he expressed his chagrin at the reports that gave all credit to the Marseillais battalion (at whose side his own had fought) for the victory of the insurgents. He suggested that no distinction be made between the armed forces of the Parisian sections and the fédérés from the various departments. All ought to share in the glory. His egalitarian instincts also led him to support suggestions that all grades be abolished among the volunteers in order to discourage the petty intrigues and ambitious rivalries that were developing in the armed forces. Moreover, the men needed arms and barracks—otherwise they could not complete the task for which they had volunteered. Mazuel suggested that suspects be disarmed and their weapons be given to the troops; the Jacobins endorsed this idea and resolved also to buy arms and distribute them among their allies. On August 29, in an impassioned speech to the society, Mazuel demanded a purge of aristocrats from the general staff of the army and called on all to respect the peasant in his cottage.[3]

Mazuel complained to the Jacobins on September 8 that the Commune still had not armed the departmental guardsmen and that Santerre had urged him to "grab some pikes and go." Santerre evidently spoke in jest, but Mazuel was too earnest to have sensed it. How can we face artillery with simple pikes? he asked, grumbling that the fédérés lacked even shoes. Santerre replied, with tongue in cheek, that patriots made war barefooted. After two members defended Santerre's patriotism and excused his "humor," Mazuel replied lamely that he had never questioned his patriotism. Four days later he informed the society of his petition to the Convention yet again requesting arms for his fédérés. On October 19 he repeated his petition to the Jacobins' affiliated societies. On October 22 he announced that the fédérés would depart for the front in a few days and requested that a ceremony mark their departure.[4]

Mazuel participated in the winter campaign of the Palatinate but spent much of his time in the popular society of Nancy. Later, when he was attacked by Fabre d'Eglantine and others, he was able to cite the testimony of the deputies André Dumont and René Levasseur concerning his republican behavior during the campaign. He returned to Paris in April, 1793, as an aide-de-camp to Bouchotte, and profited from his new position by placing many of his relatives and

3. Tuetey, *Répertoire général*, XI, lxiii–lxiv; Aulard, *Jacobins*, IV, 236–37, 246.
4. Aulard, *Jacobins*, IV, 262–65, 282, 409, 415–16.

friends in positions of administration or command. He was active before and during the insurrection of May 31, informing the Jacobins how indignant and restless faubourg Saint-Antoine was after the Girondin Maximin Isnard's threat to raze Paris. While on duty at the doors of the Committee of Twelve, Mazuel heard many Parisians repeat that if the Convention failed to save them, they would do so themselves—a threat directed at the Girondins. His exhortations to the Jacobins to expose Isnard in the sections brought about a noisy explosion in the society.

After the expulsion of the Girondins from the Convention, Mazuel was sent by Bouchotte to the Vendée, where he met and made a good impression on Ronsin and Rossignol. He returned in July and the following month was authorized to form new squadrons of cavalry. Once again he used his position to establish his friends and relatives as lieutenants in the new force, thus creating a new clientele. When the revolutionary government began to amalgamate the Hébertistes and others, it had reason, therefore, to be suspicious of this military corps that appeared to be a kind of private army commanded by Mazuel. On August 9 he was arrested arbitrarily by the revolutionary committee of section Butte des Moulins but was released immediately when the section "recognized its error."[5]

Mazuel quarreled with Guillaume Antoine Grammont, the chief of staff, and Collot d'Herbois warned him that he was undermining the reputation of his own corps in the eyes of the sans-culottes. There is little question that Mazuel was undisciplined as he journeyed from one town to another, refusing to take up his post in Lyon. Later, this dereliction, too, would be used against him at the trial: he was accused of wanting to stay close to Paris so that he could mount his alleged coup. In reality, he asked to be sent to the army in the South, not to Paris. Unfortunately for him, his request was refused.[6]

Because he was a good friend of Vincent's, Mazuel was appointed

---

5. Aulard, *Jacobins*, V, 210–11, 339. Cobb raises the important question whether Mazuel could have used this force for a coup. It seems he was limited to the two squadrons he controlled in Versailles. When Mazuel was arrested in Pluviôse, many signed the petition for his release, but the same signatures appear congratulating the Convention for unmasking "the plot" of Mazuel in Ventôse. Still, he appeared dangerous to the authorities because he had so many friends in the cavalry. He did recruit questionable people, so that it seemed he could more easily control them. Mazuel appeared to many as "a leader of a band." Cobb, *Armées revolutionnaires*, I, 136 and note 251.

6. Cobb, *Armées révolutionnaires*, I, 137.

adjutant general of the Revolutionary army. A Jacobin objected to the appointment when he learned that Mazuel lacked the military training required for this high post. Mazuel refused the appointment, however, and asked to organize six squadrons of cavalry instead. This request was granted, and by October 20, 1793, Mazuel's cavalrymen were in place to demonstrate before the Conventionnels. When the force was about to depart for Beauvais (Oise Department), Mazuel refused to travel like an enlisted man, and when admonished that officers should not enjoy greater privileges than the men, he is said to have replied that for the "15 crappy francs that the Nation allows me a day, I could just as soon leave my saber in the closet."[7] Thus, it can be assumed, he must have made the journey in a more privileged manner than the rest.

On November 7 Mazuel, together with two colleagues, presented the Convention with two boxes of gold and nineteen crosses of Saint-Louis, the result of confiscations conducted by his squadrons.[8] Any esteem he may have gained through these gifts undoubtedly diminished when on December 22 he was arrested again, for starting a fracas in a theater, an action that discredited the cavalry and aroused resentment among his own officers. Although he claimed he was being victimized because of his patriotism, and despite his many supporters, others were beginning to be critical of his conduct.[9] By the time of his arrest he had acquired some formidable enemies in the Convention, and it is possible that they were waiting for an opportunity to dismiss him from his post. The incident at the theater might have given them the opening they sought.

Fabre d'Eglantine, a friend of Danton's, had already brought charges against Mazuel as an "ultrarevolutionary." One of Fabre's supporters testified that he had heard Mazuel declare: "All that the Convention does has the effect of a conspiracy. If a deputy were to displease me, I would spit him out of it [the Convention]." Pierre

7. Aulard, *Jacobins*, V, 426; Tuetey, *Répertoire général*, X, No. 2328, XI, lxv.

8. *Procès-verbal de la Convention nationale*, XXV, 88, cited by Tuetey, *Répertoire général*, XI, lxv.

9. The original report of the revolutionary committee of section Mont Blanc is in Mazuel's dossier, 3, in F7 4774 40, AN. The committee reported not only that there was nothing suspicious in his papers but that, on the contrary, his writings expressed only patriotic sentiments. Mazuel's wife was made guardian of his effects.

In the incident in the theater, Mazuel wanted to arrest an actor by name of Elleviou of the Comédie-Italienne, who had displeased him for some reason. Tuetey, *Répertoire général*, No. 2551.

Joseph Cambon, a member of the Committee of Public Safety and its "financial expert," also denounced him and asked the Committee of General Security to examine his conduct—a plausible request considering Mazuel's riotous behavior at the theater, for which (at least purportedly) he was arrested the next day by the revolutionary committee of section Mont Blanc. Nothing suspicious was found in his papers, however, and Cambon reversed himself and apologized, calling Mazuel a warm patriot—an indication, probably, of Mazuel's popularity and influence at this time. Mazuel, meanwhile, published his own justification on January 12, 1794. Vadier of the Committee of General Security reported to the Convention that there was nothing to Fabre's accusation, another indication that Mazuel still had important support in the Convention and reflecting also the growing split between the Montagnards and the Indulgents, followers of Danton. The Convention freed Mazuel and he was sent to Lyon shortly thereafter in command of the sixth squadron.[10]

Rearrested on March 16, Mazuel faced far graver charges. A witness testified that when Mazuel heard of Ronsin's and Vincent's imprisonment, he threatened to bring his cavalry, company by company, into Paris if the two were not released, a threat that was never implemented—if it was ever made. As for Robespierre, Mazuel supposedly had called him a "Janus . . . [who] would pass away just like the others." Mazuel denied all charges and was given a defender. He was only twenty-eight when he mounted the scaffold.[11]

Mazuel's passport described him as being five feet five inches in height, with brown hair, a long, large nose, brown eyes, an average mouth, and a round forehead with a small bump. He always spoke with affection of the sans-culottes and was concerned with the well-being of the country. In character, he resembled Vincent, that "furious man of the Revolution," whose ideas he shared, including their common aspirations for the popular societies (Vincent wrote to him on the need to multiply these clubs, which Mazuel frequented in Montpellier, Nancy, Beauvais, and Paris). Mazuel was a member of the Cordeliers, but what his exact role was in that society, or how

10. Procès-verbal of the revolutionary committee of Mont Blanc, 2 Ventôse, in F7 4774 40, AN; Tuetey, *Répertoire général*, XI, lxv–lxvi, X, Nos. 2545, 2547; *Procès-verbal de la Convention nationale*, XXV, 88.

11. Tuetey, *Répertoire général*, X, Nos. 2546, 2550, 2549. The witness was Nicolas Henrion. F7 4774 40, AN, contains an entry in the margin of the first document: "Guillotiné."

active he was in it is impossible to say. In general, he looked upon popular societies as natural allies of the Revolutionary army, whose creation was largely their work.[12]

Like many other revolutionaries Mazuel was violently anticlerical in his public pronouncements, although it is difficult to say what, precisely, were his personal religious convictions. He saw the Church as the enemy of the Revolution as he addressed his men: "Brave companions in arms . . . it is against an enemy that we march, it is fanaticism and superstition that we are going to combat. . . . Everywhere danger threatens us . . . of lying Priests, whose dogma is nothing but a deception, whose mission is only an illusion, whose empire is founded only on the credulity of women, human weakness, and the ignorance of people—these are our adversaries."[13] If he rejected the promise of an afterlife, surely one reason was that he loved his own active life in the present. Among his mistresses was the talented and beautiful actress and revolutionary Claire Lacombe, with whom he undoubtedly shared common aspirations for the sans-culottes and a mistrust of the higher authorities. He knew how to spend money, once splurging almost 1,200 livres in two days on himself and his companions. None of this could have endeared him to the more ascetic Jacobins. Nor did his unstable and excitable nature contribute to the acceptance of the Revolutionary army, to which he was so ardently devoted. His militancy and ambition proved his undoing.[14]

Among the foreigners amalgamated with the Hébertistes was Anacharsis Cloots, a Prussian descended from four generations of nobility whose family background could be traced back some 450 years. Born near Clèves on June 24, 1755, he was named Jean Baptiste after his uncle, a wealthy merchant. At nine the boy expressed a desire to go to Paris, became a skeptic after reading Voltaire, and finally an atheist. He studied at Brussels, Mons, and Paris, attended the military college of Berlin, and traveled widely. At some point he adopted the name of the ancient Scythian philosopher Anacharsis. Having inherited a considerable fortune, he could afford the amenities of life

12. Cobb, *Armées révolutionnaires*, I, 138.

13. Archives [departementales] Seine-et-Oise, IV, Q 186, cited by Cobb, *Armées révolutionnaires*, I, 138n259.

14. Tuetey, *Répertoire général*, X, No. 2551; Sequestered papers of Claire Lacombe, in T 1000, Vol. I, p. 138, AN. Soboul, in *Sans-Culottes*, 786, writes that Mazuel was mistakenly characterized as second-in-command when he was arrested on March 16—which error may have led to his destruction.

Anacharsis Cloots, "burnable in Rome, hangable in London, and broken on the wheel in Vienna," faced the guillotine in Paris with his courage and his sense of irony intact.

even though he dissipated much of his wealth before long. After publishing a number of books in the 1780s, he became well enough known in foreign circles to lead a delegation on June 19, 1789, to congratulate the National Assembly. After the Bastille fell, he never wavered in his enthusiasm for the Revolution.[15]

15. Avenel, *Cloots*, I, 1–3, 8–9; Tuetey, *Répertoire général*, XI, 1. The Scythian Anacharsis, according to legend, lived about 600 B.C. He traveled to Athens, where he met

Cloots made a pilgrimage to the Bastille before it was torn down, and was deliriously happy when the National Assembly abolished feudal privileges on August 4. He saw the importance of the Club Breton—the future Jacobin Club—and moved to rue Jacob on the Left Bank because this neighborhood appeared the most advanced in Paris. Later, he bought a country house about thirty miles outside the capital. When plans for the Festival of the Federation were made, he asked that all exiles living in Paris be invited to participate, and exclaimed enthusiastically: "I am a Clèvois by birth and a Parisian cosmopolitan in ideas. Long live the Gaul! Long live humanity!" Later, he presented an eloquent address in the name of the human race.

When the Cercle Social was organized by Nicolas de Bonneville and Claude Fauchet, Cloots found it too conservative for his tastes. He attended its meeting in the Cirque National on October 13, 1790, but was disappointed in Fauchet's speech because it linked the Christian religion to Freemasonry.[16] Cloots was shocked by Louis' flight to Varennes, and after the Champ de Mars massacre he broke from the more conservative Feuillants. Still, he defended Louis and even embraced the Constitution of 1791, which sought to reimpose the monarchy. He was aware that he was among the proscribed, and during this period of repression he noted that almost all the former leaders of the popular movement had fled abroad and that the Jacobins were split over the large political questions of the day.[17]

Cloots also endorsed the war declared on Austria by the Assembly in April, 1792; he argued that it would spread the ideals of the Revolution. Robespierre, who fought valiantly against the declaration, never forgave Cloots and his coterie of "foreigners" for supporting the war. The economic difficulties resulting from the war, and the

---

Solon and was the first foreigner to become a citizen of the city. He came back to teach his own countrymen the laws and customs of the more advanced Athenians but was killed by his brother when he tried to introduce the worship of Cybele, a more rational cult than that practiced by the Scythians. See the 13th edition (1926) of the *Encyclopedia Britannica*, I–II, 906. Avenel, *Cloots*, I, 209–10, cites Cloots as saying that he was a "*Vandale*" like the ancient Anacharsis and that he had come to the modern Athens, that is, Paris.

16. Avenel, *Cloots*, I, 221–26; Tuetey, *Répertoire général*, XI, 1. The meeting in the Cirque National is described in various publications of the Cercle Social. One of them is *La Bouche de fer*, which gives a report of the gathering in its No. 3 issue (October, 1790), in LC 2 317, BN.

17. Avenel, *Cloots*, I, 291–92, 293, 297–98.

consequent political upheaval, led Cloots, like many other former supporters of a compromise with the king, to break with this policy and its defenders. He abandoned the Brissotins and became an active Jacobin.

During the spring and early summer of 1792, Cloots supported the war enthusiastically and organized the foreign residents of Paris into a "Prussian Legion." He was convinced that "the reign of the brave Sans-Culottes [had] arrived" and that he was their "unworthy spokesman." In letters to his relatives and friends he wrote that patriotic feeling among the Parisians was at a high point, and he asked his uncle to tell him how the people in Cleves felt about the recent events in France. In July he praised a friend, residing at the moment in London, for his resolve to return to France in order to join the army. And in a letter to Condorcet praising the military services of a gendarme, he declared boldly that there would be no need for such letters of recommendation "if the chateau of Tuileries" did not exist. Thus, Cloots had finally broken with the monarchy and his past policy of supporting a compromise with Louis.[18]

Cloots's new politics did not, however, reconcile him to Robespierre, of whom he wrote that "the credit of this Tartuffe is the shame of our Revolution." He charged that "king Louis XVI and king Robespierre" presented more of a threat to France than the armies of the Austrians and the Prussians, and he was convinced that Robespierre was a pensioner of the king, a puppet, or both. Who, then, was his hero of the moment? It was Lafayette, whom he called "our Fabius."[19] In short, Cloots's republicanism was still conservative.

When the attack on the Tuileries was launched, Cloots sent his two servants to join the attackers while he proceeded to the Legislature. Three days after the successful insurrection he delivered an eloquent address in the Legislative Assembly; it was published and circulated among the troops and the fédérés. On August 25, he petitioned the Assembly to give servants citizenship, ending his appeal with, "Ev-

18. Cloots's dossier, 5, in F7 4649, AN. The letter to his uncle is dated January 22, 1792; the note of praise for the chevalier d'Eon was written on July 14; and his break with the king occurred on July 24, 1792. In addition, there are a number of purely personal letters. Avenel, *Cloots,* I, 389.

19. Cloots to his friend Rongies (not dated, but it must be on the eve of August 10), in F7 4649, dos. 5, AN.

The reference to Fabius, "the Delayer," who fought Hannibal, reflects Cloots's belief that Lafayette's policy, rather than Robespierre's, would bring victory to France.

ery individual who has arms is a rich proprietor on the soil of universal law." Shortly thereafter he was granted citizenship, together with other outstanding foreigners, and he was chosen elector by his section, Quatre Nations, the future Unité. His fellow electors, in turn, recommended him for deputy to the newly formed legislative body, the Convention. Not all endorsed his candidacy: Marat rejected him and called him "a stool pigeon." Despite this opposition, he was elected from two departments, and chose to represent the department of Oise. Only Tom Paine had received more votes in the electoral college than he.[20]

In the dispute over the nature of the republic to be established, Cloots opposed a federated state—advocated by Brissot, Roland, and their partisans—in favor of a centralized one. The Jacobins endorsed this position and on November 18, 1792, agreed to publish his remarks. Many of the club's members, however, rejected the attack on Marat in Cloots's brochure *Ni Marat, ni Roland* and wanted to make clear their defense of Marat in the publication. The debate on whether to publish Cloots with or without editorial notes brought on a sharp division until Claude Basire convinced a majority that it was unimportant what Cloots thought of Marat, so long as his work against the federalists deserved to be published.[21] The society ruled, ultimately, to disseminate Cloots's *La République universelle* without reference to Marat.

Cloots argued in this pamphlet against provincial and national bodies, which he called "the plagues of mankind," in favor of "a unified nation," and suggested that French could eventually become the universal language: it had always been the mark of an educated man, but whereas it had been aristocratic in the past, today it was democratic. Then, turning to a different theme, Cloots assailed religion and

20. Avenel, *Cloots,* I, 391–92, 395–97, 403, 410, 411, 413, II, 14. Cloots declared, "At all times a Gallophile, my heart is French, my soul is sans-culotte." In a letter to Rongies, August 21, 1792, in F7 4649, dos. 5, AN, he expressed his satisfaction with the victory over the monarchy and his desire to be elected to the Convention.

21. Aulard, *Jacobins,* IV, 486–88. In a letter to General Custine, October 26, 1792, Cloots condemned "the discord of petty federative republics" in favor of his "universal republic." On December 2 he called Dumouriez "the new Messiah, liberator of the human race," etc., as he offered him his antifederalist publications. Both letters are in F7 4649, dos. 5, AN.

In *Ni Marat, ni Roland: Opinion d'Anacharsis Cloots, député de l'Oise* (Paris, 1792), Cloots called Brissot an "isolationist" (p. 8) and accused the federalists of using the September Massacres for their own purpose (p. 14).

extolled atheism. "The belief in a God produces many calamities," he declared, and proclaimed that "a religious man is a depraved animal." This was followed by a none-too-subtle attack on Robespierre: "The tyranny of sophistries is worse than the tyranny of kings. And such a man who appears, in the eyes of the vulgar, as *virtuous*, as *incorruptible*, is in my eyes the most vicious, the most corrupt of bipeds." Finally, returning to his original theme, Cloots praised Paris as the best seat from which to defend the general interests of all, rather than provincial or individual interests.[22]

Whatever praise for Cloots's defense of a unitary republic was implied in the Jacobins' decision to publish his work, Robespierre could hardly have failed to notice the personal attack on him. The antireligious sentiments of the author gave him more ammunition against the Prussian. A chauvinist appeal against a "universal" state in time of growing nationalist sentiment was also advanced against Cloots. It is surprising, moreover, that those Jacobins who were so sensitive to Cloots's assault on Marat either failed to recognize the equally bitter charge against Robespierre or were willing to ignore it. In fact, they were to elect Cloots president of the society from November 11 to December 1, 1793. It is easy to imagine what Robespierre must have thought of this development.

On November 26, 1792, the Jacobins expelled Roland, Jean-Baptiste Louvet (a bitter enemy of Robespierre's), and several others from the society. In replying to accusations that he was a "parasite," Cloots defended himself by pointing out that he could have fled to England or America. Instead, he chose to remain at his post in Paris because his principles had always included "the liberation of the world." While English creditors were pressing their debtor refugees in France, the sans-culottes, in contrast, made up but one family everywhere, he argued.[23]

When the Convention condemned Louis, Cloots voted "yes" on the king's guilt, "no" on the appeal to the people, and "death" as the punishment to be meted out. During the decisive struggle between the Montagnards and the Girondins in the spring of 1793, Cloots abandoned his former allies and called for an insurrection against

22. Anacharsis Cloots, *La République universelle; ou, Adresse aux tyrannicides* (Paris, l'an quatrième de la Rédemption [1792]). The quotations cited are on pp. 7, 27, 28. Cloots added that "the French Revolution was the beginning of the world revolution" (p. 59).

23. Aulard, *Jacobins*, IV, 485, 519, 522.

them. Shortly thereafter he protested against Marat's accusation that as a member of the Convention's diplomatic committee he must have been a friend of Minister Lebrun. He repudiated this link in the Jacobin society and declared that his brochures were disseminated by Lebrun solely as weapons of propaganda. They had nothing to do with friendship, he said, and he denied having dined with the minister at his home.[24]

During the insurrection of May 31–June 2, 1793, Cloots was too ill to leave his bed. His fever distorted events so that he was convinced the uprising had failed and that the Jacobins and the sans-culottes had been defeated. Upon regaining his health, he again began to advocate such reforms as establishing schools in order to make all Frenchmen literate. Although he was ridiculed for proposing a universal and fraternal association of all men, Cloots remained firmly wedded to his dream of a cosmopolitan state.[25] This ideal was becoming suspect as deputies, Jacobins, and ordinary Frenchmen shed their former enthusiasm for the rights of all men and embraced the narrower rights of Frenchmen alone.

In addition, Cloots's militant atheism irritated not only deists like Robespierre but also the more practical politicians who were eager to come to terms with the European powers. Desmoulins attacked Cloots as "a patriotic hypocrite" and, like Robespierre, harped on his being a "Prussian" and "a Germanic cousin" of Proly. Bourdon de l'Oise carried this "logic" further and proposed that the Convention abrogate its decrees of August 2 and 27, 1792, which had provided for special treatment of foreign deserters in an attempt to weaken the Coalition. All these enemies of Cloots made it clear that he should resign as deputy or they would expel him from the Convention. But the Jacobins rejected such base attacks on Cloots, as evidenced by their aforementioned election of him as president of the club. Moreover, Belgians, Liégeois, and Batavians rallied around him, realizing that by protecting him they were defending themselves.[26]

The pressure against foreigners, and especially against foreign

24. Cloots to Marat, May 15, 1793, in F7 4649, AN. Cloots addressed the "Belgians, Batavians, Piedmontese, and Cosmopolites" in his brochure, and wrote that he had "unmasked" the Rolands, "these two monsters." His letters to various individuals in late fall of 1792 and winter and spring of 1793 breathe a spirit of patriotism and republicanism.

25. Avenel, Cloots, II, 198, 151–52.

26. Ibid., 280, 283, 284; Vieux Cordelier, November 10, 1793, pp. 44–45.

bankers, continued to mount, however. A few days before Desmoulins' assault on Cloots, a Dutch banker named Vandenhyver was arrested for allegedly being an accomplice of Madame Dubarry's. He was guillotined on November 8, 1793.[27] Cloots had had purely business relations with him, but the growing suspicion of foreigners placed him in jeopardy, all the more so when Robespierre launched a violent attack on him in the Jacobin Club. "Can we regard as a patriot a German baron?" Robespierre asked. "Can we regard as a sans-culotte a man who possesses more than 100,000 livres? Can we believe him to be a republican, a man who associates only with bankers and counterrevolutionary enemies of France? No, citizens. Let us be on guard against foreigners who want to appear more patriotic than the French themselves." Calling Cloots a traitor, Robespierre accused him of soliciting the Committee of General Security to free "the Vandenhyvers." As for Cloots's generous gifts for various patriotic causes, Robespierre assured his hearers that they were donated only for purposes of intrigue. He further castigated Cloots for his "extravagant opinions" and denounced his "universal republic": "Despising the title of French citizen, he wants to be only a citizen of the world." Robespierre then charged Cloots with "philosophic masquerades" against religion that had alienated the Belgians. "Citizens, do you regard as a patriot a foreigner who wants to be more of a democrat than the French?" he asked again. For proof that there was "a foreign party" in their midst, Robespierre cited the election of Cloots to the presidency of the society. "Cloots is a Prussian," he concluded.[28]

The Jacobins had heard enough; they promptly expelled Cloots. He was not even permitted to reply, and after Robespierre's extraordinary attack could only ask in amazement, "Is this me?—No, it can't be me!" There is little question that the two antagonists detested each other. Cloots hated religion and supported the cult of Reason. He could hardly have done more to arouse Robespierre's dislike of him. On November 17, Cloots presented the Convention his *Certitude des preuves du mahométisme*, an attack on Christianity. This was just a few days before Robespierre indicted the dechristianizers and their cult of Reason. Cloots could hardly have chosen a less auspicious time to present his work. Furthermore, if Robespierre and his supporters thought it possible to make peace with the Coalition, as some histo-

27. Avenel, *Cloots*, II, 285.
28. Aulard, *Jacobins*, V, 555–57.

rians argue, they must have felt that the antireligious crusade had to stop, for while it continued no understanding between France and the other powers would be possible.[29]

The expulsion of Cloots from the Jacobin Club made him a suspect liable to arrest. He was interrogated on December 28 by two commissioners of section Unité's revolutionary committee, assisted by two agents of the Committee of General Security. Cloots testified that he had been in Paris since age eleven, thus for twenty-seven years. When asked about his relations with the banker Vandenhyver, he replied that he had business dealings with the bankers (in the plural), that they were not criminals, and that they had no more to do with Dubarry "than with the Virgin Mary."[30] None of this helped, of course, and he was sent to Luxembourg prison, then to Saint-Lazare.

From his cell Cloots urged "men of good will" to compare the orations of the Girondin deputy Armand Gensonné against him with the concoctions of the present, and he asked members of the Committee of General Security to examine his papers scrupulously. They would find there his religious beliefs, his political comments, and his opinions on men and events, he wrote. Once again, he repeated that his country of birth was "Gaul," and he voiced to "fair-minded citizens" his certainty that "the human race would appreciate my release."[31] Some weeks later, at the end of January, he appealed not to be clas-

---

29. Avenel, *Cloots*, II, 326; Tuetey, *Répertoire général*, XI, li. Avenel is convinced that Robespierre was willing both to settle for what Avenel calls a "defective peace" (paix platrée) and to sacrifice the sans-culottes in order to come to an understanding with the European powers; *Cloots*, II, 279, 287.

Dechristianization is one of Guérin's major themes in *Lutte de classes*—see, for example, his interesting discussion on Robespierre's peace policy in Vol. I, chap. 8, secs. 11–15. Hébert and Chaumette, together with the Jacobins, denounced Soulavie (abbé Jean Louis Giraud), France's minister in Geneva, for his "antirevolutionary intrigues." Guérin calls him "the bête noire" of the Hébertistes; *ibid.*, I, 399.

30. F7 4649, AN. Cloots reproduced the interrogation in his *Appel au genre humain, par Anacharsis Cloots, représentant du peuple sauveur*, which can be found in Michel Duval, ed., *Anacharsis Cloots: Ecrits révolutionnaires, 1790–1794* (Paris, 1979), 632–33n1.

In defending Cloots against Robespierre, Avenel refers to the latter throughout the book as "the short-sighted incorruptible," and he wonders if Paine and Cloots were arrested by order of Pitt or of Robespierre. He cites protests against the French government's betrayal of the Rights of Man from Geneva and from Scotland, where a struggle for manhood suffrage was going on. A number of Montagnard journals also attacked the government's policy. Avenel, *Cloots*, II, 336–37, 338–39, 340–42.

31. *Anacharsis Cloots aux Hommes de bonne volonté, salut*, in Duval, ed., *Cloots: Ecrits révolutionnaires*, 645–48; F7 4649, AN.

sified as a suspect and a foreigner, and asked to be released so that he could publish his *Adresse aux sans-culottes anglais,* wherein he had "unmasked the agents of Pitt."[32]

In refuting the charge that he was both a foreigner and a noble, Cloots reminded his persecutors that Lepeletier was a marquis and that Brutus was a "foreigner." Had Marat been born a half league to the east, he would have been a "Prussian." If he himself was a noble-man, it was in the same way that one was a Catholic who had refused his first communion. Asking whether the Rights of Man was limited to Frenchmen or was meant for all mankind, Cloots reminded his readers that Robespierre had defended the rights of all men in the past. The "sans-culotterie is neither French nor English; it is cos-mopolitan, universal," he wrote. As to the ongoing argument over whether a republic of atheists could exist, Cloots replied that any other republic was "a chimera." To admit "a king in heaven," he as-serted, "is to introduce within our walls the Trojan horse."[33]

The Convention's majority, having turned its back on the Consti-tution of 1789 and that of 1793, voted to exclude any deputy who had been born outside France, an act aimed at Paine and Cloots. The Committee of Public Safety was directed to prepare a report ex-cluding them from all public functions. In addition, it decided to expel all foreign deserters who had joined its armies and to allow them to remain in France only until they were exchanged.[34] What-ever sentiments of internationalism and solidarity with "the cottages against the palaces" had motivated the deputies when they com-mitted France to war in the spring of 1792 were gone. Cosmopolitan-ism now became unpatriotic.

The government began to prepare its case against Cloots. On

32. Tuetey, *Répertoire général,* X, No. 2500.
33. Avenel, *Cloots,* II, 318–19, 326–30 (summary of Cloots's "Sur les spectacles et leur influence dans l'éducation"); "Opinion d'Anacharsis Cloots, membre du Comité d'instruction publique," in Duval, ed., *Cloots: Ecrits révolutionnaires,* 641.
Cloots wrote that a noble was a valet, but that he had never served anyone. He admitted that he favored union of Clèves with France and shared with Belgians, Bata-vians, Liégeois and Clèvois the desire to chase the German enemy beyond the Rhine. See "Appel aux genre humain," in Anacharsis Cloots, *Anacharsis Cloots Oeuvres . . .* (Paris, 1980), III, 689–708. This essay was written December 12, 1793. In it, Cloots terms Robespierre "irascible."
34. Avenel, II, 332–33. Avenel comments that "in the eyes of the gentlemen of the Committee, they [the foreign deserters] were no more than disturbers of the European equilibrium."

March 7 the prosecution introduced a Prussian officer deserter, Frédéric Gugenthal, who testified that he had seen three letters written by Cloots to the duke of Brunswick at General Kalgstein's quarters. Two weeks earlier, a woman named Haquin had told the Committee of General Security that Cloots had plotted with Pereyra and Desfieux in Saint-Lazare prison to overthrow the Convention and to massacre the Montagnards, beginning with Robespierre and Barère. On March 20 Cloots was interrogated by Dobsent, was given a defense attorney, and was sent to the Conciergerie.[35]

All witnesses testify to the extraordinary courage that Cloots displayed on the eve of his death. He died the way he had lived, secure in his atheism. To the cries of his enemies, "The Prussian to the guillotine!" he replied: "To the guillotine, so be it. But you will admit, citizens, that it is quite extraordinary that the man burnable in Rome, hangable in London, and broken on the wheel in Vienna, should be guillotined in Paris, at the high tide of the republic." A number of sources report that in the midst of indignant cries against their sentence, the prisoners in Conciergerie heard the calm voice of Cloots reciting the melancholy lines "Je rêvais cette nuit que, de mal consumé, / Côté à côté d'un gueux on m'avait inhumé." Somehow this calmed everyone, and they embraced for the last time. Cloots mounted the scaffold with courage and died with dignity.[36]

In addition to the more prominent victims condemned by the Revolutionary Tribunal, another nine men and one woman were also indicted. All but one—the police spy Laboureau—were executed. Among the condemned was Jean Charles Bourgeois, who com-

35. Tuetey, *Répertoire général*, X, Nos. 2501, 2502, 2194. On the other hand, a witness named Millin, although admitting that there was fear in the prison of Saint-Lazare that the "advanced patriots" would be freed and others killed, said there was no proof that Cloots, Desfieux, and Pereyra had participated in such a plot or knew anything about it. Another witness, Cholet, named by Haquin, declared that Haquin had confused the three prisoners with "the men of blood" about whom he spoke. Cholet himself never doubted their patriotism, he testified, and had never heard them say anything unpatriotic. *Ibid.*, Nos. 2195, 2196. Millin and Cholet must have been unusually courageous and honest, considering the circumstances of their interrogation.

36. Avenel, *Cloots*, II, 459, 463. A "détenu" named Riouffe, who left a record of Cloots's last moments, wrote that Cloots showed a courage he had never suspected of him; "Mémoire d'un détenu," in Charles Aimé Dauban, *Les Prisons de Paris sous la Révolution, d'après les relations des contemporaines* (1870; rpr. Geneva, 1977), 118. In Cloots's dossier, 5, in F7 4649, AN, two deputies of the Convention, Bréard and Laloy, describe their examination and resealing of Cloots's papers in his house in section Lepeletier on June 25, 1794.

manded the armed force of section Mutius Scaevola—Vincent's section. He was twenty-five years old, a former carpenter, then an engineer, who became a civil commissioner and an elector of section Luxembourg (the future Mutius Scaevola) in 1792. He was sent on a mission to Thionville and Longwy in September by the Executive Council, and during the May 31–June 2 insurrection of the following year commanded the armed force of his section. In the Year II he was employed in the Bureau of Verification. When arrested on March 16, 1794, he demanded the affixing of seals on his papers so that he could prove his innocence. He was interrogated two days later, given a defense attorney, and condemned with the rest.[37]

Also linked to Vincent was Armand Hubert Leclerc, employed in the War Department since July 21, 1793. He was born in Cauny (the future department of Seine-Inférieure) and had been an archivist by occupation. A witness, the wife of Jean Louis Boucher, accused him of having spoken angrily against the Montagnard deputies. When asked what would become of France if all the Montagnards were guillotined, he replied: "Bah! if only one were left it would be more than enough." When interrogated, Leclerc denied plotting against the Republic or having any connection with any of the accused. He insisted that he had been too busy in the War Department to have plotted against anyone, and that he had seen Vincent only half a dozen times. In refuting Boucher's accusations he called her immoral and charged that she was widely known by the name of "lewd Sarron." Nothing helped, of course, and he was guillotined with the rest.[38]

If Bourgeois and Leclerc belonged to the middle class and "were characteristic of the revolutionary personnel of the Year II," as Soboul wrote, Jean Baptiste Ancard belonged to the lower order of sans-culottes. He was a glove cutter and day laborer by occupation.[39] Born in Grenoble in 1742, he moved to Paris and took up residence in section Unité. He was employed by Pache and sent to Mainz, then posted by Bouchotte to the army at Dunquerque before serving as Ronsin's adjutant in the Vendée. He was a member of the military commission at Tours, proof either of his competence or of his political influence. When arrested, he was employed in the office investigating émigrés.

37. Tuetey, *Répertoire général*, X, Nos. 2540–42, XI, lxiii.
38. *Ibid.*, X, Nos. 2536, 2538, 2539, XI, Nos. 225, 226, lxii.
39. Soboul, *Sans-Culottes*, 786.

Ancard joined the Cordeliers Club and became known for his forceful, even violent, expressions. He seems to have endorsed the much-discussed insurrection and made no effort to hide his feelings. A witness testified that when asked if Ancard meant a fusillade such as took place in the Vendée, he is alleged to have replied, "No, but a September 2" (that is, a massacre). The same witness reported that when all Cordeliers members rose in support of Collot d'Herbois when he denounced the alleged insurrection, only Ancard remained in his seat. Furthermore, it was alleged that he had denounced the Committee of Public Safety as another Committee of Twelve oppressing patriots. Ancard's wife supposedly was overheard saying that had the Cordeliers been less prudent, they "would have thrashed the Jacobins." [40]

Ancard was also accused of denouncing the representatives and distributing the newly published journal of the Cordeliers in cafés he frequented. One witness reported that he wanted eighty thousand heads to roll in two weeks' time, and when someone objected that two weeks was too short an interval to judge so many (evidently another two weeks for such executions would have been acceptable to the interlocutor), Ancard was quoted as saying that it didn't matter how these heads fell so long as they fell. Then he added that it was necessary for the "selfish rich to share their wealth with the Sans-Culottes." [41] Nothing was proved against him after his arrest and interrogation except his remarks, which were enough to condemn him.

A stranger to the group was Jean Antoine Florent Armand, a student of surgery born in Cheylard (the future department of the Ardèche). Before the Revolution his father, a *procureur* in the *sénéchaussée* of Villeneuve-de-Berg, employed him in his office. Shortly thereafter he became secretary of the municipality of Tours before taking up his studies. After moving to Paris, Armand seems to have plotted against the government and been naïve enough to reveal his plans to others, who informed the Committee of General Security. Those plans included the release of prisoners and the assassination

40. Tuetey, *Répertoire général*, X, Nos. 2527, 2520–22, XI, No. 227. The witnesses were Claude Tessier of section République, Jean Etienne Brochet, and a citizeness Metras (among others). Not all Cordeliers applauded Collot, as we have seen.

41. *Ibid.*, X, No. 2525. Tuetey—without showing the least skepticism—cites a number of witnesses who accused Ancard of poisoning his wife, two children, and brother, of being a thief who escaped branding only by the intervention of his brother (the same one Ancard poisoned?), and of other such unsavory behavior; *ibid.*, XI, lviii–lix.

of Hanriot, Chabot, and Barère. Armand stated that he had placarded markets in the hope of inspiring similar placarding elsewhere. When a future witness objected to the absurd nature of his plot, he assured her that it could not fail, as there were at least another forty plots like it in the capital. Armand was arrested, interrogated, and imprisoned in the Conciergerie. He was twenty-seven when he mounted the scaffold.[42] There seems to have been no connection between Armand and the Cordeliers; Fouquier-Tinville amalgamated him with the Hébertistes to show a royalist thread to the latter.

Linked to the plot was a general, Michel Laumur, the former governor of Pondicherry, India. He was born in Paris in 1730 and made his career in India. Decommissioned in 1782 because of poor health, he returned to the service in 1792 as a lieutenant colonel. His amiable relations with Dumouriez led to promotions, including the grade of maréchal de camp (brigadier general). Ultimately, however, this relationship led to his arrest. The spy Laboureau accused him of being an aristocrat who plotted against the government. Sometime in March the minister of France to Sweden, Raymond Verninac, reported a conversation in which Laumur spoke to him of the coming insurrection of the Cordeliers and the plan to appoint "a great judge," who was to be Pache. This was sufficient for the public prosecutor to have Laumur arrested on March 13, interrogated five days later, and condemned on March 24.[43]

In addition to linking the various accused to royalists, the government was at pains to show their connection to foreign bankers. Among the latter was Jean Conrad de Kock, born in Heusden, Holland, and a refugee in France since 1787. On May 15, 1791, his name appeared on a petition of the Batavian patriots presented to the Jacobins. In November, 1792, he was granted a passport to Antwerp accompanied by his wife and servant. Shortly thereafter he became one of the suppliers of Dumouriez's army, hence his frequent trips to Belgium. Desmoulins accused him of intimacy with Dumouriez, which may have been true. It seems that Hébert visited de Kock frequently

---

42. *Ibid.*, X, Nos. 2517–19, XI, lvii. Armand revealed his plot to Charles François Frédéric Haindel, former officer of the German Legion and currently commander of the 11th Regiment of hussars. Haindel's wife, Julienne Amelie Durquant, to whom Armand also revealed his plot, was assured that unlike on August 10, 1792, there was much discontent in the capital. Haindel also met femme Quétineau, who wanted to hurry the project before supplies reappeared in Paris.

43. *Ibid.*, X, No. 2383, XI, xxxviii.

at his home in Passy, and that Ronsin, Hanriot, and other officers were also frequent guests there.[44]

De Kock was arrested on March 14, 1794, and his papers were sealed. He denied all charges, declaring that he knew nothing of incendiary papers or plots against the public. He admitted that he had been at Hébert's home some four or five days earlier, when a crowd had gathered there to wait for the distribution of salt pork confiscated at the home of a wine merchant. Furthermore, he had been told that Hébert and his associates had received twenty-four pounds of salt pork, which had been distributed. Hébert had added, de Kock reported, that it pained him to see such crowds gathering (in expectation of receiving some food).[45] De Kock had given frequent contributions for various patriotic causes in section Bonne-Nouvelle, where he had his office. This was also Hébert's section. Thus, de Kock was condemned because he was a foreigner, a banker, and a friend of Hébert's.

The woman amalgamated with the Hébertistes, Marie Anne Catherine Latreille, was born in Montreuil-Bellay, near the town of Saumur. Thirty-four years old, she was the wife of General Pierre Quétineau, who was imprisoned in the Abbaye. In her anxiety to save him she became involved with Armand, who resided in the same house. It was reported that she rejoiced with Armand at the long lines of women in Les Halles who lacked food. Shortages encouraged them both to hope for an insurrection against the government.

Quétineau was arrested on March 17, 1794, and sent to the Sainte-Pélagie prison, then transferred to the Conciergerie and condemned on 4 Germinal. She declared that she was four months pregnant, which was confirmed after an examination. The Revolutionary Tribunal ordered her execution stayed until she gave birth, but shortly after this reprieve she had a miscarriage. Three weeks later, on May 11, she was executed.[46]

44. Aulard, *Jacobins*, I, 439; Tuetey, *Répertoire général*, X, Nos. 2391–93, 2405, 2211, 2214. The witnesses at de Kock's trial all spoke of these visits as "orgies." Fouquier-Tinville did not know him, as he spelled his name "Kuoff" or "Koff." See Tuetey, *Répertoire général*, X, No. 2387, for Verninac's testimony, in which he claimed that the Cordeliers planned to appoint Pache as the "great judge" during or after the insurrection.

45. Tuetey, *Répertoire général*, X, Nos. 2402–2404, 2407, 2408.

46. *Ibid.*, XI, lvi, Nos. 236–38. There is some disagreement in the sources over femme Quétineau's pregnancy. Another version is that the examination proved her not to be pregnant after all. In either case, she was certainly executed after she could no longer claim to be with child.

Among the few artisans on trial was Frédéric Pierre Ducroquet, a wigmaker and hairdresser born in Amiens and filling the post of commissioner against hoarding in section Marat. On March 5, 1794, he spoke out sharply against profiteers, contrasting their affluence with the hunger of the sans-culottes. Ducroquet was among the first to call for the veiling of the Declaration of Rights in section Marat. Among other measures, he urged sending a delegation to the Commune to see if all that could be done to supply Paris had actually been done; if not, he proposed that the section proclaim itself in insurrection. This demand led to his arrest on March 13 and interrogation five days later. A number of witnesses testified that they had heard Ducroquet call for an insurrection if provisions were not assured. He was imprisoned in the Conciergerie and his papers were sealed. On March 21 (1 Germinal) he wrote a moving letter to his wife and two children, taking his farewell. Whatever his fate, he wrote, he had been moved by love of country and his conduct had been irreproachable. He felt certain that "the Republic one and indivisible [would] not perish."[47] Soboul calls him "a true sans-culotte" and "the most modest" of those under arrest.[48]

Of the twenty on trial, only Jean Baptiste Laboureau was acquitted. A physician, he was appointed as first commissioner to the Council of Health, then as commissioner of health in the War Department. Laboureau was born in Charnay-sur-Arroux (the future department of Côte-d'Or), and was forty-one at the time of his arrest. An active member in section Marat, he became secretary of its revolutionary committee. It was said that he had displeased Robespierre, was arrested, and was pardoned after testifying against the accused in the so-called prison plot. On March 12, 1794, one of the judges on the Revolutionary Tribunal received Laboureau's declaration as to what had taken place a week earlier in the general assembly of section Marat—the session at which Ducroquet had insisted on a motion to place the section in insurrection and to veil the Rights of Man. Laboureau added Momoro's statement to the Commune on the section's unease over shortages, thus implicating him also.[49]

At a meeting of the popular society of section Marat, Amis du peuple, on March 14, Laboureau vehemently protested the arrest of Mo-

47. *Ibid.*, X, Nos. 2528, 2531, 2534, 2535, XI, No. 215, lx.
48. "Despite the sarcasm under which certain historians have covered him [Ducroquet], he remains the symbol of those humble and ardent revolutionaries, without whom the Republic could never have triumphed." Soboul, *Sans-Culottes*, 788, 789.
49. Tuetey, *Répertoire général*, X, No. 2653, XI, lxxiii.

moro and declared that if the latter's head should fall, his own would follow. He seems to have had the reputation of being Momoro's protégé, but whether this was true and he changed under the threat of his indictment, or had been a provocateur from the start, is difficult to say. In any case, he demanded that the society appoint two defenders for Momoro to learn from the Committee of Public Safety and Fouquier-Tinville what the accusations were. Laboureau himself was arrested shortly thereafter, was sent to the Conciergerie, and was interrogated on March 16. His papers were sealed three days later in his absence, which brought a complaint from his wife.[50]

On March 25—the day after most of the accused were guillotined—Laboureau wrote one of the judges of the Revolutionary Tribunal a strange letter in which he declared that prior to his arrest he knew nothing of any conspiracy. He declared, furthermore, that Vincent had never shown him the slightest confidence, but that unlike Vincent, Momoro had always shown him consideration and amity. He quoted Momoro as speaking of a "Proly faction," which Momoro thought was a remnant of Dumouriez's group, as being among the accused. As for himself, Laboureau declared that he could not distinguish who was right and who was wrong.[51]

This confession of Laboureau's is strange, indeed. Could it have resulted from a bad conscience? His testimony at the trial had helped condemn the Hébertistes and those "amalgamated" with them. He alone escaped the guillotine.

Of the twenty on trial, few can be regarded as belonging to the sans-culottes or to social strata linked to the *petites gens*. Ancard and Ducroquet were artisans. Mazuel had been an embroiderer and shoe-

50. *Ibid.*, X, Nos. 2655, 2657, XI, lxxiv.
51. *Ibid.*, X, No. 2659, XI, lxxxv. The judge who received Laboureau's letter was François Joseph Denizot. The original is unsigned. Laboureau published a brochure entitled *Rapport de ce que j'ai vu et entendu depuis ma détention,* in which, according to Tuetey, he expressed reservations about the Hébertiste "plot." Tuetey adds that much of what Laboureau wrote accords with the observations of those cited by Dauban in his *Prisons de Paris.* Dauban in fact cites (pp. 329–32) a number of quotations from Laboureau's pamphlet, including the nonsense on the "Proly faction." Some of Ronsin's conversation sounds authentic, however, and is often quoted by memorialists and others. Laboureau described him as always appearing to be gay. Ronsin understood that the trial was political and that, thus, legal arguments were of no avail. Still, he was confident of being avenged by his son and swore he would not flinch when confronted by the guillotine. At the same time he accused Hébert of babbling ("Tu as verbiagé") when he should have acted.

maker. Leclerc was an archivist, Bourgeois an engineer, and Armand a student. The last three men were linked to the Cordeliers only by their functions. Descombes was a teacher, not a sans-culotte, and no Cordelier.

Hébert, Ronsin, Vincent, Momoro (a former printer), and Laboureau were government functionaries. Cloots was an ex-nobleman, while Proly, Pereyra, and de Kock were of the haute bourgeoisie. Desfieux was a wine merchant, Laumur a general, and Dubuisson a man of letters. The last, femme Quétineau, was a housewife.

The social origins of these men and one woman did not determine their commitment to the Revolution, however. Patriotism did not flow from their social origin. It was more a result of ideals held by the individual, perhaps equally a matter of ideology (or, to use a current term, political culture). It takes little imagination, however, to note how agonizing it must have been for the patriots among the accused to become victims of a government in which they had shown such confidence. All devoted revolutionaries, not only the sans-culottes, having seen their best leaders struck down amidst calumny and vituperation, were bound to turn away from the Revolution they had embraced so ardently. Soon many retired into passivity or indifference, thus depriving the revolutionary government of their support, which alone could sustain it.

9

The Trial

If, as Marx asserts, history repeats itself once as tragedy and again as farce, the Moscow trials of the Old Bolsheviks were certainly of the former variety. The analogy between those trials and the frame-up of the Hébertistes is striking. There are the same absurd charges against individuals motivated by "reasons of state," or what were thought to be such; the same "amalgamation" of disparate individuals; the same slanders against men who sacrificed everything for the Revolution; the same attempt to find a "foreign conspiracy" behind the accused; and the same preordained outcome. If the Bolsheviks learned how to stage an uprising from "the great bourgeois revolution" of France, that Revolution also acted as a model for their destruction. Whatever reasons historians give for the trial of the Cordeliers leaders, the outcome was undeniable: it led to the destruction of "the factions" and the further strengthening of the "Republic of Virtue."[1]

It can be added, further, that the trial of the Hébertistes was inextricably linked with that of the Dantonistes. From the government's point of view both factions constituted threats to its goal of unity, essential in the war against the Coalition. And, without either party's realizing it, each depended for its existence on the continued presence of its enemy. The annihilation of one led inevitably to the demise of the other. The efforts of the two sides to destroy each other made it easier for the government to pose as the sole unifying force in the nation.

On March 14, 1794, Fouquier-Tinville announced the arrest of all "conspirators as instructed" in a letter to the Committee of Public

1. Albert Mathiez, in "Les Deux Versions du procès des Hébertistes," *Annales révolutionnaires*, XI (1919), pp. 1–27, wrote that the trial was an episode in the struggle between the revolutionary government and the moderate faction inspired by Danton (see note 46 below). This construction ignores the threat from the Cordeliers. Soboul, on the other hand, saw the trial as "an episode in the struggle . . . against the popular movement"; *Sans-Culottes*, 779.

Safety. On March 20 Couthon reported in the name of the two Committees that the trial would begin the following day (1 Germinal). The public prosecutor listed the charges against the accused and named the governments of England and the Coalition as "the real chiefs of the conspiracy."[2]

The indictment listed twenty persons, beginning with Ronsin and ending with Proly. They were charged with a plot to starve Paris, seize the government, open the prisons, massacre the representatives of the people, and circulate brochures and manuscripts that subverted liberty. The Hébertistes were specifically accused of harboring ambitions to satisfy their desire for wealth and power. In order to link them to foreign bankers, it was alleged that the plot was hatched in the home of de Kock at Passy. In addition, the prosecution claimed, shortages of essentials were to be encouraged; discord between the Jacobins and the Cordeliers was to be injected; and envoys were to spread rebellion in the environs of Paris.[3]

The arrests had taken place without resistance because the accused believed they were innocent and felt that they could prove it in court. Not one document was cited in the trial, however, doubtless because had documents been presented, the prisoners could have refuted them, whereas the often-wild allegations of "witnesses" were more difficult to challenge with cold facts. For example, one of the charges against Ronsin was that he had told a young German prisoner to hasten to Frankfurt and to inform "our enemies" of the time the conspiracy was to be executed. Ronsin noted the absurdity of this accusation in a letter to Fourquier-Tinville. The banker de Kock was

2. Débats du 1er Germinal, plaq. 1, F7 4438, AN, is an inventory of the evidence on the twenty persons indicted. The record of the Revolutionary Tribunal in W 173, AN, is a thirty-page document containing the list of the accused, résumés of witnesses, and brief summaries of the accusations against the twenty (1–3 Germinal, II); it was published by the government in *Procès des Conspirateurs Hébert, Ronsin, Vincent, Momoro, Desfieux, et complices* (Paris, 1794). The last portion of this publication, pp. 109–26, is an extremely critical summary of Hébert's life. *Jugement rendu par le tribunal révolutionnaire* ([Paris], n.d.), in Lb 41 2232, BN, is the verdict signed by A. Q. Fouquier. See also Tuetey, *Répertoire général*, X, No. 2042; *AP*, LXXXVI, 719–20; *Moniteur*, XX, No. 183 (March 23, 1794), 17–20. The indictment carried the signatures of the judges of the Revolutionary Tribunal.

3. Record of the Tribunal, in W 173, AN; *Journal de la Montagne*, No. 132 (March 25, 1794), 1066, 1072–76; *Moniteur*, XX, No. 183, (March 23, 1794), 19, 20, No. 197 (April 2, 1794), 139. Aulard, *Jacobins*, VI, 40; Wallon, *Tribunal revolutionnaire*, III, 45–47, 49, 55, 58, 59; B&R, XXXI, 360–62, 363–64, 364–69; Herlaut, *Ronsin*, 230, 231, 233. The *Bulletin* of the Revolutionary Tribunal (Nos. 1–7), published by B&R, lists the names and ages of the accused and the fourteen judges of the court.

alleged to be the intermediary between Pitt and the "conspirators," whereas Laumur, a former friend of Dumouriez's, was linked to the Hébertistes. Among other charges was the accusation that the prisoners were plotting to restore the monarchy. Couthon informed the Convention on two different occasions that the accused had hoped to place the little Capet on the throne.

The court referred to two numbers of Hébert's *Père Duchesne*, 269 and 275, to prove that its publisher had attacked the principle of concentrating all power in the hands of the Committees. Hébert defended himself by saying that one could destroy a man by quoting phrases without taking into account the circumstances under which they were written. The president of the Tribunal, Dumas, replied that since the insurrection of May 31–June 2, 1793, Hébert had been determined to disorganize all constituted authorities "and to set everything ablaze." Furthermore, he accused Hébert of receiving 100,000 livres from the national treasury to fulfill a mission that patriots performed gratis.[4]

The first witness, Louis Legendre, harking back to the acrimonious dinner party at Mayor Pache's, testified that Vincent had formerly embraced him for what he was, but that now Vincent called him a "moderate." Vincent replied that Legendre had been his friend but that their friendship had come to an end; the episode at Pache's had no other significance, he declared. Asked by the president if in ridiculing Legendre's uniform he were not ridiculing all deputies, Vincent replied that he had no such intention. He thought that the motley of colors worn by the representatives "could astonish the eyes of those unaccustomed to them," and that perhaps his remarks were thoughtless, but he had no intention of criticizing the deputies or their work.

Next to appear was Louis Pierre Dufourny, president of the directory of the Paris Department, who charged that since the May 31–June 2 insurrection Vincent had displayed publicly his hatred of all constituted authority and had tried to undermine the patriots in the popular societies. Ronsin, he declared, wanted to guillotine him (Dufourny), Robespierre, and others, had plotted to set himself up as a "Cromwell," and favored a purge of the Convention. Dufourny re-

---

4. Wallon, *Tribunal révolutionnaire*, III, 58–59. Dumas had just been ceded the presidency of the court by the former president, Martial Joseph Herman. Before the trial of the Hébertistes, Dumas had been vice-president.

ferred to an alleged letter from General Biron as proof but failed to produce the letter in court. Ronsin denied that he had ever urged the expulsion of certain leading deputies from the Convention, or that he had laughed "sardonically," another of the more absurd accusations.

Disorder broke out in the courtroom after Ronsin's testimony. Dumas accused the audience of harboring counterrevolutionaries, until all produced their cards of security. Was the outburst proof of sympathy for the accused, or were the charges regarded as being so absurd that witnesses could not contain themselves?

On March 22 some nineteen witnesses were heard, including General Louis Michel Auguste Thévenet Danican, who claimed that Ronsin had prepared a squadron of cavalry against the Convention. Ronsin replied that he had been ordered by Hanriot to send the squadrons in order to help in house searches. Danican was a royalist agent and owed his promotion to Ronsin while serving in the Vendée, but had been removed from command for cowardice at Angers.

One of the spies for Fouquier in Sainte-Pélagie prison was a Belgian named Charles Jaubert. He had been arrested as a former aide-de-camp of an Austrian general. Although released, he was badly received by the Belgian refugees in Paris, who were suspicious of him. Rearrested in 1793 by the Committee of Public Safety, he sought to save himself by accusing certain bankers of plotting against the Republic. Now he limited himself to claiming that Ronsin had spoken against the "liberticide" faction of Bourdon de l'Oise, Desmoulins, and Philippeaux, and furthermore, that Ronsin had been studying the history of England in the English language because he wanted to be a Cromwell.

Ronsin attacked Jaubert as an enemy of France. In addition, he denied reading David Hume's history, pointing out that he did not know English. As for Cromwell, Ronsin considered him an oppressor of his country, not someone worthy of emulation. This was one of the surprising twists in the testimony. The Cordeliers logically should have embraced a fellow regicide, but the fact that Cromwell was forced to govern as a dictator (Lord Protector) precluded any such approbation. To make clear his repudiation of dictatorship, Ronsin affirmed his respect for the Convention.[5]

---

5. Although there is no evidence that Ronsin ever read a biography of Cromwell, two biographies of the Lord Protector in French were published as early as 1671: François Raguenet, *Histoire Oliver Cromwel* [sic] (Paris, 1671), and F. Ferdinand de Galardi,

As for the charge that he wanted to arm the prisoners, Ronsin replied that although they were badly guarded, he had no intention of introducing arms into prison. He then demanded the appearance of various deputies, as well as Hanriot, Boulanger, and Danton's friend Saintain. He also requested that Robespierre's physician appear, evidently because the man knew things usually locked in the bedchamber. Fouquier made no response and of course had no intention of calling witnesses, some of whom might have testified in Ronsin's favor.

Dufourny then read from "notes" allegedly written by Desfieux. This "evidence" was introduced to support the charge that together with others, Desfieux had plotted to release prisoners in order to stage a counterrevolution. Desfieux replied that he did not recognize the notes. He was certain, he added, that his innocence would be proved and his calumniators confounded. Nor was he planning any "unusual movements" or desired vengeance. There were no plots, he emphasized; well-known patriots had met in his home and occupied themselves with means to raise the public spirit, that was all. Finally, he testified that he knew nothing about any armaments stolen by Mazuel (who had been implicated with Ronsin), and he denied having anything in common with Lebrun.[6]

Proly followed, accused of opposing the decree of December 15, 1792, which had annexed Belgium to France, and of having declared that Belgium should be permitted to keep its nobles and priests. He replied that he thought Belgium was not yet ripe to embrace the French Revolution and so could not abandon its nobles and priests. He was then asked if he had been Dumouriez's partisan; if he had made liaisons with Lebrun, the former minister of foreign affairs; if he had not slandered patriots; and if he had not tried to set up a new government and had not so informed the departments.

Proly admitted that at one time he had held a high regard for Dumouriez's military ability and had been misled by this, but he denied all other charges, including a statement that he had criticized the French for looting churches and had said that this must not be done in Belgium. One witness claimed that Proly had proposed unity with

---

La Tyrannie heureuse; ou, Cromwel [sic] politique (Paris, 1671). See Wilbur Cortez Abbot, A Bibliography of Oliver Cromwell (Cambridge, Mass., 1929).

6. B&R, XXXI, 369–70, 371, 372, 373–76, 377–78; Herlaut, Ronsin, 233–34, 244, 247–49. Cloots also denied he intended to corrupt Dufourny; B&R, XXXI, 376–80.

the Girondins if Dumouriez should march on Paris, and was for peace with Prussia. Others accused him of being a spy for the emperor, and libeled Ronsin and Rossignol as not interested in ending the war in the Vendée.[7]

On the next day, the Committee of Public Safety demanded that Fourqier end the trial by producing witnesses held in reserve who would divulge the plot to free prisoners and purge the Convention. Thus prompted by the Committee, Dumas asked the jurors on 4 Germinal if they had heard enough so that he could close the debate. They replied in the negative, a ruse prepared in advance, evidently, to give the appearance of a just trial. This brought the forty-fourth witness, Charles François Frédéric Haindel, a former lieutenant colonel of the German Legion, a Prussian by birth. He repeated the charges already made and implicated Armand and Quétineau. The plotting that Haindel claimed to have overheard allegedly took place on March 11, but his testimony was not corroborated by his wife until March 27—that is, three days after the execution of the prisoners. Both Armand and Quétineau had denied the charges, of course. After the jurors declared they were now sufficiently enlightened, Dumas launched a violent diatribe against the accused: "You call yourselves men of the Revolution, but you are agents of the counterrevolution. You speak of yourselves as patriots . . . and friends of the people, but you were never anything but ambitious usurpers of their confidence. . . . Villains! You shall perish!"[8]

The many trivial and absurd accusations aside, the charges against the Hébertistes can be reduced to four serious complaints: promulgating seditious posters and brochures; attempting insurrection; planning to massacre some prisoners, meanwhile releasing others in order to swell the ranks of the rebels, together with using the Revolutionary army; and trying to starve Paris. How much substance was there to these charges?

Among the posters mentioned was one by Vincent in section Quinze-Vingts that was brought to the attention of the Convention, although just what its message was is unclear. A more serious charge was leveled against unknown agitators who placarded Les Halles and denounced the shortages of supplies. Holding the Convention re-

7. B&R, XXXI, 385, 387, 394–95. A number of witnesses implicated Pache by insisting that he was to be the "great judge," or dictator, installed by the Hébertistes after the insurrection.

8. Herlaut, *Ronsin*, 250–52.

sponsible, the placard authors urged the women to march against it and to substitute a dictator for the seven hundred deputies. Decrees of the Convention were also defaced, as the revolutionary committee of section Indivisibilité demonstrated: under the names of members of the Committee of Public Safety who had signed a decree that raised the price of certain work appeared such unflattering comments, written in red pencil, as "cannibal"—this under Robespierre's name; under the names of Prieur, Lindet, and Barère was scribbled "betrayers of the people, always beastly and stupid" and "thieves and assassins." In addition, police commissioners found posters accusing the Convention of starving the people. Inflammatory posters appeared not only in the streets but also in various public establishments. Some employees of the National Treasury, for example, wrote on its walls: "Death to the Republic, Long live Louis XVII."

That these placards exploited real discontent cannot be doubted. The revolutionary committees of sections Marat and Cité, for example, had to call out their armed forces to reestablish order endangered because butter and eggs had not been distributed, as they should have been, but were stored instead in the guardhouse. Rotten food sold in markets also aggravated the situation. So did black marketing: as the jeweler Esprit Rougier testified, the transport of food was being interrupted and the goods sold in the streets, rather than in the regular markets, because the profits were higher that way. These continual shortages and interruptions of food supplies gave ammunition to counterrevolutionaries.[9]

To call for an insurrection, or even to seem to call for it under such circumstances, was extremely dangerous. A professor named Alexandre Ruelle, of section Observatoire's revolutionary committee, was surprised, he testified, to learn that according to certain police commissioners, the posters in question had been run off on the presses in Paris. He was pained, therefore, when he read in the *Moniteur* that patriots had called for an insurrection at a time when authorities were

---

9. Tuetey, *Répertoire général*, XI, nos. 1–7, 16–17, 96 (for last half of Ventôse), XI, lxxv–lxxvi, lxxix. Not all members of revolutionary committees were aware of these incendiary posters, as may be seen in the testimonies of several commissioners in sections Nord, Poissonnière, and Observatoire; *ibid.*, XI, No. 153. See also the testimony of some eight witnesses on the forced distribution of eggs and butter by hungry rioters who had interrupted suppliers of these items. Two of these witnesses thought there was a plot that explained this interruption. *Ibid.*, XI, No. 163 [misnumbered—should be 162].

struggling against counterrevolutionary enemies. The professor was not alone, of course, in believing that an insurrection indeed was being planned.

Lubin, president of the General Council, reported that he had overheard two men dressed like sans-culottes, who upon leaving the Jacobin Club discussed the need for another insurrection.[10] Although there is no proof that the Cordeliers took a single practical step to carry out an uprising, and although the word *insurrection* was often employed to mean a demonstration or some other nonviolent action, the careless attitude of the Hébertistes in appealing for such a *journée* must have frightened some, if not all, of the authorities. Moreover, even if the responsible leaders meant only a demonstration when they said "insurrection," was the same true of all their followers? Quite possibly the two men overheard by Lubin took seriously the feasibility and the need for another uprising. A revolutionary government anxious to impose "a single will" on the nation could hardly have asked for a better excuse to crush its opponents.

Although it can be argued that the calls for insurrection were purely exercises in frustration, that the violent language of the Cordeliers did not necessarily imply a serious effort to launch such a movement, these calls nonetheless occurred in moments of crisis and could add to the growing tension. Even if it were true that these threats often were made by men too drunk to know what they were about, wine can "give the tongue vows" that must not be ignored. When the Thermidorians arrested members of revolutionary committees for alleged infractions of the law, they often heard the excuse, "I drank too much."

Nor can it be doubted that an overheated imagination could invent plots. Laboureau, for example, testified on March 25 that General Westermann imagined the Cordeliers had plans for a "great judge." Ronsin was said to have declared, after reading the life of Cromwell, that he would like to be the Protector for just twenty-four hours, implying that he would have dealt with his enemies as they deserved. Perhaps the idea of a "great judge" was more imaginary than real. Still, the concept was certainly in the air. Furthermore, too many witnesses reported hearing talk of an approaching insurrection. Employees of the opera, for example, heard a horn player of the orchestra declare that soon there would be a coup in which the Convention and

10. *Ibid.*, lxxix–lxxx and No. 27.

Jacobins would be purged, and that he had spent the night making cartridges. They admitted however, that the musician was drunk when he revealed this to them.[11] But here again, such a revelation—assuming that it was such—could not be dismissed out of hand.

Further evidence of the possibility of an insurrection could easily have been discovered in a number of incidents that took place before the arrest of the accused. On February 12, 1794, Vincent read an address adopted unanimously by the Cordeliers and aimed at the sections, departments, and popular societies; it demanded the reestablishment of revolutionary laws and was leveled, evidently, at the method of rule by the Convention's Committees. When asked the difference between the former laws and decrees of the revolutionary government, Vincent replied: "Damn it, don't you see that revolutionary laws finish off everything in two weeks time, in destroying all the scoundrels, while your revolutionary government keeps you and will keep you, without ever finishing, under the most horrible despotism. You're nothing but a contemptible f——king bastard."[12] After this outburst few Cordeliers would have dared ask him to be enlightened further.

Carrier followed Vincent and revealed his surprise to find moderates among the Montagnards. He, too, had called for an insurrection in invoking Article 34 of the Declaration. Hébert also had appealed for an insurrection, as already described, and had attacked Amar for allegedly refusing to prosecute Chabot and Fabre. When charged with moderating his attack on the Indulgents, he pledged to redouble his energy and to unmask them or to perish. Boulanger was heard to remark, "Père Duchesne will write, and we will beat the drum."[13] The revolutionary government, however, was not about to march to that beat.

Other witnesses came forward who had heard the same call for an uprising. A policeman, René Charles Mercereau, quoted the agitator called Brutus as demanding another "May 31" in order to wipe out "105 rogue deputies." Another policeman, René Descoings, testified that Brutus demanded the execution of "50,000 of these fops, Feuillantins, Chapelains, [and] signers [of "anticivic petitions"]." Others verified what these two had heard.[14]

11. *Ibid.*, X, Nos. 2659, 2204.
12. *Ibid.*, XI, No. 29 (declaration of Charles Soular).
13. *Ibid.*, No. 21 and lxxx–lxxxi.
14. *Ibid.*, No. 56. Brutus' family name was Henoc. Mercereau heard Brutus say: "We need another May 31; there are 105 rogue deputies we ought to kick out." Jacot Ville-

The call for an insurrection was also heard in section Marat, as we have seen. Wouarmé, member of the General Council, testified that Ducroquet had made the motion to veil the Declaration of Rights and to pronounce the section in insurrection. Ducroquet tried to explain to Martial Joseph Herman, the former president of the Tribunal, that his motion did not mean that he intended to open the prisons and strike at the Convention; he wanted only to call the attention of the General Council to the shortages so that it would find means to stock the markets.[15] Nevertheless, he did employ the dread word *insurrection*, and the court could interpret it as it pleased.

The Tribunal must have known that not all in section Marat favored the march on the Commune. A member of the section's revolutionary committee pointed out that others had opposed it. Whereas insurrection had been necessary on August 10, 1792, and May 31, 1793, he argued, today it was essential that the government act forcefully— with "severity," as he put it. Another member of the general assembly, Antoine Simon, a municipal officer, had tried to stop the projected demonstration, warning sensibly that seizing comestibles like butter and eggs would only deprive the markets of goods. Simon's efforts had unleashed a heated shouting match as the assembly became "stormy."

Several others had recognized the dangerous implication of Ducroquet's motion and urged its defeat. Unable to overturn the resolution, a number of participants left the hall.[16] Later, the president of section Unité, Sebastien Lacroix, was said to have slandered Robespierre. Several witnesses claimed that they heard him say Robespierre was stupid for not having mounted his horse and proclaimed himself dictator after the dethronement of Louis. One of the witnesses allegedly replied, "Have we won liberty in order to create new masters?" When Lacroix intimated that Robespierre was "vindictive," another

---

neuve, age forty-nine, also heard Brutus in several popular societies, as did Guillaume Laloumet, who heard Brutus boast that he had veiled the Declaration of Rights, and who termed him "cowardly and quick-tempered."

15. *Ibid.*, No. 34. Jacques Louis Frédéric Wouarmé, employed in the War Department, did not sign the section's resolution but went to the Commune to try and tone down the controversy. Jean Jacques Roze, a merchant and member of the section's civil committee, stated that he was astonished at the "seditious proposal" of the section made to the Commune. Louis Edme Toussaint Dardelin added that when a member, Guespereau, tried to tone down the debate, Momoro interrupted him and Guespereau was forced to leave the tribune.

16. *Ibid.*, Nos. 30, 54.

witness called Lacroix a "pygmy" for attacking a man "endowed with all the virtues." Thus, there is little question that even in militant sections like Marat, Robespierre was favored over the Cordeliers leaders.[17]

In addition to the Committees' concern with a possible insurrection, they were also interested in the disposal and plans of the Revolutionary army. Westermann, the general who was linked to Danton—and therefore under suspicion—told the public prosecutor that a general whose name he had forgotten (he meant Laumur) had stated in the Cordeliers that there would be an insurrection and that the Revolutionary army would play a role in this event. Moreover, a citizen employed in the administration of military transport had repeated the same rumor. Finally, Pache was to be proclaimed dictator. It should be added that Westermann was an officer in the regular army and, as such, hated the Revolutionary army and its staff.

A witness, Jean Cordier, a basketmaker and commissioner of section Poissonnière's revolutionary committee, "alleged he had heard" that a part of the Revolutionary army was to enter Paris. There were also complaints that this force was inactive. A detachment from Finistère wrote lamenting that instead of going into the countryside to round up comestibles, they were being kept on guard duty. Detachments from sections Unité, Mutius Scaevola, and Pont Neuf, stationed at Pontoise, complained that there were plenty of hidden eggs and butter in farmers' "cupboards and barrels" and demanded permission to make house searches. Assuring their compatriots that they remained "republican Montagnards," they blamed the municipal authorities for the shortages in Paris. Fouquier-Tinville himself linked this idleness with the scarcity suffered in the capital. Undoubtedly the government feared an infiltration of the Revolutionary army into Paris. When a Sergeant Guillaume was sent on a mission by his detachment stationed in Laon, he was arrested upon entering the capital. Guillaume wrote to the public prosecutor, "Most unfortunately

---

17. *Ibid.*, No. 66. Tuetey is convinced that the call to insurrection found no echo in the masses. The demand for a "chief," or Hébert's attack on "rulers" and "high powers," or Vincent's denunciation of the "Cromwellistes"—none of this could undermine the prestige of Robespierre. *Ibid.*, lxxxiii–lxxxiv.

Sebastien Lacroix had been a commissioner of the Executive Council in the Midi and was a former friend of Danton's. Now he was linked to Vincent. He was executed shortly thereafter with Chaumette. Soboul and Monnier, *Répertoire de personnel sectionnaire*, 440.

for me, I arrived at a bad moment." He had left Laon on March 15 and arrived in Paris on the eighteenth, only three days before the trial of the Cordeliers began.[18]

In addition to the charge of creating shortages and calling for an insurrection, the Cordeliers leaders were accused of planning to massacre prisoners. There is little question that many of the imprisoned sighed with relief when the Hébertistes were arrested. Some were heard to remark that "these gentlemen would have sacrificed us." Numerous witnesses testified they had heard Ronsin and others repeat the threat of doing away with all but about "one-thirtieth" of the prisoners. Some declared that the prisoners were "useless mouths" and should be killed along with cats and dogs; others expressed their resentment that in time of shortages those in prison allegedly lacked for nothing—an all-too-common belief. An extreme expression of this discontent was voiced by a shoemaker named Bot in section Marchés; he proposed to roast the prisoners and serve them up as food for the hungry. Still others favored guillotining merchants as a solution to shortages.[19]

A number of witnesses testified that Ronsin was also drafting a list of prisoners he would release after they had submitted their reasons why they should be freed. Not one actually saw him do this, but they did "hear" of it, they claimed.[20] In an undated letter to Fouquier-Tinville, Charles Gillibert stated that a citizen named "Bonhomme" (Claude Henri Saint-Simon, the utopian socialist) could testify against Ronsin. On March 19 a Pierre Gillibert reported that Ronsin had promised freedom to Bonhomme, among others. For some reason the public prosecutor did not call any of the people mentioned. Neverthe-

---

18. Tuetey, *Répertoire général*, XI, Nos. 24, 84, 174; Soboul, *Sans-Culottes*, 801 n 162. Guillaume's letters to Fouquier-Tinville, May 7 and 18, 1794, are in W 168 and W 136, AN, respectively. Westermann related Hébertisme to military morale problems by saying that although he did not know Hébert, the man's designs were insidious and struck at the confidence of soldiers; Tuetey, *Répertoire général*, X, No. 2264 (depositions against Ronsin).

19. Tuetey, XI, Nos. 63 (long testimony of François Marie Thiéry against the "clique"), 72 (letter of Benoist, a commissioner), 73 (Marie Joseph Martin, sergeant of chasseurs, on prison conditions), 75 (Louis Claude Gilles Huyet, concierge of a detention house, and Antoine Severin Levasseur, guard in a detention house), 78 (a German musician named Buch and a printer named Tarin), and 80 (Louis Fey Duprat, no occupation given).

20. *Ibid.*, X, Nos. 2266, 2264, 2287, 2289, XI, No. 72. Much of this testimony is based on hearsay evidence.

less, this information could indicate that there had been an early connection between Saint-Simon and the Desfieux group, the "avant-garde of Hébertisme," as Mathiez characterized it. In any case, there is little doubt that the authorities took the threat of prison massacres seriously. Hanriot stationed an armed guard in Saint-Lazare prison to protect the worried inmates.[21]

More threatening to the stability of the revolutionary government were the continuing shortages of food. In addition to disruption of laissez-faire economics caused by the *maximum*, there was the interruption, or threatened interruption, to supplies arriving in Paris. Wagons would be stopped by hungry women and their contents sold, sometimes at the *maximum*, sometimes below it. Retailers complained that the cost of bringing foodstuffs from outlying regions made it impossible for them to break even, let alone to realize any profit. People stood in line for hours at a time, only to find the shelves empty when their turn had come to purchase the needed goods. The situation was made to order for authorities bent on pinning the problem on the Hébertistes. If the public could be convinced that the shortages had been created artificially—that, in other words, there was a plot to starve Paris—the government would succeed in detaching the many sans-culottes from the Cordeliers leaders.

On March 8, Fouquier-Tinville wrote to Pache that he had investigated the attempt to starve Paris by going to "the source." He had examined the communes surrounding the capital to a radius of some ten leagues, in addition to scrutinizing the method of supplying the capital. Judges of the Revolutionary Tribunal took testimony of the inhabitants of towns from Antony to Vitry. The Administration of Provisions was heard, as well as mayors of communes that were accused of withholding their supplies from the capital. A number of witnesses charged that certain individuals in various sections had aggravated the situation by threatening farmers and suppliers to the point of frightening them away from sending their supplies to Paris.[22] Ducroquet was named by a number of these witnesses. Others insisted that they had done all they could to supply the capital, but that the frequent passage of troops through their districts left little surplus

21. Albert Mathiez, "Saint-Simon et Ronsin," *Annales historiques de la Révolution française*, III (1926), 403; Tuetey, *Répertoire général*, XI, No. 80.

22. Tuetey, *Répertoire général*, XI, Nos. 161, 94 (wherein a witness named Marie Champigny stated that she heard a farmer say he preferred to sell at the *maximum* rather than have his goods requisitioned).

for Paris.[23] Rolin reported that despite all precautions taken by Hanriot, the women of surrounding communes managed to take away much of the food meant for Paris. When asked how they did it, one replied that "the bourgeois" at the barricades closed their eyes.[24]

Hébert's fulminations against commerce had discouraged merchants, but he was certainly not alone in expressing these sentiments. That greedy merchants were responsible for shortages and high prices was a popular theme. In addition to this widely held belief, there was the practice of sectional authorities, especially the commissioners on hoarding, who held that only a strict application of the measures adopted would solve the crisis. Domiciliary visits, seizures of undeclared foodstuffs, and forced sales at the *maximum* only exasperated the commercial classes.

In addition, the jealous particularism of the sections disorganized supplies. Commissioners of section Marat seized products at the barrier and sold them at the *maximum*—but this caused shortages in the surrounding sections, as Charmont pointed out, adding that section Marat's seizing of merchandise and conducting it into its own neighborhood was like a "Vendée" in the capital itself. On October 1, 1793, Ducroquet seized three dozen eggs, one rabbit, and one turkey. He distributed the eggs among thirty-six persons. Later, he argued that his sole crime lay in his desire "to make all citizens content." As for the charge ultimately brought against Descombes regarding his part in the "plot" to starve Paris, it was so badly conceived that it did not even appear in the Revolutionary Tribunal's judgment. Of course, there was no such plot, but the steps taken in the frantic search for food could be twisted to appear that those who wanted "all citizens content" were responsible for the food crisis.[25]

Furthermore, there was profiteering in foodstuffs. How could it be otherwise when drastic shortages encouraged both sales and purchases above the official price ceiling? With the army buying up much of the meat and its agents ignoring the *maximum*, prices were bound to mount for what little was available to civilians. A typical case saw a side of beef resell three times until its price had risen to 200 livres.

23. *Ibid.*, Nos. 157, 158, 123, 178, 160, 166, 170. A number of witnesses told how wagons were stopped by women and their contents sold below the *maximum*.

24. Caron, *Paris pendant la Terreur*, IV, 397.

25. Tuetey, *Répertoire général*, XI, No. 157 (four witnesses repeating the charge against Ducroquet), X, No. 2526 (the same accusation against Ducroquet). Charmont's remarks are in Caron, *Paris pendant la Terreur*, IV, 388.

The commissioners on profiteering complained of butchers in Vincennes who refused to sell to the poor because they could get so much more from the "bourgeois." A municipal officer observed that "these sort of gentlemen . . . are very dangerous, in that they recognize no other god but self-interest and their counterrevolutionary commerce; their morality is much suspect; yet one does not dare denounce them."[26]

Mayors of surrounding communes vehemently denied that food supplies were being kept from Paris. They insisted that the proprietors of goods in their communes loved the Republic, and they blamed the scarcity on army purchases. Shortages were also blamed on butchers who slaughtered cattle they had bought above the *maximum* and sold the meat, of course, above the legal price ceiling. In a few cases even national agents opposed sending all the available products to Paris. But others complained to Pache that profiteering made goods available in the countryside and deprived the capital of food. Another practice that harmed Paris was the sale by merchants of goods en route to profiteers willing to risk their necks. Yet many districts had much beef, butter, eggs, and other necessities. In other districts, although there were no profiteers (if we can believe the testimony of witnesses), shortages persisted.[27]

Questions put by Fouquier regarding the sabotage of food to be sent to Paris, or actions discouraging retailers from sending it, or buyers offering higher prices than the *maximum*, or the outright waylaying of the transports en route, all were answered in the negative. The witnesses either denied these charges or simply did not know of any such incidents. The commune of Longumeau, for example, demanded a retraction from Fouquier-Tinville after he had reported to the Convention that it had impeded supplies bound for the capital. Its revolutionary committee proved that far from discouraging transports to Paris, they had actually seized a wagon and escorted it to the city. Moreover, they insisted that the commune adhered strictly to the *maximum*—which was why they suffered, the officials added. The Paris Commune expressed its appreciation, but if the public prosecutor apologized, there is no record of his reply. The same dispute involved other communes as well.[28]

26. Tuetey, *Répertoire général*, XI, Nos. 100, 172.
27. *Ibid.*, Nos. 86, 91, 109.
28. *Ibid.*, Nos. 102, 136, 138; see also Nos. 135, 103, 158, 123, 128, 132, 148, 155. Dominique Savoure, age forty-three, a health officer and president of the popular so-

Thus, an examination of the record demonstrates how ill founded were Fouquier-Tinville's accusations. Still, the president of the court, Dumas, persisted in pressing these charges: "Did you not prepare the barbarous plan to starve the people, organize artificial shortages, and in your fury dreaded the return of abundance?" Dumas probably knew the report of the police spy Rousselin: "In almost all neighborhoods citizens said it was that scoundrel Hébert and his clique who had tried to starve us."[29] This accusation was a powerful weapon in the hands of the revolutionary government. Hungry men and women, even if they were somewhat skeptical, would more readily accept the court's condemnation.

Of course, a basic contradiction existed between the revolutionary government's need for greater productivity in order to pursue the war effort and the needs of the sans-culottes as consumers. How productive could hungry men and women be, after all? The beleaguered populace forcefully insisted on price controls and on other measures that struck at the concept and practice of the free market. Hébert, of course, expressed these sentiments aimed against merchants and farmers and widely held among the sans-culottes. This stance was certainly one reason for the popularity of his *Père Duchesne*. But it could only trouble the Committees, who needed both greater productivity and "a single will." How could farmers increase their production and merchants continue to supply the army when the very basis of their existence was becoming suspect in the eyes of the sans-culottes—suspect largely because of the fulminations of Hébert and his Cordeliers colleagues? Yet, in sacrificing these spokesmen who had harnessed and exploited the sans-culottes for their own ends, the government was to destroy the very élan and devotion that enabled it to survive. This dramatic contradiction, from which the revolutionary government could not free itself, ultimately destroyed it.

In addition to the charge of atheism, the principal accusation against Hébert was that he was part of a "perfidious system whose goal was to destroy commerce in declaiming without distinction against all citizens engaged in it." Louis Roux, a former member of

---

ciety of Longumeau, blamed the shortages on the "inequality" of the *maximum*, the poor vigilance of officials, the selfishness of wealthy proprietors, and the avarice of the commune's merchants; *ibid.*, No. 102.

29. Rousselin cited *ibid.*, xcviii (there is no report by Rousselin in Caron for March 16).

the "Provisional Commune," painted Chaumette and Hébert as daily slandering commerce and agriculture, representing merchants who supplied Paris as profiteers and cultivators and farmers as starvers of the people. Lulier, the national agent, accused them of depicting commerce in such dishonorable terms that good citizens were ashamed to pursue it. After the end of the Hébertistes, the government neglected to enforce price controls; it encouraged producers and those engaged in commerce over the needs of consumers. The sans-culottes could not maintain a balance between their earnings and "the high cost of living," which was becoming higher daily, except by pursuing the most rigorous measures. The need to enforce these measures had been systematically expressed by the leaders of the Cordeliers. "They demanded against them [the merchants and farmers]," declared Louis Roux, "the guillotine or imprisonment as suspects, the ambulatory guillotine, a revolutionary tribunal, [and] a mobile revolutionary army to inspire terror."[30]

The Cordeliers had also expressed opposition to the growing centralization of government power. The Convention and its Committees could not permit, however, the destruction of the social equilibrium that this attack threatened. The Cordeliers, of course, exploited this contradiction—something else the government could not allow. After Germinal it took the popular organizations in hand. But in condemning the Cordeliers the government condemned the political practices and aspirations of the sans-culottes as well. Thus, without denying the possibility that members of the Committees really believed in a plot to overthrow the government, one can note that the allegation of such a plot allowed them to relieve themselves of an opposition that, although often disorganized, was still dangerous because it exploited social behavior and a political attitude incompatible with the concept of a market economy and with the necessity of national defense. Having condemned the spokesmen of the sans-culottes, however, the government was bound to lose support of their rank and file as well. For despite their temporary faith in the Convention, the sans-culottes were to be disillusioned by the new social and political reality that rested on different social classes and included laissez-faire policies toward what today would be called "special interest groups": the haute bourgeoisie, well-off farmers, speculators, and so on.[31]

30. Cited by Soboul, *Sans-Culottes*, 805–806.
31. See Soboul's comments, *Sans-Culottes*, 804–806.

Of all the Cordeliers leaders, Hébert was the most feared. Unfortunately, it is difficult to assess precisely the influence of his journal because so few of his private papers remain. None of his political correspondence is available, nor his financial records. Only a few papers were returned to Hébert's executor and associate, Jacques Christophe Marquet.[32] By the summer of 1793 he had begun to criticize the concentration of power in the hands of the Committee of Public Safety, and like the Enragés, he demanded the renewal of the Convention. At the end of August he wrote, "Liberty is f——ked up when all power is placed in the hands of inviolable men," and he continued his attacks in September and October. In No. 297 of the *Père Duchesne* the following passage is bracketed, evidently by a police official, probably of the Paris Department: "If the characters who govern us, instead of wanting to devour everything like eagles and vultures, were [instead] but diligent ants like others, the republic would soon be happy and triumphant. But each one wants to have his own way; everyone wants to make the law, no one wants to obey it. We are like cats and dogs, instead of being united like brothers."[33]

There is little question that such sentiments troubled the Committees, because unlike the publications of Jean Varlet and Théophile Leclerc, the two Enragés, the *Père Duchesne* had a large circulation. That it was avidly read and its delay in arriving in army camps raised complaints can be seen in a letter of representatives-on-mission to the Army of the North. On August 23, 1793, they deplored the fact that no issue had reached their camp for three weeks. The whole army demanded it "loudly," they wrote. The journal instructed soldiers on their duties and rights, they continued, adding that they were joined in this grievance by their colleagues attached to the Army of the Ardennes.[34]

Two months earlier Vincent had asked Hébert to insert in his jour-

32. Marquet (1764–1832) was a former lawyer who printed Hébert's journal. He was elected president of the Evêché Assembly on the eve of the insurrection of May 31–June 2, 1794. Arrested and released a number of times, he also held several administrative positions in the course of his career. After the execution of Hébert and his wife, Marquet adopted their daughter. Soboul and Monnier, *Répertoire de personnel sectionnaire*, 178; Slavin, *Making of an Insurrection*, 77, and chap. 5, *passim*, for his role in the insurrection.

33. W 78, plaq. 1, p. 89, AN. The "cats and dogs" quotation appears on p. 7 of *Père Duchesne*, No. 297. This issue has a written note on its first page that reads "Journal where Hébert slanders the National Convention" and points to page 7.

34. Tuetey, *Répertoire général*, X, No. 2219.

nal a reply to the "atrocious slanders" against Bouchotte that he was a "moderate." On November 22, 1793, representative-on-mission Silvain Phalier Lejeune wrote Hébert from Laon praising him and urging him to continue exposing "intriguers and cowards" who would shackle the march of the Revolution. Lejeune assured Hébert that he would be recompensed by his fellow citizens and posterity for his devotion to the Revolution. Of the nine letters listed in Hébert's dossier, only one criticizes him (for "slandering" General Custine).[35] Of course, these letters are too few to allow an accurate assessment of Hébert's influence; nevertheless, they are revealing.[36] When Varlet attacked the decree that limited sectional assembly meetings to two a *décade*, for example, he was not harassed. But Hébert's criticism of the Committee of Public Safety was on a different scale. He was far more "accepted by the people," wrote an accuser. Thus, to his astonishment, he appeared as the principal figure charged in the trial. "For Hébert, good journalist but wretched politician and without character, it [was] the *Père Duchesne* that was being struck," wrote Soboul.[37]

If Hébert vacillated and trimmed his sails to the prevailing political wind, Ronsin, in contrast, "maintained a serenity because of his innocence or courage," testified Laboureau. The revolutionary committee of section Mont Blanc, after serving the warrant of arrest and preparing the record, sealed Ronsin's papers and delivered him to Conciergerie prison.[38] Laboureau heard him say to Momoro that for a long time now he had known that they were being pursued by a dangerous man—that is, Robespierre—and that it was useless to prepare a judicial defense because "this is a political trial." Ronsin added the same charge that he had leveled against Hébert (see chapter 8, note 51): "You talked in the Cordeliers when it was necessary to act.

---

35. *Ibid.*, No. 2228. *Ibid.*, No. 2218 is a letter by a soldier named Dolivet that defends Custine.

36. Soboul, *Sans-Culottes*, 808–809n185 analyzes these letters and concludes that they reflect a geographical and social variety.

37. *Ibid.*, 809.

38. Tuetey, *Répertoire général*, X, Nos. 2265, 2268. Ronsin's wife, Marie Angélique Lequesne, and his brother, Jean César Ronsin, a brewer of Soisson and director of military transport, were present during Ronsin's arrest. Ronsin's wife was arrested on March 21 and was not released until October 29. She was a subscriber to Babeuf's *Tribun du peuple*. Later she married General Turreau, a former friend of Ronsin's, who was made a member of the Legion of Honor by Napoleon. He became ambassador to the United States, and after his death Marie Angélique returned to that country with her four children and founded a school. Herlaut, *Ronsin*, 265–70.

This indiscreet license has undone us." Now they had to prepare to die, he said, and he swore that no one would see him falter. He was confident, moreover, that they would be avenged—a knife, he mentioned, cost only "two sols"—and he consoled himself that he had raised his adopted son in the principles of liberty.[39]

Ronsin had appealed for an insurrection in the Cordeliers, as we have seen, and had aroused opposition within the organization. Hébert had to assure his hearers that by *insurrection* Ronsin meant only that "traitors" like Fabre, Bourdon, and Chabot should be exposed. This was not true, of course, but the fact that Hébert had to sweeten Ronsin's call for an insurrection demonstrated the split within the Cordeliers. Aside from the fact that such an uprising would not have resolved either the economic or the political crisis, the uncertainty and division in the ranks of the sans-culottes and among the militants of the Cordeliers would have doomed it in advance.

As for Vincent, we have seen his intemperate outbursts and his authoritarian conduct both in the Cordeliers and in his section. Unquestionably he was devoted to the Republic and the cause of the sans-culottes. Still, his abusive language not only weakened his own role but also endangered Bouchotte and others in the War Department, as Legendre hastened to point out. Many witnesses testified to how Vincent would hold the floor, refusing to recognize those who either opposed him or simply had a different point of view. He interrupted and often insulted those who disagreed with him, treating them as stupid or worse. He was for expelling the women from the general assembly of section Mutius Scaevola, holding them responsible for the tumult that often characterized the meetings. An opponent of his testified that he withdrew a certificate of civic conduct from a man after the assembly had granted it. Another charged that when wives of soldiers at the front asked Vincent for the subsidy due them, he denounced them as counterrevolutionaries and sent them off in tears. Others told of his personal antipathy toward certain individuals, an antipathy that seemed to be based purely on personality differences that had little to do with politics.[40]

In addition, we have already seen the clash between Vincent and the deputy Legendre. Upon his earlier release from prison Ronsin

---

39. Dauban, *Prisons de Paris*, 330–31; Tuetey, *Répertoire général*, X, Nos. 29, 2290, 2659. Ronsin is quoted in Herlaut, *Ronsin*, 237.
40. Tuetey, *Répertoire général*, X, Nos. 2341, 2331, 2349.

had approached Legendre and asked him to speak to Vincent "to save him from his errors," as Ronsin put it. The dispute that broke out between Vincent and Legendre at Pache's dinner only aggravated the "errors" from which Legendre had been asked to save the young firebrand. Ronsin's remark that if Vincent were any different he would not be worth as much, if uttered in seriousness, only reflects Ronsin's lack of understanding on the need to reconcile his young friend with an important deputy. If it was essential to defeat the Indulgents in the Convention, surely deputies like Legendre would have to be won over. The threat implied by Ronsin was that if this faction were not expelled by Legendre and company, they, meaning the Cordeliers, would show them how to do it. This remark must have deepened the split between the Left Jacobins and the Cordeliers. In any case, if Ronsin meant what he said, it was impolitic of him to announce an action for which the Cordeliers had made no preparation at all. Furthermore, Legendre made it clear he had no intention of making peace with Hébert, calling him an "intriguer" and denying his patriotism. He was convinced that the *Père Duchesne* did little good in the army, in contradiction to what Bouchotte thought. As we have seen, he warned that Vincent's behavior could compromise the minister of war.[41]

When Vincent was interrogated and asked if he had conspired against the Republic, he hotly denied it, as he wrote to his wife, Nanette. He still thought that he could prove his innocence, but the next day he described the horrors of his imprisonment—the lack of communication with anyone, the foul air, the bolted doors, and the taunts of the executioner. Vincent asked Nanette to remain calm and expressed the hope that his son would be brought up to be useful to humanity as well as to the Republic. He thought that public opinion would avenge him. In his last letter, written on March 20, he expressed regret that he had caused her so much pain and asked her to console his mother. Then he took his farewells.[42]

The trial took three and a half days. All observers reported that the streets before the Palais de Justice were full. The slanders of the government had convinced the vast majority that the accused were guilty

41. *Ibid.*, No. 2329.
42. *Ibid.*, XI, Nos. 206, 207; Albert Mathiez, "Les Dernières Lettres de Vincent à son femme," *Annales révolutionnaires*, VI (1913), 250–54.

as charged. A police spy reported that "the people cannot forgive Hébert for deceiving them." Still, some were willing to defend him as a new martyr to liberty.[43]

Evidence exists that the government wanted to conclude the proceedings as soon as possible. Robespierre, if we believe Avenel, was eager to speed up the trial. He felt that unlike Dumas, other judges would balk at condemning the innocent. To learn how some of them felt, he took one of the judges, Gabriel Toussaint Scellier, to dinner. When Robespierre complained at the slowness of the proceedings, Scellier replied that the law strictly defined the forms that judges were to follow so that the innocent might not suffer. He then made it clear that he regarded any violation of those norms as odious and intolerable. Robespierre retorted that they would pass a law excusing the court from adhering so strictly to these procedures. At these words the judge remained silent.

Nor could Robespierre be certain that the jury would condemn the accused. In order to intimidate its members, the government decided on March 20 to arrest a juror named Antonelle, who had had the courage to resign rather than play the government's game. He had published a work entitled *Observations du juré,* with commentaries, in which he argued that often man was better than his actions seemed to imply.[44]

Thus, with the Committees pressing the Tribunal to make quick work of the affair, with the jury aware of Antonelle's arrest, and with the swelling crowds outside convinced that the Cordeliers leaders had plotted against their interests, the accused were brought into the hall where only the jurors sat. Naturally, they felt isolated and alone. At the same time the government made sure that the clerks and scribes touched up all remarks in its favor. One juror alone, Naulin, wrote truthfully what had occurred, but his account was only a historical narrative after the event was over.[45]

43. Wallon, *Tribunal révolutionnaire,* III, 62.

44. Avenel, *Cloots,* II, 442–43.

45. *Ibid.,* 451. Albert Mathiez, in "Les Deux Versions du procès des Hébertistes," argues that there were two versions of the trial, an official and an unofficial. The latter was a "Dantoniste" version in which both Pache and Hanriot were implicated. In order to avoid indicting them, the Committee of Public Safety, and especially Robespierre, substituted the testimony against Pache so as to make it appear to be against Danton. In addition—for example—Dufourny's lengthy testimony in the unofficial version was

When Vincent, Momoro, and others demanded to have Pache and Hanriot brought in as witnesses, Dumas refused.[46] Hébert's writings were used out of context against him. In vain did he protest that at the time he wrote the articles quoted, Danton was a member of the Committee of Public Safety and Chabot was in the Comité de sûreté. Nothing helped. When other defendants demanded that Collot, Carrier, Pache, and Hanriot be called, they were removed by the gendarmes. The trial was closed by a violent attack on the accused by Dumas. After the jury had declared that it was sufficiently enlightened to render a verdict, the accused attempted to speak but were drowned out by shouts of "Long live the Republic!" Hébert reportedly was so depressed during the trial that he lost all his former combativeness. When it ended he had almost to be carried out by the gendarmes.[47]

To the question "Was there a design and provocation to an insurrection?" the jury replied, "Yes." The court declared that the condemned had planned to use the excuse of food shortages and the perceived "need" to punish traitors as the basis for the insurrection. They had also hoped to purge the Convention of its "rogues" and had accused the government of provoking another massacre like that of the Champ de Mars. As to the means of executing their plan, the court held that the accused meant to use the Revolutionary army, massacre prisoners, "unleash" 20,000 women, and deprive Paris of food. Finally, on the goals of the insurrection, the Tribunal announced that the accused had intended to execute the majority of the Convention, destroy the two Committees, crush the Jacobins, do away with the Executive Council, set up a "great judge" as dictator, and reestablish royalty.[48] All but Laboureau were condemned to death. The execution was set for that same day, 4 Germinal—March 24—at 4 P.M.

---

much reduced in the official journal. In short, the "grand judge," who was supposed to have been Pache, became Danton instead. Mathiez points out that the Hébertistes never attacked Danton, and furthermore, that contemporaries believed the two had an understanding against the Committee of Public Safety.

46. Lecointre devotes twenty-six individual paragraphs, each a specific accusation, to members of the two Committees. Paragraph 13 charges them with being responsible for the refusal to allow the sixteen deputies demanded by the accused Hébertistes to testify in their behalf, and with having substituted a false report in order to demonstrate that they were in rebellion against the law. *Dénonciation faite à la Convention nationale . . .* , in Le 38 2175, BN.

47. Wallon, *Tribunal révolutionnaire*, III, 63–64, 65.

48. Tuetey, *Répertoire général*, XI, No. 214.

JUGEMENT
RENDU
PAR LE TRIBUNAL
RÉVOLUTIONNAIRE,

ÉTABLI PAR LA LOI DU 10 MARS 1793, SÉANT AU PALAIS, A PARIS,

Q U I, *sur la déclaration du Jury du jugement, portant :*
« Qu'il est constant, 1°. qu'il a existé une conspiration contre
» la liberté et la sûreté du Peuple Français, tendant à
» troubler l'Etat par une guerre civile, en armant les ci-
» toyens les uns contre les autres et contre l'exercice de
» l'autorité légitime; par suite de laquelle, dans le cou-
» rant de Ventôse dernier, des conjurés devoient dissoudre
» la représentation nationale, assassiner ses membres et
» les patriotes; détruire le gouvernement républicain, s'em-
» parer de la souveraineté du Peuple, et donner un tyran
» à l'État; 2°. que Jacques-Réné HÉBERT, Charles-
» Philippe RONSIN, François-Nicolas VINCENT,

» Antoine-François MOMORO, Frédéric-Pierre DU-
» CROQUET, Jean Conrade KOCK, Michel LAUMUR,
» Jean-Charles BOURGEOIS, Jean-Baptiste MAZUEL,
» Jean-Baptiste ANCARD, Armand HUBERT-LE-
» CLERC, Jacob PEREYRA, Marie-Anne LA-
« TREILLE, femme QUETINOT, CLOOTZ, dit
» ANACHARSIS, François DESFIEUX, Antoine DES-
» COMBES, Jean-Antoine-Florent ARMANT, Paul-Ulric
» DUBUISSON, Pierre-Jean BERTHOLD-PROLY,
» sont convaincus d'être les auteurs ou les complices de cette
« conspiration;
» CONDAMNE lesdits HÉBERT, RONSIN, VINCENT,
» MOMORO, DUCROQUET, KOCK, LAUMUR,
» BOURGEOIS, MAZUEL, ANCARD, HUBERT-
» LECLERC, PEREYRA, la femme QUETINOT,
» CLOOTZ, DESFIEUX, DESCOMBES, ARMANT,
» DUBUISSON et BERTHOLD-PROLY, à la peine
« de mort, conformément à la loi du seize Décembre,
« mil sept cent quatre-vingt-douze.

*Du 4 Germinal, l'an deuxième de la République française,
une et indivisible.*

AU NOM DU PEUPLE FRANÇAIS.
Le Tribunal révolutionnaire a rendu le jugement suivant :

Vû par le Tribunal révolutionnaire, établi à Paris, par décret
de la Convention Nationale, du dix mars 1793, l'an deuxième
de la République, sans aucun recours, au Tribunal de cassation;

The judgment of the Revolutionary Tribunal condemning to death Hébert
and his codefendants for "conspiracy against the liberty and security of the
French people."

Fouquier-Tinville had written to Hanriot to take measures against attempts to rescue the accused. No such measures proved necessary. It seems that the government's massive propaganda had convinced the vast majority of people, including many of the sans-culottes who had been staunch supporters of the Cordeliers, that their former spokesmen had indeed betrayed them. Too many agreed with the sans-culotte who was quoted as saying: "The committees of Public Safety and of General Security . . . there's my jury. They've never betrayed me." Others reported on "the joy of the people" at seeing "conspirators" condemned to the guillotine. A few raised questions regarding Bouchotte, who had kept Vincent in the War Department so long, and still others showed their suspicion of Pache and Santerre.[49]

Even before the trial, all the former friends of the Hébertistes had begun congratulating the Convention. Only the Commune kept quiet. But after Léonard Bourdon on March 19 expressed his astonishment that the General Council had not come forth, a delegation headed by Pache arrived with their congratulations. Then followed the department of Paris and a part of the Revolutionary army. A police spy revealed that "in all the streets, in all public places, everywhere where two or three persons met, they spoke of the conspirators, and their death was voted unanimously."[50] Whatever exaggerations may appear in this observation, little doubt exists that the overwhelming majority of the people, sans-culottes and their allies in other groups, were convinced of the government's justice.

After the verdict, having been returned to prison to await execution, Hébert bewailed his fate. Turning to Ronsin, he declared that liberty was now lost. Ronsin replied: "You don't know what you're talking about. Liberty cannot be destroyed now. The party that sends us to our death will follow there in turn and it won't be long now." Meanwhile, when Laboureau appeared in the Jacobins he was universally applauded, according to the record. Yet one wonders: could the Jacobins, who surely were aware of raisons d'état and of revolutionary politics in particular, have been so naïve as to accept the condemnation of the Cordeliers leaders without some painful questions?

At 4 P.M. the condemned were placed into three carts and taken in the midst of great crowds and hostile cries to the guillotine. At the foot of the platform the men embraced. Ronsin exhibited great

49. Wallon, *Tribunal révolutionnaire*, III, 45, 66.
50. *Ibid.*, 43–44.

Detail of an engraving purporting to show Hébert, Vincent, and others being borne to the guillotine.

courage. The crowd showed its appreciation for the calm and banter with which he met his end, but it was especially hostile to Hébert. Women cried out, "But this is no man; he's a little runt!" The executions took but seventeen minutes, and as each head fell in the basket people cried, "Long live the Republic!"[51]

Quétineau was returned to prison on her claim that she was pregnant, but her reprieve from the guillotine would be brief (see chapter 8). This still left the wives of the condemned. The wives of Hébert, Momoro, and Ronsin were arrested by order of the Committee of General Security and defamed. The committee's journal slandered them, as did others. Hébert's wife, Marie Marguerite, was executed on April 13, 1794, an indication of the special hatred (and fear?) the government felt for her husband. Momoro's wife was freed on May 27, 1794, Ronsin's spouse not for another five months.[52]

Perhaps the most depressing outcome of this affair was the relative ease with which so many ordinary sans-culottes, members of the sections, and political sympathizers were convinced to abandon their longtime friends. Understandably, men and women who feared for their own or their families' lives would make no protest. But it is difficult to believe that after so many months of revolutionary activity and proof of commitment to the Republic by the Cordeliers leaders, the accusations against them, including even the charge that they wanted to restore royalty, should win such widespread credence. Can the government's campaign have been that effective? More likely, when it came to a choice between believing the men of the Great Committees or the Hébertistes, the sans-culottes elected the former. The prestige of Robespierre and his colleagues could not be undermined by Hébert or Ronsin.

This is not to say that the Cordeliers leaders did not have a core of supporters that remained loyal to them to the end. The police spy Béraud wrote that Hébert's partisans, heard at the National Garden, continued to defend him.[53] Another reported, "It seems that he [Hébert] has his proselytes." Bacon wrote that some persons admitted

51. Walter, *Hébert et le "Père Duchesne,"* 268; Herlaut, *Ronsin,* 253, 254, 255. Hébert's execution was especially cruel. As he lay tied to the plank with his head under the blade of the guillotine, Sanson, the public executioner, passed the *bonnet rouge* several times under his nose.

52. Herlaut, *Ronsin,* 254, 255–56.

53. Caron, *Paris pendant la Terreur,* VI, 3.

that despite their confidence in the government, they would not be convinced of the Hébertistes' guilt unless they saw the evidence with their own eyes.

Some workers at the arms factory spoke of *Le Sappeur Sans-Culotte,* a journal put out by a soldier who wanted to replace Hébert's paper. A crude publication that repeated the slanders of the government and was subsidized by the authorities, it sought to imitate the style and language of the *Père Duchesne* and appealed to the sans-culottes against their former spokesmen. The first number opened by saying that people were no longer deceived, that Hébert was "a great rogue," and that "the guillotine was too good for such a scoundrel." [54] It accused Hébert of laying a sumptuous table for himself and his guests and of being subsidized by England and Austria, and it denounced Hébert's wife, whom it called "a defrocked nun . . . ugly as mortal sin, wicked, cantankerous, insolent, [and] in a word, the scum of the earth." The next number spoke of "the great joy" at learning that Chabot, Delaunay, Fabre d'Eglantine, and their accomplices in the Indies Company scandal had been arrested. The third number was also happy to inform its readers that Hébert had been made "to sing" during his interrogation, and to assure them that the heads of the accused had been "divorced from their bodies" as all danced "the Carmagnole." [55]

Bacon made a significant observation: "I see the little people. Well, what do they think? Hébert still has a considerable party among such citizens." There was a rumor, moreover, that some three hundred partisans of his from Saint-Antoine would appear at the Palais de Justice in his support. Rolin wrote on 4 Germinal that "Hébert and his associates had many citizenesses" who supported their party.[56]

Nor were all Cordeliers intimidated by the arrest of their leaders. A letter written to the society by one Robert, a rank-and-file member, reveals much of what the others must have been thinking during the

54. *Le Sappeur Sans-Culotte,* "Premier numéro" [March 18, 1794], in Lc 2 2596, BN. Its content may be gauged from the following caption: "Great anger of the people against the infamous Père Duchesne, and his accomplices, who wanted to release from the Temple [prison] the wolf-cubs [Louis' children], to let all the conspirators jailed in Paris roam freely, to massacre members of the National Convention, and to proclaim as king the son of the tyrant Capet."

55. *Ibid.,* Nos. 2 and 3.

56. Caron, *Paris pendant la Terreur,* VI, 1, 33–34, 89.

trial. He headed the three-page document with "Paris this 1 Germinal the last year of liberty if our enemies triumph." Then he addressed the society:

> Immortal Cordeliers, if the rights of man are no longer in your hearts liberty is finished. If you examine, citizens, all [past] revolutions, you will see in all of them some factions that have destroyed the Philosophes whom we today call Patriots; accordingly your members have committed no other crime than to remain warm and true patriots, a powerful faction has sworn their destruction and they will *perish* if the Brave Fouquet de tinville [Fouquier-Tinville], the honest judges and true Republicans of the jury do not take heed and a firm stand against a part of the people whom they have criminally misled against their most ardent defenders. . . . *Robespierre, couton* [Couthon], *and billos de varennes* [Billaud-Varenne] are fooled, and you also, intrepid Cordeliers, you are in a stupor greater than that of Champ de Mars.

Robert adjured his readers to raise their voices and demand justice. "If you remain silent before the wicked, they will destroy you," he warned. He concluded: "Why hasn't justice been rendered to the petition twice presented regarding the 62 deputy conspirators [Girondins] while they accord hardly 5 to 6 days to our friends who are as good as Chalier. Republicans, what has become of your oaths? You have been reduced to silence and to baseness, to opprobrium and to slavery. You have sworn a hundred times to die, well die then, for you no longer have any liberty." He signed his letter, "Robert cordelier," with a subscript: "those who do not see the revolution are blind."[57]

Robert was not alone, of course, in his support of the Cordeliers. Latour-Lamontagne reports a dramatic confrontation between a supporter of the Cordeliers and his opponent, a confrontation that on the one hand proves there were individuals who spoke up in favor of the accused, but on the other hand demonstrates their isolation. On March 22 Latour overheard people complaining on the Place de la Révolution about the way the trial of the Hébertistes was being conducted. "They don't allow them . . . the freedom to defend themselves; the president [of the court] talks harshly to them. It's yes or no, that I demand of you, he says to them each time; it's not a question here of [subtlety] of phrases, etc." Another complained that the court was behaving "contrary to the dictates of humanity and of

---

57. Robert's letter to the Cordeliers, March 21, 1794, is in W 126, AN.

Paris ce I^r Germinal l'an dernier de liberté si nos ennemis triomphe

Immortels Cordeliers si les droits de l'homme ne sont plus dans vos cœurs la liberté est anneantie

Si vous examinez, citoyens toutes les revolutions, dans toutes vous y verrez des factions qui ont écrasé les Philosophs ce que nous appellons aujourd'hui Patriotes; Consequament vos membres n'ont d'autre crime que d'être chauds et vrais patriotes, une faction puissante a juré leur perte et ils periront si le Brave Fouquet de tinville, les honnêtes juges et vrais Republicains du juré n'y prenent garde et ne se rordissent fortement contre une portion du peuple qu'on a criminellemê égaré contre ses plus ardens deffenseurs non jamais non, il n'a montré le même acharnement contre aucun de ses ennemis les plus averés. Robespierre couton ebillot devarenne, sont trompés, et vous aussi intrépides cordeliers, vous êtes dans une stupeur plus grande que celle du champs de mars. Les hipocrites m^{des}, Aristocrates, Ruyalistes et moderés se rejouissent et sont insolents. je ne vous dirai pas insurgez vous; mais au moins élever la voix de manie a faire voir que vous n'êtes pas muet pour redamer la justice, si vous vous taisez devant les mechants ils vous écraseront

21

on fait un decret l'aprés midi et dans la nuit suivante on arrête
vos freres et des le lendemain sont sortis contre eux eux
des panflets insolents et les plus noires calomnies
lancées par une portion du peuple qu'on égare
et qu'on lance comme des lions rugissants, ensuite
tous les aristocrates de toutes les sections, vont
bassement flagorner la convention à qui vous avez donné
le droit de vous enchêner; Enfin toutes les loix de
l'humanité et de la justice sont violées, avez vous
fait attention à ce rouge qui a fait la motion de se
plaindre de ce que la commune n'avait pas été les flagorner
— si vous ni prenez garde on forcera peut-être
votre conscience et vos deffenseurs seront
victimes. Pourquoi n'a t on pas fait droit
a la demande qu'on a faite 2 fois relativement
aux 62 conspirateurs députés, on a toujours refusé
pendant qu'on accorde a peine à 6 jours à nos
emis qui sont autant de chaliers. Republicains
que sont devenus vos sermens, vous voila

réduits au silence ou a la bassesse a l'opprobre
et a l'ésclavage vous avez juré xvv fois de
mourir eh bien mourez donc car vous
n'avez plus de liberté".

Robert cordelier

ceux qui ne voyent pas
la revolution sont
aveugles

justice." He was interrupted by a sans-culotte who declared that this was the first time he had heard complaints against the court. Perhaps, he said, his opponent would have applauded if the Convention and the Jacobins were on trial and the court were equally severe. This brought applause from the crowd, and the individual who had made the first objection disappeared.[58]

The next day Rolin wrote that Hébert's partisans were encouraged by the paucity of proof against him, and that "insinuating themselves everywhere ("ils se glissent partout"), they "pretended" he was guiltless. They were convinced that the accused "would come out of the Revolutionary Tribunal in shining glory."[59] The chief of security in the Office of Administration of Police, Legrand, had reported on the growing tension in public opinion during the first two days of the trial. He admitted that "a quiet agitation reigns that is impossible to define," and that it was important to speed up the trial. At the same time it was essential to make Hébert's conduct clear to the populace "in order to avoid the agitation of a part of the people which is very prejudiced in his favor."[60] But Purvoyeur defined Hébert's defenders as only "the forty-sous people."[61]

As a result of these observations the police took precautionary measures. They declared that in order to discourage efforts at rescue, an imposing armed force was essential. After the sentence they feared trouble at the execution, but no effort was made to rescue the condemned men. Still, a few voices were heard in their favor at the very doors of the Tribunal.[62]

Thus, a minority of the sans-culottes, or at least a minority conscious of the politics of the Committees, remained loyal to their former comrades and to the goals they championed. Many, of course,

58. Caron, *Paris pendant la Terreur*, VI, 34.

59. *Ibid.*, 71.

60. Legrand is quoted in Soboul, *Sans-Culottes*, 815n209. Legrand's report of March 22 stated that in regard to provisions there were groups of malevolent characters who were dangerous because they discouraged the people by their surreptitious agitation: "The presence of the armed force prevents the evil [from erupting] but does not destroy it"; *ibid.*

61. Caron, *Paris pendant la Terreur*, VI, 69.

62. On March 24 a man tried to provoke the people against the gendarmes in order to rescue the condemned; in W 174, AN, cited by Soboul, *Sans-Culottes*, 816n214. The next day a woman was arrested for making "counterrevolutionary proposals" during the execution of Hébert and his accomplices; in Commune de Paris, Département de Police, A A/17, p. 65, APP.

were confused, and former activists who remained silent must have felt depressed and anguished. Suspicion of their old colleagues now began to poison relations among them. Bacon, for example, reported a new silence—in contrast, obviously, to a former confidence and ebullience. He described François Xavier Audouin, son-in-law of Pache and adjutant to Bouchotte, as "so sad at present that he astonishes everyone." He continued: "Since the death of Hébert, I have noticed that in the cafés, the men who spoke out much, are [now] silent."[63]

Section Faubourg Montmartre's congratulatory address spoke of "the people's anxiety without support [that is, without reason] after so many crimes" (by the Hébertistes).[64] A report of March 30 admitted, "There are still people who are convinced that Hébert was a victim of his patriotism; but they say this in a low voice." There were also complaints about moderates now being chosen to sit on juries and revolutionary committees, about the dissolution of the Revolutionary army and "of everything that carries the revolutionary name," as Latour-Lamontagne wrote, citing an observer.[65]

The Jacobins, too, took their cue from the court. During the club's session of March 23, the accused were attacked as plotters in "the foreign conspiracy" ready to turn over frontier posts to the enemies of France.[66] The arrest of Danton during the night of March 30–31, less than a week after the executions, increased the confusion. Grivel observed the astonishment among the sans-culottes.[67] Police reports spoke of the anxiety and stupor that struck the public. What could be said, when those who had denounced the Dantonistes had already been guillotined? This new action of the Committees disoriented the sans-culottes further. Public opinion could not help but be troubled.[68]

The indictment of the Dantonistes had been foreshadowed on March 19 when Collot d'Herbois gave a long address in the Jacobins warning that "another faction" (he called them "moderates") wanted

63. Caron, *Paris pendant la Terreur*, VI, 117, 118–19. Audouin, twenty-eight years old, was a former vicar of Saint-Eustache and was to be persecuted with Pache in 1795. *Ibid.*, V, 403n1.

64. Faubourg Montmartre, plaq. 1045, p. 8, 1 Germinal, in C 299, AN.

65. Caron, *Paris pendant la Terreur*, VI, 190; but after saying this, the man hastily left.

66. Aulard, *Jacobins*, VI, 10–11.

67. Caron, *Paris pendant la Terreur*, VI, 226.

68. Soboul, *Sans-Culottes*, 818.

to take advantage of the Hébertistes' arrest. At the same time he defended the Paris Commune by saying that one should not strike indiscriminately at this institution because in addition to "conspirators" there were "men of August 10" in it.[69] This meant that both the Indulgents and the General Council were to be purged.

As could be expected, not only moderates, but royalists as well, profited from the repression of the Cordeliers. Robert pointed this out in his letter. In section Lepeletier a servant named Vuillemot was arrested for openly praising Hébert—not out of regard for Hébert's opinions, but because he believed that had the Hébertistes succeeded, the Convention, the Jacobins, and the patriots would have been butchered and royalty restored. On March 25 Soulet reported that in all public places aristocrats and moderates rejoiced over Hébert's execution and affected "much patriotism." Soulet added a most revealing observation: the patriots also rejoiced, but they watched each other.[70] One can understand just how sincere their "joy" must have been. Similarly, on March 20 Rolin had reported joy at the arrests of Hébert and Ronsin on the part of merchants, "who pretended" that the two had intended to pillage them. A few days later the police spy observed that "aristocrats" who had never appeared in sectional assemblies since August 10 were rejoicing over the execution "of the scoundrels who wanted to reestablish royalty." He noted their "aristocratic smile" as they predicted that all the "scoundrels" would disappear.[71]

Among these "scoundrels," naturally, were those who had been close to Hébert—Pache, Hanriot, Bouchotte, Chaumette, and Santerre. Even members of the Committee of Public Safety came under attack. On March 27 it was announced in a café that Collot d'Herbois had been arrested. Not a single patron protested the rumor, which would not have passed by before the trial. The Committee of Public Safety of the Paris Department, after being informed that rumors were abroad regarding the arrest and fear of arrest of patriots, decided to publish 2,000 handbills reassuring them that they need not be afraid: "Let us reject the slanderous rumors spread by the counterrevolutionaries, that this or that patriot will be or has been ar-

69. Aulard, *Jacobins*, VI, 2–3.

70. Revolutionary committee of section Lepeletier on Joseph Vuillemot, in W 34, dos. 2138, AN; Caron, *Paris pendant la Terreur*, VI, 117.

71. Caron, *Paris pendant la Terreur*, V, 442, VI, 44.

rested . . . ; the patriots have nothing to fear, the conspirators alone should tremble."[72]

On March 24 Grivel noted that three witnesses at the trial had testified that the "conspirators" planned to make Pache the *grand juge*." He speculated that this was food for thought because Pache was in touch with Bouchotte, thus he could have held the threads of the conspiracy in his hands. Three days later Soulet wrote that people were impatient to learn who were Hébert's accomplices and to see them guillotined.[73]

Counterrevolutionaries were emboldened now to attack the memory of Marat. They saw him as Hébert's inspirer, as one who had preached violence and in whose footsteps the Enragés had allegedly followed before Hébert took their place. Prevost reported he had heard some say that were Marat alive, he too would have been guillotined; they spoke of him as having been a warm partisan of the Cordeliers. On March 20 Bacon revealed that Marat's portrait had been dragged through the mud and that the Convention was about to remove his remains from the Panthéon. Charmont wrote that some were saying it was Marat who had conceived Hébert's plot, and that it was a good thing he had been assassinated, as otherwise he would have been guillotined with the Hébertistes. Monic added that Marat's bust had been thrown out of windows like Mirabeau's before him. People were heard to declare that they had lost confidence in all men, since Marat, too, had betrayed them. Bacon reported on March 26 that in a café of Saint-Denis when someone spoke of removing the remains of Marat from his resting place, another chimed in that it was to be hoped they would remove Lepeletier's as well.[74]

This campaign against "the martyrs of liberty" alarmed spokesmen of the government and their loyal supporters. Bertrand reported that police in section Tuileries had ordered the removal of Chalier's bust (a charge repeated by Collot on March 29 but denied by the police). Dumas saw the maneuvers of "aristos" in this attack on the martyrs of the Revolution, and Legendre warned against attempts "to counterrevolutionize the tombs." Collot defended Chalier in the Jacobins

---

72. Tuetey, *Répertoire général*, X, No. 2019.

73. Caron, *Paris pendant la Terreur*, VI, 79, VI, 138. Grivel ended his remarks by writing that "people suspected them [Pache and Bouchotte] for a long time of being the true authors of the discord."

74. *Ibid.*, V, 373, 428, VI, 8, 63–64, 118.

and warned against moderates who were attempting to take advantage of the government's strike against the Hébertistes. Anyone who questioned the esteem of Jacobins for Marat and Chalier, declared Collot, was a counterrevolutionary.[75]

This kind of threat, and the arrest of Danton, put a temporary end to the campaign against the memory and busts of Marat and Chalier. The Thermidorians went on to carry out the proposals initiated by their moderate predecessors. Robespierre's fall was only some four months away, and with his death the busts and the memory of former "martyrs" would also come to an end. More important, with suspicion and confusion rife in the ranks of those sans-culottes who, for whatever reason, had supported the Cordeliers, the government was now under pressure from the moderates and those to their right. It could no longer balance them with the Hébertistes. If not quite at the mercy of the moderates, it could do little to suppress them for good. The former militants either disappeared from the political scene by going into hiding or, if they still appeared in the general assemblies, kept silent. Moreover, in revolutionary politics whoever says "A" must say "B" as well. Now no militant was safe.

75. *Ibid.*, VI, 191; Aulard, *Jacobins*, VI, 29–32; *Moniteur*, XX, No. 192 (April 1, 1794), 93, No. 193 (April 2, 1794), 106–107.

10

The Repression

Reports from representatives-on-mission prove that the Hébertistes were supported by allies in various provincial towns, not only in Paris.[1] These partisans of the Cordeliers leaders were suppressed shortly after the sections of the capital launched their own purges of the condemned faction. Although some sought the protection of revolutionary committees in the small communes around Paris, few escaped the police. Shortly before Robespierre fell, Claude Javogues estimated that 20,000 persons had been arrested as Hébertistes.[2]

Without exception, the men purged had participated in all the important *journées* of the Revolution. In section Révolutionnaire three founders of its popular society were imprisoned on trumped-up charges.[3] In section Contrat Social a commissioner of the revolutionary committee was arrested for declaring that he did not think Hébert was a criminal. In Hébert's section, Bonne-Nouvelle, three sans-culottes were accused of charges so vague that the men were simply released several days later.[4] Generally, the repression against revolutionary committees was limited. Nevertheless, *Hébertisme* became a word with which to stigmatize any political and social behavior of the sans-culottes that was incompatible with Jacobin concepts and with those of the government committees.

Chaumette, who had been the symbol of the popular movement, was arrested March 18, 1794. He was accused of plotting against the

1. Aulard, *Actes du Comité de salut public*, XII, 30, 160, 196, 245, 472, 473–75, 557, 561; XIV, 143, 674.
2. Caron, *Paris pendant la Terreur*, V, 384–85, VI, 27, 166; Aulard, *Jacobins*, VI, 241.
3. Joseph Bodson the younger, Jean Charles Chemin, and Pierre Tarreau. Soboul and Monnier, *Répertoire de personnel sectionnaire*, 416, 417, 418.
4. *Ibid.*, 417, 146, 175, 176; Wallon, *Tribunal révolutionnaire*, IV, 507; *La Section de Bonne-Nouvelle, à toutes les sections et autorités constituées de la Commune de Paris* (Paris, n.d.), in Lb 40 1746, BN.

government and of advocating atheism. Twenty-five individuals were indicted along with him, including the former bishop of Paris Jean Baptiste Joseph Gobel and Hébert's widow.[5] On March 31 Saint-Just reported on the "conspiracy" of the Dantonistes. Camille Desmoulins and other friends of Danton were also indicted and "amalgamated" with foreign bankers and deputies involved in the Indies Company affair. Less than two weeks after the execution of the Hébertistes, the Dantonistes were delivered to the guillotine.[6] Eight days later, on April 13, it was the turn of Chaumette and his codefendants.[7]

Of course, the government could not allow the repression of the sans-culotte leaders to go too far because this would only have encouraged the moderates and counterrevolutionaries. This seems to have been the reason for the authorities' refusal to prosecute Pache, Hanriot, and Bouchotte. The government purged the General Council, however, and deprived the sections of their representatives. The central authorities also dismissed former police administrators and appointed new men in their place. Pache was arrested on May 10, 1794, and not freed until the amnesty of October 26, 1795.[8] His arrest further alienated the sans-culottes from the government. The former magistrates of the people were no longer their representatives, but rather mere functionaries and appointees of the central authorities.

All former militants in the sections now came under attack. As Rolin observed, "The revolutionary committees are losing their credit every day."[9] In section Unité, for example, several moderates denounced their committee as being linked to the former Hébertistes. The committee counterattacked, however, and arrested its accusers.

5. Arrest warrants, in F7 4435, pl. 3, AN; Tuetey, *Répertoire général*, XI, Nos. 882, 891; *Moniteur*, XX, No. 200 (April 9, 1794), 166–67, No. 203 (April 12, 1794), 191–92, No. 205 (April 14, 1794), 203–205.

6. *AP*, LXXXVII, 629–38, LXXXVIII, 151–52, 159, "Pièces annexes"; *Moniteur*, XX, No. 192 (April 1, 1794), 97–104.

7. See the following for Chaumette: *Chaumette procureur de la Commune à ses concitoyens* (Paris, n.d.), in AD I 50, AN; *Moniteur*, XX, No. 97 (December 27, 1793); Albert Mathiez, "Chaumette franc-maçon," *La Révolution française*, XLIII (1902), 121–41; Albert Mathiez, *Contribution à l'histoire religieuse de la Révolution française* (Paris, 1907), 136–59; Aulard, *Le Culte de la Raison*, 82; Frédéric Braesch, ed., *Papiers de Chaumette* (Paris, 1908), Introduction, 90; Maurice Dommanget, *Sylvain Maréchal l'égalitaire, "l'homme sans dieu": Sa vie, son oeuvre (1750–1803)* (Paris, 1950); Soboul, *Sans-Culottes*, 828.

8. Albert Mathiez, "L'Arrestation de Pache," *Annales révolutionnaires*, VIII (1916), 147–48. Jean Jaurès thought Pache played a fine role during the insurrection of May 31–June 2, 1793; see *Histoire socialiste*, VII, 448–49.

9. Caron, *Paris pendant la Terreur*, VI, 224.

It appealed to the Committee of General Security to examine its conduct, thus bypassing the general assembly of the section in fear of encouraging the moderates. This tactic only strengthened the government's control of the section.[10]

A similar dispute occurred in section Brutus. A leading member of its revolutionary committee, Charles Chardin, clashed with Jean Leymerie, a physician expelled from the section's popular society. Leymerie was jailed, but his partisans persuaded the Committee of General Security to free him and imprison Chardin instead. Leymerie then attacked his enemies in the section, declared that they should not mix in politics, and concluded by pronouncing that "the shoemaker ought not to raise himself higher than [the soles] of his shoes."[11] Yet his political biography was no less "revolutionary" than that of those he despised. Evidently, he reflected a class bias that divided the so-called patriots of '89 from those of '93.

This conflict continued until Pierre Moussard, a spokesman of the section's popular society, entered the dispute. "In a monarchical state barbers are absolute nullities," he declared, "but in a Republic they are intelligent beings who must exercise their reason." Replying to Leymerie's attempt to link the section's revolutionary committee to the Hébertistes, he proved that the section had been the first to present a petition to the Convention against the "impious faction." Jean Philippe Victor Charlemagne, president of the section, seconded Moussard's effort and helped halt the section's drift to the right. Chardin was acquitted and Leymerie imprisoned instead.[12] Yet, again, the latter was no less devoted to the Revolution than his opponents.

The government thought it could limit the repression, but its un-

10. See dos. 3994, 27 Ventôse (March 17, 1794), in W 74, AN, for a denunciation by Jean Robert, a wine merchant, of Louis David Sandoz, a merchant engaged in printing and engraving who had a long revolutionary career behind him. Others accused were Bereytter, a leader of the section's popular society, and Marie Charles Roulx, a sculptor, who opposed removing Marat's bust; Tuetey, *Répertoire général*, XI, No. 894; Soboul and Monnier, *Répertoire de personnel sectionnaire*, 440, 444, 445.

11. Tuetey, *Répertoire général*, XI, Nos. 931, 946; MS 118, fol. 35, in Bibliothèque Victor Cousin, cited by Soboul, *Sans-Culottes*, 834–35.

12. *Section de Brutus. Mémoire instructif sur la conduite de Leymerie* (Paris, 20 Germinal II), in Lb 40 417, BN; Tuetey, *Répertoire général*, XI, Nos. 967, 1816, 2038; Soboul and Monnier, *Répertoire de personnel sectionnaire*, 166 (Duperon), 164 (Sarrette), 167 (Moussard), 166 (Charlemagne), 163–64 (Leymerie). Leymerie was deported to French Guiana (1801–1802), from which he escaped to the United States; he finally returned to France in 1812.

controlled attack on the Hébertistes encouraged the spirit of personal vengeance in the sections. To the apathy and suspicion that now permeated them was added personal malice whose origin had little to do with politics but whose evolution became mixed up with factional animosities. All of this only added to the confusion surrounding the trials of Hébert, Danton, and Chaumette and gradually destroyed the link between the Committees and the militants who had supported them.

The experience of Jean Mathieu Brichet, assistant to the head of the Department of War and thus linked to Vincent, illustrates the danger faced by former militants in displeasing Robespierre and the Jacobins. Brichet was a member of section Mail's revolutionary committee and secretary of the Jacobin Club who had been praised as "an excellent citizen" and for "regenerating section Mail." After he proposed that the arrested Girondins be tried and deputies of the Center be expelled from the Convention, Robespierre denounced these extreme suggestions and had him ejected from the Jacobins without a hearing. Shortly thereafter, the Jacobins resolved that no one expelled from their society could be employed by the government. This resolution led to Brichet's arrest and execution (July 9, 1794).[13]

Having had personal relations with the Cordeliers leaders was now enough to condemn a man. Of the sixteen employees in the War Department, nine were arrested on the basis of only one denunciation; it was enough that they had been employed by Vincent. The wife of a member of section Bonnet Rouge's revolutionary committee confessed what many must have felt: "You will see in a short time the best patriots of Paris destroyed; so my husband and I will retire from all society and we shall no longer see anyone. My husband will leave the Cordeliers because we have no desire to go to the guillotine."[14]

This fear and apathy destroyed the political life of the sections. Their general assemblies now devoted time to purely administrative and local affairs. The stormy debates and passionate discussions of the past were finished. The assemblies occupied themselves with reading official decrees, laws, and pronouncements. Arming "cava-

13. Brichet, Mathieu Jean, dos. 1, in F7 4617, AN; *Moniteur*, XIX, No. 144 (February 12, 1794), 443–45; Aulard, *Jacobins*, V, 643–46, 670; Wallon, *Tribunal révolutionnaire*, IV, 454.

14. Soboul, *Sans-Culottes*, 850 n 92. For other individuals, *ibid.*, 846–48; Soboul and Monnier, *Répertoire de personnel sectionnaire*, 426, 471, 475, 483; and Cobb, *Armées révolutionnaires*, I, 822, 823.

liers" and performing other patriotic tasks under the direction of the central authorities replaced the former initiative of the sections.[15]

Even members of the government were not immune from the Terror that, in Saint-Just's words, "chills the heart." As Legendre had predicted, Bouchotte felt compromised by his appointment of Vincent. In a remarkable letter to Robespierre, the minister of war now justified his former support of Vincent and the subsidy of Hébert's *Père Duchesne*.[16] Interestingly, his letter is addressed not to the Committee of Public Safety but to Robespierre alone.

On March 27, 1794, the Convention dissolved the Revolutionary army. Delegates from the disbanded force protested that Ronsin had seldom visited them, and they sought to demonstrate their loyalty to the Convention.[17] The popular movement was dealt a further blow when the General Council abolished commissioners against hoarding. Its members were disoriented by the trial of the Cordeliers and had been attacked for not congratulating the Convention soon enough for uncovering the "plot" of the Hébertistes. Bourdon de l'Oise had even called them accomplices of "the faction." The Commune's spokesman, Lubin, "explained" that the reason the General Council had failed to appear earlier was that its members felt they had to remain at their post until the "conspiracy" had been unmasked. This fooled no one, but the Commune had saved itself for the time being.[18]

Among the last of popular institutions to suffer the government's attack were the popular societies, especially those limited to individual sections. In his report of March 13, Saint-Just acknowledged their former important role but declared that now "the people" were

15. Bacon reported on April 24 that several sections were busily discussing the purchase of two horses and the arming of two "cavaliers," adding that "almost the whole session was devoted to patriotic speeches." Rolin noted that in section Panthéon-Français "everything passed in tranquillity worthy of true republicans." Caron, *Paris pendant la Terreur*, VI, 72–73, 90–91, 136.

16. Bouchotte to Robespierre, 5 Prairial (May 24, 1794), pl. 4, pp. 164–65, in F7 4436 4, AN. This letter is published in E. B. Courtois, *Rapport fait au nom de la commission chargée de l'examen des papiers trouvés chez Robespierre et ses complices* (Paris, Nivôse, an III), 125–26. For changes in the Revolutionary army's chief of staff, see Cobb, *Armées révolutionnaires*, I, 93.

17. *Moniteur*, XX, No. 188 (March 28, 1794), 67–68.

18. *Ibid.*, No. 183 (March 21, 1794), 17, No. 191 (March 31, 1794), 91–92; *ibid.*, XIX, No. 179 (March 19, 1794), 730; *ibid.*, XX, No. 181 (March 22, 1794), 3–4; Tuetey, *Répertoire général*, X, Nos. 2084, 2089.

absent from them. These societies, he charged, wanted to mold public opinion under the pretext that they were acting "in a revolutionary manner." Soon others joined the attack, accusing the clubs of harboring "aristocrats and counterrevolutionaries" subsidized by "English money."[19]

The well-known arrogance and spirit of exclusiveness that frequently characterized members of sectional societies provided their enemies with ammunition. Not only moderates but ordinary citizens resented them. A measure defeated in the general assembly would often be passed in the sectional society during the interval between meetings of the former. Thus, the will of the assembly frequently would be frustrated by a popular society. Police spies testified that many citizens of the sections opposed these clubs. Charmont, for example, revealed that "most citizens who are not members of popular societies shun those who are." Béraud reported that the measures proposed by Saint-Just against them "were universally applauded." Pourvoyeur added that people were saying the popular societies "are less popular assemblies than a collection of conspirators."[20]

In an effort to demonstrate the purity of their morals, the Cordeliers ruled that all members must give an account of their possessions before the Revolution and their worth at present.[21] The pressure to dissolve popular societies continued, however. As early as November, 1793, as we have seen, Robespierre had criticized them for lack of patriotism. In December he had opposed the affiliation of section Invalides' popular society to the Jacobins. Sectional societies, he pronounced, were "the ultimate resource of the malevolent opposed to liberty," and he called them "bastard societies" that did not merit the "sacred name" *popular*.[22]

On May 15, 1794, the Jacobin Club ruled that its members could no longer belong to sectional societies and gave them ten days to withdraw from the latter or lose their Jacobin membership. Under these

19. *Moniteur*, XIX, No. 174 (March 14, 1794), 686–92; *ibid.*, XX, No. 187 (March 27, 1794), 49–51. Collot d'Herbois attacked the "audacious men" who frequented these societies and called on the Jacobins to combat them; *ibid.*, XX, No. 205 (April 9, 1794), 202–203.

20. Caron, *Paris pendant la Terreur*, V, 202, 313, 42.

21. *Ibid.*, VI, 142, 224.

22. Aulard, *Jacobins*, V, 503–504; *Moniteur*, XVIII, No. 71 (December 1, 1793), 549; *ibid.*, XX, Nos. 236, 238, 240 (May 15, 17, 19, 1794), 467–68, 482–83, 498–99; *Journal de la Montagne*, Nos. 45, 46 (December 28, 29, 1793), 356–58, 363–64.

continued attacks sectional societies began to close their doors. Typical of their attempts to maintain dignity in defeat, the society of section Arcis informed the Convention that although it had never abandoned its republican principles, it dissolved itself "out of regard for public opinion."[23] Shortly thereafter most of the remaining sectional societies dissolved themselves.[24]

Male prejudice had shown itself in the fall of 1793 when the women's club Républicaines révolutionnaires, led by Claire Lacombe and Pauline Léon, was banned after Amar's report of October 29. Now even the oldest feminine organization, Société fraternelle des deux sexes, established in 1790 and sitting in the premises of the Jacobin Club, came under attack.[25] As the government and the Jacobin Society continued their attacks, sectional societies notified the Convention when they ended their existence.[26] Several clubs whose membership had not been limited to a single section tried to maintain themselves despite the mounting pressure. But with the Jacobins monopolizing political life, they too were doomed. By June, 1794, Vadier of the Committee of General Security declared that popular societies were no different from sectional ones. Only "the first and legitimate Society"—that is, the Jacobins—should exist.[27] In less than six months the Jacobins themselves would no longer be "legitimate."

Thus, the revolutionary government, in its effort to establish a unitary and centralized republic, began by outlawing the Cordeliers,

23. Caron, *Paris pendant la Terreur*, IV, 222. For Guillaume Tell, see fol. 6, April 29, 1794, in A A/266, APP; for section Arcis, MS 119, fols. 105–106, May 18, 1794, in Bibliothèque Victor Cousin.

24. *Adresse de la section de la Fontaine-de-Grenelle composant la Société des Amis des loix révolutionnaires, à la Convention nationale* (Paris, 18 Floréal II), in Lb 40 1832, BN. Many of the dissolving groups are listed by the *Moniteur*, XX (various dates), no. 237, pp. 474–75; No. 240, pp. 499, 501, 516; No. 242, p. 518; No. 243, p. 522; No. 252, p. 598; No. 262, p. 680; No. 263, p. 689. See also Aulard, *Jacobins*, VI, 143; *Pétition de la section des Tuileries . . .* (Paris, 1er Sans-Culottide II), in Lb 40 526, BN; and *Moniteur*, XXI, No. 363, 3e sans-culottide II (September 19, 1794), 784.

25. See Morris Slavin, "Feminists and Antifeminists in the French Revolution," in *Women in History, Literature, and the Arts*, ed. Thomas Copeland and Lorrayne Y. Baird-Lange (Youngstown, Ohio, 1989), 17–42.

26. Harmonie sociale of section Arsenal is in C 303, plaq. 1113, p. 23, AN; for Société populaire et républicaine of section Bon-Conseil and Société populaire de l'Ami du peuple of section Marat, respectively, *ibid.*, pl. 1114, pp. 9 and 13.

27. Aulard, *Jacobins*, VI, 181. In contrast to Vadier, Pache argued that free men need to communicate with one another over public affairs. *Observations sur les Sociétés patriotiques, par J. N. Pache, citoyen.* (Paris, n.d.), in Lb 39 5788, BN.

struck at the Indulgents and their moderate supporters, and finished by destroying all organs so painfully established by the popular movement. It is doubtful that winning the war required such unanimity. It is even more doubtful that the Revolution could have been victorious in its early days without the contribution of the popular movement and, above all, of the popular societies.

CONCLUSION

The Hébertistes defy simple defini-
tion. Like many revolutionaries, they harbored contradictions of character and of principle. As imperfect spokesmen of the sans-culottes,
they reflected paradoxical views and actions. They could hardly have
been consistent in their social and political ideals and, like Hébert
himself, expressed their "great anger" or their "great joy." If there is
an element of the irrational in their behavior, this too was a character-
istic of sans-culottisme.

Although championing egalitarianism and democracy in their relationship to the sectionnaires of Paris, the Cordeliers leaders excluded the vast majority of the French people, the peasants and farmers, from these twin ideals. Their movement, like sans-culottisme
itself, was wholly an urban expression. Yet even this statement must
be modified. The Hébertistes regarded the commercial classes with
the same suspicion they applied to peasants, whose goods their
Revolutionary army did not hesitate to requisition. But since a great
many sans-culottes were themselves petty merchants or peddlers or
were linked to commerce and trade by family ties, an attack on commercial activity must have alienated those who otherwise might have
been sympathetic. Moreover, the Cordeliers' indictment of commerce
raised the question of just what kind of an economic program they
could have proposed to substitute for the one they attacked.

It is true, of course, that concepts of private property and laissez-
faire were profoundly modified by the revolutionary regime. The
maximum was adopted by the Montagnards even though they did
not believe in it. It eased the immediate economic plight of the sans-
culottes in the larger towns of France, but it could not provide the
goods of prime necessity that the sans-culottes as consumers needed.
Here the Hébertistes failed utterly. They made no effort to develop a
program that would raise the productivity of the countryside and at
the same time generate needed manufactured goods in the towns to
exchange for the products of the soil.

The intensive effort to dig out saltpeter and to forge pikes failed to stimulate the Cordeliers spokesmen's interest in the production of nonmilitary goods. Requisitioning, after all, was a desperate measure that could not solve the fundamental contradiction between the town and the countryside. The Hébertistes, of course, could not jump over a whole historical epoch with its emphasis on consumption and the physiocrats' exaggerated concept of the "net product." Not having an economic program for the sans-culottes, the Hébertistes had to rely on purely political and moral measures instead. But this approach left them isolated from their base and only compounded their problem of trying to contend with the Convention and its Committees for the continuing support of the sans-culottes.

Were the Hébertistes victims of the "bourgeoisie," whose historical defenders the Jacobins were? To begin with, it must be admitted that many historians question the traditional view that the bourgeoisie's social and economic aspirations were expressed by the Jacobins. Still, unless one rejects the idea that the French Revolution was a social revolution, that social classes with different economic, political, and cultural interests clashed in 1789, it is difficult to deny that the long-range historical interests of France's middle classes were, consciously or unconsciously, expressed by the Montagnards. Thus, though it can be argued that the egalitarian and democratic goals of the sans-culottes menaced the bourgeoisie and its spokesmen, the Jacobins/Montagnards faced a concrete, immediate threat of "factionalism" that was undermining the war effort.

Just as the threat of "federalism" inspired by the Girondins after the insurrection of May 31–June 2, 1793, aroused a reaction against its supporters, so the continued party strife called out a countermove by the revolutionary government. There is little doubt that the Jacobins/Montagnards were concerned, above all, about winning the war. If sans-culottisme had to be sacrificed and its spokesmen curbed in order to establish that "unity and indivisibility" that defined the Republic, so be it. In this respect the government acted, it appears, not from any abstract class bias but from the immediate need to support the war effort. Robespierre was not alone in his obsession with "a single will."

Hébert paid the price for challenging that "will." Too many historians and biographers, however, including his own contemporaries, have been convinced that he lacked "character." This is a harsh judgment and deserves some modification. Perhaps it would be more correct to say that he lacked firmness in circumstances that called for it. There was a kind of naïveté on Hébert's part in thinking that after challenging Robespierre and the Committees he would be left alone. His dechristianization crusade, assault on commerce, obsessive insistence on executing the imprisoned Girondins, feud with Desmoulins, and call for an insurrection—even in normal times these would have caused uneasiness in a government trying to establish a republic "one and indivisible." In time of war, foreign and domestic, Hébert's efforts, even though confined to words—albeit words that were most influential—were bound to bring a counterstroke.

None of this denies his virtues. If anyone helped give the sans-culottes a sense of dignity and worth, it was Hébert and his *Père Duchesne*. The fact that his journal was written in the patois of the streets does not lessen its contribution. Besides, even though Hébert was ambitious for a governmental office—the ministry of the interior, to be specific—his popularity rested on his championing of the egalitarian and democratic ideals of his readers. Whether he would have continued to defend the sans-culottes as a minister is not possible to answer. It was enough for the central authorities to realize that Hébert, because of his past, would continue to appear as the spokesman for the popular movement. Under such circumstances he could not be relied on to do the Committees' bidding. It was one thing to have a Bouchotte in the ministry; it would have been quite a different thing to have had Hébert in the government.

Those who believe that raising the political consciousness of the masses and encouraging their participation in government are worthy goals find Hébert's role, if not quite admirable, still deserving of respect. It may be true that some of his politics were demagogic, but his very ambition was bound to encourage the popular movement to take an independent course. Moreover, he had experienced the pangs of hunger and knew "the proud man's contumely." Surely this was reason enough to make common cause with the sans-culottes and to express their "great anger" and share their "great joy." In addition, Hébert as a person was interesting and cultured. There is no indication of vulgarity in his behavior at home with either his friends or his guests. Too much is also made of his alleged cowardice at the moment of death. Hébert loved life too much to leave it at an early age. Besides, it is more important to know how well he lived, not whether he died, like Ronsin, with aplomb.

It is quite likely that Hébert used the food crisis for his own, political ends. Nevertheless, because it was a real crisis—an even greater one than the war—he was able to rivet the attention of the sans-culottes on their immediate needs. Of course, both crises fed on each other. Military defeats heightened the uneasy feeling in the capital, and the belief that shortages were artificially created—that but for the counterrevolutionaries, France could feed itself—aggravated the difficulty, made for intolerance of dissent, and aroused suspicion against political opponents. Thus, on the one hand, there was a popular base to be exploited by any party that could channel the dissatisfaction against the authorities. Conversely, an unscrupulous government could use the discontent against any party that threatened it.

It is doubtful if the Cordeliers would have enjoyed the influence in the sections had it not been for the scarcity of essentials. At the same time, the club's leaders did not know how to link the food crisis to their political goals. The *journées* of September 4 and 5, 1793, had given the Commune, the Cordeliers Club, and the militant members of the sections important concessions. The Convention had bowed, however reluctantly, to the will of the sans-culottes, but in addition to the weaknesses and imperfections of the Law of the Maximum, the law against speculation and hoarding could not be enforced. Besides, the need to supply the armies above all made for neglect of the civilian sector. Requisitions, the purchase of supplies by the army's agents above the *maximum*, the draft of men and horses for the armed forces, England's blockade—all depressed the agricultural sector. The Cordeliers had no solution for this crisis.

This economic emergency had its parallel in the political events shaped originally in the Vendée. The dispute on strategy that pitted the sans-culotte generals Ronsin and Rossignol, supported by the representatives-on-mission Choudieu, Richard, and Bourbotte, against professional military officers like Generals Biron and Westermann, backed by deputies Philippeaux, Bourdon de l'Oise, and the two Goupilleaus, was not limited to military matters alone. The quarrel had deeper political and social implications.

It could be argued, of course, that an important military campaign had to be put into the hands of the most capable military leaders. Since, obviously, a civilian like Ronsin and a simple noncommissioned officer like Rossignol lacked the training and experience of the professionals, they should not have been in charge of such a campaign. Were military competence alone to be considered, this argument would be a valid one. The real problem, however, was that decisions about strategy, and even about tactics, were shot through with politics.

The more conservative deputies were not anxious to enhance the reputations of sans-culotte officers. They realized, of course, that the latter's political success could only be advanced by their military success. Bitter opponents of the sans-culottes and the Cordeliers, the Indulgents were willing to risk defeat for republican arms rather than allow the sans-culotte commanders to reap the fruits of victory in the Vendée.

In addition, there was the matter of valuable property possessed by the Goupilleaus. Ronsin and Rossignol showed no intention of compromising on their scorched-earth policy against the rebels in order to save some properties of the two deputies. Here, too, was reason enough to develop sharp differences on how to command the army. Of course, it must not be forgotten that even from the purely military point of view, the strategy of the Indulgents proved costly to republican arms. The Vendée, then, gave birth to the two factions that fought each other to the death.

Ronsin's appointment as commander of the Revolutionary army a month after the demonstrations of September 4 and 5 was probably the high tide of sans-culottisme. By November, after Robespierre's speech against dechristianization, the Commune was forced to retreat. In December the Paris Commune was dealt another blow when it was forced to surrender its control of the sections' revolutionary committees. National agents, directly responsible to the Convention, now became instruments of centralization at the expense of local initiative. On December 17, 1793, Ronsin and Vincent were arrested and remained in prison until February 2, 1794. Thus, Ronsin's triumph was of short duration.

Although all revolutionary parties praised excessively the ancient Greek and Roman "republicans," they denounced and misunderstood Cromwell's historic role. The Cordeliers should have adopted this regicide and founder of the Commonwealth as their own—even if he did purge Parliament and, ultimately, was forced to govern as a military dictator. Ronsin evidently could not read English, yet he still had to deny specifically that he had perused Hume's life of Cromwell—evidence of a strong fear of militarism in French society at this time. Given this fear, could he have used his Revolutionary army against the Convention, assuming that the Cordeliers had made determined plans to launch an insurrection? It is more than doubtful.

The Cordeliers leaders dreamt of insurrection, but they did nothing practical to carry it out. Still, it is not surprising that another insurrection would appeal to them. They had been participants in three successful uprisings in the past: July 14, 1789; August 10, 1792; and May 31–June 2, 1793. Each time the position of the sans-culottes seemed to have improved. Another revolt might bring the long-sought solution to their economic and political problems. But instead of the careful preparations they had made for such actions in the past, this time the Hébertistes organized nothing and no one.

They did talk of insurrection, of course, and this was their fatal error. Carrier, Hébert, and Ronsin threatened and blustered that another uprising was needed, but when asked against whom the insurrection was to be launched and what its goals were, they remained tongue-tied. An insurrection against the moderates made no sense; the moderates were not in power. A revolt against the Montagnards who directed the Convention and its two Committees made even less sense to the sans-culottes and, for that matter, to members of the Cordeliers Society. They had contributed to the expulsion of the Girondins and had helped place the Montagnards in power. Supposing they were successful in overthrowing the government—what then? Could they have shortened the war or brought an end to food shortages? They possessed no magic formula for either.

Who would have followed the Hébertistes, even if they attempted to organize such a *journée*? Hébert was popular enough in some neighborhoods of Paris, but the police reports and other sources show that his popularity did not compare with Robespierre's. If forced to choose between the two individuals, few militants would have followed Hébert against Robespierre.

The government, moreover, was playing a clever game. There is little indication that the Ventôse decrees were more than skillful propaganda. It was enough, however, to have promulgated the goal of distributing confiscated lands and other property among the indigent patriots. The Convention had won them over. A government that was pursuing an energetic policy to beat the Coalition, that was successfully appealing to young and old for patriotic contributions, and that alone appeared to represent stability in an unstable world—such a government was bound to enjoy the support of the sans-culottes.

The Cordeliers leaders fell between two stools. They could neither organize an insurrection nor keep quiet in face of the shortages and other frustrations. Whatever popularity they enjoyed in the sections, popular societies, and among individual militants, they could not turn this advantage against the Committees and the Convention. The Cordeliers might veil the Rights of Man, and section Marat might demonstrate its discontent before the Commune, but the real power and popularity were with the revolutionary government.

Collot d'Herbois, among others, enjoyed this popularity. Yet he embodied a paradox, for he owed his appointment on the Committee of Public Safety to the mass demonstration of the sans-culottes in early September. Among the leaders of the demonstration had been the Cordeliers and their allies in the General Council. Moreover, upon his return from Lyon, this "giant" attacked the moderates and their supporters in the Convention no less vehemently than did the Hébertistes. But at the decisive moment, just when the Cordeliers felt certain he was on their side, he became the spokesman and defender of the Committees against Hébert, Ronsin, Momoro, and their followers.

What caused this change? Did he calculate the parallelogram of forces and find that the Cordeliers were too weak? Or was he really convinced that their policy would lead to disaster for the Revolution? It is impossible to say. But that his role up to the break with his former comrades had spurred on the Cordeliers leaders can hardly be doubted. With the Committee and the Jacobin society behind him, Collot's confrontation with Momoro, after the disastrous session of the Cordeliers on 14 Ventôse, could have led only to the latter's defeat. Resolutions of amity between the two popular societies merely papered over the cracks.

The fracas over Hébert's twenty-four pounds of meat added to the discomfiture of his followers. The defender of sans-culottisme who thundered constantly against hoarding was now put on the defensive and had to justify this "gift" to hungry sans-culottes. Certainly no greater gift could have been presented to Hébert's enemies. The police report that portrayed so graphically the sans-culotte who scratched his head, upon reading Hébert's justification, caught the latter's dilemma exactly. Whom to believe? That was the question.

Could the publication of the Cordeliers' *l'Ami du peuple* have strengthened their position in public opinion? It is doubtful. What could this journal have said that Hébert's *Père Duchesne* did not say? Moreover, how much confidence did its publishers have, when they themselves refused to sign their names to the articles? No anonymity was possible in any case. The agents of the Committees knew the authors well and had no need for legal niceties.

Equally revealing was the enthusiasm with which the sections welcomed Saint-Just's speech on "the foreign conspiracy." The great majority fell in behind the government, with few voices of dissent raised against the Committee's monstrous charges against the Hébertistes. Not all of this support can be attributed to fear. Confidence in the government's spokesmen and in its revelations of a "conspiracy" won over many sans-culottes and paralyzed its opponents. This was perhaps the most depressing result of Saint-Just's address.

Still, it must not be forgotten that there were dissenters, as the police reports make clear. If some historians, like Mathiez, find hardly a ripple in the normal life of the sections when the arrests of the Hébertistes became known, others, like Guérin, exaggerate the support the accused enjoyed. The more perceptive militants in the sections knew without a doubt that the imprisoned Cordeliers were patriots and, thus, victims of the government. Individuals made some foolhardy statements about launching a rescue operation, but there could not have been any serious effort to organize such a coup.

Were Collot and Billaud-Varenne involved in the "plot" of the Cordeliers? There is some evidence to sustain this possibility, but surely those two were shrewd enough not to risk their political careers and their lives in such a hopeless cause. They could exploit the popular movement for their own ambition, but they could never allow it to attack the Committee of which they were an integral part.

Mayor Pache's role is also unclear, but there is enough evidence to link him to the Hébertistes. The reports of police spies repeatedly cite various individuals as speaking of his supposed role in a Hébertiste coup, as the future "great judge." The idea of a dictator after a military coup was not unfamiliar to Parisians. Marat, too, had spoken of a "chief" who would take power upon the removal of the Girondins. Furthermore, the lack of documents in Pache's dossier points to a deliberate destruction of whatever evidence existed against him. The fact that he, together with Hanriot and Santerre, had escaped arrest astounded many contemporaries. Yet there is little doubt that by arresting these three the Committees would have broken their links to the popular movement. It was enough to have crippled the movement for the time being. The Thermidorians were to finish what the Committees had begun.

It must have been deeply depressing for the arrested Cordeliers to see how effective was the government's campaign against them. Aside from their loyal followers and some skeptics in the popular societies and the sections, the vast majority seem to have accepted the public prosecutor's charges against their former spokesmen. Even without the modern means of communication, the government enjoyed a near monopoly on the "news" it wished to give out. With the arrest of Hébert, his journal no longer appeared, and the Cordeliers' *Ami* never saw the light of day after the second number. Who was there to defend the Cordeliers? Besides, even the expression of confidence that the court would free the accused was itself now suspect. Above all, why should the ordinary man and woman in the street have doubted the pronouncements of their elected representatives?

The report of the Cordeliers' "astonishment" at the charges against their leaders should be accepted with some skepticism. It is difficult to believe that the Cordeliers were naïve enough to be "astonished." They surely realized this coup was political and that the trial was to be a political, not a judicial, proceeding. Chenaux's "astonishment" that not a single member of the society had expressed support for the arrested leaders seems equally naïve. Of course, fear played a role in the Cordeliers' reactions. The apparatus of repression was by then fully in place, and to have challenged the government at this point would have brought on fierce reprisals. To risk arrest by a Girondin Committee of Twelve when the great majority of sans-culottes, sections, and popular societies were in strong sympathy with the imprisoned was quite different from a situation in which many of the popular organizations were on the side of the authorities.

The resolutions of support for the government and the execrations of the sections as they vied with one another for who could be fiercest in denouncing the imprisoned Cordeliers must have added to the mood of depression of all but the stoutest revolutionaries. The demise of the Cordeliers and the apology of section Marat for its general assembly's having been fooled by "intriguers" demonstrated that it was impossible to stand up in defense of the arrested Hébertistes. It is true, of course, that the tardiness of a few sections in expressing their joy at the actions of the government illustrates that some of the more militant sectionnaires did not capitulate without some effort to maintain their dignity. But within forty-eight hours whatever opposition remained in the sections and popular societies to the central authorities vanished as the general and popular assemblies joined the officially orchestrated chorus.

Momoro's and Vincent's leadership of the Cordeliers stands in sharp contrast to that of the Chenauxs, Brochets, and Prétots. In his support of Ronsin and Rossignol, Momoro had proved his commitment not only to the Republic but to the spirit of egalitarianism that he championed so warmly in his brochures and pronouncements. His social and philosophical principles were markedly to the left of the Jacobins, and his proposals in connection with the *maximum* show that he had given some thought to the economic problems that such a measure would pose. Momoro's conviction that society had prior rights to products of the soil, as against the right of private ownership, was shared by a number of *philosophes* (like Rousseau), social reformers (like Fauchet and Bonneville), and political activists (like Roux and Varlet). Momoro, however, as president of the Cordeliers and leader of section Marat had political influence that the others lacked. His Rights of Man underscored the emphasis he placed on the social factor as against the individual and private. Several of his principles favored the poor against the propertied, and his nod to "the forty-sous people" assured him a ready base in the section. His egalitarian principles did not apply to the way he presided over the sectional assembly, however: there is little doubt that he led the section with a high hand.

Equally intolerant of dissent was his colleague Vincent. Younger by a dozen years than Momoro, Vincent also had a base in the War Department, as well as in section Mutius Scaevola. His uncontrolled outbursts against opponents, or those perceived by him to be such, were due partly to his passionate nature and partly to his youth. Saint-Just was also young, but unlike Vincent he could curb his feelings and discipline them to serve his reason, or what he perceived to be reasons of state. Historians have commented on Vincent's violent language, which erupted even in the most elegant of his addresses on the floor of the Convention. Like the diatribes of *Père Duchesne*, Vincent's expressed the zeal of the sans-culotte committed in struggle to preserving the Republic. Nor should it be forgotten that both Momoro and Vincent had put their lives in danger more than once in the cause of the Revolution.

Equally committed to the Revolution were the men who were arrested with Momoro and Vincent. Desfieux, Pereyra, and Proly had long revolutionary careers and had carried out dangerous missions for the government. None of the three was a sans-culotte; all were middle class in origin and were linked to commerce or banking. Similarly, Dubuisson and Descombes possessed some education and were members of the liberal professions. Mazuel alone could be regarded as a sans-culotte—at least in his early days. Upon assuming command of a cavalry squadron, however, he changed his social status as well.

That the Revolution should be led by members of the middle class is not surprising, of course. Such leadership is a common character-istic of modern revolutions, bourgeois or proletarian (or what passes for these definitions). The sans-culottes, lacking education, leisure, and political experience, could not be leaders of first rank. Nor, until they gained political and administrative experience, could many com-pete with the revolutionaries just named.

The arrest of these men and the cynicism with which they were sacrificed are hardly equaled until our own century. Was there a more ardent French patriot than Anacharsis Cloots? By social origin he was a noble, by birth a Prussian, by politics a moderate, by inclination a cosmopolitan. Yet in his foreign policy he was a French imperialist. That French nationalism had turned into chauvinism under the inspi-ration of Robespierre is clear when we examine the charges of the latter against "poor Cloots," as Louis Blanc called him. The universal Rights of Man, as Cloots pointed out in a question to Robespierre, had turned into the rights of Frenchmen alone. The politics of impe-rialism are hidden in Robespierre's indictment aimed at Cloots.

As for "amalgamating" people who had no relation with the Hé-bertistes, the same political trick is common in our own times. To destroy the political reputation of the Cordeliers by slander, they had to be surrounded by criminals of as low a type as possible. Thus, by giving the latter a "political" role and endowing the former with a criminal role, the public prosecutor created a perfect amalgamation. The trial of the Hébertistes, like that of the Dantonistes, was a frame-up pure and simple. It had nothing to do with judicial process but, as Ronsin understood, was a political proceeding. Like the Old Bolshe-viks on trial under Stalin, the Hébertistes were slandered, abused, reviled, and finally, condemned and executed.

Some of the accusations against them were so absurd that if the outcome of the trial had not been so tragic, the charges would have seemed amusing. Vincent had ridiculed the uniform of Legendre; suddenly this became a serious charge and was trumpeted into an attack on the dignity of the Convention. Reading the life of Cromwell was proof that Ronsin wanted to imitate the Protector of the Com-monwealth. Momoro's arbitrary behavior in denying his opponents the floor was cause to send him to the guillotine. Proly, who knew the Belgians better than his interrogators, thought the former should be allowed to keep their nobles and priests; this "moderate" view was enough to help condemn him.

The antipopular nature of the repression was best expressed in the arrest and condemnation of Chaumette. To call him an "ultra" was to tar all egalitarians with the same brush. His influence in the General Council helped assure support of the Parisian authorities for the Montagnards. If he was a radical it was only in his anticlerical feelings. As the chief official of the municipality he expressed and defended the dreams of the sans-culottes for a more meaningful life. Chaumette's execution was a direct blow against the popular institutions, those who staffed them, and the mass of Parisians who had sacrificed so much to establish an independent municipal government.

The many witnesses that the court heard seemed to be ordinary men and women engaged in commerce, the crafts, or the liberal professions, or who held modest government posts. There is little question that they understood what the authorities wanted of them. This in no way precludes their effort to give an honest testimony. The problem was that so much of it was based on hearsay evidence, and there is no record of a cross-examination by the defense attorneys of these witnesses, if it was ever made.

The condemnation and execution of the Hébertistes and those amalgamated with them ended the popular phase of the French Revolution. Former activists and spokesmen for the sans-culottes now went into hiding or dropped out of the movement. The Revolution became a bureaucratic affair, led into safe channels that excluded the initiative from below. The élan and zeal of the sans-culottes, which men like Robespierre recognized and had paid homage to in the past, disappeared from the scene. The Paris Commune, the sectional assemblies, and even the Jacobin Club—all were tamed now.

Popular societies, where so many innovations had been born, now found themselves on the defensive. It was the revolutionary government, it should be recalled, that had begun the attack on them by dissolving sectional societies first. The difference between them and the older popular societies was often so obscure that members of both organizations had to examine their early beginnings in order to be sure whether they were one or the other. True, the older clubs tended to reflect the outlook of their founders, who often went back to 1789, as against the new sectional assemblies of 1793. But here again, just as the Thermidorians were to amalgamate the "devoted patriots" with their moderate opponents, the deputies of the Right did not distinguish between the patriots of '89 and those of '93. In a few short months the long-established clubs were also closed down, finally ending with the demise of the Jacobins themselves. Thus, the dissolution of the sectional societies and the domestication of the Cordeliers foreshadowed the end of "the Mother Society" itself. Equally important, the suppression of the popular movement as expressed by the Cordeliers/Hébertistes led directly to Thermidor. The latter, in turn, changed the nature of the Revolution.

The Hébertistes had no aims fundamentally different from those of the Convention and its Committees. Still, from their point of view, the main task was to satisfy the confused social and political aspirations of the sans-culottes. Their failure brought in its train the end of Jacobinism as well. For despite the different "historic tasks" that each party set for itself, Jacobinism and Hébertisme proved to be interdependent. If the Jacobins wished to remain in power, they needed the popular movement behind them. But the latter was led by the Hébertistes. When they destroyed the Cordeliers, the Jacobins undermined their own position as well. Thus, ultimately, Père Duchesne had his revenge.

BIBLIOGRAPHY

PRIMARY SOURCES

Archival Sources

Archives Nationales

Série C documents, containing resolutions and addresses to the National Convention by various sections and popular societies:

290, plaquette 990, section Arsenal

295, plaq. 991, section Faubourg du Nord

295, plaq. 995, section Poissonnière; revolutionary committee of section Homme Armé; popular society Amis du peuple of section Marat

299, plaq. 1045, p. 8, section Faubourg Montmartre's address to the Convention; p. 32, section Cité's address to the Convention

300, plaq. 1057, section Gardes-Françaises deposits saltpeter

303, plaq. 1099, section Brutus; plaq. 1113, popular society Harmonie sociale of section Sans-Culottes; plaq. 1114, popular society (La Société populaire et républicaine) of section Bon-Conseil

Série F7 documents, pertaining to individuals:

4435, plaq. 1, Fouquier-Tinville's "Justification"

4435, plaq. 3, Chaumette's arrest warrant

4435, plaq. 7, Fouquier-Tinville to the Committee of Public Safety regarding De Koff (*sic*)

4436 4, plaq. 4, Bouchotte's letter to Robespierre

4438, plaq. 1, Inventory of documents on the persons indicted

4617, dossier 1, Brichet, Mathieu Jean

4649, dos. 5, Cloots, Anacharsis

4672, dos. 1, Descombes, Antoine Ignace François

4672, dos. 2, Desfieux, François

4774 40, dos. 3, Mazuel, Albert

4774 67, dos. 2, Pereyra, Jacob

4774 83, dos. 1, Proly, Pierre Berthold

4775 48, dos. 2, Vincent, François Nicolas, and Ronsin, Charles Philippe

Série W documents, relating to the Revolutionary Tribunal:

34, dos. 2138, revolutionary committee of section Lepeletier on Joseph Vuillemot

74, dos. 3994, Robert's denunciation of section Unité's revolutionary committee; on members of section Unité

77, plaq. 379, testimony of Mathias Halm

136, Sergeant Guillaume's letter to the public prosecutor

168, another letter by Sergeant Guillaume

173, record of the Tribunal on the accused, witnesses, and accusations

Other documents:

AD I 50, Chaumette's defense of his political conduct

AD I 55, Maurin's reply to charges against him

AF II* 286, Committee of General Security to revolutionary committees of the sections

AF II* 294, release of Vincent and Ronsin, 14 and 15 Pluviôse, Year II

BB 3 58, dos. Pache

D III, dos. 4, letter of Descombes' wife

T 1000$^{1-3}$, sequestered papers of Claire Lacombe

Published document:

Procès des conspirateurs Hébert, Ronsin, Vincent, Momoro, Desfieux, et complices. Paris, An II. 126 pp.

Bibliothèque Nationale

Manuscripts in Nouvelles acquisitions françaises (Nouv. acq. fr.):

2662, folios 63, 72, 73, 155, 156

Brochures of Antoine François Momoro:

Lb 40 542, *Section du Théâtre-Français dite de Marseille.* Paris, April 15, 1793. 2 pp.

Lb 41 2978, *De la Convention nationale . . . Déclaration des droits.* Paris, n.d. 7 pp.

Lb 41 3324, *Rapports des événemens relatifs à la visite faite par le Général en chef Rossignol, des differentes divisions composants l'armée des côtes de la Rochelle.* [Paris], n.d. 6 pp.

Lb 41 3389, *Rapport sur l'état politique de la Vendée, fait au Comité de salut public . . .* Paris, 22 [Vendémiaire], An II. 36 pp.

Lb 46 3219, *De Saumur.* [Paris], August 13, 1793. 3 pp.

Ld 4 3556, *Réflexion d'un citoyen sur la liberté des cultes religieux, pour servir de réponse à l'opinion de M. l'abbé Sieyès . . .* [Paris], 1792. 8 pp.

Le 38 2461, *Opinion de Momoro, administrateur et membre de directoire du département de Paris.* [Paris], n.d. 14 pp.

Ln 27 14429, *Pétition à l'Assemblée nationale.* [Paris], n.d. 3 pp.

Other published sources:

Lb 39 5788, *Observations sur les sociétés patriotiques, par J. N. Pache, citoyen.* Paris, n.d. 8 pp.

Lb 40 417, *Section de Brutus. Mémoire instructif sur la conduite de Leymerie.* Paris, 20 Germinal [An II]. 8 pp.

Lb 40 526, *Pétition de la section des Tuileries* . . . Paris, 1er sans-culottide [An II]. 2 pp.

Lb 40 1746, *La section de Bonne-Nouvelle, à toutes les sections et autorités constituées de la Commune de Paris.* Paris, n.d. 4 pp.

Lb 40, 1727, *Extrait du registre et déliberations de la section de Bon-Conseil.* Paris, 10 Ventôse [An II]. 4 pp.

Lb 40 1818, *Soutiens aux patriotes, guerre aux modérés* . . . Paris, 5 Ventôse [An II]. 8 pp.

Lb 40 1832, *Adresse de la section de la Fontaine de Grenelle* . . . Paris, [18 Floréal, An II]. 7 pp.

Lb 40 1891, *La Section d'Indivisibilité à la Convention nationale.* Paris, 30 Pluviôse [An II]. 8 pp.

Lb 40 2194, *Liberté, égalité. Société républicaine de l'ami du peuple.* Paris, 9 Ventôse [An II]. 4 pp.

Lb 40 2438, *Discours prononcé par C. Camus* . . . Paris, 11 Ventôse [An II]. 8 pp.

Lb 40 2457, *Société fraternelle des deux sexes du Panthéon-Français. Adresse présentée le 27 Ventôse, par cette Société, à la Convention nationale.* [Paris]. 1 p.

Lb 41 1040 B, *Réponse de Philippeaux à tous les défenseurs officieux des bourreaux de nos frères dans la Vendée, avec l'acte solennel d'accusation, fait à la séance du 18 nivôse, suivie de trois lettres écrites à sa femme, de la prison.* Paris, l'an III. 97 pp. Published by Philippeau's widow with a two-page introduction.

Lb 41 1679, *J. Bouchotte, ex-ministre de la Guerre, à ses concitoyens.* Au chateau de Ham, 12 Ventôse, l'an troisieme. 8 pp.

Lb 41 2232, *Jugement rendu par le tribunal révolutionnaire.* [Paris, n.d.]. 15 pp.

Lb 41 4809, *Réponse de J. R. Hébert, auteur du "Père Duchesne," à une atroce calomnie.* [Paris]. 1 p.

Le 38 1280, *Discours prononcé à la Convention nationale dans la séance du 20 Ventôse, l'an III, par Sieyès.* [Paris], Germinal, An V. 4 pp.

Le 38 2175, *Denonciation faite à la Convention nationale, par Laurent Lecointre, de Versailles, député de département de Seine-et-Oise, contre Billaud-Varenne, Collot d'Herbois, et Barère, membres du Comité de salut public, Vadier, Voulland, Amar, et David, membres du Comité de sûreté générale.* [Paris], n.d. 10 pp.

Le 39 64 bis, *Pierre Choudieu à ses concitoyens et à ses collegues* . . . [Paris], n.d. 47 pp.

Ln 27 8243, *Jean Baptiste Olivier Garnerin electeur de Bon-Conseil de 1792.* Paris, n.d. 8 pp.

Ln 27 18956, *Notice sur la vie de Sieyès, membre de la première Assemblée nationale et de la Convention.* Paris, 1794. 66 pp.

Archives de la Préfecture de Police

A A/266, p. 6 [dossier Arcis, nos. 1–17].

A A/17, p. 65, Commune de Paris, Département de Police.

BOOKS

Aulard, Alphonse. *Recueil des actes du Comité de salut public avec la correspondance officielle des représentants en mission et le registre du conseil exécutif provisoire.* 28 vols. Paris, 1889–1951.

————. *La Société des Jacobins. Recueil de documents pour l'histoire du Club des Jacobins de Paris.* 6 vols. Paris, 1889–97.

Barrière, J. F., ed. *Mémoires particulières de Mme de Rolland.* Paris, 1847.

Barrucand, Victor, ed. *La Vie véritable du citoyen Jean Rossignol (1759–1802).* Paris, 1896.

Berville, Saint-Albin, and Jean Francois Barrière, eds. *Collection des mémoires relatifs à la Révolution française. . . .* Paris, 1828. Vol. LVIII of Berville and Barrière, eds., *Débats de la Convention nationale.* 2d ser.; 65 vols.

Braesch, Frederic, ed. *Papiers de Chaumette.* Paris, 1908.

Brissot de Warville, J. P. *Sur la propriété et sur le vol.* 1780; rpr. Brussels, 1872.

Buchez, P. J. B., and P. C. Roux, eds. *Histoire parlementaire de la Révolution française.* 40 vols. Paris, 1834–38.

Calvet, Henri. *L'Accaparement à Paris sous la Terreur: Essai sur l'application de la loi du 26 juillet 1793.* Paris, 1933.

Caron, Pierre. *Paris pendant la Terreur: Rapports des agents secrets du ministre de l'intérieur.* 6 vols. Paris, 1910–64.

Charavay, Etienne, ed. *Assemblée électorale de Paris, 18 novembre 1790–15 juin 1791 . . .* 3 vols. Paris, 1890.

Cloots, Anacharsis. *Anacharsis Cloots Oeuvres. . . .* 3 vols. Paris, 1980.

————. *La République universelle; ou, Adresse aux tyrannicides.* Paris, [1792].

————. *Ni Marat, ni Roland: Opinion d'Anacharsis Cloots, deputé de l'Oise.* Paris, 1792. 16 pp.

Courtois, E. B. *Rapport fait au nom de la commission chargée de l'examen des papiers trouvés chez Robespierre et ses complices.* Paris, Nivôse III (December, 1794–January, 1795).

Dauban, Charles Aimé. *Les Prisons de Paris sous la Révolution d'après les relations des contemporaines.* 1870; rpr. Geneva, 1977.

Duval, Michel, ed. *Anacharsis Cloots: Ecrits Révolutionnaires, 1790–1794.* Paris, 1979.

Fortescue, J. B. *The Manuscripts of J. B. Fortescue, Esq., Preserved at Dropmore.* 10 vols. London, 1892–1927.

Hamel, Ernest. *Papiers inédits, trouvés chez Robespierre.* 3 vols. Paris, 1828.

Mably, Gabriel Bonnot, de. *De la législation; ou, Principes des loix.* 2 vols. Lausanne, 1777.

Mathiez, Albert. *Le Club des Cordeliers pendant la crise de Varennes et le massacre du Champ de Mars.* Paris, 1910.

Mavidal, M. J., M. E. Laurent, *et al.*, eds. *Archives parlementaires de 1787 à 1860: Recueil complet des débats législatifs et politiques des chambres françaises.* Series I, 90 vols. Paris, 1879–.

Momoro, Antoine François. *Traité élémentaire de l'imprimerie; ou, Le Manuel de l'imprimeur.* Paris, 1796.

Rapports de Grivel et Siret, commissaires parisiens du conseil exécutif provisoire sur les subsistances et le maximum . . . Paris, 1908.

Schmidt, Adolphe. *Tableaux de la Révolution française.* 3 vols. Leipzig, 1869.

Senart, Gabriel Jérôme. *Révélations puisées dans les cartons des comités de salut public et de sûreté générale; ou, Mémoires inédits de Senart.* 2d ed. Paris, 1824.

Tourneux, Maurice. *Bibliographie de l'histoire de Paris pendant la Révolution française.* 5 vols. 1890; rpr. Paris, 1968.

Tuetey, Alexandre. *Répertoire général des sources manuscrits de l'histoire de Paris pendant la Révolution française.* 11 vols. Paris, 1890–1914.

JOURNALS

L'Ami du peuple par le club des Cordeliers
La Bouche de fer
Journal de la Montagne
Journal de Paris
Le Publiciste de la République française
Le Père Duchesne
Le Sappeur Sans-Culotte
Le Vieux Cordelier
Réimpression de l'ancien Moniteur

SECONDARY SOURCES

BOOKS

Afanassiev, Georges. *Le Commerce des céréals en France au dix-huitième siècle.* Translated under the direction of Paul Boyer. Paris, 1894.

Aulard, Alphonse. *Histoire politique de la Révolution française: Origines et développement de la démocratie et de la république, (1789–1804).* Paris, 1901.

———. *Le Culte de la Raison et le culte de l'Etre suprême (1793–1794).* 2d ed. Paris, 1904.

Avenel, Georges. *Anacharsis Cloots: L'Orateur du genre humain.* 2 vols. Paris, 1865.

Barante, Amable Guillaume Prosper Brugiere, baron de. *Histoire de la Convention nationale.* 6 vols. 1851–53; rpr. New York, 1976.

Blanc, Louis. *Histoire de la Révolution française.* 12 vols. 2d ed. Paris, 1864–70.

Bloch, Camille. *La Monnaie et le papier-monnaie.* Paris, 1912.

Caron, Pierre. *Le Commerce des céréals.* Paris, 1907.

———. *Tableau de dépréciation du papier-monnaie.* Paris, 1909.

Cobb, Richard. *Les Armées révolutionnaires: Instrument de la Terreur dans les départements, avril 1793–floréal an II.* 2 vols. The Hague, 1961–63.

————. *The People's Armies: Instrument of the Terror in the Departments* (New Haven, 1987).

Dommanget, Maurice. *Sylvain Maréchal l'égalitaire, "l'homme sans Dieu": Sa vie, son oeuvre (1750–1803).* Paris, 1950.

Edmonds, W. D. *Jacobinism and the Revolt of Lyon, 1789–1793.* New York, 1990.

Furet, François. *La Gauche et la Révolution française au milieu du XIXe siècle: Edgar Quinet et la question du Jacobinisme.* Paris, 1986.

Furet, François, and Denis Richet. *La Révolution des Etats généraux au 9 thermidor.* 2 vols. Paris, 1965.

Gerbaux, Fernand, and Charles Schmidt. *Procès-verbaux des comités d'agriculture et de commerce. . . .* 4 vols. Paris, 1908.

Godechot, Jacques. *La Contre-révolution: Doctrine et action, 1789–1804.* Paris, 1961.

Guérin, Daniel. *La Lutte de classes sous la première république: Bourgeois et "bras nus" (1793–1797).* 2 vols. Paris, 1946.

Hamel, Ernest. *Histoire de Robespierre.* 3 vols. Paris, 1865–67.

Harris, Seymour E. *The Assignats.* Cambridge, Mass., 1930.

Hatin, Eugene. *Histoire politique et littéraire de la presse en France. . . .* 8 vols. Geneva, 1967.

Herlaut, General. *Le Général rouge Ronsin (1751–1794): La Vendée, l'armée révolutionnaire parisienne.* Paris, n.d.

Jacob, Louis. *Hébert Le Père Duchesne: Chef des sans-culottes.* Paris, 1960.

Jaurès, Jean. *Histoire socialiste de la Révolution française.* Edited by Albert Mathiez. 8 vols. Paris, 1924; rpr. with notes by Albert Soboul, New York, 1973.

Lamartine, Alphonse de. *Histoire des Girondins.* 8 vols. in 4 tomes. Brussels, 1847.

Lefebvre, Georges. *Etudes sur la Révolution française.* Paris, 1963.

————. *La Révolution française.* Paris, 1951. Vol. XIII of Louis Halphen and Philippe Sagnac, eds., *Peuples et civilisations.* 20 vols. (ongoing).

————. *Documents relatifs à l'histoire des subsistences dans le district de Bergues . . .* 2 vols. Lille, 1914–21.

Markov, Walter. *Maximilien Robespierre, 1758–1794: Beiträge zu seinem 200. Geburtstag.* Berlin, 1958.

Mathiez, Albert. *Contribution à l'histoire religieuse de la Révolution française.* Paris, 1907.

————. *La Révolution française.* 3 vols. 10th ed. Paris, 1951.

————. *Un Procès de corruption sous la Terreur: L'Affaire de la compagnie des Indes.* Paris, 1920.

————. *La Vie chère et le mouvement social sous la Terreur.* Paris, 1927.

Michelet, Jules. *Histoire de la Révolution française.* Edited by Gérard Walter. 2 vols. Paris, 1961.

Mignet, François A. M. A. *Histoire de la Révolution française depuis 1789 jusqu'en 1814.* 2 vols. 2d ed. Paris, 1869.

Palmer, R. R. *Twelve Who Ruled: The Year of the Terror in the French Revolution.* Princeton, 1941.

Quinet, Edgar. *La Révolution.* 2 vols. Paris, 1865.

Rose, R. B. *Gracchus Babeuf, the First Revolutionary Communist.* Stanford, 1978.

Sainte-Claire Deville, Paul. *La Commune de l'an II: Vie et mort d'une assemblée révolutionnaire.* Paris, 1946.

Sewell, William H., Jr. *Work and Revolution in France: The Language of Labor from the Old Regime to 1848* (Cambridge, Eng., 1980).

Slavin, Morris. *The French Revolution in Miniature: Section Droits de l'Homme, 1789–1795.* Princeton, 1984.

———. *The Making of an Insurrection: Parisian Sections and the Gironde.* Cambridge, Mass., 1986.

Soboul, Albert. *Les Sans-Culottes parisiens en l'an II: Mouvement populaire et gouvernement révolutionnaire, 2 juin 1793–9 thermidor an II.* Paris, 1958.

Soboul, Albert, and Raymonde Monnier. *Répertoire du personnel sectionnaire parisien en l'an II.* Paris, 1985.

Sybel, Heinrich von. *Geschichte der Revolutionzeit von 1789 bis 1795.* 5 vols. 3d ed. Düsseldorf, 1866–70.

Taine, Hippolyte Adolphe. *Les Origines de la France contemporaine.* 6 vols. 11th ed. Paris, 1879–94.

Thiers, Adolphe. *Histoire de la Révolution française.* 10 vols. 3d ed. Paris, 1832.

Tissot, Pierre François. *Histoire complète de la Révolution française.* 6 vols. in 3 tomes. Paris, 1834–36.

Tridon, G. *Les Hébertistes: La Commune de Paris de 1793.* 2d ed. Paris, 1871.

Wallon, Henri. *Histoire du tribunal révolutionnaire de Paris.* 6 vols. Paris, 1880–82.

Walter, Gérard. *Hébert et le "Père Duchesne" (1757–1794).* Paris, 1946.

———. *Histoire de la Terreur, 1793–1794.* Paris, 1937.

ARTICLES

Cobb, Richard. "Note sur Guillaume Bouland de la section du Finistère." *Annales historiques de la Révolution française,* XX (1950), 152–55.

Duval, Louis. "Hébert chez lui." *La Révolution française,* XII (1886), 961–81, XIII (1887), 4–65.

Faye, Jean Pierre. "Les Grandes Journées du Père Duchesne, maître poêlier et fils du sacripant." Paris, 1981.

Guilhaumou, Jacques. "L'Effet populaire dans le *Père Duchesne:* L'Exemple de la figuralité du corps." *Les Intermédiaires culturels* (1981), 403–23.

———. "Le mise en scène de l'anglais dans le *Père Duchesne* d'Hébert (juillet 1793–février 1794): Le Jacobinisme à l'épreuve du paradoxe." *Komparatistische Hefte,* No. 2 (1979), 102–15.

———. "Le 'Moment actuel' et processus discursif: Le *Père Duchesne* d'Hébert et le *Publiciste de la République française* de Jacques Roux (14 juillet–6 septembre 1793)." *Bulletin du centre d'analyse du discours*, III (1975), 147–73.

———. "Les Mille Langues du Père Duchesne: La Parade de la culture populaire pendant la Révolution." *Dix-huitième siècle revue annuelle* (1986), 143–54.

———. "L'Idéologie du Père Duchesne: Les Forces adjuvantes (14 juillet–6 septembre 1793)." *Le Mouvement social*, No. 85 (October–December, 1973), 81–116.

Lafargue, Paul. "La Langue française avant et après la Révolution." In Lafargue, *Marxisme et linguistique*. Paris, 1977.

Manfred, Alfred. "La Nature du pouvoir Jacobin." *La Pensée*, CL (April, 1970), 62–83.

Mathiez, Albert. "L'Arrestation de Pache." *Annales révolutionnaires*, VIII (1916), 147–48.

———. "L'Arrestation de Santerre." *Annales révolutionnaires*, VIII (1916), 149.

———. "Chaumette franc-maçon." *La Révolution française*, XLIII (1902), 121–41.

———. "Les Dernières Lettres de Vincent à sa femme." *Annales révolutionnaires*, VI (1913), 250–51.

———. "Les Deux Versions du procès des Hébertistes." *Annales révolutionnaires*, XI (1919), 1–27.

———. "Les Droits de l'Homme voilés au club de Sédan en pluviôse." *Annales historiques*, III (1926), 495–96.

———. "Saint-Simon et Ronsin." *Annales historiques*, III (1926), 493–94.

———. "Trois discours inédits de Momoro." *Annales historiques*, III (1926), 484–87.

Rose, R. B. "The 'Red Scare' of the 1790s: The French Revolution and the 'Agrarian Law.'" *Past and Present*, CIII (May, 1984), 114–30.

Slavin, Morris. "Feminists and Antifeminists in the French Revolution." In *Women in History, Literature, and the Arts*, edited by Thomas Copeland and Lorrayne Y. Baird-Lange. Youngstown, Ohio, 1989.

———. "Théophile Leclerc: An Anti-Jacobin Terrorist." *Historian*, XXXIII (May, 1971), 398–414.

Sonenscher, Michael. "The *Sans-Culottes* of the Year II: Rethinking the Language of Labour in Revolutionary France." *Social History*, IX (October, 1984), 301–28.

INDEX

Chabot, François (Jacobin involved in Indies Company scandal), 22, 100
Chardin, Charles (member of revolutionary committee of section Brutus), 247
Charlemagne, Jean Philippe Victor (president of section Brutus), 247
Chaumette, Pierre Gaspard (*procureur* of Paris Commune and leading dechristianizer), 15, 18, 71, 92, 138, 245, 264
Chenaux, Louis Barthélemy (president of Cordeliers after arrest of its leaders), 147–48, 149
Choudieu, Pierre René (deputy-on-mission in Vendée and supporter of Ronsin), 61
Cloots, Anacharsis (Jean Baptiste): origin and early politics of, 190–93; as supporter of war, 193; on Robespierre, 193; election of to Convention, 194; political and religious opinions of, 194–96; as victim of chauvinism, 197–99; arrest and execution of, 200
Collot d'Herbois, Jean Marie (leading Montagnard and on Committee of Public Safety): in support of Rossignol, 84; ambivalent role of, 85, 87–88, 259; as delegate to Cordeliers, 109–14, 121
Cordeliers Club: as opponents of moderates, 54–55; in split with Jacobins, 55–57, 85–86; and revival of *l'Ami du peuple*, 98, 124–25; talk of insurrection in session of 14 Ventôse, 98–101, 258; police reports on, 101–102, 115–17; delegation of to Jacobins, 116; in session of 19 Ventôse, 120; Chenaux's report to, 125–26; helplessness of in face of arrests, 147–49; supports of in crisis, 149–51, 234–41; surrender of, 151, 156–57, 159–62; charges against at trial, 224; policy failures of, 253–54
Couthon, Georges Auguste (member of Committee of Public Safety), 92, 158–59, 209, 210
Cromwell/Cromwellistes, 115, 121, 210, 215, 257, 263

Danton, Georges: as criticized by Hébert, 19, 20; in collaboration with Robespierre, 28, 30, 85; and characterization

of Hébertistes as "ultrarevolutionaries," 50; in conflict with Robespierre, 58; as criticized by Vincent, 115–16; arrest of, 241
Deforgue, François Louis Michel (minister of foreign affairs), 175
Descombes, Ignace François (commissioner of supply, Paris Commune): origins and political life of, 179–80; efforts of to supply Paris, 180–81; arrest and interrogation of, 181–82
Desfieux, François (Jacobin and Cordelier activist): political life of, 170–72; arrest of and charges against, 173; in refutation of charges, 212
Desmoulins, Camille (journalist and anti-Hébertiste), 22–25, 27, 246
Didot, Aristarque (secretary of section Réunion), 49, 50
Dubuisson, Pierre Ulrich: political life of, 178–79; denunciation of by Robespierre, 179
Ducroquet, Frédéric Pierre (commissioner on profiteering, section Marat): as proponent of insurrection and veiling Rights of Man, 103, 205
Dufourny, Louis Pierre (president of Paris Department and opponent of Hébert), 82, 157, 173, 210–11, 212
Dufriche-Desgenettes (author of *souvenirs* on Hébert), 16
Dumas, René François (president of Revolutionary Tribunal at trial of Hébertistes), 170, 211, 213
Dumouriez, Charles François (general attacked as traitor by revolutionaries), 16, 17, 58

Enragés: Lefebvre's opinion of, 2–3; and concern about shortages, 34; leaders of, 34–35, 91, 110; among Républicaines révolutionnaires, 146–47, 251. *See also* Popular Societies
Evêché (archbishop's palace): Club électoral in, 55

Fabre d'Eglantine (leading Dantoniste involved in Indies Company scandal), 22, 72, 76, 77, 100